Essential Articles:
for the study of
English Augustan Backgrounds

Edited by **Bernard N. Schilling**

Professor of English
University of Rochester

ARCHON BOOKS   Hamden, Connecticut   1961

Library of Congress Catalog Card Number: 61-15683
Printed in the United States of America

CONTENTS

SCHILLING

THEORY AND GENERAL IDEAS

INTRODUCTION

Immense resources are by now available for literary study in England and America. Contributions to scholarship and criticism are numerous and often so valuable that a student preparing himself for a career in literary teaching and learning is embarrassed, not to say overwhelmed. Yet from the mass of commentary certain titles have emerged which seem to compel attention. If one offers a seminar for example, in one of the standard areas or periods of English literature, the syllabus will show year after year some items that cannot be omitted, things that every serious student should know. Beyond special editions, books and monographs, a number of articles in learned journals have tended to achieve classical status and are to be found invariably on shelves of reserved books. Apart from physical deterioration brought on by repeated use, the many volumes containing these pieces take up a great deal of space, and being withdrawn from general access they do not carry out their proper function in the library. A practical solution to this problem would clearly appeal to students, professors, and librarians.

Confining our selections to the so-called "learned journals" will exclude some of the best things on our subject — things that demand the attention of all serious students. But if we do not try for an ideal coverage, we may still achieve our goal of utility and convenience. We propose then to choose from various periodicals some of the items essential to a given course of study. Hence the title Essential Articles whose meaning we would interpret literally, even though we cannot pretend that these are all the articles that everyone would consider "essential." For the background of the great English Augustans, Dryden, Swift and Pope, let us choose from the articles which time has sanctioned, and let us draw these into a single volume of convenient size. This offers a clear gain in simplicity and usefulness. The articles chosen make up a body of knowledge that cannot fail to be valuable, and they act as models of the kind of contribution to learning which we are training our graduate students to make themselves. If a similar concentration of articles is made for each of the major Augustans, we may conduct the study of these writers with greater confidence, knowing more fully the extent and kind of reading that we can take for granted.

The problem of choice has its usual embarrassments here, and students may wonder at the omission of famous articles by, for example, R. S. Crane, C. A. Moore, A. O. Lovejoy. These either bear equally upon the middle and late 18th century, or derive most of their examples nearer the age of Johnson. Despite clear overlapping, such work might better appear in another general volume covering the period directly following the English Augustans.

It may be objected that many of the articles here chosen have already been reprinted, thus relieving the strain on the periodical volumes from which they were taken. Why not replace these with other items, not as yet so widely available? The answer might be that frequent reprinting merely shows the accuracy of the general title — that these articles are indeed "essential" and belong in every new collection. Further, reprinting in numerous other volumes leaves the articles still scattered in as many different places as ever — these being simply not the same places as at first. To put ten items on reserve that have been often reproduced, requires ten separate volumes still, instead of only one. The immense gain in having the articles conveniently in one place, each to be studied alongside and in the context of the others, is surely important. Such a volume can also be available in two or three copies for a seminar of good size, whereas duplication would run to twenty or more volumes otherwise. If all the pieces are together furthermore, they can be purchased for one's permanent professional library and used as a ready source or support at various levels.

While individual practice must vary greatly, perhaps we can agree on the importance of prose style, of couplet verse, of the satiric genre, and of certain general ideas and critical theories. These will establish the lines passing into Dryden, Swift, and Pope themselves, and will enable the student to make his way more certainly into any aspect of the period he may wish to study in depth.

I should like to acknowledge here the excellent work done by my assistant, Harry Rusche, in helping to prepare this volume for the press.

Bernard N. Schilling

PROSE STYLE

"ATTIC PROSE" IN THE SEVENTEENTH CENTURY

Morris W. Croll

I

Two terms present themselves to the literary historian seeking a name for the new kind of style that came into general use in Latin and all the vernacular languages at the end of the sixteenth century.[1] 'Anti-Ciceronian prose' has the merit of indicating the character of the controversy out of which the new tendency emerged victorious: it connects the successful movement led by Lipsius, Montaigne, and Bacon with the frustrated efforts of Erasmus, Budé, and Pico early in the sixteenth century. But it is open to several objections. In the first place, it indicates only revolt, suggests only destructive purposes in a movement that had a definite rhetorical program. Secondly, it may be taken as describing a hostility to Cicero himself, in the opinions of the new leaders, instead of to his sixteenth-century "apes," whereas in fact the supreme rhetorical excellence of Cicero was constantly affirmed by them, as it was by the ancient Anti-Ciceronians whom they imitated.[2] And thirdly, it was not the term usually employed in contemporary controversy, and was never used except by enemies of the new movement. The only name by which its leaders and friends were willing to describe the new style during the century of its triumph, from 1575 to 1700, was "Attic."

For these reasons "Attic" is the preferable term, and should take its place in literary history as the name of the dominant tendency in seventeenth-century prose-style in contrast with that of the sixteenth century. To use it at the present time, however, for this purpose, without a full and clear explanation of the meaning attached to it could only cause positive misunderstanding or utter confusion. For it is a word that has suffered vicissitudes. In current and uncritical literary writing of the last two centuries it has often been employed to designate a style conformed to the conversational customs of a well-trained and sophisticated society – the society of Paris in the eighteenth

Reprinted by permission from Studies in Philology, Vol. 18 (1921), pp. 79-128.

century rather than of Athens in the age of Pericles. This meaning, it is true, was imposed by a later age than the seventeenth
century and might safely be disregarded, the more safely, indeed,
because it does not correspond to any of the more important
meanings recognized as sound by the best students of antiquity.
But unhappily in the usage of classical scholars themselves the
word does not now carry a single and definite meaning; and the
most recent researches tend to add complexity rather than
clearness to its history. For the truth is that it was never a
formalized word of rhetorical theory in ancient criticism, such
as can be used for definition; it always tended to be a nickname
of compliment or eulogy, and was subject to the variations of
meaning that we may observe in many similar words of the
modern critical vocabulary. There was a disposition, it is true,
to associate it in Roman criticism with one of the two great
"characters of style" of which we will speak presently. But on
the other hand it might denominate a quality of style, vaguely
associated with Athens in the time of its glory, which neither
of the "characters" could afford to neglect and which might appear equally well in either. Or again it could be used in its exact geographical sense, of any author who lived at Athens, without reference to either the quality or the character of his style.
    All the trees in this forest have again been studied close-up
by recent scholars; and we are now no more competent to give
a comprehensive definition of 'Attic' than the ancients themselves were. Evidently any one who wants to use the term at
the present time for the purpose of identification must explain
what he means by it. If this involved an attempt to discuss the
many questions still in controversy among the classicists, or
to adjust the relations of the various ancient meanings of the
word that have been mentioned, it would be too pretentious an
undertaking for one who is not a trained classicist. But we are
not concerned here with any of these thorny problems. Our business is to understand 'Attic' as the seventeenth-century critics
did; and they at least had a clear idea of what they meant by it,
and used it to define the stylistic purposes of their own age. It
meant in their critical vocabulary one of two kinds or characters of style made familiar to them in modern and vernacular
use by the imitation of antiquity since the beginning of the Renaissance, and corresponding, as they saw, roughly but definitely
enough with the two leading "characters," or genera dicendi,
distinguished by ancient criticism. [3] This limitation of meaning will serve as a clue to guide us through all complexities.

"ATTIC PROSE" IN THE SEVENTEENTH CENTURY

Classical scholars may not, therefore, feel highly rewarded by the present survey, and it is not in their interest that it is undertaken. Yet it may have some value even for them. For the word 'Attic' had a lively, contemporary interest in the seventeenth century that it has never had since, and was used by men whose own writings were, by intention at least, direct continuations of ancient Latin literature. Their knowledge was limited in its range as compared with that of the most accomplished modern classicists; but as far as it went it was both sounder and more vivid than that of any later generation. It is possible that their use of the term we are considering will help to simplify a problem which has been greatly confused by the investigation of details; and it is certain that it is truer to ancient usage than that which has been current in popular criticism since the eighteenth century.

II

The seventeenth century, then, regarded the history of ancient prose-style chiefly as a story of relations and conflicts between two modes of style, which — for the sake of the utmost simplification — we may characterize at once (in modern terms) as the oratorical style and the essay-style, and may describe by the kind of ornament most used in each. The oratorical style was distinguished by the use of the schemata verborum, or 'schemes,' as we may call them, which are chiefly similarities or repetitions of sound used as purely sensuous devices to give pleasure or aid the attention. The essay-style is characterized by the absence of these figures, or their use in such subtle variation that they cannot easily be distinguished, and, on the other hand, by the use of metaphor, aphorism, antithesis, paradox, and the other figures which, in one classification, are known as the figurae sententiae, the figures of wit or thought. [4] — But of course such characterizations are mere caricature, and serve only as convenient labels. The form and history of the two styles must be fully considered.

The first is of earlier origin: it is the style in which prose first came to be recognized as a proper object of artistic cultivation among the Greeks. According to the sketchy and untrustworthy reports of ancient literary historians, Gorgias was its "inventor"; but this may mean no more than that he first formulated and systematized for teaching purposes the 'schemes' which serve to ornament it, and especially the three most important

of these, which still go by his name in rhetorical theory: and
it is almost certain that even these figures originated long before Gorgias' time, in certain liturgical or legal customs of
the primitive Greek community. [5] The next stage in its history
is associated with the name of Isocrates, a disciple of Gorgias,
to whom is always attributed the elaboration of the form of the
rhythmic "period" and the subordination to this, in their proper
artistic relation to it, of the 'Gorgianic schemes.' Isocrates
was the most important of all that class of teachers to whom
Socrates and Plato have given a much worse reputation than
they deserve. The sophistic scheme of education included a
great use of oratory because it was founded on a study of politics; the individual man was conceived as a kind of mirror reflecting the character and interests of his town or state, and
his literary education was wholly determined by the customs of
the forum and the public uses of rhetoric. [6]

In spite of all opposition from the philosophers this type of
education spread generally throughout the Greek world, in the
colonies perhaps even more widely than in the home cities, and
was disseminated in the Hellenistic period throughout the greater part of the Mediterranean world. And with it, of course, went
the 'sophistic' rhetoric everywhere, now exfoliating in cultus
and flamboyancy under the influence of provincial tastes, now
degenerating into a merely puerile and academic employment
of the schemes, or again assuming the normal grandeur of its
proportions and the purity of its design, but preserving through
all variations the essential features of its form as they had been
perfected by Isocrates. In fact the conventionalized oratory of
the sophistic schools must be considered not only the most conspicuous contribution of the Greeks to the prose-style of Europe, but also the standard and normal form of their own prose,
of which all other forms are variations, and to which it always
returned as to the true rhetorical point of departure. Nor did it
perish with the passing of classical Greek culture. It lived again
in the Roman rhetoric which culminated in the oratory of Cicero,
and survived, to enjoy still longer and stranger destinies, in
the teaching of the Christian schools of the Middle Ages.

The form of Isocratean rhetoric need not detain us long here;
we are concerned with it only in its relation with the style that
arose in opposition to it, and the only point that it is necessary
to emphasize here is the sensuous character of its appeal to its
audience. Its "round composition" and the "even falling of its
clauses" do not always satisfy the inward ear of the solitary

reader. Heard solely by the reflective mind, it is an empty, a frigid, or an artificial style. But it is not meant for such a hearing. It is addressed first, like music, to the physical ear; and the figures with which its large and open design are decorated have been devised with a reference to the attentive powers and the aural susceptibilities of large audiences, consisting of people of moderate intelligence, and met amid all the usual distractions of public assemblage—as Cicero says, in sole et pulvere.

In their appropriate place they are the legitimate resource of a great popular art, and their fitness for their ends is vindicated by the fact that they reappear whenever the necessary conditions of popular eloquence are satisfied. But it is evident that their literary adaptability is strictly limited. They offer nothing that is pleasing to an intellect intent upon the discovery of reality; and a people like the Greeks, in whom philosophic curiosity was quite as strong an incentive to literary art as the love of sensuous forms, would not long resist the temptation to ridicule or parody them, and to study modes of expression deliberately contrasted with them. The beginning of the history of the essay-style among them follows hard, as we should expect, upon that of the oratorical, in the lifetime indeed of the reputed founder of the latter.

In his dialogue named from the orator, Plato relates a conversation that is supposed to occur on a visit of Gorgias to Athens in about the year 405, when Gorgias was perhaps eighty years of age. Socrates had been invited to meet him at dinner and hear him deliver a new oration that he had prepared. Socrates avoided the proffered entertainment, probably with some malice; but, either by accident or design, met the dinner party on its way home, and was again invited to hear an oration by the master — this time at Callicles' house. Socrates went with the party, but asked whether Gorgias would not consent to converse with him instead of speaking to him. In the long conversation that followed the philosopher succeeded by his unequalled dialectic art in making Gorgias and one of his disciples acknowledge that the true aim of education is not the art of persuasion, but how to see and like the truth, how to know right from wrong and love it; and gave an original turn to the whole theory of style by showing that it is at best a kind of cookery which makes things palatable whether they are good for us or not, whereas the study of morality is like medicine, which puts the soul in a state of health and keeps it there.

In this dialogue of Plato's, and in the Phaedrus, which treats the same theme, are laid the foundations of a new interpretation of the functions of rhetoric, wholly different from those of oratory, and of the practise of a style appropriate to these functions. But it is not fair to say that Plato and Socrates foresaw such an outcome of their controversy with the sophists, or would have been pleased by it if they had done so. Cicero complained that it was Socrates who first instituted the opposition between philosophy and oratory which, as he properly observed, is fatal to the highest development of the latter; and this statement seems to represent the attitude of Socrates in the Gorgias with substantial correctness. The purport of his argument is almost certainly that in the public life of a sound commonwealth, and, with still more reason, in the private activities of its citizens, there would be no use of an art of rhetoric of any kind. The Protestant, or Puritan, divorce of spirit and sense is apparent in his treatment of the subject, and he has apparently not thought of the possibility that a new theory of style could be erected on the foundation of his opposition to oratory and its forms.

History shows, however, that when you put rhetoric out at the door it comes in at the window, and the inevitable next step in the development of the ideas of Socrates and Plato was their systemization with reference to an art of prose composition. Aristotle effected this in the first two Books of his Rhetoric, which have served as the starting point of all subsequent theories of style that have called themselves "modern." This book was a wholly new thing in the world; for the theory of rhetoric was here worked out for the first time, not on the basis of the susceptibilities of audiences, and the aural effect of language, but on the basis of the processes of reasoning and in strict relations with the science of logic. Speaking roughly, we may say that the Rhetoric treats for the first time the art of writing, as opposed to the art of speaking. [6a]

This statement will have to be very carefully guarded, however; for there is an astonishing inconsistency in the work, which it will be useful to consider here for a moment. After treating style in the first two books as dependent upon the forms of thought, Aristotle discusses, in the third book, which is about style, a form which is not distinguishable from the Isocratean oratorical style, except that he lays an emphasis perhaps on shorter periods and treats the oratorical figures very simply. The explanation is probably to be found in the fact that the two parts were composed for different purposes at different times. The first is the work of a philosopher seeking to explain the part that

8

rhetoric is observed to play in the life of man, and is not meant
to have anything to do with the practise of the art; the second is
a purely objective description of the form of style which he saw
in actual use, the only describable, conventionalized form then
in existence. [7] Of course this explanation does not get rid of the
essential inconsistency of his two modes of treatment. Nothing
can do that; for it is involved in Aristotle's theory, and we encounter here for the first time a phenomenon that meets us at
every point in the later history of the intimate or essay-style,
namely, the slipperiness of all rhetorical theory when it tries
to establish itself on anything other than the sensuous character of language and the social conventions that give it opportunity and effect. When it aspires to be the art of presenting things
or thought in their essential character and their true linea-
ments, rhetoric at once begins to lose its identity and be dissolved into one or another of the sciences. It is an art, in short,
and every art is a social convention.

But we need go no further into this subject at present; what
concerns us is that Aristotle's Rhetoric exactly represents the
state of unstable equilibrium which had necessarily followed
Plato's attack upon oratory. A new use of prose-style had now
attained general recognition as a form of art — in brief the use
of style for the purposes of philosophy and as closely related to
the art of dialectic; and on the basis of this new conception of
the purpose of prose-discourse Aristotle had erected the theory
of the art of rhetoric. But in the meantime the older, traditional, oratorical customs had not yielded to the vigor of Plato's
attack, but on the contrary were as flourishing as ever, and
were universally recognized, even by Aristotle, as displaying
the form of style which, in a purely rhetorical sense, is the
ideal and abstract best. In other words, theory and the tradition of practice were in conflict, and Aristotle had done nothing
to reconcile them.

The recognition of this difficulty was what determined the
next step in the development of Greek rhetorical theory. The
followers of Aristotle resolved it in a purely empirical way by
recognizing a division of prose-style into two distinct characters or genera, which henceforward played the leading rôle in
all the rhetorical criticism of antiquity. At a later stage in the
development a third "character" was added and appears in all
Latin criticism; but in the most recent and much the best treatment of the subject this addition is considered as a makeshift
which tends to confuse the principle on which the original division

9

was based. [8] We shall have to speak of it in its place; but the main facts of modern stylistic history, as of the ancient, are best represented by a consideration of the two characters which first make their appearance in Theophrastus and are more clearly defined in later successors of Aristotle.

The first was known as the genus grande or nobile. It was the rhetorical style of the Gorgianic tradition, and the adjectives used to describe it indicate the character it was originally supposed to have. When it was practised independently of the social and political conditions upon which it depends for its greatest success, its elaborate form and ornamental figures, studied merely for their own charm, gave it a character of cultus, or empty ornateness; and it was so portrayed at certain periods by its opponents. But the true nature of the genus grande is to be broad and general in its scope, large and open in design, strong, energetic, vehement. Tacitus ridicules its degenerate practitioners as minstrels or dancers, in allusion to the musical beauty of their rhythms;[9] but Cicero in more than one passage compares the true orator with the tragic actor, in allusion to the breadth and passion of his portrayal of life.[10]

The newer style, which had appeared in opposition to this, was known as the genus humile or submissum (demissum), but its quality is better indicated by the more descriptive appellations often given to it, or to branches or varieties of it: lene, subtile, insinuating, flexible, subtle. A style of this general character would naturally have many particular forms. It might, for instance, become a deliberately rude, formless, negligent style — décousu, as Montaigne says of his own — in order to express contempt for cultus, or even for rhetoric itself, and a love of "honest" simplicity; on the other hand, it might emulate the colloquial ease and mondanité of good conversation, in intended contrast with the vulgar pomp of public oratory, and be distinguished as elegant, graceful, nitidus; or again it might declare its superiority to popular tastes, as in the hands of the Stoics, by affecting a scornful and significant brevity of utterance. All of these and other species of the genus were recognized by the ancients as actually existing, or as having existed at different times and places, and were distinguished by appropriate terms. [11] But the genus as a whole is properly characterized by its origin in philosophy. Its function is to express individual variances of experience in contrast with the general and communal ideas which the open design of the oratorical style is so well adapted to contain. Its idiom is that of conversation or

is adapted from it, in order that it may flow into and fill up all
the nooks and crannies of reality and reproduce its exact image
to attentive observation. [12]

As to its specific rhetorical forms nothing needs to be said
here; they will be considered fully elsewhere. But a general
point must be urged which is often, or usually, ignored by ad-
mirers of a genus humile, and even by those who practise it,
though the neglect of it is a prolific source of aberration both
in theory and practise. And this is the point that its rhetorical
forms are modifications, adaptations of those of the oratorical
style. The ancients were very slow to recognize any kind of literary customs other than oral ones; and even in the genres that
were obviously meant for silent reading, such as the letter, the
form of the style was controlled by the ear. This is a sound
principle at all times, and for all kinds of style, and its operation cannot be escaped even though it is forgotten or denied.
There is only one rhetoric, the art of the beauty of spoken sounds.
In oratory this beauty displays itself in its most obvious, explicit, exfoliated forms; in the genus humile in much more delicate,
implicit, or mingled ones. But the forms are ultimately the
same, and whatever beauty of style we find in the most subtle
and intimate kinds of discourse could be explained—if there were
critics skillful and minute enough—in terms of oratorical effect.

The history of Greek and Roman style is chiefly the story of
the relations of the genus grande and the genus humile. Theoretically the two kinds are not hostile or exclusive of each other;
Cicero is always anxiously insisting that they are both necessary in their proper places and relations to the oratory that he
dreamed of as the perfection of literary art. But in fact they
almost always proved to be rivals; and different schools, even
long and important literary periods, distinguish themselves by
their preference for one of them, their dislike of the other.

III

It proved to be so again during the formative period of modern prose-style. The literary movement which is the subject of
the present discussion was a successful attempt to substitute
the philosophical genus humile for the oratorical genus grande
in the general practice of authors and the general favor of readers.

Both the customs and the spirit of sixteenth-century life demanded literary expression in oratorical forms. It was a period
of social unity, or at least of social unities. Brittle, temporary,

illusory, these unities were; yet they were effective and brilliant while they lasted, and created the congregational and social customs which are favorable to a spoken literature. Even the religious controversy, so destructive of European society in the long run, had the opposite effect at first. For it consolidated large masses of people in devotion to a common cause, and gathered them together in popular assemblies which listened with a new motive for attention to discourses in the traditional forms of popular oration.

More important than all partisan loyalties, however, was the new feeling of national unity which made itself felt almost everywhere during this century. Whatever divisive forces were latent in the religious controversy were controlled and subordinated by centripetal tendencies in the political world; and the bitterest sectarian foes were compelled to share, with at least a semblance of concord and common loyalty, in the dazzling social and public life that centered in the courts of princes and in the cities that swarmed about them and took them as their models of conduct and manners. We hear remarkably little, during this period, of solitary and contemplative existences, of local characters, or of the self-dependent individualism of the country-house. Everyone was present, either in fact or in idea, at court, and the most striking opportunities for literary distinction were offered at the constant gatherings, public or semipublic, more or less formal, which attended its various ceremonies and progresses and procedures. The occasions for the public display of stylistic art in the presence of the sovereign or one of his (or her) greater satellites were many: in the minor circles of courtiers and ladies-in-waiting they were innumerable. We should doubtless be greatly astonished, if we were able to recover a complete picture of the court-life of the time, to observe how many of the uses of books like Il Cortegiano, Guevara's Libro Aureo, the Arcadia, and Euphues were oral rather than literary. It is probable that these books — and there is no reason why we should not add Ariosto's and Spenser's epics — were habitually read aloud in assemblies of which we can now form but a faint picture in our minds, and were indeed composed chiefly with a view to such performance. When we add that solitary reading with the eye was only beginning to be a customary form of entertainment, we are prepared to understand why the literary education of the Renaissance was almost wholly conducted by means of the practise of oratory.

The various forms of prose-style that resulted from this

training need not be distinguished here. They were as various,
of course, as the elements of the literary tradition in which the
Renaissance was living. They were partly (indeed chiefly) medieval, partly classical, partly popular or folk forms. But it is
enough for our present purpose to observe that all of them, by
whatever channels they had come to the culture of the sixteenth
century, had their ultimate origin in the Gorgianic, or Isocratean type of oratory that we have been discussing in the preceding section. That this is true of the style taught by the orthodox
humanists is well-known: their aim was to teach their pupils to
"write Cicero." But it is also true of the many kinds of style
due to the survival of medieval educational customs and social
modes: the forms of preaching-style, for instance, that were
prevalent until after the middle of the century, both in Latin and
the vernacular; the style employed in letters composed for social display or amusement; the aureate style affected by those
accustomed to Renaissance courtly ceremony, as in the show-
speeches of knights in tournaments, or in begging or complimentary addresses to sovereigns; and the literary cultismo
practised in many moral treatises and romances, as by Guevara, Sidney, and Lyly. However unclassical all these may be in
their effect upon our ears and taste, they have one character in
common: they are all arrived at by the elaboration of the
"schemes," or figures of sound, that have been described as
the chief ornaments of the Isocratean oratory. And that is all
that is necessary in order to fix them in their place in the one
great European tradition of oratorical style.

Against the literary tyranny of this tradition, and more particularly against its sixteenth-century efflorescence, the representatives of the modern spirit of progress were in revolt
during the last quarter of the century. The temporary unities
of the Renaissance were evidently breaking up; and the literary
customs that had flowered upon them responded immediately to
the tokens of their decay. The historian versed in the poetry of
this period can detect the coming of the severer air of the seventeenth century in the new distaste that declares itself everywhere for the copious and flowing style of Ariosto and Spenser,
and the "tedious uniformity" of Petrarcanism: the student of
prose-style is made aware of it at an even earlier date by the
eager malice with which some of the new leaders recognize the
artificiality of the oratorical customs of their time.

It was Muret, it seems, that remarkable prophet of seventeenth-century ideas, who first tossed this straw into the wind.

In one of the latest and boldest of his academic discourses he
asserts that the reasons for the practise of oratory in the time
of his rhetorical predecessors, Bembo and Sadoleto, are no
longer of any effect in the present age, because the real concerns of political life, and even the most important legal questions, are no longer decided in the public audience-chambers
of the senates and courts, but in the private cabinets of ministers of state and in the intimacy of conversation.[13] It was a
cynical observation, perhaps, but a true one, justifying Machiavelli's wonderful realism at last, and foretelling the Richelieus,
Bacons, and Cecils of a later generation.

Like his fellows in the new rationalism Muret arrived at his
ideas by the first-hand study of facts. But he was like them too
in that he desired to support his case by classical authority. The
source of the passage just alluded to seems to be the discussion
at the opening of the Rhetoric in which Aristotle explains that
the justification of oratory is to be found in the imperfection
and weakness of judgment characteristic of an uneducated public, incapable of distinguishing truth from error by the tedious
processes of reason. Aristotle was perhaps the only ancient
author whose authority was great enough to stand against that
of Cicero on a question of this kind, and this famous statement
in the Rhetoric was eagerly seized on by the anti-oratorical critics of the seventeenth century: its echoes are heard from Muret and Bacon to Pascal and Arnauld. But the same idea came
to the Anti-Ciceronian leaders from other ancient sources; and
it is to be observed that they find a more specific appropriateness to the circumstances of their own time in the magnificent
description of the decline of Roman oratory during the Empire
which Tacitus puts into the mouth of Maternus in his Dialogue.[14]
This passage played a great part in forming Muret's ideas; but
the first clear intimation of its vital relation to modern life is
found in Montaigne's essay on The Vanity of Words (I, 51). After some introductory words suggested by the Gorgias of Plato,
and the passage of Aristotle already mentioned, Montaigne goes
on to say that oratory has flourished most in states where "the
vulgar, the ignorant, or the populace have had all power, as in
Rhodes, Athens, and Rome," and in periods of turmoil and civil
strife, as at Rome during the Republic; "even as a rank, free,
and untamed soil," he continues, "beareth the rankest and strongest weeds.

Whereby it seemeth that those commonweals which

14

depend of an absolute monarch have less need of it than
others. For that foolishness and facility which is found
in the common multitude, and which doth subject the same
to be managed, persuaded, and led by the ears by the sweet-
alluring and sense-entrancing sound of this harmony, without duly weighing, knowing, or considering the truth of
things by the force of reason: this facility and easy yielding, I say, is not so easily found in one only ruler, and it
is more easy to warrant him from the impression of this
poison by good institution and sound counsel.

Is he looking back toward the Roman Empire or forward to
the régime of absolutism beginning to be established in his own
time? One cannot tell. In the literature of the period that was
then beginning these two historical phenomena are always presenting themselves side by side. For example, in a passage of
Etienne Pasquier, plainly suggested by the same discourse in
Tacitus' dialogue: "Tels fanfares sont propres, en une demo-
cratie, a un orateur en tout voue et ententif a la surprise du
peuple par doux traits et emmiellement de sa rhetorique: Ce
qui ne se presenta onc entre nous."[15]
Political motives, however, were not the ones that weighed
most with the Anti-Ciceronian leaders. Their scientific interests and above all their universal preoccupation with moral
questions played a still greater part in determining their rhetorical program. The old claims of philosophy to precedence
over formal rhetoric, long ago asserted by Plato, are revived
by them in much the old terms, and the only justification they
will admit for the study of style is that it may assist in the attainment of the knowledge of oneself and of nature. "The art of
writing and the art of managing one's life are one and the same
thing" is the motto of Montaigne and all his followers. "As for
me," writes Lipsius to Montaigne in 1588, "I mightily scorn all
those external and polite kinds of studies, whether philosophical
or literary, and indeed every kind of knowledge that is not directed by prudence and judgment to the end of teaching the conduct of life."[16] Bacon deprecates the harsh treatment of rhetoric by Plato and labors its justification in the Advancement of
Learning; but he treats it as a subordinate part of dialectic or
logic, as Aristotle does, and in certain portions of its subject-
matter as identical with moral or political philosophy.[17] Le
Mothe le Vayer is more express and clear than any of his predecessors. They have all praised the new genres, the letter and

the essay; but he professes at the beginning of his discussion of rhetoric[18] to treat of written style alone, la rhetorique des livres, a style to be read, not heard: all that has to do with speaking he repudiates.

This is the general attitude of the leaders of opinion in the first half of the century. In the second half it is not changed, but, on the contrary, is more clearly defined. Bayle speaks of the faux éclat of oratory. "Ces messieurs la (les orateurs) ne se soucient guère d'éclairer l'esprit ... ils vont droit au coeur, et non pas droit a l'entendement: ils tachent d'exciter l'amour, la haine, la colère,"[19] Bayle displays the scorn and intolerance that have always been characteristic of the scientific rationalist; but with proper deductions his opinions may be taken as characteristic of the age of La Bruyère, Arnauld, Fénelon, and Malebranche, of the Port-Royal community and the Royal Society of London. The temporary success of Puritanism and Quietism, the rapid progress of scientific method, and the diffusion of Cartesian ideas, all in their different ways helped to create a taste for a bare and level prose-style adapted merely to the exact portrayal of things as they are. The severest theorists indeed can hardly be brought to recognize a difference between logic and rhetoric; while even the most liberal would exclude the characteristic beauties of oratorical form from the legitimate resources of literary art. Persuasion is indeed the object of rhetoric. But the legitimate means of attaining this end, they constantly assert, is not by the sensuous appeal of oratorical rhythm, but, on the contrary, by portraying in one's style exactly those athletic movements of the mind by which it arrives at a sense of reality and the true knowledge of itself and the world.[20] Fénelon is the harshest critic of Isocrates and his school — he was aware that this included Bossuet — that the century produced;[21] and Malebranche proposed to correct the too-imaginative prose of the age of Montaigne and Bacon by applying to it its own rationalistic criticism with a rigor that Montaigne and Bacon never dreamed of.[22]

In short, though this was the period when the Isocratean model was revived by Bossuet, the critics were all on the side of the severer style, and most of them were either hostile or indifferent to oratory in all its forms. The doctrine of the genus humile was taught everywhere.

Up to this point we have not mentioned the word Attic, which is the object of the discussion. We have considered only the two great modes of style, the grand and the familiar, and the relation of the ancient rivalry between them to the theory of modern Anti-Ciceronianism. This, however, is the proper approach to our subject. For in the controversies of the Anti-Ciceronians "Attic style" means to all intents and purposes the genus humile or subtile, "Asiatic" describes the florid, oratorical style of Cicero's early orations or any style ancient or modern distinguished by the same copious periodic form and the Gorgianic figures that attend upon it. 'Attic' is always associated with philosophy and the ars bene vivendi, 'Asiatic' with the cultus of conventional oratory. This is not the usual modern method of relating the two terms. Probably the fault now most commonly associated with Asianism is one to which the Anti-Ciceronians of the seventeenth century were themselves peculiarly liable when they used the characteristic forms of their art for oratorical purposes. We think of the tumor, the exaggerated emphasis, the monstrous abuse of metaphor in the preaching of the first half of the century in all the European countries; or of qualities dangerously related to these in the non-oratorical prose writings of Donne, Gracian, Malvezzi, and other masters of the 'conceit'; or even of tendencies of the same kind that we may observe in writers so normal as Lipsius, Bacon, Balzac, and Browne. There is a kind of Asianism, in short, that arises from a constant effort to speak with point and significance, as well as from an excessive use of the ornate figures of sound, from too much love of expressiveness as well as from the cult of form; and inasmuch as this vice was more familiar to the reformers at the end of the century than the other, and was the one that was in immediate need of correction at that time, it has taken its place in our traditions as typical Asianism. But the Anti-Ciceronians were not aware that they were falling into error through an excess of their own qualities; they called themselves "Attic" because they avoided certain traits of style which they disliked, and did not observe that they sometimes ceased to be Attic through avoiding and disliking them too much. It is true therefore that their use of the terms was a one-sided and inadequate interpretation of their meaning in ancient criticism. [23] But on the other hand, it is fair to remark that so is the present use, and indeed that the seventeenth century was far more nearly in accord with the ancient ideas of the character of Attic prose than we are. Through the influence of eighteenth-century tastes we have come to associate it with the laws of taste and good form imposed by a slightly frivolous, or at least not very intellectual, social custom; and have lost sight of the fact that it had

CROLL

its original in philosophy rather than in the manners of "the
world," and preserved its philosophical associations in antiquity
through all its transmutations. This fact the Anti-Ciceronians
of the seventeenth century never forgot. It was the basis of their
distinction between Attic and Asian prose.

The evidence on this point is clear and decisive, and begins
with the earliest phases of the sixteenth-century Ciceronian
controversy. Erasmus, however, is the only witness that we
shall need to cite from the first period. Throughout the Cicer-
onianus 'Attic' denotes opposition to the copiousness of Cicero,
and fondness for a scientific or philosophical brevity, marked
by the same tendency toward ingenuity and point which accompanied the genus humile in ancient times. Speaking of the humanist Lazare de Baïf, one of the interlocutors says: "He prefers
to be pointed [argutus], it seems, Attic rather than Ciceronian."24 William Grocyn "was always inclined to the epistolary
pointedness, loving laconism and appropriateness of style;25
in this genre certainly one would call him nothing but Attic; indeed he aimed at nothing else, and when he read any writings
of Cicero would say that he could not endure his fulness of expression."26 Linacre, again, "surpasses an Attic in the repression of his feelings . . . ; he has studied to be unlike Cicero."27
Scaliger, answering Erasmus, bullies and berates him for calling Cicero "redundant and Asiatic."28 Improperly of course;
for Erasmus is using these opprobrious words only in echoing
Cicero's own criticism of his earlier orations, and is careful
to point out the variety of styles in his works. Still Cicero is
prevailingly a copious and ornate orator. Controversy is never
nice and discriminating; and Cicero continues 'Asian' to the end
of Anti-Ciceronian history. Lipsius, for example, writes in
1586; "I love Cicero; I even used to imitate him; but I have become a man, and my tastes have changed. Asiatic feasts have
ceased to please me; I prefer the Attic."29

'Attic,' however, by this time was beginning to be more fully defined, and all its ancient associations re-awakened in defense of it. Erik van der Putten (or Puteanus), evidently a follower of Lipsius, publishes a rhetoric of 'Laconism,' in which
he marshals an array of "brief" ancient writers, Thucydides,
Cato, Tacitus, especially, who are properly called Attics, he
says, because they are so reticent, so incisive, so significant.
But this term is inadequate to express their true glory; they
may better, he thinks, be called the Spartans. 30 Later Balzac
in the Preface to his Socrate Chretien (1652), makes the same

distinction. "Que si nostre zele ne peut s'arrester dans nostre
coeur: Qu'il en sorte a la bonne heure! Mais qu'il se retranche
dans le stile de Lacedemone: Pour le moins dans l'Atticisme:
Au pis aller, quil ne deborde pas par ces Harangues Asiatiques,
ou il faut prendre trois fois haleine pour arriver a la fin d'une
periode." Further on he is more exact, and speaks of the "At-
tiques de Rome, qui contrefaisoient Brutus, et n'imitèrent pas
Ciceron," meaning Seneca and his school.

Great progress in critical discrimination and historical knowledge has evidently been made since the sixteenth century. This
progress continues in a later generation; and the clearest witness of all is Père Bouhours. He has the prose of the century
in perspective: its faults and dangers are vividly before his
mind, and he sees that they are immediately connected with the
imitation of the ancient models of the acute and subtle genus
humile, Tacitus, Lucan, Seneca: yet, he says, I am still an
Attic in my tastes; and what he means by that is exactly shown
in a passage from an earlier work, [31] every sentence of which
is important for our purpose. He is speaking of the French language, and says that what he admires most in it is "that it is
clear without being too diffuse (étendue). (There is perhaps
nothing that is less to my taste than the Asiatic style.) It takes
pleasure in conveying a great deal of meaning in a few words.
Brevity is pleasing to it, and it is for this reason that it cannot
endure periods that are too long, epithets that are not necessary,
pure synonyms that add nothing to the meaning, and serve only
to fill out the cadence (nombre) .... The first care of our language is to content the mind (esprit) and not to tickle the ear.
It has more regard to good sense than to beautiful cadence. I
tell you once again, nothing is more natural to it than a reasonable brevity." The form of the opposition between 'Attic' and
'Asian' in the seventeenth-century mind is more exactly expressed in the various phrases and turns of this passage than in
any other that we shall be likely to find.

IV

The aim of the literary historian is the utmost simplification that is consistent with the actual variety of the facts he
deals with; and in the preceding pages we have been trying to
make our generalization broad enough to include all the significant facts of seventeenth-century prose-style. But on the other
hand, the uniformity of any large set of phenomena is only

CROLL

interesting in relation with their diversity. The genus humile
had a history in antiquity running through seven or eight centuries, and during that period developed various phases of theory and various forms of style, most of which were known to
the leaders of Anti-Ciceronianism and played their different
parts in the drama of rhetorical controversy in the seventeenth
century. To distinguish these phases, and the character and extent of the influence that each of them had in the period we are
studying, is no less important than to observe the general tendency that is common to them all; and this will be the purpose
of all the rest of our discussion.

The earlier Greek phases of this history — the only ones that
we have considered up to this point — were of minor importance
in determining the actual forms that prose-style took in the seventeenth century; and if we only wanted to know what models it
could imitate we might confine our attention to the Stoic school
of rhetoric that triumphed over Ciceronian oratory in the first
century of the Roman Empire. But, on the other hand, the critics whose business it was to defend and explain it were well
acquainted with its purer sources in the classical period of
Greek culture; and they very often, one might say usually, defended or concealed their real use of the inferior "Atticism" of
Seneca and Tacitus by claiming the sanction of greater names
than these. Unless we can interpret the disingenuousness of
men laboring under the imputation of literary heresy we shall
constantly be puzzled in reading their manifestoes. Three names
associated with three phases of the history of genus humile in
the classical Greek period occur with some frequency in their
writings, those of Plato (or Socrates), Aristotle, and Demosthenes; and in the present section we will take up briefly each
of these phases, with reference to its place in seventeenth-
century prose-criticism — reserving for the proper point the
explanation of the paradox of describing the style of Demosthenes as a phase of the genus humile.

1. Of the first not much needs to be said. The nature of the
controversy recorded in the Gorgias and Phaedrus was of course
known to the Anti-Ciceronian leaders; and they knew perfectly
well, moreover, that the Isocratean, or Gorgian rhetoric was
of essentially the same kind as the Ciceronian rhetoric taught
by the orthodox humanists of the sixteenth century. It would
have been strange if they had not used the name of Plato in pro-
pagating their new taste for a philosophical and intimate prose,
or had not detected the similarity of the aims of their opponents

20

to those of the ancient sophistic rhetoricians. It was in fact
their occasional practise to apply to these teachers and their
seventeenth-century successors the old name of "sophists."[32]
There was an additional motive, however, for the revival of
this ancient controversy, which will strike the modern reader
as a curiosity of literary history. The new "Attics" were nine-
tenths Stoic in their morals, as they were in their rhetoric.
But Stoicism was stigmatized as heresy — especially when it
called itself "Christian" — at every distributing center of Catholic orthodoxy; at Rome itself it was under constant surveillance.
In these circumstances the name of Socrates was a convenient
disguise, partly because it was not hard to wrench his philosophy into a Stoic form, and partly because his conduct on his
trial and the manner of his death had long given him a place
among those who had fallen as martyrs of the struggle against
conventional sentimentality. Quevedo occasioned no surprise
when he linked the names of Socrates, Cato, and Job in his
Stoic hagiology;[33] and Balzac's title Le Socrate Chrétien could
easily be read in its real sense of le stoique chrétien.
For these reasons, then, we occasionally meet with the
names of Plato and Socrates in the propaganda of the new school.
But as far as the form of its style was concerned the earliest
masters of Attic had but little influence upon it. In the first half
of the century it is almost safe to say that they had none. In the
second, on the other hand, there were several ambitious revi-
vals of Hellenism, both in England and France, and the name
of Plato is often heard as that of a writer and a model to be imitated. Thus the Chevalier de Méré proposes a purely Greek literary program: Plato in prose and Homer in verse are the
preferred models, and next to these (since one must do lip-service, at least, to oratory) Demosthenes.[34] But there is some
disingenuousness in this and similar professions. The actual
style of de Méré does not differ in kind from that of St. Evré-
mond, for example, which was formed in the "libertine" school
of the first half of the century and "corrected" by the new mondanité of the second. Like other representative critics of his
century, de Méré calls himself an Attic; but he had already discovered the eighteenth-century formula in which Atticism is
identified with the "agreeable" style of l'honnête homme; and
this is a style very different from Plato's.
With less emphasis the same statement can be made of the
style of Fénelon in his Dialogues. Though it superficially resem-
bles the model it imitates, its Platonism is but a thin disguise

of the romantic and Christian poetry that we are familiar with
in his other prose writings. Indeed there is but one prose-style
of the seventeenth century that will stand a comparison, either
in kind or quality, with that of Plato: the prose-style of the
Lettres Provinciales; and Pascal is neither deceived nor disingenuous about the sources of this. He acknowledges that it
has been formed by the imitation of the same Stoic models that
were in favor in the first half of the century. [35]

The most important part played by Plato was to perpetuate
the idea of an "Attic" style, with new and somewhat different
associations, in the second half of the century, at a time when
the Latin models of such a style, heretofore in favor, had begun to be discredited.

2. The part played by Aristotle was much greater. Of course
neither his Rhetoric nor any other of his surviving works could
serve as a model for stylistic imitation, as the works of Plato
could. Yet it is probably correct to say that certain forms of
seventeenth-century prose-style are chiefly due to the attempt
to apply directly, in practise, ideas concerning the relation between logic and rhetoric gathered from the first two books of
the Rhetoric. This is probably true of styles so different in
their associations as that recommended by the Royal Society of
London and often used by its scientific contributors and that imposed upon the writers of the Port Royal Community by their
teachers. Both of these are characterized by a deliberate plainness which Aristotle would have been far from recommending
for literary use; but they both seem to rest finally on Aristotle's
resolution of the forms of rhetorical persuasion into forms of
syllogistic reasoning.

The importance of his influence upon the forms of style was
as nothing, however, when compared with that of his influence
on the theory of the Attic school. The advocates of a style suited
to philosophical thought needed a classical authority for their
support as unquestionable and orthodox as that of Cicero, and
Aristotle's Rhetoric provided them with what they needed. The
rhetorical aphorisms and discussions in Seneca's letters expressed their ideas, it is true, in popular and telling ways. They
served the purposes of Attics who did not need to profess any
great amount of classical learning or any profound knowledge of
rhetorical theory. But Muret, Bacon, Hobbes, and the teachers
of Port Royal – the men whose task was to lay the philosophical
foundations of seventeenth-century style – were all Aristotelian
at first hand, while many others, Lipsius, Descartes, and so on,

obtained their ideas from the same source, though perhaps less directly. To show adequately the relation of each of these philosophers to the Rhetoric would be a task far beyond our present limits; but at least it may be taken for granted that seventeenth-century Anti-Ciceronianism, like all other historical movements of protest against the excessive study of rhetorical form, derives its ultimate authority from the first two books of that work. [36] Even its third book proved useful. For its description of the usual Isocratean oratorical forms was taken for what it was, a mere conventional recognition of existing customs; whereas its highly original treatment of Enthymemes was often employed for guidance in the art of forming aphorisms and antitheta in which the seventeenth century arrived at absolute perfection, and its treatment of the metaphor was often appealed to by the new Attics in defence of their favorite figure. [37] It is somewhat astonishing to find Aristotle quoted in justification of the devices of style by which concettismo achieves its dubious effect of power; but concettismo is, in fact, implicit in any "rhetoric of thought," such as Aristotle's was.

3. The third phase of Greek influence, namely that of Attic oratory, requires a larger discussion; for it involves the reopening of the subject of the genera dicendi. Hitherto we have considered only two genera, or 'characters, ' and this, as we have said, appears to have been the original form of the classification. The genus humile arose in opposition to oratory, as the appropriate language of intimate philosophical discussion; and the Gorgianic kind of rhetoric which was then regarded as the only, or at least the typical, form of oratorical style, then properly assumed the name of the genus grande in contrast with it. But a kind of oratory arose at Athens during the fourth century which was not open to the charges brought against the Gorgian rhetoric by Socrates and Plato, which, on the contrary, had some of the same qualities that the masters of the genus humile arrogated to themselves, an oratory disdainful of the symmetries and melodious cadences of the Isocratean model and professing to make its effect by the direct portrayal of the mind of the speaker and of the circumstances by which he has been aroused to vehement feeling. This later type of oratory was of course familiar to the post-Aristotelian theorists who adopted the bipartite division; but so strong was the tradition of the earlier type of oratory that they took no account of it in their theory. They merely wished to represent the dichotomy of style in its original and most striking form. When, however, the oratory

of Lysias and Demosthenes and their school had at last taken so firm a place in the tradition that they could no longer be disregarded in the doctrine of the genera, a curious situation presented itself. For now a mode of style had to be recognized which was allied in its rhetorical form and procedure with the genus humile, yet was unmistakedly grander than the genus grande and had the same uses. Nothing but disorder could result from such an anomaly; and in fact the adjustment that was finally made was little better than a confused and illogical working arrangement. The "Attic" oratory of Demosthenes usurped the title of the genus grande; the genus humile remained undisturbed in its old functions and character; and a third genus was added to take care of the Isocratean oratory, and was given the name of the genus medium (modicum, temperatum, etc.), though this name does not appropriately represent either the historical or the formal relation of the Isocratean style to the other two. In the time of Cicero it had become customary to define the character of the three genera more fully by a reference to the effect of each upon the audience. The genus humile is best adopted to teaching or telling its hearers something; the genus medium delights them or gives them pleasure; the genus grande rouses them and excites them to action. 38

It is true that this explanation of the development of the tripartite classification is not so clearly documented as we should like to have it. It is only probable. But it is the result of what seems the best investigation of the subject, and it at least explains. We may now add that the treatment of the three styles in the seventeenth century tends to confirm it, because it shows a similar solution of the problem by men placed in a situation strikingly like that of the ancient theorists.

The aim of the founders of seventeenth-century prose style was to domesticate a genus humile. The movement inaugurated by the Anti-Ciceronian leaders, Bacon, Montaigne, Lipsius, was like that of Plato and Socrates and their followers in that it was meant to make and legalize a breach between oratory and philosophy, and to establish in general use a style meant to express reality more acutely and intimately than oratory can hope to do. And the form of oratory which was present to their eyes in the usage of their own age was, as we have seen, the same Isocratean form that the founders of the ancient genus humile had before them. But the seventeenth century could not sacrifice its love of grandeur and nobility to its love of philosophic truth any more than the Athens of the fourth century could. It was, indeed, an age that for peculiar reasons, affected solemnity, a kind of somber magnificence, in all the forms of its artistic expression. It was the immediate heir of the Renaissance, for one thing, and came naturally by a taste for pomp and grandiosity; but, furthermore, the peculiar political and religious temper of the time, especially as it came under Catholic and Anglo-Catholic influence, tended to strengthen these inclinations and to give them a special character. "Persuade the King in greatness," said Bacon in the confidence of his private journal; and the words might be taken as an index of the temper in which some of the most representative art of his age was produced. It was the age of the Baroque in sculpture and architecture; of the intense and profound Catholicism of El Greco; of the conscious Romanization of moral ideals; of the dogma and ceremony of absolutism; and of the elaboration, in sermon and essay, of a sombre liturgy of Death.

Such an age could not be satisfied with the intimate and dialectic uses of prose alone. It needed them and made the most of them; but its rhetorical preceptors must also hold up before it the image of a great and noble oratory, greater and nobler even than the Ciceronian, but as free from Cicero's 'Asianism,' as 'Attic,' as their own philosophical essay-style. They need not actually achieve this style, it is true, in their own practise; but even though it should prove to be far beyond its powers, the seventeenth century demanded the contemplation of such a model as the ideal form to "persuade it in greatness."[39] The name of Demosthenes therefore appears in the writings of the Anti-Ciceronian rhetoricians from the beginning of the century to the end as the symbol of the genus grande in the Attic manner. Bacon, in a letter written in the name of Essex, says that if one must study oratory, Demosthenes (not Cicero) is the model to be imitated.[40] Fénelon, opposing the Isocrateanism of preaching style – which had been revived in the eloquence of Bossuet and his followers – eloquently proclaims the superiority of the greater Attic orator. [41] And between these two great critics there are many that utter the same sentiment. But it was Balzac who made the name of Demosthenes his trademark or heraldic device. The sum and substance of his writings on the subject of style is that he aims to produce a union of Attic quality with the grand manner of a "heroic" oratory, to combine the virtue of Brutus's style, as he says in one place, with that of Cicero's, the naturalism, that is, of the one with the eloquence of the other. For the purposes of this program the authors who served as the models of his own style — Seneca, Tacitus, and Tertullian — were ill-adapted, and he publicly repudiated them — with a disingenuousness which was justified perhaps by a lofty purpose — as inferior and debased Attics, professing to find the only model of the true heroic style in Demosthenes, or perhaps in the late 'Attic' orations of Cicero against Antony. [42]

Balzac took all this program with a grand seriousness worthy of it. It expressed a genuine will toward la grande éloquence. But judged by his practise, or that of any one else of his time, it has as much significance as a flare of trumpets or a pyrotechnic display. The kind of Attic practised in the seventeenth century could not combine with the magnificence of oratory to advantage, and the bizarre effects so common in the sermons and panegyrics of the first half of the century are the monstrous births that proceeded from the unnatural union between them. The taste of the age was not equal to the Athenian feat of being simple and grand at once; and when Bossuet turned from his early studies in Attic ingenuity and point to the reform of oratorical style, it was not the example of Demosthenes or Lysias that served his turn, but the old conventional oratorical model of Isocrates, and the medieval preachers.

The professed study of Demosthenes' oratory, in short, had but little practical effect upon seventeenth-century prose; and the same thing is true of all other Hellenistic programs of style in France and England during the period of Balzac and the generation that immediately followed him. Some of them were important as indicating new turns of thought and a widening of literary horizons; but none of them and not all of them taken together, had a decisive influence on the form of vernacular style, or provided models that could be effectively imitated. Concerning the first half of the seventeenth century and the generation that preceded it a much stronger statement than this must be made. The truth about this period can only be expressed by saying that it was anti-Greek. The study of Hellenistic culture had become associated with the ornamental learning, the flowery science, of the humanists. "The wisdom of the Greeks," said Bacon, "was rhetorical; it expended itself upon words, and had little to do with the search after truth." This statement has a strange sound in modern ears; and in fact Bacon would have expressed the opinion of his age better if he had made it more carefully. We could not object if he had said that the Greeks were speculative and rhetorical; and the age of Bacon, Montaigne, and Descartes was equally averse to disinterested speculation and disinterested rhetorical beauty. The new rationalists were incapable, in short, of understanding the value of Greek culture; and even though they had been able to form a juster estimate of it, they would still have rejected it merely on the practical ground that it was too remote, too ancient, conveyed in a language too foreign to their own. It is thus that we are to explain the bravado of Burton and Descartes, and several other great scholars of the time, who professed that they knew no Greek or had forgotten what little they had been taught. [43]

The culture of the period from 1575 to 1650 is almost wholly Latinistic; and we must seek for the models on which it chiefly formed its style in the forms of Latin prose which it considered Attic.

V

The history of Latin prose-style during the classical period displays the same constant tendency to a rivalry and opposition between two great characters of style that prevailed in Greece; and indeed from the time that the facts begin to be clear enough for exact historical statement this rivalry is conducted under the direct influence of Greek theory and largely in imitation of it. But there was a difference, due to a difference in the characters of the two races, which manifests itself especially in the associations that attached themselves to the genus humile. In Greece, as we have seen, this 'character' of style originated in philosophy and arose, later than the other, out of a protest against the emptiness and unreality of oratory. In Rome, on the other hand, it had its roots in the very beginnings of Roman life, and was originally the expression of the practical and unphilosophical nature of the Roman people. In its first phases it was certainly not a literary style at all, or at least owed nothing to formal rhetorical method; and the beauties that were later seen or imagined in it were merely the natural expressions of the soldierly and rustic character of the early Roman gentlemen, the accidental effects of art that sometimes arise spontaneously from a Spartan or Puritan contempt of art.

So at least we may suppose. Almost nothing remains to show what it actually was, and we cannot say with assurance how much of the character attributed to it was due to the philosophic theories of the days when Roman thought had already been profoundly affected by the Stoicism of later Greek culture. Probably there is general truth in the idea then prevalent that there had been a severe early Roman prose expressive of the national character; and whether there was or was not the belief in it had its effects upon the later prose, and the genus humile at Rome took from it associations of virility and sturdy practical purpose, associations with primitive and archaic forms of virtue, which always made it something different from its Greek counterpart even after Roman culture had been generally Hellenized. To these associations the genus humile owed part of its great success during the Empire, largely because they transported the men of that age to a different world from their own; and it had the same value once again in the seventeenth century to those who were reviving at that time "Roman" and Stoic conceptions of literary style. But even in a somewhat simpler and more classical period than either of these, in the pre-Augustan age of Cicero and Brutus, the genus humile was already supposed to have a peculiarly Roman and primitive character. In the style of the Commentaries of Caesar, as manly and efficient, men have always said, as his legionaries themselves, it was believed that the national genius still survived, though Caesar had in fact studied rhetoric assiduously in the schools; and in Brutus' treatise De Virtute — whose non-survival was the occasion of many Stoic tears in the seventeenth century — we might be able to behold an image of the early Roman through all the sophistication of a philosophical and rhetorical theory. [44]

We cannot in fact tell when or how the native tendencies of Latin style blended with foreign influences, or what forms of national prose they might have produced if they had been left to exfoliate in their own manner. What we do know is that Roman rhetoric became outwardly well Hellenized during the last century of the Republic, that the theory of the rhetorical genera was established in the same form that it had then come to have in Greek practise, and that henceforward the history of the genus humile in Latin prose — like that of its rival, the grand oratorical style of Cicero — has to be written chiefly in terms of Greek rhetorical theory. The Greek genus humile was not now, however, what it had been in the time of Aristotle; during the two centuries that had intervened it had undergone important changes in its technique and had acquired new associations, all of which are exactly reproduced in the Latin style that represents it. We must turn back to the point where we left off the account of its development and consider these changes.

We have seen that Aristotle first developed into a system the theory of style as it is determined by the processes of thought and that in the generations immediately after him a place was found in rhetorical teaching for a kind of style, known as the genus humile, founded upon this way of looking at rhetorical phenomena. We have now to observe that the great increase in the interest in philosophical studies in Greek communities during the third and second centuries was the cause of an increased attention to this genus humile and of interesting developments in its theory and practise, and that the occasions for the proper and healthy use of the more popular oratorical style were at the same time greatly reduced as a result of changed political conditions in the Greek world. Whether this change is to be regarded as a beneficent consequence of the restoration of order by absolute authority, as the Romans of the first century and most seventeenth-century observers considered it to be, or was, on the other hand, a lamentable indication of the decay of character that follows the loss of liberty, as Milton, for instance, undoubtedly thought it was, we will not stop to inquire. It is the fact alone that concerns us, and we will proceed at once to specialize it still further by noting that the important rhetorical fact is not so much the spread of philosophical interest in general, as the remarkable diffusion of the principles of the Stoic sect. This does not mean necessarily that Stoicism was in itself the most important philosophy of the age — though that also may be true — but only that it had clearer and more systematic theories than the other sects with regard to the form of a philosophical style, and was able to speak, at least on most points, as the general rhetorical representative of them all.

Aristotle describes two essential virtues of style: clearness and appropriateness. But his method of treating the theory of rhetoric in the first two books implies another of almost equal importance, namely, brevity; and in his immediate followers this virtue assumes actually a coördinate place with the other two in the description of the genus humile. Upon his analysis, modified in this way, the Stoic rhetoric depends; and the three qualities — clearness, brevity, and appropriateness — appear and reappear in it, usually in the order named, and with only such additions and subtractions as always occur in a traditional formula. Each of them, however, is interpreted in a particular way and takes on a special meaning in the Stoic system. [45] We will consider the three in order, and what they meant in Stoic practise.

1. Aristotle places clearness first. The Stoics often — though not always — give it the same titular position. But, whether they

CROLL

do so or not, it is never first in their affections. There were two features of Stoic thought that tended to reduce this virtue to a subordinate rank, or even to give a positive value to its opposite. Clearness is evidently the first merit of an exposition of objective reality, as in the statement of facts and laws of natural science; Aristotle occasionally had such exposition in his mind, and, partly on his authority, there have been in modern times several attempts to erect the theory of style on the foundation of mere scientific clearness. But the kind of truth that the Stoics chiefly had in mind was moral and inward. It was a reality not visible to the eye, but veiled from common observation; hidden in a shrine toward which one might win his way, through a jostling, noisy mob of illusory appearances, by a series of partial initiations. This kind of reality can never be quite portrayed of course, because ultimate knowledge of the mystery of truth is never attained. But it is at least possible to depict the effort of the athletic and disciplined mind in its progress toward the unattainable goal. And this effort of the mind was the characteristic theme of the Stoics, and the object of their rhetorical art. Though by the rigor of their theory they were bound to a cold passionless objectivity, they really aimed at a highly imaginative portrayal of their relations with truth; and even those who professed to strive for clearness, and in fact did so, could not resist the temptation to convey the ardor of their souls in brevities, suppressions, and contortions of style which are in fact inconsistent with a primary devotion to the virtue of perspicuity.

In the second place, the Stoic sage was always, by his own account, a foreigner in the world. His outward fortunes were bound up in every conceivable way with powers and conventions which were alien to his soul; and the form in which the problem of life presented itself to him was how to reconcile his inward detachment and independence with his necessary outward conformity to the world, or even with the desire — which he usually professed — to be of service to it. Obscurity, therefore, might be useful to him in two ways. Sometimes it was a necessary safeguard of the dangerous truths he had to utter; sometimes it was a subtle mockery of the puerile orthodoxies of society.

Clearness is a virtue, then, to which the Stoics pay lip-service, which they more honor in the breach than the observance; and its value in the criticism of their prose consists chiefly in the fact that it enables us to distinguish two classes of writers among them. One consists of those who studiously defy it for the reasons just mentioned. Tacitus — le prince des ténèbres — Persius, and Tertullian are of this class, and their imitators in the seventeenth century, Donne (in his letters), Gracian, Bacon, Malvezzi, etc., may easily be distinguished by their cult of significant darkness. The other is of those who studiously cultivate clearness, not for its own merits, but as a wise corrective to the other qualities of Stoic prose, brevity and appropriateness, which they love better. Seneca and the seventeenth-century writers who directly imitate him, such as Lipsius and Bishop Hall, and Montaigne and Browne in some of their writings, are representative of this class.

2. Aristotle's second virtue is brevity, and this the Stoics liked so well that they sometimes actually put it first, in the place of clearness.[46] It is a quality that is almost necessarily involved in the attempt to portray exactly the immediate motions of the mind. In the history of all the epochs and schools of writing it is found that those which have aimed at the expression of individual experience have tended to break up the long musical periods of public discourse into short, incisive members, connected with each other by only the slightest of ligatures, each one carrying a stronger emphasis, conveying a sharper meaning than it would have if it were more strictly subordinated to the general effect of a whole period. Such a style is a protest against easy knowledge and the complacent acceptance of appearances. It was of course a style loved by the Stoics. But there was a feature of their discipline which gave a particular value to the virtue of brevity; for they made greater use than any of the other sects of the art of condensing their experience into "golden sayings," dicta, maxims, aphorisms, sententiae. Chrysippus, working perhaps on hints received from Pythagoras, gave directions for the manufacture of sententiae, and the use of them in moral discipline, directions which are familiar to modern readers through Bacon's reproduction and expansion of them in his De Augmentis, unhappily without due credit given to his predecessor.[47] It is not enough to say of Stoic style that it tends toward brevity. In its most characteristic forms it tends toward the sententia, which is as properly to be called its ideal form as the rhythmic cumulative period is that of the Ciceronian style.

3. The quality of appropriateness is not so easy to deal with, for it has been the subject of puzzled discussion, and has assumed a Protean variety of forms. Yet it is of the utmost importance in the interpretation of Stoic style. Aristotle does not

clearly enough define what he means by it, but it is evident that
he thinks chiefly of appropriateness to the character of the audience addressed and the nature of the occasion: a style should
adapt itself to the social requirements of discourse, and not be,
for instance, either too lofty or too mean for the kind of audience
contemplated. Through the recognition of this virtue of style, it
seems, he is able to introduce into his Rhetoric the description
of the Isocratean model of oratory which occupies his Third
Book. [48] But in this use of the word there was an obvious danger to the Stoics; for it might be used as an open door for the
entrance of those modes of popular and sensuous appeal which
they deprecated in public oratory and carefully excluded from
their own private discourses. They gave to the quality of appropriateness, therefore, a meaning more suitable to the theory
of a style which was to concern itself intimately with experience.

The statement of it by Lipsius will serve to present their
view briefly. [49] Appropriateness, he says, has two aspects, appropriateness to thing and to person. The former we will consider first for a moment. It is evident that taken in its strict sense
appropriateness to the thing has nothing to do with rhetoric. If
(as Lipsius defines it) "everything is said for the sake of argument (or subject)," and "the vesture of sentence and phrase
exactly fits the body of the thing described," thought and discourse are exactly identical, and there is only one science of
both, which we may call logic or dialectic, or what-not. The
proper outcome of the doctrine of "appropriateness to the thing"
is such a mathematical style as was contemplated by Bayle, and
some seventeenth-century Cartesians, a style admirable of
course for scientific exposition, but limited to uses in which art
has no opportunity. In short this phase of the Stoic doctrine of
style exactly illustrates the instability of an anti-oratorical theory of style, which we have already noted in other connections.
But, as we have also observed, practise never squares exactly
with a theory; and insistence upon the more literal truth of language has often served as a wholesome corrective or a partisan
challenge in periods sated with the conventional ornaments of style.

Secondly, there is appropriateness to person; and this, says
Lipsius, has two phases: appropriateness to the person or persons addressed, and appropriateness to the speaker or writer
himself. In the former phase it may be taken as justifying the
study of the abstract rhetorical beauties of oratory. So Aristotle
seems to take it. But the Stoics lay all the emphasis on the other phase, namely, the exact interpretation in one's expression

of the mode of one's thought; or rather they identify the two phases, the proper and effective mode of impressing one's hearers being, in fact, to render one's own experience in the encounter with reality as exactly, as vividly, as possible. And here we must return to what was said a moment ago concerning the character of Stoic morality, in order to show how this interpretation of appropriateness brings into play the rhetorical artifices which are characteristic of the Stoic style and were often so overdone in the periods that we are chiefly concerned with. If truth and reality were easily come at and declared themselves in the same unmistakable uniform terms to all inquiring minds, their expression in language would be a comparatively simple task. The style appropriate to the thing would be almost the same as that appropriate to the mind of the speaker. But it is not so, of course. The secrets of nature are made known only to attentive and collected minds, prepared by a long preliminary training in habits of exclusion and rejection; and even to them but partially, and in moments of rare and peculiar illumination. A style appropriate to the mind of the speaker, therefore, is one that portrays the process of acquiring the truth rather than the secure possession of it, and expresses ideas not only with clearness and brevity, but also with the ardor in which they were first conceived. It is no more a bare, unadorned, unimaginative style than the oratorical style is; it aims, just as oratory does, to move and please, as well as to teach, but is distinguished from oratory by the fact that it owes its persuasive power to a vivid and acute portrayal of individual experience rather than to the histrionic and sensuous expression of general ideas.

The figures it uses, therefore, are not the "schemes," or figures of sound, which characterize oratory, but the figures of wit, the rhetorical means, that is, of conveying thought persuasively. Antithesis is one of the chief of these, not however as a figure of sound, which it may be, but as a means of expressing striking and unforeseen relations between the objects of thought. Closely connected with this is the study of "points,"or argutiae; for the effect of points or turns of wit is found to be due nearly always to an open or veiled antithesis. These two, antithesis and point, are the chief means employed in the art of aphoristic condensation, which, as we have seen, is the normal form of Stoic rhetoric. Of equal importance with these, and of greater literary value, is the metaphor. If Aristotle first expounded the uses of this figure, the Stoics of the late Greek period, and especially those of the Roman Empire, may have the credit of having first shown fully in practise its marvelous expressive powers. It is the greatest of the figures by which literature may interpret the exact realities of experience; and is as much the characteristic possession of the essay style as the musical phrase is of the oratorical. [50]

It has been necessary to enter into these details concerning the Stoic rhetorical technique because all subsequent practise of the genus humile was affected by it; in the Stoics of the late Greek period, of the first and second centuries of the Roman Empire, and of the seventeenth century we encounter the same traits of style.

We return now to the history of the genus humile at Rome.

How much progress the opponents of the Ciceronian type of oratory had made during the last century of the Republic in domesticating the devices of Stoic rhetoric which have just been described we cannot say with definiteness, because the remains of the literary activity of the circles of the Scipios and Laelius, and of Brutus and Pollio, are singularly few and fragmentary. It may be that the example of Cato and the image of the primitive Roman gentleman preserved a simpler and plainer character in their prose, and made them chary of adopting too freely methods of expression which had the double taint of foreign culture and philosophic sophistication. We cannot say with certainty. But we know that in its theory and general outlines the Stoic rhetoric was approved and imitated by them. Cicero's testimony makes this sure. For he calls the kind of rhetoric which was usually (but without his approval) set in contrast with his own almost indifferently by the names genus humile or stilus Stoicus, and the terms in which he describes it in his rhetorical treatises show that it had the same general features that the genus humile had assumed in Greece during the third and second centuries: its brevity, its significant abruptness, its tendency to sententiousness, and its preference of the "figures of thought" to the "figures of sound."

This form of style had, as we have seen, all the advantage of being associated in men's minds with the native Roman tradition. It was the "ancient" style in contrast with the Ciceronian model, which bore the imputation of Asianism and novelty. Why, we may well inquire, was it so slow in winning its way to a position of preeminence in Roman letters ? When we read in Cicero's writings the names of the authors who represented it in his own time and the century before him we cannot fail to see that they are both more numerous and vastly more respectable and Roman

than those of their literary opponents. Indeed if the name of
Cicero himself is eliminated from the history of the grand style,
a comparatively small number of important names remains to
it. Yet this is unquestionably the style that won the greater suc-
cesses during the pre-Augustan age and even in the Augustan
age itself, whereas the Stoic style did not attain its proper triumph until a later generation and after it had submitted itself
to the process of regularization and conventionalization in the
schools of declamation.

The explanation may be found in the uncompromising haughti-
ness of its pretensions during the earlier periods. It was in-
transigeant in two senses, both as Stoic and as 'ancient Roman.'
Cicero's great success was due to his sympathy with popular
tastes; and his own confidence and joy in the rightness of the
rhetorical appeal which the people loved saves him from the imputation of insincerity. The Stoics, on the other hand, may have
suffered from an excess of scruple. Their unwillingness to confess the aid of rhetoric or to study their characteristic modes
of expression in the systematic and deliberate way in which they
were later studied in the schools of declamation may have cost
them their chance to be heard either in their own time or by
later generations.

These are mere speculations concerning an interesting fact.
What is clear and certain is that Stoic style entered on a new
and brilliant phase of its history with the foundation of the
"schools of declamation," which first made their influence felt
during the Augustan age, and later came to control the style of
almost all Roman literature for more than two centuries.

If there is a common misunderstanding in the mind of the
general reader of the character of the training in the schools of
declamation, the blame must be imputed to the scholars who
have written on the subject. The fault commonly attributed to
the teachers in these schools is too great a fondness for rhetorical artifice and the love of it for its own sake; and this is a
sound indictment. But without the critical specifications that
might be expected to accompany it in the statements of scholars
it is more misleading than helpful; for it might more justly be
brought against the masters of the style that the new schools
repudiated and supplanted than against those that accepted their
training and practised according to their precepts. A reader,
for instance, who accepted the careless, denunciatory language
of most modern historians on this subject — rather than their
actual meaning — would suppose that Seneca wrote with more

CROLL

rhetorical exuberance and display than Cicero, that Tacitus'
style reflected a less exact image of the actual world than that
of Livy, and that Juvenal and Persius are characterized by an
habitual use of the flaccid ornaments of conventional rhetoric![51]
It is necessary, therefore, to point out that the purpose of the
schools of declamation was to train their pupils in the practise
of the genus humile — de re hominis magis quam de verbis agi-
tantis. Their pretension was realism; their program the cultivation of all the means of individual expression at the expense
of conventional beauty. It is true that they studied for this purpose the figures and devices that had been conventionalized by
the rhetoricians of the Stoic schools of Greece; they even practised them with a more conscious art and found in them new resources for purely literary and rhetorical pleasure. But these
figures and devices were metaphor, antithesis, paradox and
"point" — the appropriate means for the literary expression of
ingenious thought and acute realism.

The name by which these schools were known has doubtless
done much to create a prejudice against them; but the general
custom of denunciation is due in a still greater degree to the
fact that the period in which their influence culminated and produced its greatest results is conventionally treated as a period
of literary decadence. That there was a general depreciation of
moral values in the public and social life of the age of Nero and
Domitian no one will deny; and it is probable that the literature
of such an age reflects some of its evil conditions even in the
character of works which are designed to correct them. But
there is often an undue readiness to distribute the honors of de-
generacy; and it is fair to recall that in great measure the literature of the silver age was a literature of protest. The first
fruits of the schools of declamation came to maturity during the
Augustan age, in the writings of Ovid; and in the constant stylistic trickery, combined with the soft delicacy of sentiment and
the absence of ideas that characterize these exercises in poetry
there are grounds for the expectation of a literary decline. But
the characteristic products of the next century are not at all in
that vein. On the contrary they are nearly all the new births of
a union between the forms of style taught in the schools of declamation — Stoic, as we have seen, in their origin, but not necessarily so in their application — and a genuine and powerful
movement of Stoic philosophy, which derived its impetus from
a revolt of the best ideas of the age against the corruption prevalent in society. The style of the schools of declamation gained

36

a new value, a new meaning, from this happy alliance. In the
writings of Seneca, Tacitus, Lucan, and Juvenal it served to
recall the ideas of an age of Rome that seemed almost as primitive then as the Middle Ages do to us now, and reaped the advantages of that association with early native forms of prose
which the Stoic style had always enjoyed. To this association,
indeed, it partly owed its tremendous success. But on the other
hand it might claim at the same time the honors of a "modern"
style in a sense that that term has enjoyed in almost all periods; for its expressive and piquant forms lent themselves admirably to the needs of the new rationalists and their independent criticism of contemporary society.

VI

In previous sections of this paper we have seen that "Attic
prose" in the seventeenth century denoted the genus humile, or
philosophical essay-style, in contrast with the Ciceronian type
of oratory; and have discussed the influence of the earlier Greek
theorists and exemplars of this genus upon it. We have now to
observe that the forms of the genus humile that were of practical use to it as models for its own imitation were the Roman
forms whose history has been outlined in the preceding section.
This statement must be made still more specific, however.
The prose that actually determined the forms of its style was
that Stoic prose of the first century of the empire — along with
some later prose of the same school — which was alembicated
in the schools of declamation. The traditions of the Republic on
which "Silver-age Latinity" rested, to which it always referred,
were valuable, it is true, to the seventeenth century, and it is
for that reason that it has been considered so carefully here.
The example of Brutus, for instance, was of incalculable advantage to it both in morals and rhetoric when it wished to describe
in the clearest and purest terms the ideal to which it aspired,
or to express most unequivocally the motives of its opposition
to an oratory of pure display; and we have seen that Balzac
spoke of "the style of Brutus" as if it were a familiar form that
could be studied at large in existing documents. The example of
Caesar again served their purposes in the same way. That he
did not actually belong to a particular school of philosophy or
style made no difference. For his conduct, and that of his legionaries, were regarded as the counterparts in practise of the
heroic virtue which Epictetus and Seneca portray in its moral

37

and inward effects;[52] and his style, virile and soldatesque, like
his life, would have been taken by Montaigne and Bacon as the
model of their own, in preference to that of Seneca or Tacitus,
if they had not been compelled by the spirit of their age to be
rhetoricians malgré soi.[53]

But seventeenth-century writers could not imitate Brutus or
Caesar or Cato in their own style. The explicit and inartificial
candor of the Republic was the quality that some of them loved
best, but none of them could emulate it in their own manners,
because they were living in a different kind of an age and were
wholly conscious of the difference. They felt sincerely, almost
instinctively indeed, that they were living in a period of decline.
There had been a culmination of energy and confidence in the
sixteenth century; but the external unities of the Renaissance
were dissolving, and the most striking phenomenon of the new
age was the division between their outward and inward interests
and allegiances which revealed itself to its wisest minds. As in
the first century, authorities and orthodoxies were establishing
themselves in the corporate political and spiritual life of the
age which derived their sanction from its weaknesses rather
than from its strength; and these the 'good man,' the 'sage,'
felt himself bound to support or obey because they were the only
safeguards against the evils which the divisions and corrupt tendencies of the time would bring in their train if they were left
free to work out their natural results. But his true devotion
was given elsewhere; his true ideals were not embodied in the
external forms and symbols of the age; his real standards could
not be made manifest by signs which would be visible to the
crowd.[54] In such an age the true literary modes are those that
serve the purposes of criticism, protest, individual intelligence.
The ideal form of style to which it refers is of course the "natural" style which expresses naïvely the candor of the soul. But
in fact the style it demands for its self-expression is one that
has been wrought upon with subtle art to reveal the secret ex-
periences of arduous and solitary minds, to express, even in
the intricacies and subtleties of its form, the difficulties of a
soul exploring unfamiliar truth by the unaided exercise of its
own faculties.

It was not only its social and political state, however, that
turned its literary tastes in the direction of the inferior Atticism
of the Empire. An explanation that lies nearer the surface of
things is found in the state of its artistic culture, the character
of its literary tastes as determined by its historical position.

38

"ATTIC PROSE" IN THE SEVENTEENTH CENTURY

It was still in the Renaissance, or at least was its immediate
successor, and it had not yet cast away the love of rhetorical
ornament for its own sake which had descended to the Renaissance from the middle ages. Its purpose indeed was to escape
from this tradition, to represent things as they are, to be as
little ornate and rhetorical as possible; but it could not express
even this purpose except by means of artifice, mannerism, device. It was still somewhat "Gothic" in spite of itself; and the
rhetoric elaborated in the schools of declamation offered it exactly the opportunity it needed to indulge what was most traditional, most unclassical in its tastes under the protection of
classical authority.

For these, and doubtless for many other, reasons there was
a revival of silver-age literature in the seventeenth century, or
in the period from 1575 to 1675 which we are treating here as
the seventeenth century. Many of the isolated facts which are included in this general statement and justify it have been noted
of course by literary history. But the disingenuous or merely
traditional orthodoxy which runs through the age has partly
veiled the actualities of its taste and practise from the eyes of
modern students. And it is partly at least for this reason that
the period (1575-1675) between the Renaissance, properly so-
called, and the neo-Classical age has never been clearly differentiated in literary history, although in the other arts, in sculpture, painting, and architecture, its character has been recognized and described. We shall not understand the seventeenth
century, we shall not know the exact meaning of the eighteenth
century, until we have come to realize more clearly than we
now do that a century intervened between the eighteenth and the
sixteenth in which Lucan had a more effective influence on the
ideas and the style of poetry than Virgil did; in which Seneca was
more loved and much more effectively imitated in prose-style
than Cicero had been in the previous generations; in which Tacitus almost completely displaced Livy as the model of historical
and political writing; in which Martial was preferred to Catullus,
and Juvenal and Persius were more useful to the satirists than
Horace; in which Tertullian, the Christian representative of the
Stoic style of the Empire – notre Sénèque, as he was called –
exercised a stronger power of attraction over the most representative minds than St. Augustine, who is the Cicero and the
Ciceronian of patristic Latin.

These are the great names. But the movement of imitation
and rehabilitation extended the broad mantle of its charity over

minor works which have not at any other time been well regarded by the modern world. Velleius Paterculus' odd mixture
of anecdote and aphorism[55] and Pliny's unpleasing Panegyric
to Trajan[56] played their several parts, and not unimportant
ones, in seventeenth-century prose history; and it would be possible to add interesting details concerning the taste of this period for other minor authors of the first century. But space must
be reserved even in so general a survey for the mention of two
Greek writers, by no means minor, who were at Rome during
the period of Seneca and Tacitus and display in different ways
the spirit of the Roman culture of their time. Plutarch's Morals
and Epictetus' Discourses, known chiefly in translation, exercised an enormous influence upon the moral ideas, and only a
little less upon the literary ideas, of the generation from Montaigne to Pascal.

The zeal of this revival was not more remarkable than its
success. It is probably true that no other modern period has
so thoroughly domesticated in its own literary productions the
thought and the style of a period of antiquity; and the title of the
Silver Age of modern literature as applied to the period of European literature beginning about 1575 would have considerably
more in its favor than nicknames given by this method of nomenclature usually have.

To prove the soundness of assertions sweeping over so wide
an area as this would of course be impossible within the limits
of a single paper; and even the evidence concerning prose-style,
which is all that we are concerned with here, would only be convincing through its cumulative effect in a series of chapters.
There is no more than room here to gather together a few of
the passages in which the dependence of the age upon first-cen-
tury models is most broadly depicted.

François Vavasseur, the French Jesuit rhetorician of chief
authority in the middle of the century, may almost be said to
have devoted his literary career to the exposition of the silver-
age proclivities of his time and an attack upon them. His admirable treatise on the Epigram is meant to show, among other
things, the superior excellence of Catullus over Martial, and
that on the Novum Dicendi Genus is an accurate and sweeping
description of the preference of the age for the Latin authors
of the Decadence. [57] All this is echoed, but less clearly and
with less candor, in the later opinions of Balzac, who probably
learned more from Vavasseur than his critics have confessed.
But Balzac is torn between his romantic tastes and his classical

judgment; and the perspective is better preserved in two critics
of the latter half of the century. In describing the taste of Prio-
lo, the historian, for the ancient Anti-Ciceronians of the first
century, Bayle allows himself to enlarge his theme into a discussion of the contrast between the three Augustans, Cicero,
Livy and Virgil, who have an eloquence of the same general kind,
he says, and Seneca, Pliny, Tacitus, and Lucan, whose style
he describes in striking terms of denunciation, and adds: "The
French begin to be sick of the same distemper." One questions,
after reading what he says of Mdlle. de Gournai and Montaigne,
and other writers of the earlier part of the century, whether he
does not mean the word begin ironically. [58] Father Bouhours, at
least, has no doubt of the cause of the distempers which have appeared for a century in French style. In his various critical writings he constantly draws a parallel between a certain class of
ancient authors, in which Seneca, Tacitus, Lucan, and Tertullian are the chief names, and the authors of the century past.
At different places he includes on the modern side of the parallel Montaigne, Lipsius, Balzac, the concettisti of Spain and
Italy, especially Gracian and Malvezzi, and a great array of
other writers of the seventeenth century. And in his best-known
work he represents Philanthe, the voice of the common tastes
of his time, as saying that he finds his opinions beginning to
change: he does not despair of some day coming to prefer Virgil
to Lucan, Cicero to Seneca. [59]

Poets and prose-writers are mingled in these citations indis-
criminately; and in this respect they correctly represent the
criticism of the time, which usually makes no distinction between them in discussions of style. There is no lack of witnes-
ses, however, who are concerned wholly with questions of prose;
rather there is an embarrassment of riches. We need not cite
the polemics of Muret and Lipsius, who were engaged in a deliberate attempt to rehabilitate Seneca, Tacitus, and the whole
school of silver-age Latinity, or of Montaigne, who was just as
consciously the propagandist of the influence of Plutarch and
Seneca. For these are controversialists whose testimony is pre-
judiced. The comments of later writers who have observed the
current of their times serves our purpose better. In the Latin
translation of his Advancement of Learning, published nearly
twenty years after the English version, Bacon added a significant passage to his famous denunciation of Ciceronianism, which
has wholly escaped the attention of critics. Here he describes
another styli genus, characterized by conciseness, sententiousness,

41

pointedness, which is likely to follow in time upon a period of oratorical luxury. Such a style is found, he says, in Seneca, Tacitus, and the younger Pliny, "and began not so long ago to prove itself adapted to the ears of our own time."[60] If this passage had not been concealed in Latin it would have had a greater influence upon our reading of the seventeenth-century prose. It is admirably confirmed by what Father Caussin said in France in 1619: he describes the new form of style in the same way, mentions the same ancient models, adding Sallust to the list, and says it is the style that everyone now covets.[61]

From the middle of the century an interesting array of parallels in ancient, Biblical, and seventeenth-century literature drawn up by the libertine scholar Gabriel Naudé must suffice. Naudé puts Seneca and Plutarch in the first rank of his preference, as a Montanist should; and with them Epictetus and Aristotle; the Wisdom of Solomon he thinks has the same value; and the chief modern authors of like quality are Montaigne, Charron, and Du Vair.[62]

After 1650 the knowledge of what has been happening in prose grows steadily clearer; the defects and errors of the first half of the century are under correction, but it is generally recognized that the same models are still preferred, the same "Attic" tendency prevails. Perhaps the most interesting comment of all, because of the genius of its author, is the fragment of Pascal's, cited on a former page, in which he asserts that the spirit of the time has all been favorable to an intimate style, which portrays things in their familiar form and as they are known as first hand, and that the style of Epictetus, Montaigne, and Louis de Montalte (that is of Pascal himself in the Lettres) is of this kind.[63] Pascal, it is true, derives his Stoicism, and the intimate style appropriate to it, partly from the Greek spring of Epictetus, but even he was more influenced by the style of his French translation, says Strowski, than by the original; and, as we have had occasion to observe, the Latin sources of neo-Attic were those that availed most for the uses of the seventeenth century. Malebranche, looking back over its history and criticizing it from the angle of a "mathematical" Cartesian, sees three great literary influences, all of the same kind, that have constantly been in operation. Tertullian, Seneca, and Montaigne are the members of this interesting trio; all of them, as he says, enemies of clear thinking and pure reason, because they have more fancy than judgment and dress the truth in colors of imagination.[64]

"ATTIC PROSE" IN THE SEVENTEENTH CENTURY

Finally, in the last year of the century, Shaftesbury sums up the history of Senecan imitation in his Characteristics. He describes accurately the form of the familiar essay in the manner in which Seneca had written it, and says: "This is the manner of writing so much admired and imitated in our age, that we have scarce the idea of any other model.... All runs to the same tune and beats exactly one and the same measure."[65]

It may be expected by the reader that in order to round off our argument we shall give illustrations of the use of the word "Attic" in the seventeenth century as applied specifically to the style of Seneca and Tacitus and their contemporaries. Many passages could be cited, of course, in which this attribution is implied; but those in which it is expressly stated would not be very numerous. For the age was aware, as our own is, that "Attic" had certain associations which made it seem inappropriate to authors so fond of rhetorical artifice as the Stoics of the first century were, even though it recognized that their philosophical and intimate manner gave them a general right to this appellation when they are contrasted with the Ciceronian and Isocratean kind of orators. "Attic" in short named in their use a genus dicendi that was very general in its character and very inclusive, and they were reluctant, just as the ancients were, to apply it to particular schools of writers. But this need not greatly trouble us. It is not so important for our purpose to defend our use of the term "Attic" as it is to indicate the relation between ancient forms of style and those prevalent in the seventeenth century. And this relation is exactly expressed by saying, first, that "Attic" meant in the seventeenth century the genus humile, and secondly, that the form in which the ancient genus humile was actually imitated in its own practise was the form in which it appeared in the prose and poetry of the silver age of Latin literature, and especially in the prose of Seneca and Tacitus. The term "Attic" is, in truth, not wholly satisfactory; but it is the only one that seems to be available to describe the dominant tendency of the seventeenth-century style, and was also the only one generally used for the purpose in the seventeenth century itself.

NOTES

1   It is perhaps necessary to say that the present paper is part of a more extended study with the same title, the object of which is to show that the successful Anti-Ciceronian movement inaugurated by Muret, Lipsius, Montaigne, and Bacon, in the last quarter of the sixteenth century, gave a new direction to European prose-style and determined its characteristic forms throughout the seventeenth century. For the history of this movement and the description of the forms of style which it created, the reader must be referred to other parts of this study, not yet published.

Various discussions of the Ciceronian movement of the Renaissance are familiar, and in all of these the earlier phases of the opposition to it — led by Erasmus, Pico, and others — receive due attention. On the other hand, the decisive Anti-Ciceronian movement of the last quarter of the century has heretofore received but cursory mention, as by Norden (Die Antike Kunstprosa, 778-9), Sandys (Ciceronianism, in Harvard Lectures on the Revival of Learning), and Izora Scott (Controversies over the Imitation of Cicero, 106-111). Miss Scott concludes with the unhappy statement that "barring a few individual dissertations .... controversial writing on the question ceased with the contribution of Muretus." An account as full as the limits of my subject permitted is given in my paper in the Revue du Seizième Siècle (II, 1914, 200-242) on Juste Lipse et le Mouvement Anti-Cicéronien.

2   Montaigne is franker than any other of the leaders in expressing a dislike of Cicero. Yet he admires his eloquence. "There is no real excellence in him," he says, "unless his eloquence itself is so perfect that it might be called a real and substantive excellence." Of course part of the point of this is, however, in the implied doubt of the value of pure eloquence, in itself; for no Ciceronian would think of doubting it.

3   Of course in the matured ancient theory there are three characters. See explanation, however, below, footnotes 8 and 37.

4   The division of the figures into schemata verborum and figurae sententiae is here adopted because it represents the opposition of styles that we are concerned with. There were, of course, other classifications in antiquity, based on other principles.

5   They are: — 1) Isocolon, approximate equality of length between members of a period; 2) Parison, similarity of form between such

equal members, as in the position of the nouns, verbs, adjectives, etc.; 3) Paromoion, likeness of sound between words thus similarly placed. Descriptions of them may be found in Volkmann's Rhetorik d. Griecher u. Römer, pp. 40-49, in Landmann's Euphuismus, Child's John Lyly and Euphuism, in the Introduction to Lyly's Euphues, ed. Croll and Clemons, or better in a number of the medieval treatises collected in Halm's Rhetores Latini Minores. They may be briefly described as the chief figures by which oratorical concinnity is effected.

6   E. M. Cope's Introduction to his translation of the Gorgias (London, 1883) gives a clear statement of the character of sophistic education.

6a   For the relation between the ideas of Plato and those of the Rhetoric see Cope, Gorgias, xxv-xxvi, and Hendrickson, Origin and Meaning of the Characters of Style, Amer. Journal of Phil., XXVI, 249-251.

7   On the inconsistency spoken of see Henrickson, as above, 254-5. Norden speaks of inconsistencies of the same kind between the Rhetoric and other works of Aristotle (see Antike Kunstprosa, 125-6).

8   In all that concerns the history of the three characters of style and the relations between the genus grande and the genus humile in ancient theory, I follow the convincing article by Professor G. L. Hendrickson cited in the preceding notes, and its companion, The Peripatetic Mean of Style and the Three Stylistic Characters, in vol. XXV of the same publication.

9   Plerique jactant cantari saltarique commentarios suos. Dial. de Or., 26. It is interesting that the reformers of style in the Rennaissance compared the corrupt medieval form of the genus grande to minstrel's elocution. See my Introduction to Lyly's Euphues, p. xlii.

10   For example, in Brutus 201: Grandis et, ut ita dicam, tragicus orator.

11   See, for instance, the classification by Demetrius: graceful, plain, and arid; all of these being species which, in a different classification from Demetrius', would form parts of the genus humile. See also Diogenes Laertius, Life of Zeno, and Quintilian, XII, 10, 20-27.

12 Quintilian's metaphor (XII, 10, 37) is beautiful. Advising the Romans to cultivate the grand style rather than the 'Attic,' he says: "Greek keels, even the little ones, know well their ports; let ours usually travel under fuller sails, with a stronger breeze swelling our canvas.... They have the art of threading their way through the shallows; I would seek somewhat deeper waters, where my bark may be in no danger of foundering."

13 Oration of 1582, introducing his course on the Epistolae ad Atticum; see also his double oration of 1580, defending himself for the public teaching of Tacitus, which had made him the object of open attack and secret intrigue.

14 Chapters 36-41. Rigault, La Querelle des Anciens et des Modernes, Chapter I, has made an admirable use of this dialogue as one of the starting-points in antiquity of the modern idea of progress. An interesting paper might be written on the effect of the Anti-Ciceronian agitation on the growth of this idea.

15 Works, Amsterdam ed. of 1723, I, 2 (ed. Feugère, Letter 1). Andreas Schott develops at length the relation between the decline of oratory and the political conditions at the downfall of the Republic, in the prefatory letter (to Lipsius) of his edition of the elder Seneca.

16 Epp. Misc., II, 41.

17 Book II (De Augmentis Scientiarum, VI, chap. 3). "For although in true value it is inferior to wisdom, ... yet with people it is the more mighty." Its function is "to contract a confederacy between the Reason and Imagination against the Affections"; and again: "Logic handleth reason exact and in truth, and Rhetoric handleth it as it is planted in popular opinions and manners." The chief defect that he notes in the study of rhetoric is that too little attention has been paid to the study of private modes of discourse. In this art orators are likely to be defective, "whilst by the observing their well-graced forms of speech they lose the volubility (i. e., the subtlety or flexibility) of application." He then proceeds to supply this defect in part by making a collection of aphorisms and antitheses on the moral and political life of man, which he greatly extended in the De Augmentis, observing that whether this belongs to politics (prudential wisdom) or to rhetoric is a question of no importance.

18 De l'Eloquence Françoise (Works, IV, Paris, 1684), pp. 4-7. He also has a treatise Sur la Composition et sur la Lecture des Livres (Works, vol. XIII). Whether a work had ever been written

before on this subject I cannot say.

19   Oeuvres Diverses, III, 178. Compare same, I, 645, vi; and his Dictionnaire, s. v. Pitiscus, A.

20   "La principale partie de l'éloquence consiste à concevoir fortement les choses et a les exprimer en sorte qu'on en porte dans l'esprit des auditeurs une image vive et lumineuse, qui ne présente pas seulement les choses toute nues, mais aussi les mouvements avec lesquels on les conçoit." Arnauld, Logique, III, chap. 9. Compare Fénelon, Dialogues sur l'Eloquence II: "Toute l'éloquence se réduit à prouver, à peindre et à toucher." And again: "La vive peinture des choses est comme l'âme de l'éloquence."

21   See a passage near the beginning of the first dialogue, and a more interesting one near the end of the second, in which Fénelon seems to apprehend not only the connection between Bossuet and Isocrates, but the Isocratean character of medieval Latin preaching-style.

22   See the passages of La Recherche de la Vérité cited on a later page (p. 52, n. 64).

23   In antiquity, however, there was much the same variation of usage as that described in the text. The opponents of Cicero always tended to identify Asianism with the oratorical cultus, just as the modern Anti-Ciceronians did; but of course the prevalent doctrine was that there are two ways of becoming Asian: aut nimio cultu aut nimio tumore; either by studying too zealously the orationis cultus (as Bembo, Lyly, and many sixteenth-century writers did) or by exaggerating the sententiarum venustas (as Montaigne, Lipsius, Browne did in the seventeenth century). See Hendrickson, XXVI, p. 287, where the appropriate passages from Diomedes, Cicero, and St. Augustine are cited.

24   Opera Omnia, Leyden 1703-1710, vol. I, col. 1012A.

25   Proprietatem sermonis: on the technical meaning of this term in the theory of the genus humile see below, pp. 31-34.

26   Col. 1012 E.

27   Ib., ib. In Column 989 F, paraphrasing Horace's description of the brief style that tends to obscurity, he calls it Atticism, though Horace has nothing to suggest this.

28 Pro M. T. Cicerone, Paris 1531, section 68 and elsewhere.

29 Epp. Misc., II, 10.

30 De Laconismo, Louvain 1609. Van der Putten was Lipsius' successor in the chair of rhetoric at Louvain, and was one of those
disciples of his who caused his contemporaries to speak of him
in the terms that Quintilian used of Seneca, as "the man upon
whose faults a sect was founded." Ideas adapt themselves to the
size of the minds they find a lodging in, and it is not Lipsius'
fault altogether that concettismo of one kind or another makes its
appearance so soon in the style of his followers. Van der Putten
thinks (p. 78-9) that there is too much copia in Demosthenes and
the other Attic orators!

31 Entretiens d'Ariste et d'Eugène, 1671.

32 See Balzac, De la Grande Eloquence, Works 1665, vol. 2, pp.
518 ff., and the works of Naudé, passim.

33 See E. Mérimée, La Vie et les Oeuvres de ... Quevedo, Paris
1886, p. 288.

34 Méré's "Atticisme mondain" is very exactly described and placed
in its true relations by Strowski, Pascal et son Temps, vol. II,
chapter 8, and vol. III, chapter 7.

35 "La maniere d'écrire d'Epictète, de Montaigne, et de Salomon
de Tultie (that is, of Pascal himself in the Lettres Provinciales)
est le plus d'usage, etc." Pensées, I, 18, ed. Brunschvig, p.327.
See also his Entretien sur Epictète et Montaigne.

36 Muret's dependence upon Aristotle has been mentioned on an
earlier page. One of the characteristic expressions of his irony
was his choice of the Rhetoric instead of a Ciceronian subject
for his course in 1576-7, when he had been badgered into a temporary renunciation of the new anti-rhetorical studies of the rationalists. See Dejob, M. A. Muret, Paris 1881, pp. 293-6. Dejob fails to interpret Muret's career in an intelligible fashion because he does not understand the "Attic" movement and its intellectual implications. – Aristotelianism manifests itself clearly
in the subordinate relation of rhetoric to dialectics and ethics in
Bacon's Advancement and in the Port Royal treatises. On this
point see Jacquinet, Baconi de re litteraria judicia, Paris 1863,
pp. 48-51.

37 The raptures of the concettisti in praise of metaphor may be stu-

died in Gracian, Agudeza y Arte de Ingenio, Madrid, 1642, 1648, etc., passim; in Pallavicino, Trattato sullo Stile e sul Dialogo, 1646, etc., chapter 7 ("si chiama reina delle figure"); and in Tesauro, Il Cannocchiale Aristotelico, 1654, p. 316 ("il più pellegrino e mirabile ... parte dell' umano intelletto"). But Bouhours, the determined corrector of concettismo, is not less an admirer. See La Manière de bien Penser, 1687, pp. 20-21. The whole theory of concettismo is derived from Aristotle, especially Book II, chapters 22-24 (on Enthymemes) and Book III, chapter 2, sections 8-15 (on Metaphors). This point has been admirably brought out in the old work by Ferri, De l'Eloquence, Paris, 1789, pp. 228-233, the only discussion I know of in which the preëminence of prose over poetry in any proper consideration of the seventeenth-century conceit is observed.

38 This interpretation of the relation of the three characters follows that of Hendrickson in the articles mentioned in a former note (see p. 45, n. 8).

39 Compare with this phrase of Bacon's one of Balzac's, wholly characteristic of him. In his later works, he says, he has written most on political themes, and his aim in these productions has been to express himself "de ce qu'il y a de plus magnifique et de plus pompeux en la vie active."

40 Spedding's Life and Letters, II, 21-26.

41 Dialogues sur l'Eloquence I, near the beginning, II, near the end. Lipsius, in his Judicium supra Senecam, prefixed to his edition of Seneca (1605), anticipates Balzac's theory. See also the same use of Demosthenes' name and credit in Caussin's Eloquentia Sacra et Humana (1619), II, chapter on the Anti-Cicerones.

42 Avant-propos to his Socrate Chrétien, and Paraphrase, ou de la Grande Eloquence; also the attack of an enemy in the Lettres de Phyllarque à Ariste, and Ogier's answer in his Apologie pour M. Balzac.

43 Montaigne's reason for not reading Greek is characteristic of the period; "I am not satisfied with a half-understanding" (II, 10; see also I, 26). On the Latinization of culture in this age see an excellent passage by Nisard, La Litt. Fr., I, 429-30; also Brunetière, l'Evolution des Genres, p. 53; Spingarn, Literary Criticism in the Renaissance, p. 186.

44 Norden identifies Roman "Atticism" with the archaizing movement. With all deference to his authority, the reader is com-

pelled to feel he has made his point only as regards the second century, and has introduced new confusion into the history of the term Attic.

45   The clearest statements of the form of Stoic style in antiquity are in Diog. Laer. (Life of Zeno), VII, 59; Cicero, De Oratore (which Zielinski, with some exaggeration, describes as an exposition of Stoic theory), and Quintilian, XII, 10. In the modern period, Lipsius' treatise on style, Institution Epistolica, and La Mothe le Vayer's l'Eloquence Française (Oeuvres IV) rest directly on ancient Stoic authority. The clearest recent statement is by Hendrickson (as above, Am. J. of Phil. XXVI, pp. 257-61, 272, 284).

It should be said that in Diogenes Laertius another virtue, purity of language as determined by the usage of good society, precedes these three. This, however, proved so foreign to other ideals of the Stoic school that it was often omitted, and when it appears and is made prominent, as it is in the Roman Stoics of the second century, it is interpreted in such a way that it falls into virtual coincidence with the quality of appropriateness. Its history in the seventeenth century would make an interesting chapter, but must be omitted here.

46   So, for instance, Lipsius, Instit. Epist., ch. VII: Prima illa, prima mihi, sermonis virtus est.

47   Book VI, ch. 3. La Mathe le Vayer is more candid: see his l'Eloquence Fr., pp. 16, 57, etc. The source is Chrysippus as reported by Plutarch in his Controversies of the Stoics; but Aristotle's analysis of the enthymeme also contributed to the discussions of Bacon and La Mothe le Vayer.

48   See Hendrickson, as above, XXV, 135-6; XXVI, 254.

49   Instit. Epist., ch. 10.

50   See note 37, p. 48.

51   Boissier's essay on the Schools of Declamation is very misleading in this way.

52   In a sea-letter to his father the sailor-son of Sir Th. Browne is naïvely delighted with the spirit of the old Caesarian legions as portrayed in Lucan's Pharsalia. "It would have served [us] well," he says, "and had probably concluded the war in our fight with the Dutch." Works of Sir Th. B., ed. Wilkins, London, 1842, I, p. 142-3.

53   Daniello Bartoli (I Precepti, chap. 7), describing the "modern"
      style (a name often given to the new "Attic"), says: "Its beauty
      does not rob it of its strength. It can make the same boast that
      Caesar's soldiers did, who were able etiam unguentati bene pug-
      nare. Bacon's Secretary names Caesar with Seneca and Tacitus
      as his favorite authors. Montaigne's almost poetic praises of
      him are well known.

54   This view is more rigorously asserted in Fulke Greville's neg-
      lected prose-classic A Letter to an Honourable Lady than al-
      most anywhere else. But it is implied in the voluntary retire-
      ment of Montaigne and Charron, Lipsius and Balzac, Greville
      and Browne, to mention only a few of the philosophical solitaries
      of this age.

55   In Boccalini's Ragguagli di Parnaso, I, 23, Velleius Paterculus
      carries Lipsius' works to Apollo to receive immortality, and
      leads the author himself into the presence, between "Seneca the
      moralist" and "Tacitus the politician." There is an allusion here
      to Lipsius' Commentary on Paterculus. Gracian the concettisto
      finds in Paterculus a store-house of examples of his loved Agu-
      deza.

56   Dom Jean Goulu, the translator of Epictetus, published a long
      eulogy and analysis of the Panegyric to Trajan (Lettres de Phyl-
      larque à Ariste, 1628, Seconde Partie). Lipsius made a commen-
      tary on the work, and analyses of it were common in Italy and
      Spain, as were imitations. For an English imitation see Wotton's
      Panegyrick to King Charles.

57   Vavasseur (Vavassor), F., Oratio Tertia, Contra Novum Dicen-
      di Genus, Opera Omnia, 1709, pp. 201-209.

58   The references are all to the Dictionnaire. See also the articles
      on Balzac, Goulu, and Javersac.

59   La Manière de bien Penser dans les Ouvrages d'Esprit, ed. 1715,
      p. 445, Third Dialogue, at the end especially. Compare also
      p. 514: "Plus capable de préférer les pointes de Sénèque au bon
      sens de Cicéron, et le clinquant de Tasse à l'or de Virgile."

60   De Aug. Sc., I (ed. Spedding, Boston, 1865, vol. II, p. 127).

61   De Eloquentia Sacra et Profana, II, chapters 14-16.

62   Bibliographica Politica, p. 25 (in Grotii et Aliorum Dissertation-
      es, Amsterdam, 1645). See also his Syntagma de Studio Liber-
      ali, p. 79, and elsewhere.

63   See note 35, p. 48.

64   Recherche de la Vérité, Eng. Translation, 1694, Book II, Part
     3, Chap. 3, "Of the Force of Some Authors' Imagination." Also
     an additional Illustration of this chapter, pp. 144-47.

65   Miscellany, Book I, Chap. 3 (Works, ed. Robertson, 1900, Vol.
     II). Also I, 1.

RES ET VERBA: WORDS AND THINGS

A. C. Howell

Sometimes a phrase appeals to men and becomes a commonplace because it seems to meet a need they have experienced.
The pair of terms under consideration, words and things, had
an interesting history during the seventeenth century because
it served as a corrective comment on the heavily ornamented
style of writing then in vogue. It is the purpose of this paper to
trace briefly through the seventeenth century the use of this
combination of words and the idea represented by it. Although
the passages quoted do not by any means exhaust the possibilities of its use, they very probably represent a cross-section
and tend to demonstrate a changing conception of style and a rising interest in the technical study of words in terms of meaning.
As will appear, the term res, meaning subject-matter, seems
to become confused with res meaning things, and the tendency
to assume that things should be expressible in words, or con-
versely, words should represent things, not metaphysical and
abstract concepts, may be discerned. The controversy has
some current interest because of the present concern with semantics and the problem of meaning discussed by Alfred Korzyb-
ski, C. K. Ogden, I. A. Richards, S. I. Hayakawa, Stuart Chase,
and others.
    The origin of the use of this pair of words is, of course, clas-
sical; and it was from their study of classical rhetoric that seventeenth-century critics learned of it. An early expression of
the idea, with the two words in close juxtaposition, is the statement attributed to Cato the Elder: "Rem tene, verba sequen-
tur,"[1] which may be translated, "take hold of things and words
will naturally follow, or will take care of themselves." In the
rhetorical writings of Cicero the pair of words appears frequently, usually in expressions concerning the relation of style to
subject-matter, for which res was the normal rhetorical term.
In such sentences as this: "Ergo utimur verbis aut eis quae pro-
pria sunt at certa quasi vocabula rerum paene una nata cum rebus ipsis; aut eis quae transferuntur ..."[2] – translated in the

Reprinted by permission from English Literary History, Vol. 13
(1946), pp. 131-142.

Loeb Classical Library edition, "The words we employ then are
either the proper and definite designations of things, which were
almost born at the same time as the things themselves; or terms
used metaphorically ..." etc. – in such sentences Cicero seems
to recognize the distinction between words as representing things
and words used metaphorically, a distinction which will be noted
later. Again, commenting on the five ornaments of oratory, he
names as one of them the quality of brevity and goes on, "Brevitas autem conficitur simplicibus verbis semel una quaque re
dicenda, nulli rei nisi ut dilucide dicas serviendo."[3] Here again
res and verba are paired, and the meaning seems to be that brevity is attained by using simple words, saying each thing once,
and observing nothing except that you speak with lucidity. Cicero
does not suggest that words should represent things merely; he
was more interested in ornamentation than in the plain style.
When he used the term res, he was normally referring to subject-matter. However that may be, readers of Cicero often
meet with the pair of words under discussion.

But the phrasing with which Quintilian expressed the relationship of words and things seems to have made the strongest impression on seventeenth century readers and may have been the
basis for their use of the pair of words in relation to style. In
the Institutes Quintilian advised the writers: "Curam ergo verborum rerum volo esse sollicitudinem. Nam plurumque optima
rebus cohaeret et cernuntur suo lumine,"[4] which Professor C.S.
Baldwin translates as follows: "Let care in words be solicitude
for things. For generally the best words are inseparable from
their things and are discovered by their light."[5] It is possible
here to translate the term rerum as subject-matter, as does
the Loeb Classical Library translator; yet it remains a fact that
res and verba appear together in the Latin, which every seventeenth-century reader would have used, and consciously or unconsciously he would have recalled the simple meaning of the
two terms, things and words.

But the rhetoric of Cicero prevailed during the Renaissance,
to the general neglect of Quintilian's admonition, with only a
rare voice raised in opposition. Thus, when Donne began to
preach, he was only following the prevailing style when he chose
words for sound and for their ornamental value as well as for
their meaning. It was Francis Bacon who began the condemnation of Ciceronianism, and perhaps first used res and verba in
a contemporary discussion of style. But his condemnation did
not begin to take effect until the Restoration, as will be noted.

The point to note here is the use of the terms. Discussing the first distemper of learning in The Advancement of Learning, Bacon first mentions the causes of Ciceronianism, then goes on:

> ... these four causes concurring, the admiration of the ancient authors, the hate of the schoolmen, the exact study of the languages, and the efficacy of preaching, did bring in an affectionate study of eloquence and copy of speech.... This grew speedily to an excess; for men began to hunt more after words than matter. [6]

When Bacon turned The Advancement of Learning into Latin under the title De Augmentis Scientarum, he translated the last phrase quoted above as "... atque hinc factum est, ut paulo postea major apud plurimos coeperit haberi verborum cura quam rerum. "[7] – using the exact phrase of Quintilian, "Curam ergo verborum rerum." In the next section of the Advancement Bacon again uses the terms and goes on to point out a distinction of which Hobbes was to make vigorous use. "Here then is the first distemper of learning," said Bacon, "when men study words and not matter... for words are but the images of matter...."[8] In the Latin this becomes "Hic itaque cernere est primam literarium intemperiem, cum (ut diximus) verbis studetur non rebus... quid enim aliud sunt verba quam imagines rerum...."[9] Thus, for Bacon the pair of words, res and verba, matter, or things, and words was clearly associated with a way of writing which did not approve of words used as ornament, "full of sound and fury, signifying nothing."

His voice was raised in protest even at the moment when the preaching of Donne and Andrews was popular, and the pursuit of words, rather than things was considered the proper ornament of style. In 1629, however, another voice was raised in protest, using the same pair of words to plead for a simpler style. Sir John Beaumont sounded the warning, echoing Quintilian, in a poem which anticipates a number of the conceptions of style which were to be in vogue in the Restoration. In his poem "To His Late Majesty, Concerning the True Forme of English Poetry," he advised the poet to seek:

> ... pure phrase, fit epithets, a sober care
> Of metaphors ...   (lines 51-52)
> Strong figures drawn from deepe invention's springs
> Consisting less in words and more in things
> A language not affecting ancient times
> Nor Latin shreds, by which the pedant climbs ... [10]
>   (lines 55-58; italics mine)

Although Ben Jonson has much to say about style in his Timber, he seems not to have used the pair of words under discussion. Perhaps he comes closest to it in such statements as, "In all speech, words and sense are as the body and the soule."[11] and "Pure and neat language I love, yet plain and customary."[12] The quotations are cited from the section entitled "De Stylo, et Optimo Scribendi Genere, " which, according to Spingarn, is almost literally translated from Quintilian's Institutes.[13] That he knew the passage may be gathered from other evidence. He cites a statement attributed to Julius Caesar, "Verborum delectus origo est eloquentia, "[14] and in the margin refers the reader to "Quintil. L. 8. " He also told William Drummond of Hawthornden in the "Conversations" that "Quintilian's 6, 7, 8 books were not only to be read but altogether digested. "[15] Certainly he would have agreed with Beaumont that good style should consist "less in words and more in things. "

No reader of early seventeenth-century prose needs illustrations of the extravagant over-use of words, the evident love of words for themselves, which marks the sermons and essays of the period. The authors were hunting more after words than matter, to use Bacon's phrase, and paid small attention to Beaumont's suggestion. The trick of the redoubled phrase, common in Donne and Browne, the piling up of alliterative synonyms of which Taylor and Donne were often guilty, the choice of strange, unusual terms often without meaning to their auditors — all these can be abundantly illustrated in the prose published between 1620 and 1660. Four sentences may therefore, serve as examples of the usages against which Quintilian's admonition, "let care of words be solicitude for things, " was directed.

> (John Donne) ... we have no such rule or art to ground a presagition of spiritual death, and damnation ... for the mercies of God work momentanely, in minutes ...
> [Sermon 158][16]

> (Sir Thomas Browne) ... But who were the proprietaries of these bones, or what bodies these ashes made up, were a question above antiquarism; not to be resolved by man, nor easily perhaps by spirits, except we consult the provincial guardians, or tutelary observators.... [17]
> [From Hydrotaphia, or Urn-Burial, Chapter 5]

> (Jeremy Taylor, telling the story of three false witnesses

who swore oaths) ... the first wishing that, if he said
false, God would destroy him with fire; the second, that
he might die of the King's evil; the third, that he might be
blind: and so it came to pass; the first, being surprised
with fire in his own roof, amazed and intricated, confound-
ed and despairing, paid the price of his slander with the
pains of most fearful flames; and the second perished by
pieces, and chirurgeons and torment; which when the third
saw, he repented his fault ... but wept so bitterly, that
he found at the same time the reward of his calumny, and
the acceptance of his repentance 18
    [Sermon 24, from Twenty-five Sermons preached at
                               The Golden Grove]

(John Gauden) ... darkness and disputes, division, distractions, dissatisfactions, and confusions must needs follow ... [any opposition to Apostolic Succession] 19
       [Funeral Sermon for Dr. Brownrig, London, 1660]

With Hobbes the distinction between "words," Bacon's "images of things (or matter)," and the "things" themselves becomes clearer as he champions the cause of the simple, plain
style in his Leviathan (1651). His keen interest in clarity and
definition led him to deplore the use of words which had vague
referents, to use the term of modern writers on semantics. He
attacks vagueness and absurdity in language and drives home
his point by singling out for particular sarcasm the writers on
divinity, and by implication the preachers. Thus in Chapter 3
of the Leviathan he takes up the problem of classification of
nouns, concluding that words are only "wise men's counters,"
having no value if not related to verifiable facts. Discussing absurdities in language, he remarks that the cause of the seventh
absurdity is the use of "names that signify nothing; but are taken
up and learned by rote from the schools, as 'hypostatical,' 'tran-
substantiate,' 'consubstantiate,' 'eternal-now,' and the like
canting of schoolmen."20 Again, he concludes: "the light of human minds is perspicuous words, but by exact definitions first
snuffed, and purged from ambiguity ... and on the contrary,
metaphors, and senseless and ambiguous words are like ignes
fatui...."21 Later, he remarks on "another fault in the discourses of some men; which may be numbered amongst the sorts
of madness; namely the abuse of words ... and that is, when
men speak such words, as put together, have in them no signification

at all...." That his readers may "be assured their words are
without anything correspondent in the mind ..." he proceeds to
give examples of such combinations of words which have no referents in the minds of readers, from "the schoolmen," such
as the title of a chapter in Suarez's book, "The first cause does
not necessarily inflow anything into the second, by force of the
essential subordination of the second cause...." And, concludes
Hobbes, not without a slight dig at theologians in general, "When
men write whole volumes of such stuff, are they not mad?"[22]
And mad, or at least "enthusiastick," to use a term then coming into vogue, [23] these writers were beginning to be considered
by the rising generation which produced the Royal Society.

Hobbes, then, approved of a style "consisting less in words
and more in things," and his powerful influence sounded the
deathknell of the ornate style, especially in preaching. Jeremy
Taylor, writing "Rules and Advices to the Clergy," which appeared after his elevation to the Bishopric of Down and Connor
in 1660, had by this time seen the need for a less ornate style;
and hence cautions the preacher as follows: "In your sermons ...
use primitive, known, and accustomed words, and affect not the
new fantastical, or schismatical terms."[24] Coming from Taylor, the most ornate preacher of the period, this advice surely
marks the advent of a new style in preaching, where words are
no longer to be fantastical or unknown to the auditory.

Other essays on preaching contained the same advice in more
detail, advocating the doctrine that words should move nearer
to things and that vague, abstract terms should be avoided. John
Eachard, writing in 1670, condemns the high-flown style popular in the universities; saying, "... for the most part, an ordinary cheesmonger or plum-seller, that scarce ever heard of a
university, shall write much better sense and more to the purpose than these young philosophers, who, injudiciously hunting
for great words, make themselves learnedly ridiculous...."[25]
Continuing the theme, Eachard attacks ornate preaching:

> Among the first things that seem to be useless, may be
> reckoned the high tossing and swaggering preaching....
> For there be a sort of Divines, who, if they happen of an
> unlucky hard word all the week, they think themselves not
> careful of their flock, if they lay it not up till Sunday, and
> bestow it amongst them in the next preachment....
>   Those that are inclinable to make these useless speech-
> es ... do it, for the most part, upon one of these two

considerations. Either out of simple phantastic glory. . . .
Or else, they do this to gain a respect and reverence from
their people. . . . For if the Minister's words be such as
the constable uses: his matter plain and practical, such
as comes to the common market: he may pass possibly
for an honest and well-meaning man, but by no means for
a scholar! Whereas if he springs forth, now and then, in
high raptures towards the uppermost heavens; dashing, here
and there, an all-confounding word! . . . if he soars aloft
in unintelligible huffs! preaches points deep and mystical
and delivers them as darkly and phantastically! "this, is
the way," say they, "of being accounted a most able and
learned Instructor."[26]

The obvious irony needs no comment, but the use of the terms
words and matter brings in a strong echo of the commonplace
which the century could not forget. [27]

It was the poet Abraham Cowley, however, who was next after Beaumont to use the actual pair of words under discussion.
Familiar as he was with the idea of Bacon and Hobbes and the
dear friend of Bishop Thomas Sprat, historian of the Royal Society, Cowley was much concerned with the problem of language.
It was natural, therefore, for him to consider words and things
when he wrote his "Ode to the Royal Society." Stanza 4 of the
Ode begins:

> From Words, which are but Pictures of the Thought,
> (Though we our Thoughts from them perversely drew)
> To Things, the Mind's right Object, he it brought. . . .[28]

The "he" refers to Philosophy, a fact which the poet is at some
pains to establish in a previous stanza. As will appear shortly,
the use of words and things may have occurred to Cowley as the
result of the deliberations on style in the Royal Society, for Bishop Sprat was to make the pair famous in his History. The lines
also recall Bacon's statement that "words are but images of
matter," and Hobbes's insistence on a distinction between words
and objects of reality.

Another member of the Royal Society caught the phrase – perhaps not unaware that he was echoing Quintilian, Beaumont, and
Cowley – when he wrote in his "tagged" version of Milton's Paradise Lost, which he made into a sort of drama and entitled
"The State of Innocence," the following lines:

> From words and things, ill sorted and misjoined
> The anarchy of thought and chaos of the mind. [29]

John Dryden did not find his phrase about words and things in
John Milton's poem, but he may have heard it discussed at the
meetings of the Royal Society, where he was one of those particularly concerned with the problem of language and style.

For in the deliberations of that important body is found the
clearest expression of a growing desire to make words represent things. This interpretation may not have been what Quintilian meant when he used the phrase "Let care in words be solicitude for things"; but the statement phrased by Sprat and embody-
ing the pair of words under consideration did mean that words
should stand for things and has become almost a classic definition of the plain style advocated by Hobbes and other Restoration critics.

As Bacon had traced in the Advancement of Learning the rise
of Ciceronianism, Sprat in the History of the Royal Society traces the rise of the ornate style. He notes that after the days of
Henry VIII the language "received many fantastic terms, which
were introduced by our Religious Sects; and many outlandish
phrases, which several Writers, and Translators, in that great
hurry, brought in, and made free as they pleased...."[30] As a
result of this confusion in the use of terms, the Royal Society,
he remarks, "did not regard the credit of Names, but Things:
rejecting or approving nothing because of the title which it
bears...."[31] When he comes to discuss "Their Manner of Discourse"[32] he notes that they have been "most sollicitous [sic]"
in regard to it, because:

> ... unless they had been very watchful to keep in due tem-
> per, the whole spirit and vigour of their design, had been
> soon eaten out, by the luxury and redundance of speech.
> The ill effects of this superfluity of talking, have already
> overwhelmed most other Arts and Professions.... Noth-
> ing may be sooner obtain'd than this vicious abundance of
> Phrase, this trick of Metaphors, this volubility of Tongue,
> which makes so great a noise in the World....[33]

But they have agreed upon a style which corrects these evils,
he says:

> They have, therefore been most rigorous in putting in

execution, the only Remedy, that can be found for this extravagance: and that has been, a constant Resolution, to
reject all the amplifications, digressions, and swellings
of style: to return back to primitive purity, and shortness,
when men deliver'd so many things, almost in an equal
number of words. . . . [34]

To illustrate that the Royal Society meant what it said when
it demanded "so many things almost in an equal number of
words," Bishop Sprat explains how the reports of the Society,
called "Histories" are collected "by the plainest Method and
from the plainest Information . . . from . . . experienc'd Men of
the most unaffect'd, and most unartificial kinds of life." By
"experienc'd" the Bishop meant, of course, practical men. He
then proceeds to give a number of samples of such "Histories,"
from which are taken the following sentences illustrating the
style of reporting:

In the Month of May the Oysters cast their Spaun (which
the Dredgers call their Spat;) it is like a drop of candle,
and about the bigness of a half-penny. The Spat cleaves to
Stones, old Oyster-shells, pieces of Wood, and such like
things, at the bottom of the Sea, which they call Cultch. . . . [35]

The use of words which may be identified with things, in full ac-
cordance with the Society's instructions, is here plainly evident.
But attention to things to the exclusion of words, which the
Royal Society both preached and practiced, "soon grew to an excess" as Bacon remarked of the opposite tendency a century
earlier. Consequently it, too, was condemned — and by no less
a person than the satirist Swift. Readers will recall the passage
in Gulliver's Travels, Book 3, the Voyage to Laputa, where Gulliver visits the Grand Academy, a generally recognized satire
on the Royal Society. Section four of the fifth chapter entitled
"Gulliver's visit to the Laboratories of the Grand Academy of
Lagado," gives an account of a device for framing a universal
language.

The other project was a scheme for entirely abolishing
all words whatsoever; and this was urged as a great advantage in point of health as well as brevity. . . . An expedient
was therefore offered, that since words are only names for
things, it would be more convenient for all men to carry

about them such things as were necessary to express the
particular business they are to discourse on ... many of
the most learned and wise adhere to the new scheme of expressing themselves by things. [36]

Here Swift, satirizing the style of the Royal Society, picks
up for special attention Bishop Sprat's phrase "so many things
almost in an equal number of words," and produces one of the
most delightful passages in his book. Noticeable also are the
side glance at Bacon's "words are only images of matter" and
Hobbes's emphasis on concrete words in Swift's phrase, "words
are only names for things."

Thus a simple pair of words, used technically by classical
writers on rhetoric, was picked up in the seventeenth century,
expanded into a commentary on style, made a rallying cry for
the new plain style, adopted by the Royal Society, and was finally laid low by the trenchant pen of Swift. Or was it? Perhaps
it was only scotched; for the semantic writers have resurrected
the spirit of the phrase when they point out the dangers of "high
order abstractions" and agree with Hobbes that the use of words
which have no communicable meaning leads to absurdity and
madness. They praise "pointer-words," that is, words which
stand for things, as did the Royal Society. And once more the
poet comments — a modern Beaumont this time, writing another
essay on the true form of English poetry. So Karl Shapiro brings
the wheel full circle when in his Essay on Rime he writes:[37]

> The question is one of language. No conception
> Too far removed from literal position
> Can keep its body. Ideas are no more words
> Than phoenixes are birds. The metaphysician
> Deals with ideas as words, the poet with things,
> For in the poet's mind the phoenix sings.

Thus perhaps in spite of Swift's strictures, the words of Quintilian are still in point, "Curam ergo verborum rerum volo esse sollicitudinem."

RES ET VERBA: WORDS AND THINGS

NOTES

1 Found in C. Julius Victor, Ars Rhetorica, Cap. 1.

2 Cicero, De Oratore, 3. 149. The translation is that of E.W.Sutton, in the Loeb Classical Library (Cambridge: Harvard Univ. Press, 1942), 2. 118-119.

3 Cicero, De Partitione Oratoria, 19. (Op.cit. 2. 326). Other illustrations of the use are in Orator, 40.9; and De Oratore, 3.19.

4 Quintilian, Institutes of Oratory, Lib.8, Proem, 20. 21.

5 C.S.Baldwin, Ancient Rhetoric and Poetic (New York, 1924), p. 78.

6 Francis Bacon, The Advancement of Learning, edited by William Wright (Oxford, 1920), p. 29.

7 Bacon, Works. Edited by James Spedding, Robert L. Ellis, and D.D.Heath (London, 1858), 1. 451.

8 Bacon, Advancement of Learning, Ed.cit., p.30.

9 Bacon, Works, loc.cit.

10 "The Poems of Sir John Beaumont," in English Poets, Edited by Alexander Chalmers (London, 1810), 6. 30-31.

11 Joel E. Spingarn, Critical Essays of the Seventeenth Century (Oxford, 1908-1909), 1. 36.

12 Loc. cit.

13 Spingarn, op.cit., 1. 224.

14 Ibid., 1. 37.

15 Ibid., 1. 218.

16 John Donne, Works, edited by Henry Alford (London, 1839), 6. 289.

17 Sir Thomas Browne, Works, edited by Simon Wilkin (London, 1900), 3. 42.

18   Jeremy Taylor, Works (London, 1880), 1. 748.

19   Cited by Caroline F. Richardson, English Preachers and Preaching, 1640-1670 (New York: Macmillan, 1928), p. 85.

20   Thomas Hobbes, Leviathan. Edited by Henry Morley (London, 1889), p. 14.

21   Ibid., p. 30.

22   Ibid., p. 42.

23   George Williamson, "The Restoration Revolt against Enthusiasm." SP, 30 (1933), 571-603.

24   Jeremy Taylor, op. cit., 3. 712.

25   John Eachard, The Grounds and Occasions of the Contempt of the Clergy and Religion (London, 1670). Reprinted in Critical Essays and Literary Fragments (English Garner), edited by John Churton Collins (New York, n.d.), p. 259-260.

26   Ibid., p. 264.

27   Joseph Glanvil published two essays in 1678 which also favored the new style and advised the use of plain words. The titles are: "A Seasonable Defence of Preaching and the Plain Way of it," and "An Essay on Preaching." In this latter he has a division entitled "The Preacher should use Plain Words:", in which he advocated "a manly unaffectedness and simplicity of speech ..." (Reprinted in Spingarn, op. cit., 2. 273.)

28   The Works of Abraham Cowley. The Tenth Edition. (London, 1707), 2. 603.

29   The speech is a part of Lucifer's soliloquy in Act 3, Sc. 1. Looking on Adam and Eve sleeping, Lucifer remarks:

    Their reason sleeps, but mimic fancy wakes
    Supplies her part, and wild ideas takes,
    From words and things ill sorted ... etc.
                                        (lines 140-144)
(Works of John Dryden, edited by Scott and Saintsbury [Edinburgh, 1883] 5, 147) The soliloquy is, of course modelled on Paradise Lost 4, lines 803-808, which runs as follows:

> Him ... they found assaying [to] forge
> Illusions as he list, phantasms and dreams
> Or if, inspiring venom, he might taint
> The animal spirits, that from pure blood arise
> Like gentle breaths from rivers pure, then raise
> At least distempered, discontented thoughts
> Vain hopes, vain aims, inordinate desires ...

30 Thomas Sprat. The History of the Royal Society (London, 1667), p. 42.

31 Ibid., p. 105.

32 Part 2, Section 20.

33 Ibid., pp. 111-112.

34 Ibid., p. 113.

35 From "The History of the Generation and Ordering of Greenoysters, commonly called Colchester-Oysters." Ibid., p. 307.

36 Jonathan Swift, Gulliver's Travels (Edited by G. Ravenscroft Dennis). In Prose Works of Jonathan Swift (London, 1899), 8. 192, 193.

37 Karl Shapiro, Essay on Rime (New York: Reynal & Hitchcock, 1945), p. 1.

SCIENCE AND ENGLISH PROSE STYLE IN THE
THIRD QUARTER OF THE SEVENTEENTH CENTURY

Richard F. Jones

Literary style, like human personality, is a compound exceedingly difficult of analysis, for when its more obvious constituents are made clear, there still remains an illusive element, consciousness of which leaves the analyst with the unpleasant sensation of not having reached the bottom of the matter. As the most complex phenomenon in literature, style is the resultant of all the forces, known and unknown, underlying literary development, and the method and extent of the contribution made by each of these forces are a matter of probable inference rather than of positive demonstration. For that reason, any attempt, however ambitious, to account for the style of a literary epoch must be content with pointing out those more obvious influences that are combined and reflected in speech and writing, and with ignoring other factors which may escape detection. Under the protection of this confession I shall attempt to make manifest what seems to me the most important influence instrumental in changing the luxuriant prose of the Commonwealth into that of a diametrically opposite nature in the Restoration.

To one who is familiar with the writers of the Puritan régime, it would be rash to maintain that the style of this period is homogeneous, but probably every one can agree that the dominating manner of writing was that revealed in the great figures of Jeremy Taylor, Sir Thomas Browne, and John Milton, and lesser writers like Nathanael Culverwell. As is well known, this style is characterized by various rhetorical devices such as figures, tropes, metaphors, and similes, or similitudes, to use a term of the period. The sentences are long, often obscurely involved, and rhythmical, developing in writers like Browne a stately cadence, which, in the studied effect of inversions, is the prose counterpart of Milton's blank verse. The penchant for interlarding a work with Latin and Greek quotations is also apparent. The diction reveals a host of exotic words, many Latinisms, and frequently poetic phraseology of rare beauty. Against this style there arose a movement which later became an organized revolt,

Reprinted by permission from Publications of the Modern Language Association, Vol. 45 (1930), pp. 977-1009.

and which in the course of its condemnation of the old developed for itself a new standard of expression. The spirit animating the revolt had its origin in the scientific movement that determined the intellectual complexion of the seventeenth century. It is the purpose of this article to show that the attacks on the old, as well as the formulation of a new, style find consistent expression in those associated with the new science, that the first organized scientific body in England, the Royal Society, definitely adopted a linguistic platform which exerted a powerful influence on the style of its members even in writings other than scientific, and that the foremost exponents of the new style were members of this society and in most cases deeply interested in science.

Since Bacon stimulated and, to a certain extent, determined the scientific development of this period, one should search first in his writings for evidence of a stylistic standard. Without insisting upon a direct connection between his views and the movement that arose near the middle of the century, it would be foolish to underestimate the possible influence of one whose words were reverenced by later scientific reformers of style. At the very outset, however, we may say that his own style was quite different from that advocated by the scientists. "Ornamented with the riches of rhetoric," as it is, it everywhere reveals tropes, figures, and similitudes. For this reason his followers, though worshipping his ideas, never refer to his manner of expression as a model. Sprat, it is true, cites him as an example, but for poets and wits, not for writers of serious prose.[1] Rawley, Bacon's chaplain and biographer, represents his patron as opposed to fine writing, and tells us that in composing his works, the philosopher "would often ask if the meaning were expressed plainly enough, being one that accounted words to be but subservient or ministerial to matter, and not the principal."[2] Yet even Rawley must have been aware that plainness is not a characteristic quality of Bacon's prose, for he immediately adds the rather meaningless statement, "And if his style were polite, it was because he would do no otherwise." Regardless of his own style, however, Bacon attacks all manner of rhetorical devices because they lead to the first distemper of learning, "when men study words and not matter," and he holds that similitudes and ornaments of speech render the detection and correction of errors very difficult.[3] Moreover, near the beginning of the Magna Instauratio he reveals a stylistic attitude, which, though not apparent in his own practice, is essentially the same as that later maintained by his followers. "It being part of my design," he

says, "to set everything forth, as far as may be, plainly and
perspicuously (for nakedness of the mind is still, as nakedness
of the body once was, the companion of innocence and simplicity)
let me first explain the order and plan of the work."[4] While his
antagonism to rhetoric and his advocacy of a naked style may
not have inspired the stylistic revolt, they had their origin in
the same scientific spirit that animated the later reformers of
prose, who express views similar to his.

The immediate influence of Bacon's words must have been
slight for the exuberant prose of the Elizabethans continued on
to the more highly developed and poetic style of the Commonwealth. In 1646, however, is heard again the plea for a plain
style; this time in John Wilkins' Ecclesiastes, or a Discourse
concerning the Gift of Preaching. Wilkins, who later became
the prime mover in the establishment of the Royal Society, had
been for a number of years deeply interested in science, and
was at this moment an enthusiastic member of a small group of
men who met weekly in London to put into practice the Baconian experimental philosophy. It was the spirit of the latter that prompted
him to say, as regards the "phrase" that should be used in preaching,

> It must be plain and naturall, not being darkned with
> the affectation of Scholasticall harshnesse, or Rhetoricall
> flourishes. Obscurity in the discourse is an argument of
> ignorance in the minde. The greatest learning is to be seen
> in the greatest plainnesse.... When the notion is good, the
> best way to set it off, is in the most obvious plain expres-
> sion.... And it will not become the Majesty of a Divine
> Embassage, to be garnished out with flaunting affected el-
> oquence. How unsuitable it is to the expectation of a hung-
> ry soul, who comes unto this ordinance with a desire of
> spiritual comfort and instruction, and there to hear onely
> a starched speech full of puerile worded Rhetorick? 'Tis
> a sign of low thoughts and designs, when a mans chief study
> is about the polishing of his phrase and words.... Such a
> one speaks onely from his mouth, and not from his heart.

The same opinion is continued in another passage, concerning
which we must remember that the epithet "solid" was so consistently applied to the new philosophy as opposed to the old,
that the expression "solid business" is equivalent to scientific
matters. "It must be full, without empty and needlesse Tauto-
logies, which are to be avoided in every solid business, much

more in sacred. Our expressions should be so close, that they may not be obscure, and so plain that they may not seem vain and tedious."[5] A glance at Wilkins' own writings discovers a practice consistent with his theory, and William Lloyd, in a funeral sermon on him, truly says,

> He spoke solid truth, with as little shew of Art as was possible. He exprest all things in their true and natural colours; with that aptness and plainness of Speech, that grave natural way of Elocution, that shewed he had no design upon his hearers. His plainness was best for the instruction of the simple.... He applied himself rather to the Understanding than Affections.... In his Writings he was judicious and plain, like one that values not the circumstances so much as the substance.

Two years later the same contempt for the superficial fineries of verbal dress appears in William Petty, one of the outstanding members of the little group who, about the middle of the century, met weekly in Petty's lodgings at Oxford, for the purpose of carrying on experiments, a group that later merged with a similar body in London to form the Royal Society. Petty was especially interested in the practical aspect of science, devoting much of his time to inventions of various sorts. In communicating some matters of scientific nature to Samuel Hartlib, he says,

> I shall desire you to shew them unto no more than needs you must, since they can please only those few that are real Friends to the Design of Realities, not those who are tickled only with Rhetorical Prefaces, Transitions and Epilogues, and charmed with fine Allusions and Metaphors.[6]

The expression "Friends to the Design of Realities" is interesting in this case, for it means nothing more than subscribers to the new philosophy, and thus the quotation shows that Petty makes style a distinguishing mark between the experimental philosophers and those who held to the old tradition. This remarkable sensitiveness to matters of style on the part of the scientists, which is revealed in their thinking it necessary to confess, and vindicate, their lack of rhetorical ornament, appears again in a work by Francis Glisson, a famous physician of the time, and a prominent member of the London group of

Baconians which was formed in 1645. He concludes his preface
in the following manner:

> Finally expect no flashes of Rhetorick and Courtly-Language;
> Nobis licet esse tam dicertis,
> Musas qui colimus severiores.
> And indeed the conditions of the matter forbids all such paint-
> ing; in such a manner,
> Ornari res ipsa negat, contenti doceri. [7]

The next opposition to rhetorical ornament is discovered in
Hobbes' Leviathan, 1651. Though now chiefly remembered for
his psychological and political philosophy, Hobbes was, according to his own statement, most interested in natural science. [8]
His philosophical interests were developed in France along with
Descartes, Gassendi, and Mersenne, but in his earlier years
he had been a companion of Bacon, and from the latter he may
have caught his scientific enthusiasm. In his characteristically
blunt fashion, Hobbes tells us that there is nothing he distrusts
more than elocution, and that he has rejected the ornament of
classical quotations because there is no longer any virtue in ancient authority. [9] He permits a counsellor to use only significant, proper, and brief language, and forbids them "obscure,
confused, and ambiguous Expressions, also all metaphoricall
Speeches tending to the stirring up of Passion," which are useful only to deceive. [10] In speaking of that antithetical pair dear
to the seventeenth-century critic, judgment and fancy, he lays
down the law, as the Royal Society did later, that —

> In Demonstration, in Councill, and all rigorous search
> of Truth, Judgement does all; except sometimes the under-
> standing have need to be opened by some apt similitude;
> and then there is so much use of Fancy. But for Metaphors,
> they are in this case utterly excluded. For seeing they op-
> enly professe deceipt; to admit them were manifest folly.

And again, "in a Sermon, or in publique, or before persons unknown, or whom we ought to reverence, there is no Gingling of
words that will not be accounted folly." [11] Among the four abuses of speech, he lists the metaphorical use of words, "that is,
in other sense than that they are ordained for; and thereby deceive others." [12] He insists that "Metaphors and Tropes of
speach are no true grounds for reasoning," and one of the causes

for absurd conclusions he ascribes "to the use of Metaphors, Tropes, and other Rhetoricall figures in stead of words proper."[13] He concludes by saying:

> The Light of humane minds is Perspicuous Words, Reason is the Pace; Encrease of Science the way; and the benefit of man-kind the end. And on the contrary, Metaphors, and senseless and ambiguous words, are like ignes fatui; and reasoning upon them, is wandering among innumerable absurdities.[14]

The same scientifically induced materialism so characteristic of Hobbes appears in John Webster's Academiarum Examen, 1653. Webster was a chaplain in the Parliamentarian army, and an early and ardent follower of Bacon. In the work mentioned above he vehemently attacks the old philosophy, and fervently recommends a reformation of the universities in the way of the substitution of experimental science for the Aristotelianized divinity and natural philosophy dominant there. But he is not content with attacking these only; he would place distinctly below the new science such subjects as rhetoric, oratory, and the like, which, he says,

> serve only for adornation, and are as it were the outward dress and attire of more solid sciences; first they might tollerably pass, if there were not too much affectation towards them, and too much pretious time spent about them, while more excellent and necessary learning [i. e. experimental philosophy] lies neglected and passed by: For we do in these ornamental arts, as people usually do in the world, who take more care often time about the goods of fortune, than about the good of the body it self or the goods of the mind, regarding the shell more than the kernel, and the shadow more than the substance.[15]

A similar dislike for an ornate style and a corresponding approval of plainness in expression may be found in Robert Boyle, a scientist so illustrious it would be impertinent to comment on his connection with the new movement. In his Some Considerations Touching the Style of the Holy Scriptures, written about 1653 though not published until 1663, he expresses the view that when verbal ornaments are spared, they are not missed, and that some writings expressed in the plainest language outshine other subjects decked with the gaudiest expressions. Nor does he ascribe any importance to an objection that the Bible is destitute of eloquence and unadorned with the flowers of rhetoric, an objection which, he says, "a philosopher [i.e. a scientist] would not look upon as the most considerable."16

We also find the Baconian spirit stirring in out-of-the-way places. In 1660 Joshua Childrey published his Britannia Baconia, which is in reality a natural history of England, Scotland, and Wales, and the title of which indicates its connection with the new science. The author worshipped Bacon, and regarded his words with almost superstitious awe, trying in all humility of spirit to put into practice the precepts of the great master. He, too, was imbued with a scorn of fine language, and with a feeling that science demanded a style more suited to its purposes. "I have endeavour'd," he says in the preface, "to tell my tale as plainly as might be, both that I might be understood of all, and that I might not disfigure the face of Truth by daubing it over with the paint of language." He then proceeds to emphasize the fact that clear and accurate expression is just as essential to the communication of truth as careful observation is to its discovery, and he implies his conviction that the prevailing style was inimical to its proper presentation. A like attitude continues to be manifested in this branch of science, if for the moment we may step beyond the chronological limits of this article. Robert Plot, in the Natural History of Oxfordshire, 1676, says,

> And these [natural and artificial phenomena] I intend to deliver as succinctly as may be, in a plain, easie unartificial Stile, studiously avoiding all ornaments of Language, it being my purpose to treat of Things, and therefore would have the reader expect nothing less than words. 17

Ten years later, in the Natural History of Staffordshire, he is still making the same stylistic pronouncement, though the need for it had long ceased to exist. Certainly hostility to the style of the Commonwealth must have been deeply imbedded in scientists to cause this one to say in 1686, at a time when rhetoric was no longer in favor with any one of importance,

> I shall make all Relations (as formerly) in a plain familiar Stile, without the Ornaments of Rhetoric, least the matter be obscured by too much illustration; and with all the imaginable brevity that perspicuity will bear. 18

The foregoing quotations are sufficiently numerous and emphatic to indicate that repugnance to the prevailing style and a feeling for the need of a simpler, more direct manner of expression were a characteristic feature of the new science from its very inception. To us it seems quite natural that science should be antipathetic to rhetoric, but in this period some unique factors tended to accentuate this antipathy. Above everything else, the experimental philosophy was characterized by a savage attack upon "Aristotelity," to use Hobbes' term, in the course of which the chief charge was brought against the wordiness of peripateticism. [19] Again and again the new scientists stigmatized the traditional philosophy for being concerned only with words having no concrete significance and representing only figments of the imagination. Thus verbal superfluity became suspect. Allied to this attitude was the feeling for concrete reality, which naturally eschewed the verbal luxuriance of figurative language and the more subtle effects of imaginative expression. All this led to an insistence upon a direct unadorned style which should be concrete in idea, and clear and economical in expression, in short, to use a phrase of the period, "the marriage of words and things."[20]

When the experimental philosophers were joined in a royally protected society, 1662, it was inevitable that what had been the more or less sporadic and scattered, but still representative, attacks on prose expression should be combined and strengthened into an organized revolt. So we are not surprised to find that in the statutes of the Royal Society, published in 1752, chapter V, article IV reads:

> In all Reports of Experiments to be brought into the Society, the matter of fact shall be barely stated, without any prefaces, apologies, or rhetorical flourishes, and entered so in the Register-book, by order of the Society.

But the full importance of this requirement is not revealed until we read Thomas Sprat's History of the Royal Society, 1667, in an oft-quoted passage of which the author makes clear the society's intense opposition to rhetorical prose, and outlines the ideal of a new style which had already crystalized and upon which it was vehemently insisting. Sprat's words throw so much light on the movement which we are tracing, that I shall give them in full, even at the risk of bringing before the reader's eye that with which he is already familiar.

73

Thus they have directed, judg'd, conjectur'd upon, and
improved Experiments. But lastly, in these, and all other
businesses, that have come under their care; there is one
thing more, about which the Society has been most sollicitous; and that is, the manner of their Discourse: which,
unless they had been very watchful to keep in due temper,
the whole spirit and vigour of their Design, had been soon
eaten out, by the luxury and redundance of speech. The ill
effects of this superfluity of talking, have already over-
whelm'd most other Arts and Professions; insomuch, that
when I consider the means of happy living, and the causes
of their corruption, I can hardly forbear recanting what I
said before; and concluding, that eloquence ought to be banish'd out of civil Societies, as a thing fatal to Peace and
good Manners. To this opinion I should wholly incline; if
I did not find, that it is a Weapon, which may be as easily
procur'd by bad men, as good: and that, if these should
onely cast it away, and those retain it; the naked Innocence
of vertue, would be upon all occasions expos'd to the armed
Malice of the wicked. This is the chief reason, that should
now keep up the Ornaments of speaking, in any request:
since they are so much degenerated from their original
usefulness. They were at first, no doubt, an admirable
Instrument in the hands of Wise Men: when they were onely employ'd to describe Goodness, Honesty, Obedience: in
larger, fairer, and more moving Images: to represent
Truth, cloth'd with Bodies; and to bring Knowledge back
again to our very senses, from whence it was't first deriv'd
to our understandings. But now they are generally chang'd
to worse uses: They make the Fancy disgust the best things,
if they come sound, and unadorn'd: they are in open defiance
against Reason; professing, not to hold much correspondence with that; but with its Slaves, the Passions: they give
the mind a motion too changeable, and bewitching, to consist with right practice. Who can behold, without indignation, how many mists and uncertainties, these spacious
Tropes and Figures have brought on our Knowledg? How
many rewards, which are due to more profitable, and difficult Arts, have been still snatch'd away by the easie vanity of fine speaking? For now I am warm'd with this just
Anger, I cannot with-hold my self, from betraying the shal-
lowness of all these seeming Mysteries, upon which, we
Writers, and Speakers, look so bigg. And, in few words,

I dare say; that of all the Studies of men, nothing may be sooner obtain'd, than this vicious abundance of Phrase, this trick of Metaphors, this volubility of Tongue, which makes so great a noise in the World. But I spend words in vain; for the evil is now so inveterate, that it is hard to know whom to blame, or where to begin to reform. We all value one another so much, upon this beautiful deceipt; and labour so long after it, in the years of our education: that we cannot but ever after think kinder of it, than it deserves. And indeed, in most other parts of Learning, I look on it to be a thing almost utterly desperate in its cure: and I think, it may be plac'd amongst those general mischiefs; such, as the dissention of Christian Princes, the want of practice in Religion, and the like; which have been so long spoken against, that men are become insensible about them; every one shifting off the fault from himself to others; and so they are only made bare common places of complaint. It will suffice my present purpose, to point out, what has been done by the Royal Society, towards the correcting of its excesses in Natural Philosophy to which it is, of all others, a most profest enemy. [21]

This earnest indictment of the earlier mode of expression does not represent the sentiments of Sprat only. The History was written at the instigation and under the auspices of the Royal Society, was closely followed by the members during its composition, and when finished was heartily approved by the same body, so that we may look upon his attitude as typical of that of his colleagues. [22] Furthermore, in the next paragraph Sprat describes in terse and effective manner the style required by the Society of all papers presented to it.

They have therefore been most rigorous in putting in execution, the only Remedy, that can be found for this extravagance: and that has been, a constant Resolution, to reject all the amplifications, disgressions, and swellings of style: to return back to the primitive purity and shortness, when men deliver'd so many things, almost in an equal number of words. They have exacted from all their members, a close, naked, natural way of speaking; positive expressions; clear senses; a native easiness: bringing all things as near the Mathematical plainness, as they can: and preferring the language of Artizans, Countrymen, and Merchants, before that, of Wits, or Scholars.[23]

The great importance of this discussion of style relative to other matters canvassed in Sprat's History, is made clear by comments upon the book itself, in which the manner of expression is the characteristic most remarked. In an ode, which was prefixed to the History, and which will later be treated more in full, Cowley notices, and with great praise, only the style of the work. In the next year Glanvill thinks it necessary to praise its stylistic qualities in a passage which expresses the desired ideal as elucidated by Sprat and renders a fairly accurate criticism of the latter's prose. The book, he says,

> is writ in a way of so judicious a gravity, and so prudent and modest an expression, with so much clearness of sense, and such a natural fluency of genuine eloquence: So that I know it will both profit and entertain you. And I say further, that you may remember to do your self this right, That the Style of that Book hath all the properties that can recommend any thing to an ingenious relish: For 'tis manly, and yet plain; natural and yet not careless: The Epithets are genuine, the Words proper and familiar, the Periods smooth and of middle proportion: It is not broken with ends of Latin, nor impertinent Quotations; nor made harsh by hard words, or needless terms of Art; Not rendred intricate by long Parentheses, nor gaudy by flanting [sic] Metaphors; not tedious by wide fetches and circumferences of Speech, nor dark by too much curtness of Expression: 'Tis not loose and unjointed, rugged and uneven; but as polite and as fast as Marble; and briefly avoids all the notorious defects, and wants none of the proper ornaments of Language.[24]

It is remarkable how sensitive the scientists were to the problem of expression. We may say without exaggeration that their program called for stylistic reform as loudly as for reformation in philosophy. Moreover, this attitude was in the public mind indissolubly associated with the Society.[25]

Such then was the stand firmly taken by the first scientific society in England as regards expression in prose composition. Naturally its stylistic ideal was reflected in the scientific writings of its members.[26] The question next arises, Did it actually influence the style of non-scientific writings of the day?

Fortunately we have two examples, one of which is remarkable, of men whose style was radically changed under the pressure exerted by the Society. In 1661 Joseph Glanvill, later the most ardent defender of the Royal Society, published his Vanity of Dogmatizing, the contents of which time prevents me from describing, except to say that within its narrow compass it gathered all the new threads of philosophical thought that traversed the mid-seventeenth century. It is written in an highly rhetorical, exuberant, one might even say flamboyant, style, animated by an enthusiasm great enough to justify the charge of its being rhapsodical. The modern note sounded by Glanvill, however, must have brought him into sympathetic contact with some fellows of the Royal Society, and thus have whetted his desire to become a member of that body. At any rate, when, near the end of 1664, he published a second edition entitled Scepsis Scientifica, [27] he prefixed an "Address to the Royal Society," in which he eulogized the new philosophy in general and that company in particular. This composition has all the ear-marks of being a bid for an invitation to join the philosophers, and such an inference is borne out by the fact that on December 7, 1664, Lord Brereton presented the book to the Royal Society, and, after the "Address" had been read, proposed the author as a candidate for membership. [28] What especially interests us in the dedication is the following passage found near the conclusion:

I found so faint an inclination [toward publishing the work again] that I could have been well content to suffer it to have slipt into the state of eternal silence and oblivion. For I must confess that way of writing to be less agreeable to my present relish and Genius; which is more gratified with manly sense, flowing in a natural and unaffected Eloquence, than in the musick and curiosity of fine Metaphors and dancing periods. To which measure of my present humour, I had indeavour'd to reduce the style of these Papers; but that I was loth to give my self that trouble in an Affair, to which I was grown too cold to be much concern'd in. And this inactivity of temper perswaded me, I might reasonably expect a pardon from the ingenious, for faults committed in an unmaturity of Age and Judgment, that would excuse them. [29]

Here we have a man desiring admission to the Royal Society, who with humility of spirit apologizes for his past sins,

and with obvious alacrity swears allegiance to a stylistic creed
that might otherwise have barred his entrance. I would not wish,
however, to insinuate that his conversion was not sincere, for
later events prove otherwise. But though he had evidently come
under the influence of the scientists, and had experienced a true
change of heart in stylistic matters, his open apology was evidently intended to serve a purpose. When we remember that less
than four years separated the two editions, the reference to the
immaturity of youth provokes a smile. It is significant that a
man seeking admission into the society considered it necessary
to place himself in the proper position as to style. [30]

A number of changes are introduced into the Scepsis, but, as
the author states, very few as regards style, and they are concerned only with the substitution of simpler and more usual
words for coined words or unusual Latinisms. [31] This change,
however, reveals that he was moving in the direction of the new
manner of expression demanded by the scientists. It is a stroke
of good fortune for our purposes that in 1676 Glanvill published
a third abbreviated version of the Vanity of Dogmatizing, as the
first of seven essays combined to form a volume with the title,
Essays on Several Important Subjects in Philosophy and Religion. [32] A comparison of this essay with the first version af-
fords nothing short of a revelation. Under the influence of the
Royal Society the author's changed stylistic standards had established complete control over his writing, and had caused him to
revise with a ruthless hand work written under the inspiration
of the great prose writers of the Commonwealth. Furthermore,
though in the second edition he had contented himself with an apology, leaving the style little changed, he would not permit the
treatise to go forth again until it had become "quite changed in
the way of writing." It is hardly necessary to do more than display parallel passages to show what science was doing to prose.

That all bodies both Ani-
mal, Vegetable, and Inanimate,
are form'd out of such particles of matter, which by reason of their figures, will not
cohaere or lie together, but
in such an order as is necessary to such a specific formation, and that therein they
naturally of themselves con-

curre, and reside, is a pretty conceit, and there are exper-iments that credit it. If after a decoction of hearbs in a Winter-night, we expose the liquor to the frigid air; we may observe in the morning under a crust of ice, the perfect appearance both in figure, and colour, of the Plants that were taken from it. But if we break the aqueous Crystal, those pretty images dis-appear and are present dissolved.

Now these airy Vegetables are presumed to have been made, by the reliques of these plantal emissions whose avolation was prevented by the condensed inclosure. And therefore playing up and down for a while within their liquid prison, they at last settle together in their natural order, and the Atomes of each part finding out their methodical Situation till by breaking the Ice they are disturbed, and those counterfeit composi-tions are scatter'd into their first Indivisibles.
Vanity, p. 46.

And there is an experiment... That after a decoction of Herbs in a frosty Night, the shape of the Plants will appear under the Ice in the Morning: which Images are supposed to be made by the congregated Ef-fluvia of the Plants themselves, which loosly wandring up and down in the Water, at last settle in their natural place and order, and so make up an appearance of the Herbs from whence they were emitted.
Essays, p. 11.

Gone is the Brownesque "swelling" sentence at the beginning of the first passage, and the touch of beauty that adorned the account of the experiment has vanished; while the "vicious abundance of phrase" and "volubility of tongue" that charac-terize the remainder of the quotation have given way to the "plain and familiar words" and the "close, naked, natural way of speaking" of the later version.

But this is so largely prose-
cuted by that wonder of men,
the Great Des-Cartes, and is
a Truth that shines so clear
in the Eyes of all considering men; that to goe about in-
dustriously to prove it, were
to light a candle to seek the
Sun. Vanity, p. 28.

Upon which position all the
Philosophy of Des-Cartes
stands: And it is so clear, and
so acknowledg'd a Truth, among
all considering Men, that I need
not stay to prove it.
Essays, p. 5.

For body cannot act on anything but by motion; motion
cannot be received but by
quantitative dimensions; the
soul is a stranger to such
gross substantiality, and
hath nothing of quantity, but
what it is cloathed with by our
deceived phancies; and therefore how can we conceive under a passive subjection to
material impressions.
Vanity, p. 29.

For Body cannot act on anything, but by Motion; Motion
cannot be received but by Matter, the Soul is altogether im-
material; and therefore, how
shall we appreciate it to be
subject to such Impressions.
Essays, p. 6.

If we will take the literal evidence of our Eyes; the Ae-
thereal Coal moves no more
than this Inferior clod doth.
Vanity, p. 78.

To Sense the Sun stands still
also; and no Eye can perceive
its Actual motion. Essays, p. 20.

And thus, while every age is
but another shew of the former, 'tis no wonder that Science hath not outgrown the
dwarfishness of its pristine
stature, and that the Intellectual world is such a Micro-
cosm. Vanity, p. 138.

And thus while every Age is
but another shew of the former, 'tis no wonder that human
science is no more advanced
above its ancient Stature.
Essays, p. 10.

In these passages there is an obvious change from "specious
tropes" and "vicious abundance of phrase" to a primitive purity
and shortness, " in which "positive expressions" and "native
easiness" are manifest. The reduction of these "wide fetches

and circumferences of speech" to a direct and "natural way of speaking" brings out in vivid relief not only the way in which the scientific spirit was destroying the sheer joy in language, but also how the definite linguistic stand taken by the Royal Society was producing results. [33]

Nor is the composition of our bodies the only wonder; we are as much nonplust by the most contemptible Worm and Plant, we tread on. How is a drop of Dew organiz'd into an Insect, or a lump of Clay into animal Perfections ? How are the Glories of the Field spun, and by what Pencil are they limn'd in their unaffected bravery ? By whose direction is the nutriment so regularly distributed into the respective parts, and how are they kept to their specifick uniformities ? If we attempt Mechanical solutions, we shall never give an account, why the Wood-cock doth not sometimes borrow colours of the Mag-pye, why the Lilly doth not exchange with the Daysie, or why it is not sometime painted with a blush of the Rose ? Can unguided matter keep it self to such exact conformities, as not in the least spot to vary from the species. That divers Limners at a distance without either copy, or designe, should draw the same Picture to an undistinguishable exactness, both in form, colour, and features; this is more conceivable, then that matter, which is so diversi-

Blind Matter may produce an elegant effect for once, by a Chance; as the Painter accidentally gave the Grace to his Picture, by throwing his Pencil in rage, and disorder upon it; But then constant Uniformities, and Determinations to a kind, can be no Results of unguided Motions.
Essays, p. 11.

81

fied both in quantity, quality,
motion, site, and infinite other circumstances, should
frame it self so absolutely according to the Idea of it and
its kind. And though the fury
of Appelles, who threw his
Pencil in a desperate rage upon the Picture he had essayed
to draw, once casually effected those lively representations, which his Art could not
describe; yet 'tis not likely,
that one of a thousand such
praecipitancies should be
crowned with so an unexpected an issue. For though blind
matter might reach some ele-
gancies in individual effects;
yet specifick conformities can
be no unadvised productions,
but in greatest likely hood, are
regulated by the immediate
efficiency of some knowing
agent. Vanity, pp. 44 ff.

Here, indeed, is merciless pruning. The "amplification of style"
found in the extended illustrations, touched with beauty, of the
composition of bodies, has been unhesitatingly cut away, for
Glanvill's changed standard reveal in it only a "trick of flaunting
metaphor," "specious tropes and figures," and he now feels that
the discussion has been rendered "tedious by wide fetches and
circumferences of speech." Certainly condensation could go no
further than is manifested in the later version. How completely
has vanished the feeling for beauty in language, as well as a
spirit of enthusiasm and imaginative activity.

The process that had been inaugurated in the Scepsis Scientifica of reducing exotic and unusual words, or "hard words," to
more natural terms, as well as a constant striving for a simpler, more direct expression, is carried still further in this last
version, as is made clear by the foregoing quotations and may
be emphasized by further passages. "Which to us is utterly oc-
cult, and without the ken of our Intellects" becomes "to which

82

we are strangers;" "those abstrusities, that lie more deep, and
are of a more mysterious alloy" = "the Difficulties that lie more
deep;" "those principiate foundations of knowledge" = "The Instruments of knowledge;" "Plato credits this position with his
suffrage; affirming" = "Plato affirms;" "is a difficult which confidence may triumph over sooner, then conquer" = "is hardly to
be conceived;" "is but as the Birth of the labouring Mountains,
Wind and Emptiness" = "stands yet unresolved;" "preponderate
much greater magnitudes" = "outweigh much heavier bodies."[34]
And there are many verbal changes, always making for greater
simplicity or brevity, which may be represented by the following: "our employed mindes" = "we;" "material ἔιδωλα" =
"material Images;" "bodily distempers" = "diseases;" "doth
much confer to" = "makes;" "education-prepossessions" = "first
opinions;" "praeterlapsed ages" = "past ages;" "world's Grand-
aevity" = "greatest antiquity;" "midnight compositions" = "dreams."
    While it is true that Glanvill is reducing a book to the dimen-
sions of an essay, and thus he omits many ideas in toto, the
comparisons placed before us reveal not a change in or omission
of ideas, but an alteration in treatment and expression only.[35]
In sentence-structure the Brownesque inversions, as well as
Browne's habit of overloading the first part of a sentence at the
expense of the latter, are ironed out and straightened into a natural order in which verb follows subject, and object verb. Exclamatory sentences and rhetorical questions are subdued to direct assertions, the length of sentences is perceptibly decreased,
and oratorical cadence has almost disappeared. The verbal reform, begun in the Scepsis, is continued in the substitution of
simpler, more current words for the unusual Latinisms and
exotic terms characteristic of Browne, while emotional and extravagant expressions are greatly tempered. There is general
condensation in expression, an economy of words which deflates
the verbosities and superfluous terms of the earlier style. Figurative language and poetic imagery, whether extended or brief,
are abolished, curtailed or restrained. Illustrations, in the description of which Glanvill had shown a feeling for beauty, are
purged of all qualities except the essential one of expository
clearness. All the glories of enthusiastic expression and all joy
in beauty have faded into the common light of day. We find in a
comparison of the two versions not only a change in style but a
vivid picture of the spirit of one age yielding to that of another.[36]
    We have in the essays of Abraham Cowley what I take to be
another example of the direct influence which the sentiments and

regulations of the Royal Society were exerting upon writers. That there was a decided change in style between his early and later prose has been recognized by more than one scholar. Mr. A. A. Tilley in the Cambridge History of English Literature asserts that Cowley furnished a complete transition from the old to the new style in prose, his early work revealing stiff, cumbrous, and involved sentences, nearer to Jeremy Taylor than to Dryden, and unlike the conversational ease of the later essays composed during the last four or five years of his life. Mr. Tilley calls especial attention to the fine example of rhetorical prose in the latter part of A Vision Concerning Oliver Cromwell, published in 1661 though composed in 1659, contrasting with that the style of the Essays, which is neither stiff nor slovenly, and in which the use of metaphors is strained, and the sentences well turned.[37] Dr. A. B. Gough, in his edition of Cowley's prose works, also thinks that the style of the Essays reveals a decided advance in clarity and ease over the earlier prose.[38] Cowley's first biographer, in the year after the former's death, pointed out "that in the Prose of them [essays], there is little Curiosity of Ornament, but they are written in a lower and humbler style than the rest, and as an unfeigned Image of his Soul should be drawn without Flattery." Several passages in the essays themselves bear witness to the author's acquired depreciation of eloquence, in one of which he speaks slightingly of "Figures and Tropes of Speech" as only adorning discourse,[39] and in another he refers scornfully to the "tinckling" of oratory.[40] But the best expression of his changed attitude appears in "The Garden," composed in 1666 and addressed to John Evelyn, where after an opening paragraph, which misses much of being as rhetorical as the Vision, the author says, "You may wonder, Sir (for this seems a little too extravagant and Pindarical for Prose) what I mean by all this Preface."[41]

This change has generally been attributed to French influences, especially Montaigne, but we must remember that when the Vision and earlier prose works were written, Cowley had for some years been exposed to French influence without results. What possible factor comes into play between 1659, when the Vision was composed, and the composition of the Essays? In February, 1660, Cowley was proposed, and in the following March was elected, to the "invisible college" that was soon to become the Royal Society.[42] In 1661 he published a Proposition For the Advancement of Experimental Philosophy, which was an elaborate plan for a "Philosophical College," and to which the structure of the Royal Society owed much. Upon his retirement into the country he severed formal relations with the society, since he could no longer attend the meetings, and was not reckoned a member after the passing of the second charter of April 22, 1663. But his contact with the members was by no means broken nor his interest in science lost. In fact, Sprat says, "This labour about Natural Science was the perpetual and uninterrupted task of that obscure part of his Life." On December 7, 1664, at the same meeting at which Glanvill's Scepsis was presented to the Society, a committee was appointed to improve the English tongue, composed of more than a score of men, among them Dryden, Evelyn, Sprat, and Waller. [43] Naturally, Cowley, not being a member, does not appear in the list but we learn from excellent authority that he met with them. On August 12, 1689, Evelyn wrote to Pepys,

> And in deede such [improving the English tongue] was once design'd since the Restauration of Charles the Second (1665), and in order to it three or fowre Meetings were begun at Grey's-Inn, by Mr. Cowley, Dr. Sprat, Mr. Waller, the D. of Buckingham, Matt. Clifford, Mr. Dryden, & some other promoters of it. But by the death of the incomparable Mr. Cowley, distance and inconvenience of the place, the Contagion and other circumstances intervening, it crumbled away and came to nothing.

The important place here granted Cowley in the scheme is borne out by what Sprat says in his Life of the poet: "we [Clifford and Sprat] had persuaded him ... to publish a Discourse concerning Style." At the very time Sprat was writing the History of the Royal Society with its pronounced opinions on style, he was conferring with Cowley about improving the language and persuading him to write a discourse on style. Certainly Cowley must have been brought into direct and stimulating contact with the stylistic convictions of the new philosophers. This is made all the clearer by his "Ode to the Royal Society," prefixed to Sprat's history, in which he ardently praises Bacon, the new philosophy, and the Society. One stanza, however, is devoted to praise of Sprat's work,

> And ne're did Fortune better yet
> Th' Historian to the Story fit:
> As you [Royal Society] from all old Errors free
> And purge the Body of Philosophy;

> So from all Modern Folies He
> Has vindicated Eloquence and Wit.
> His candid Stile like a clear Stream does slide
> And his bright Fancy all the way
> Does like the Sun-shine in it play;
> It does like Thames, the best of rivers, glide
> Where the God does not rudely overturn
> But gently pour the Crystal Urn,
> And with judicious hand does the whole current guide.
> T'has all the Beauties Nature can impart,
> And all the comely Dress, without the paint of Art.

From this stanza we see that the only aspect of Sprat's volume which the poet notices is its style, that he attributed to his future biographer credit for purifying prose as the scientists had purified natural philosophy, and that he evidently approved Sprat's indictment of the traditional prose style and subscribed to the new standard that the scientists had formulated. Thus Cowley must have been keenly and sympathetically aware of the efforts made by the experimental philosophers to discredit the old methods of expression, and he must have come under the same influence that metamorphosed Glanvill. To seek for the cause of his stylistic evolution in any other quarter seems to me far-fetched, if not futile.

With the example of Glanvill and Cowley before us, may we not infer that the same pressure toward stylistic reform must have been brought to bear upon all members of the society, [44] and through them even upon the world outside? Furthermore, when we consider the notable array of men of affairs, noblemen, clergymen, and writers who were members of the society, we must believe that the influence of the latter was indeed far-reaching. The many-sided Isaac Barrow, divine, mathematician, and classical scholar, by virtue of being professor of geometry at Gresham College, Lucasian professor of mathematics at Cambridge, 1663, and a very early member of the Royal Society, could hardly have escaped being influenced by the stylistic attitude of the society. John Tillotson, another great exponent of the new style, "whose sermons at Lincoln's inn and St. Lawrence Jewry attracted large congregations," and became a stylistic pattern for the whole nation, was not elected a member of the society until 1672. [45] Yet in another way he had come under its influence. As a son-in-law of John Wilkins, he was associated with the latter in the composition of An Essay towards a real

SCIENCE AND ENGLISH PROSE STYLE 1650-1675

Character and a Philosophical Language, 1668.[46] This remarkable project had long been in Wilkins' mind, and in 1662 he was
prodded to develop it by the Royal Society, the members of which
were deeply interested in the matter.[47] The study of language
naturally involves consideration of style, and we are not surprised to find the stylistic attitude of science reflected in various parts of the Essay.[48] In this way Tillotson must have had
impressed upon him the stylistic values of the new philosophy.[49]

Finally, Dryden, who asserted that whatever talent he had
for English prose was due to his having often read the works of
Tillotson,[50] was in a position to be even more directly influenced
by the persistent efforts of the scientists to purify prose expression. He joined the Royal Society the same year in which it received the patronage of Charles II, and the poem addressed to
Dr. Charleton bears eloquent testimony to his admiration of and
interest in the new science. He, too, was a member of the committee appointed to improve the tongue, at the meetings of which,
we may infer, he discussed stylistic matters with Cowley, Clif-
ford, and Sprat. That he was no indifferent listener to the scientific discussions of the society is revealed in his answer to
the charge of being magisterial, preferred against him by Sir
Robert Howard: "I must crave leave to say, that my whole discourse was sceptical according to the way of reasoning which
was used by Socrates, Plato, and all the Academics of old, ...
and which is imitated by the modest inquisitions of the Royal
Society."[51] If he was so influenced in the method of presenting
his ideas, would he not likewise be influenced in the manner of
his expression, a matter considered no less important by the
scientists ?

Before concluding this article it may be advisable to distinguish between the revolution in style which we have outlined and
another stylistic movement of the century.[52] The Anti-Ciceronian movement was the rhetorical counterpart of the revolt against
that body of orthodox ideas, gathered largely from antiquity, in
which the Renaissance was complacently resting. The rationalistic spirit of inquiry, especially in moral and political matters,
which demanded a turning away from what appeared to be only
the forms of knowledge to direct observation and the realities
of life, also found it necessary to revolt against the Ciceronian
style that was closely associated with orthodox philosophies. In
the same way, the scientific movement, in the main engineered
by Bacon, represented the abandonment of empty theories of nature for observation and experiment. It also announced a stylistic

program, but one distinctly different from the Anti-Ciceronian. In short, the desire to discover knowledge which would more fully satisfy the demand for reality was responsible for both revolutions, but the stylistic movements that accompanied them pursued different and divergent courses. The Anti-Ciceronian style found its theories in Aristotle and its models in such Latin writers as Lucan, Juvenal, Persius, Tacitus, Pliny, and especially Seneca; science renounced Aristotle and all his works, and sought for no models in the ancients. Instead of a conscious literary style, such as the other movement was developing, the new philosophy found in the very nature of its material a manner of expression characterized by the lack of literary qualities. The former style, which was far from denying itself the assistance of rhetoric, made use of aphorism, antithesis, paradox, and especially metaphors; the latter, which eschewed all rhetorical flourishes, laid not the slightest claim to these qualities, and against metaphors, as this article has revealed, carried on constant and uncompromising warfare. Again, neologizing was a distinct characteristic of the Anti-Ciceronians, and freakish Latinisms and strange words were admitted into their works; the scientists, on the other hand, abhorred all such Importations, preferring "the language of Artizans, Countrymen, and Merchants" to the "hard" words of scholars. Bacon, Hall, Jonson, and Wotton have been considered the Anti-Ciceronian leaders in England, but there is nothing that relates the last three to the stylistic propaganda of science. Bacon, it is true, attacked the study of style for its own sake, which, he claimed, was fostered by study of the classics, and his own style reveals Anti-Ciceronian characteristics, but in at least one passage in his works[53] he condemns this style — in fact, he considers it one of the distempers of learning — and elsewhere, as revealed near the beginning of this article, he states with approval the characteristics which were later embodied in the stylistic ideal of the scientists, and which do not belong to the other movement. Other examples of Anti-Ciceronianism in England are Donne, Burton, and Browne, with the first of whom the scientists were in no way concerned, while against the style of the latter two they were in open revolt. In fact, the inclusion of these men among the Anti-Ciceronians coerces the belief that one object of the scientific attack was not Ciceronianism but Anti-Ciceronianism. Finally, the absence of any reference on the part of the scientific reformers either to the movement in general, or to single representatives of the movement, strongly argues their indifference to, if not ignorance of, the movement as such.

There are, to be sure, certain resemblances between the two stylistic attitudes. In both "reality" is emphasized, but with the scientists the term generally means a material reality, while the Anti-Ciceronians used it to refer much more widely to rationalistic explanations of human experience. Though in both "things" are preferred to "words," the experimental philosophers had concrete objects in mind, while the others were thinking of intellectual or moral conceptions. Indeed, as has been said, both attitudes had their origin in that element in the Renaissance which turned from reliance on the authority of the ancients and their unsatisfying philosophy to a rationalistic examination of actual experience, but they developed in quite different directions. Neither is it significant that both object to musical phrases and pronounced rhythm in prose, though the Baconians were consistent in their practice, as cannot be said of the Anti-Ciceronians. Likewise, the former constantly emphasize clearness, which together with plainness was the cardinal tenet in their creed, but the latter, though sometimes including the word in their terminology, frequently did not exemplify it in their practice. To the scientist brevity meant the excision of all rhetorical devices; to the others it meant studied brevity such as aphorisms, point, and the like. Again, appropriateness, propriety, is a term so general and common that its use by both parties is hardly indicative of any relationships, and, in fact, it signified one thing in science and another in moral matters, which constituted the most important element in the revolt against Cicero. One must be cautious in arguing a relationship from the mere occurrence of similar terms, for terms have a way of detaching themselves from their first use and of becoming common property, a fact which may be illustrated by examples given earlier in this article. Alexander Ross objects strenuously to the "Tullian pigments" in Browne's style, an expression that seems immediately to identify him with the Anti-Ciceronians, but Ross was the most orthodox of the orthodox, vociferously opposed to everything new in science and philosophy, and so by no stretch of the imagination can he be included in that group. Browne, on the other hand, was not a Ciceronian, as the charge would imply, but an Anti-Ciceronian. Another example is revealed in the passage quoted from Samuel Parker, in which the expression "scheme of words" is used, and which thus would seem to place him among the enemies of Cicero, since the latter especially objected to the schemata verborum in the Ciceronian style. But

89

Parker employs the term with reference to metaphors, which
are one of the figurae sententiae, and these latter are characteristic of the Anti-Ciceronians.

By far the clearest and most consistent explanation of the attacks of science upon rhetorical prose is discovered in the nature of the scientific movement. Above everything else the new
science insisted upon the necessity of abandoning the empty notions of traditional philosophy, which seemed far removed from
material objects, and of observing carefully and recording accurately all physical phenomena. In the concrete nature of the
experimental philosophy is to be found the secret of the craving
for a clear, accurate, plain style and the belief that such a style
was essential to the attainment of scientific goals. [54] This ob-
session with the actual nature and appearance of things caused
them to resent the interposing of any possible obstruction between observation and description, and gave rise to a stylistic
taste which decreed that a rhetorical style, with its figurative
language and musical cadence, was the product of folly, vanity,
and immaturity, and was not appropriate to serious discourse.
Furthermore, the interest in science, together with the wider
growth of rationalism, tended to create a distrust of the imagination, a distrust which in some cases was deepened by the
growing feeling that fancy was associated with the passions, and,
therefore, was a dangerous faculty of the mind. This latter attitude appears infrequently in the scientific revolt, but plays a
great part in the attack on pulpit eloquence. Finally, scientific
materialism exerted a distinct influence on ideas regarding the
nature of language. A suggestion of this appears in Bacon, but
it finds clear and definite expression in Hobbes, who claims that
words are only the marks of things. [55] Thus the connotative value of words and their power to invest the creations of the imagination with life and being are summarily cast into the discard.
Hobbes' idea is implied in the words of many of the scientists,
and in Samuel Parker is again clearly stated. [56] Its most remarkable manifestation, however, is in John Wilkins' Essay
towards a real Character and a Philosophical Language, 1668,
in which words are literally reduced to marks, and which frankly confesses to making no provision at all for such creatures of
the imagination as fairies, fauns, and the like on the ground
that they have no existence in nature. With this conception of
language in the background, is it strange that science came to
grips with imaginative prose ?

There were, of course, other factors cooperating with science in the simplification of English prose. Rationalism and the steady growth of the classical spirit made against all extravagancies. In explaining the attacks on intricacies of style, Mr. Spingarn mentions the substitution of general for technical terms, the preference for sceptical as opposed to dogmatic modes of thought and speech, the horror of pedantry, the trend toward precision of word and idea, and the attempt to make literature approximate conversation. In most of these matters the presence of the two factors just mentioned may be noted, but it should be remarked that science also was very much concerned with all but the last. Two characteristics of the scientific revolt, however, distinguish it from other stylistic influences, and justify the opinion that science exerted by far the most powerful force upon prose. First, the thorough-going nature of the stylistic reform advocated by the experimental philosophers, which, rejecting any compromise whatsoever with rhetoric, insisted upon an undefiled plainness, caused the issue at stake to be outlined sharply and distinctly. Perhaps of greater importance is the fact that reformation of style was a very significant part of a definite program adopted by a closely organized society of prominent men who were aggressively active in promulgating their views. The extent to which Glanvill's style changed under their discipline is a fair gauge of the influence that must have been exerted upon all the members of the society, and, through them, upon the outside world.

NOTES

1   History of the Royal Society, pp. 416-17. Earlier in the volume he had found in Bacon's prose traits quite different from those demanded by the Royal Society. See p. 36. See also R. Boyle, Works, ed. T. Birch, V, 39.

2   The Works of Francis Bacon, ed. Spedding, Ellis, and Heath, new ed., 7 vols., 1879-1890, III, 11.

3   Ibid., III, 282-4, 330. The first reference contains his famous explanation of, and attack on, Ciceronianism. Though his own prose reveals elements that ally him to the Anti-Ciceronians, his emphasis upon a plain style is quite foreign to them; furthermore, as will be noted later, he was so far from approving their style that he considered it one of the distempers of learning.

4   Ibid., IV, 22. In a Preparative towards a Natural and Experi-
     mental History he lists rhetorical ornaments among the factors
     which increase the difficulty of, while adding nothing to, the
     work. "And for all that concerns ornaments of speech, simili-
     tudes, treasury of eloquence, and such like emptiness, let it be
     utterly dismissed" (IV, 254).

5   Ecclesiastes, or a Discourse concerning the Gift of Preaching
     as it falls under the Rules of Art, 1646, p. 72.

6   The Advice of W. P. to Mr. Samuel Hartlib, for the Advance-
     ment of some particular Parts of Learning. London, 1648, Har-
     leian Miscellany, vol. 6, p. 2.

7   A Treatise of the Rickets, 1651. (This is a translation of the
     Latin edition which appeared the preceding year.) Mention might
     here be made of John Drury's The Reformed School (c. 1649), a
     passage from which (p. 49) reads: "Whatsoever in the teaching
     of Tongues doth not tend to make them a help unto Traditionall
     knowledge, by the Manifestation of Reall Truths in Science, is
     superfluous, and not to be insisted upon, especially towards
     Children, whence followeth that the Curious study of Criticisms
     and observations of Styles in Authors and of straines of wit,
     which speak nothing of Reality in Sciences, are to be left to such
     as delight in vanityes more than in Truths." Drury belonged to
     that group of educational reformers which centered around Co-
     menius, and to which Samuel Hartlib also belonged. Their phil-
     osophy, which is shot through with the spirit of scientific utili-
     tarianism, was largely inspired by Bacon, and properly falls
     in the scientific movement. Drury's emphasis upon "reality"
     manifests the same attitude as is revealed in the quotation from
     Petty, and clearly indicates that the materialistic nature of the
     new science, with its insistence upon direct sense-observation
     of natural phenomena, was the chief source of this craving for
     a plain style. For an extended discussion of the influence of the
     Baconian philosophy upon educational theory, see Foster Watson,
     The Beginning of the Teaching of Modern Subjects in England,
     chap. VI.

8   See end of the Leviathan.

9   Leviathan, ed. A. R. Waller, pp. 526-7.

10   Idem, p. 185.

11   Idem, pp. 43-44.

12   Idem, pp. 14-15.

13   Idem, pp. 21, 25.

14   Idem, p. 26.

15   P. 88.

16   Pp. 295, 301. See also Boyle's Works, ed. T. Birch, II, 92, 136; III, 2, 512: V, 54.

17   P. 2.

18   P. 1.

19   Numerous references might be given to support this statement, but I shall quote only one writer, who figures in this study. "Aristotelian Philosophy is a huddle of words and terms insignificant." And again, speaking of entities, modes, and formalities, "What a number of words here have nothing answering them.... To wrest names from their known meaning to Senses most alien, and to darken speech by words without knowledge; are none of the most inconsiderable faults of this Philosophy.... Thus these Verbosities do emasculate the Understanding; and render it slight and frivolous, as its objects." Joseph Glanvill, Vanity of Dogmatizing, 1661, pp. 150 ff. He also speaks of the verbal emptiness of Aristotle's philosophy.

20   One stylistic vice obviously came under the ban of the experimental philosophers. The latter's violent attack upon the ancients and upon authority in general did much to depreciate the value of Latin and Greek quotations. Glanvill in the Vanity of Dogmatizing, attacks this habit on the ground that reliance on antiquity is no longer to be countenanced, so that appeals to it are impertinent and futile. "'Twas this vain Idolizing of Authors, which gave birth to that silly vanity of impertinent citations; and inducing Authority in things neither requiring, nor deserving it. That saying was much more observable, That men have beards and women none; because quoted from Beza; and that other Pax res bona est; because brought in with a said, St. Austin," pp. 142 ff. In 1678 he says that "the custom is worn out everywhere except in remote, dark corners." An Essay Concerning Preaching, pp. 11 ff. See also Hobbes' view of the same matter given earlier in this article.

21   Pp. 111-113.

22   Cf. Thomas Birch, History of the Royal Society, II, 3, 47, 51,
      138, 161, 163, 197.

23   P. 113. Sprat believed that English writers in general were
      freer from stylistic vices than the French. "There might be,"
      he says, with an eye on France, "a whole volume compos'd in
      comparing the Chastity, the newnesse, the vigour of many of
      our English Fancies, with the corrupt, and the swelling meta-
      phors, wherewith some of our Neighbors, who most admire
      themselves, do still adorn their books." And again, "We have
      had many Philosophers, of a strong, vigorous, and forcible
      judgment, of happy and laborious hands, of a sincere, a modest,
      a solid, and unaffected expression, such who have not thought it
      enough to set up for Philosophers, only to have got a large stock
      of fine words, and to have insinuated into the acquaintance of
      some great Philosophers of the age." Observations on Monsieur
      de Sorbier's Voyage into England, 1665, pp. 265, 671. See also
      Hist. of Roy. Soc., pp. 40-1. Evelyn expresses the same senti-
      ment, only he makes a luxuriant prose style a characteristic of
      the whole French nation. "The Reader will find," he remarks in
      the preface to his translation of a French treatise on painting,
      "in this discourse (though somewhat verbose, according to the
      style of this overflowing nation) divers useful remarks." Mis-
      cellaneous Writings of John Evelyn, ed. W. Upcott, 1825, p. 559.
      Another sturdy Englishman expresses the same sentiment in
      more emphatic words. "And indeed however our smoother tongued
      Neighbors may put in a claim for those bewitcheries of speech
      that flow from Gloss and Chimingness; yet I verily believe that
      there is no tongue under heaven, that goes beyond our English
      for speaking manly strong and full." Nathaniel Fairfax, A Trea-
      tise of the Bulk and Selvedge of the World, 1674, "To the Read-
      er." In view of the common opinion that French influence played
      a great part in the simplification of English prose, these quota-
      tions are worthy of note. Furthermore, not a single stylistic re-
      former in England, as far as my knowledge extends, ever refers,
      directly or indirectly, to any influence from across the Channel.

24   Plus Ultra, p. 84.

25   The following quotation from Sprat's History clearly evinces the
      important place granted style in the obligations of the scientists.
      In fact, it shows that the experimental philosophers considered
      a reformation in current methods of expression essential to the
      advancement of science. "Their [members of the Royal Society]
      purpose is, in short, to make faithful Records, of all the Works
      of Nature, or Art, which can come within their reach: that so
      the present Age, and posterity may be able to put a mark on the

Errors, which have been strengthened by long prescription: to restore the Truths, that have lain neglected: to push on those, which are already known, to more various uses: and to make the way more passable. to what remains unreveal'd. This is the compass of their Design. And to accomplish this, they have indeavour'd to separate the knowledge of <u>Nature,</u> from the colours of <u>Rhetorick,</u> the devices of <u>Fancy,</u> or the delightful deceit of <u>Fables.</u>" Pp. 61-2.

26   See P. H. Hembt, "The influence of Early Science on Formative English, 1645-1675," <u>Journal of Chemical Education</u>, III, 1051, and C. S. Duncan, <u>The New Science and English Literature,</u> pp. 147-54.

27   This version is accessible in a modern edition by John Owen, 1885. All references are to this edition.

28   See Birch, <u>op. cit.</u>, I, 500. Glanvill's purpose is also suggested by a change introduced in the body of the work. A passage in the <u>Vanity,</u> p. 240, reads, "And the sole Instances of those illustrious Heroes, <u>Cartes, Gassendus, Galileo, Tycho, Harvey, More, Digby,</u> will strike dead the opinion of the Worlds decay, and conclude it, in its prime." In the <u>Scepsis,</u> p. 209, there is substituted for the names given above "that Constellation of Illustrious Worthies, which compose the Royal Society."

29   In an earlier passage he gives another excuse for this style, though at the same time suggesting the immaturity of youth as one. After speaking of some ingenious people laboring under the prejudices of education and customary belief, he says, "For Such it was then that the ensuing Essay was designed; which therefore wears a dress that possibly is not so suitable to the graver Geniuses, who have out grown all <u>gayeties of style and youthful</u> relishes; But yet perhaps is not improper for the persons, for whom it was prepared. And there is nothing in <u>words</u> and styles but <u>suitableness,</u> that makes them <u>acceptable and effective.</u> If therefore this Discourse, such as it is, may tend to the removal of any <u>accidental</u> disadvantages from <u>capable Ingenuities,</u> and the preparing them for <u>inquiry,</u> I know you have so noble an ardour for the benefit of Mankind, as to pardon a <u>weak</u> and <u>defective</u> performance to a laudable and <u>well-directed</u> intention." P. liv. In still another passage he touches upon this all-important matter: "And 'Tis none of the least considerable expectations that may be reasonably had of your Society, that 'twill discredit that <u>toyishness</u> of <u>wanton fancy;</u> and pluck the misapplyed name of the <u>Wits,</u> from those conceited Humourists that have assum'd it; to bestow it upon the more <u>manly spirit</u> and

genius, that playes not tricks with words, nor frolicks with the
Caprices of froathy imagination." P. lxv. These words clearly
indicate the popular association of stylistic reform with the society, and the important place such a reformation occupied in
the scientific movement.

30   This case furnishes strong support to Herford's contention that
Browne's style was the obstacle in the way of his joining the
Royal Society. Browne had early become notorious for his style.
In Medicus Medicatus, 1645, an attack on the Religio Medici,
Alexander Ross says, "Your Rhetoricall descriptions (which
are both useless in and destructive of Philosophy) make the soule
sometimes equal with God, sometimes no better than a corrup-
tible body, ... If you lay the fault of this upon your Rhetoricall
expressions, I must answer you, that Rhetorick in such a subject may be well spared: use your Rhetorick when you will work
upon the affections, but not when you will informe the understanding. Rhetoric ... ought not to be used, but with great discretion,
especially in abstruse questions.... If you will dispute like a
philosopher, you must lay aside Rhetorick, and use Philosophical termes; otherwise you will do as the fish Sepia, to wit, you'l
so thicken the waters of your discourse, with the liquor that
cometh out of your mouth, that you will make your self invisible,
and delude the Reader, which is the fashion of those, who dare
not confide in the strength of their arguments; whereas naked
truth cares not for such dressings, nor seeks she after such
corners." P. 92. Ross has nothing but scorn for "Rhetoricall
flourishes" and "Tullian pigments." See C.H. Herford's edition of Browne's works, Everyman's Library, p. xiv.

31   Ferris Greenslet in Joseph Glanvill, 1900, pp. 200-201, has
listed all such verbal changes, which amount to less than a
score. Doctor Greenslet notices the difference between Glanvill's early and later work in the matter of diction, clearness,
and simplicity, as well as in the quality of imagination. But
since he failed to compare the Vanity with the version that appeared in the Essays, he did not perceive the extent or fully understand the nature of the author's stylistic evolution. Though
he attributes the change in part to the influence of science, he
failed to perceive the conscious and decisive nature of the influence which the Royal Society exerted on Glanvill. He is correct in detecting Bacon in the concrete imagery and balanced
brevity of sentence structure, but he limits Browne's influence
too narrowly to words. Though he accurately characterizes
Glanvill's later style as simple, plain, reasonable, he is not sufficiently aware of the profound change that had taken place. See
Chapter VII.

32 Concerning this essay, "Against Confidence in Philosophy," a
    passage in the preface to the volume reads: " [It] is quite
    changed in the way of Writing, and in the order. Methought I
    was somewhat fetter'd and tied in doing it, and could not express
    my self with that ease, freedom, and fulness which possibly I
    might have commanded amid fresh thoughts. Yet 'tis so alter'd
    as to be in a manner new." A Comparison of the two versions
    reveals that chapters XVI, XVII, XVIII, and XIX, attacking Aris-
    totle and the peripatetic philosophy, as well as chapters I, II,
    VI, XI, XX, XXI, and XXII, have been omitted almost in toto;
    that there is much beneficial rearrangement of material; and
    that much other material has been either left out or highly con-
    densed. These changes, together with the compression in style
    have caused the treatise to shrink to a fourth or a fifth of its
    first dimensions. A passage in the "Epistle Dedicatory" again
    calls attention to a change in his stylistic taste: "They [essays]
    were some of them written several years ago, and had trial of
    the World in divers Editions: Now they come abroad together
    (with some things that are new) reduced to such an Order, as is
    most agreeable to my present judgment."

33 Likewise the enthusiastic, exclamatory, and picturesque ele-
    ments of the following passage are strangely subdued to a quiet-
    er level. "What cement should unite heaven and earth, light and
    darkness, natures of so divers a make, of such disagreeing at-
    tributes, which have almost nothing, but Being in common; This
    is a riddle, which must be left to the coming of Elias. How
    should a thought be united to a marble-statue, or a sun-beam to
    a lump of clay! The freezing of the words in the air in the
    northern climes, is as conceivable as this strange union. That
    this active spark, this σύμφυτον πνεῦμα (as the Stoicks call
    it) should be confined to a Prison it can so easily pervade, is
    of less facile apprehension, then that the light should be pent up
    in a box of Crystall, and kept from accompanying its source to
    the lower world: And to hang weights on the wings of the winde
    seems far more intelligible." (Vanity, p. 20.) "So that, what
    the Cement should be that unites Heaven and Earth, Light and
    Darkness, viz. Natures of so divers a make, and such disagree-
    ing Attributes, is beyond the reach of any of our Faculties: We
    can as easily conceive how a thought should be united to a Sta-
    tute, or a Sun-Beam to a piece of Clay: How words should be
    frozen in the Air, (as some say they are in the remote North)
    or how Light should be kept in a Box; as we can apprehend the
    manner of this strange Union" (Essays, p. 4).

34 Vanity, pp. 26, 27, 28, 29, 53, 137; Essays, pp. 5, 6, 13, 25.

35   It would be easy to quote many more parallel passages illustra-
     ting this change, but the reader should compare the two versions
     himself in order to realize fully the transformation that has tak-
     en place. It is hardly necessary to point out that all Glanvill's
     later works reveal the same stylistic evolution.

36   Later Glanvill joined in the attack on pulpit eloquence, which
     arose about 1668, and which will be treated in a future article,
     and his words show that science was by no means without its
     influence upon this attack. Furthermore, the terms used by the
     reformers of the pulpit are startingly similar to those with which
     the scientists have made us familiar. See Glanvill, Philosophia
     Pia, pp. 73, 90-1; the last essay in Essays on Several Import-
     ant Subjects, 1676; and An Essay Concerning Preaching, 1678,
     pp. 11-51. For an account of Glanvill's vigorous defense of the
     Royal Society, consult the present writer's "Background of the
     Battle of the Books," Washington University Studies, VII, Hu-
     manistic Series, No. 2 (1920), 125-129.

37   VIII, 431-433.

38   P. 310.

39   Abraham Cowley, The Essays and Other Prose Writings, ed.
     A. B. Gough, 1915, p. 143.

40   Ibid., p. 199.

41   Ibid., p. 169.

42   Birch, Hist. Roy. Soc., II, 200-202.

43   Ibid., I, 499. The late Professor Emerson in "John Dryden and
     the British Academy" (Proceedings of the British Academy, X,
     1924) calls attention to the fact that Cowley was not a member
     of this committee, and thinks that Evelyn's memory had played
     him false in mentioning Cowley. But we must remember that
     Evelyn does not say that Cowley and the others were members
     of the committee, and that there is no reason why both the poet
     and Clifford, who also was not a member, should not have met
     with the committee.

44   Another possible example of the influence of the Royal Society in
     sobering the style of its members is found in Samuel Parker,
     later bishop of Oxford, who in 1666 published A Free and Impar-
     tial Censure of the Platonic Philosophie, dedicated to Bathurst,
     then president of Trinity College, Oxford, and formerly a member

of the Oxford group of Baconians, to which reference has already been made. Both in the dedication and in the body of the work (pp. 2, 64) Parker expresses his gratitude to Bathurst for turning him from the unprofitable study of the old scholastic philosophy to the new experimental science. Though disclosing the influence of both Hobbes and Descartes, the Censure reveals chiefly the influence of Bacon and his followers. Parker brings to bear upon Platonism the same arguments which the experimental philosophers had used, and were using, against Aristotelianism; namely, that, as regards natural phenomena anyway, its empty notions could not be tested by sense-observations or experiments, the criteria of truth. From this attack on a philosophy which presumably is mainly words, he passes naturally to an onslaught upon a wordy and figurative style, which is fully in keeping with the attitude of the scientists, and in the composition of which he undoubtedly had an eye on the Cambridge Platonists. These latter, he says, "put us off with nothing but rampant metaphors and Pompous Allegories, and other splendid but empty Schemes of speech, ... True Philosophie is too sober to descend to these wildernesses of the Imagination, and too Rational to be cheated by them. She scorns, when she is in chase of Truth, to quarry upon trifling gaudy Phantasms: Her Game is in things not words.... I remember I had not long conversed with Platonick Authors, when I took occasion to set it down as a note to my self, that though a huge lushious stile may relish sweet to childish and liquorish Fancies, yet it rather nauceates a discreet understanding then informs and nourishes it.... And to discourse of the Natures of things in Metaphors and Allegories is nothing else but to sport and trifle with empty words, because these Schemes do not express the Natures of Things but only their Similitudes and Resemblances." (Pp. 73 ff.) And he continues his attack on metaphors at great length. But in spite of this expressed antipathy to rhetorical prose, the style of the Censure is far from being bare and unadorned. (Note, for instance, the following: "But when they pretend to be Nature's Secretaries, to understand all her intrigues, or to be Heavens Privadoes, talking of the transactions there, like men lately drop'd thence encircled with Glories, and cloathed with the Garments of Moses & Elias," etc., p. 73.) He had been for only a short time a member of the Royal Society, and perhaps its influence had not had time to bear fruit. In his next important works, however, A Discourse of Ecclesiastical Politie, 1670, and A Defence and Continuation of the Ecclesiastical Politie, 1671, we note a decided toning down of his enthusiastic language, though he himself claims that he is pursuing a middle way between a bare and an ornate style. (A Defence, pp. 97-8.) Parker will be treated more at length in my article on pulpit eloquence.

45   <u>Cam. Hist. of Eng. Lit.</u>, VIII, 346, 423.

46   "His [Tillotson's] joining with Dr. Wilkins in perfecting the
      scheme of a <u>real character and philosophical language</u>, the es-
      <u>say</u> towards which was publish'd in 1668, led him to consider
      exactly the truth of language and style, in which no man was hap-
      pier, or knew better the art of uniting dignity with simplicity,
      and tempering these so equally together, that neither his thoughts
      sunk, nor style swell'd; keeping always a due mean between flat-
      ness and false rhetoric.... Together with the pomps of words
      he cut off likewise all superfluities and needless enlargements.
      He said what was just necessary to give clear ideas of things,
      and no more. He laid aside long, and affected periods. His sen-
      tences were short and clear; and the whole thread was of a piece,
      plain and distinct. No affectations of learning, no torturing of
      texts, no superficial strains, no false thoughts, nor bold flights.
      All was solid and yet lively, and grave as well as elegant ... he
      retrenched both the luxuriance of style, and the length of ser-
      mons:" Thomas Birch, <u>The Life of the Most Reverend Dr. John</u>
      <u>Tillotson</u>, 2nd ed., London, 1753, pp. 22-23.

47   Birch, <u>Hist. Roy. Soc.</u>, I, 119; II, 265, 281, 283.

48   In the Dedication a passage reads, "To which it will be proper
      for me to add, That this design will likewise contribute much to
      the clearing of some of our Modern differences in Religion, by
      unmasking many wild errors, that shelter themselves under the
      disguise of affected phrases; which being Philosophically unfold-
      ed and rendered according to the genuine and natural importance
      of Words, will appear to be inconsistencies and contradictions.
      And several of those pretended, mysterious, profound notions,
      expressed in great swelling words, whereby some men set up
      for reputation, being this way examined, will appear to be, either
      nonsence, or very flat and jejune." Later he speaks of "the Com-
      mon mischief that is done, and the many impostures and cheats
      that are put upon men, under the disguise of affected insignifi-
      cant Phrases." On pages 17-18, he says, "As for the ambiguity
      of words by reason of <u>Metaphor</u> and Phraseology, this is in all
      instituted languages so obvious and so various, that it is needless
      to give any instances of it, ... And although the varieties of
      Phrases in Language may seem to contribute to the elegance and
      ornament of Speech; yet, like other things of fashion, they are
      very changeable, every generation producing new ones; witness
      the present Age, especially in the last times, wherein this grand
      imposture of Phrases hath almost eaten out solid knowledge in
      all professions; such men generally being of most esteem who
      are skilled in these Canting forms of speech, though in nothing
      else." The same values that appear in the previous discussions

of style also appear in the use of such terms as brevity, perspicuity, significancy, and facility of expression, and the like. See pp. 319, 443, 447.

49   That the Royal Society looked upon Wilkins as specially qualified for the study of language or style is revealed in the fact that, though he was not appointed on the committee to improve the language, perhaps because he was too busy with the Essay, he was ordered to attend the first meeting of the committee and outline to them the proper method of procedure. Birch, Hist. Roy. Soc., II, 7.

50   Congreve's dedication of Dryden's Dramatic Works, quoted by Ker, Essays of John Dryden, I, xxvii n.

51   "Defense of an Essay of Dramatic Poesy," Essays of John Dryden, ed. Kerr, I, 124. Dryden in the preface to Religio Laici called himself a sceptic in philosophy, and Kerr, I, xv, speaks of him as "sceptical, tentative, disengaged." How much of this quality was due to the scepticism of science that stretched from Bacon to the Royal Society? See Bredvold's "Dryden, Hobbes, and the Royal Society," Mod. Phil., XXV, 417-38.

52   In discussing this paper, a fraction of which was read before one of the groups of the Modern Language Association at Toronto, 1928, one scholar maintained that there was some relation between the two movements and referred to Professor Morris Croll's very able articles on Anti-Ciceronianism. During my own investigations I had discovered no such relationship, and a close study of the problem has confirmed me in the belief that the two movements were separate and distinct in that the scientific demand for stylistic reform neither had its origin in, nor drew support from, the Anti-Ciceronian revolt. For Professor Croll's theories consult the following: "Juste Lipse et le Mouvement Anti-Ciceronien," Revue du Seizieme Siecle, II, 1914; "'Attic' Prose in the Seventeenth Century," Stud. in Philol., XVIII, April, 1921; "Attic prose: Lipsius, Montaigne, Bacon", Schelling Anniversary Papers, 1923; "Muret and the History of 'Attic prose'," P M L A, XXXIX (1924).

53   See Schelling Anniversary Papers, pp. 138-9.

54   Probably the most remarkable example of this passion for concrete, material reality in language as well as in philosophy, is discovered in the startling proposal advanced by Nathaniel Fairfax in the preface to A Treatise of the Bulk and Selvedge of the World, 1674. Fairfax displays a violent antipathy to all imported words in the English language, and in his own work he tries as

far as possible to substitute English coinages for words of foreign origin, with grotesque results in some cases. Since he was a great admirer of the Royal Society and the experimental philosophy, which impressed him with its practical and utilitarian character, it is not strange to find him proclaiming an interest in things, not words. Thus he advocates the purification and enlargement of the English vocabulary, made necessary by the activities of the new scientists, through the introduction of plain homely words, gathered from the fields and shops. He wishes to realize literally Sprat's "so many things in the same number of words," not difficult Latinisms but the common words of daily use, "words that answer works, by which all Learners are taught to do, and not make a Clatter." More of his sentiments are worth quoting. "Now the Philosophy of our day and land being so much workful as the world knows it to be, methinks this of all times should be the time, wherein, if ever, we should gather up those scatter'd words of ours that speak works, rather than to suck in those of learned air from beyond Sea, which are as far off sometimes from the things they speak, as they are from us to whom they are spoken. Besides, it may well be doubted, whether Latine can now be made so fit to set the writings of a Working Philosophy by, as our own Speech.—For we must know that almost all the old pieces of good Latine that we draw by, have been taken up by that sort of learning that is wont to be worded in the Schools, and spent in the setting to sale of such things as could best be glazed with the froth of ink, by the men of the Closets. Whence he that is best skill'd in it, is so hard put to it, in the kitchin, the shop, and the ship; and ever will be, though Plautus should be as well understood as Tully. For the words that are every day running to and fro in the Chat of Workers, have not been gotten into Books and put abroad for other Lands until this way of Knowing by Doing was started amongst us. — But as Learnings being lockt up in the Tongues of the Schools, or Love's being lickt up in more womanly simprings of the lips, and the smiling kissing speeches of some others abroad, have been enough to enkindle in us a panting after, and fondness for some of those Outlandish dynns: So if the works of our own men shall be shipt over by words of our own tongue, it may happily make others who have love enough for things, to seek as much after our words, as we upon other scores have done after theirs; the first draught being English, name and thing, doing and speaking." Cf. what Sprat says about the Royal Society's "preferring the language of Artizans, Countrymen, and Merchants, before that of wits, or Scholars."

55 Leviathan, ed. A. R. Waller, p. 14.

56 A Free and Impartial Censure, p. 61.

THE ATTACK ON PULPIT ELOQUENCE IN THE RESTORATION: AN EPISODE IN THE DEVELOPMENT OF THE NEO-CLASSICAL STANDARD FOR PROSE

Richard F. Jones

One of the interesting phenomena in literary history is the sudden and decided change that came over English prose in the third quarter of the seventeenth century. [1] This stylistic revolution finds a ready, if not always a clearly realized, explanation in the rationalistic temper of the age, which demanded of prose a fitter medium for the expression of thought, and discountenanced appeals to the imagination and emotions. Hence the inference might easily be drawn that the change represented an unconscious substitution of one style for another, in that prose was naturally reacting to the altered intellectual outlook of men. Yet seldom indeed are literary revolutions achieved in such a manner, for they are as much the products of conscious effort as of unconscious change. Men are not so oblivious of their own standards nor so unobservant of their changing intellectual environment as to pass through a transition period without noting its character or deliberately assisting the cause to which they are bound. Such certainly was not the case with seventeenth-century prose. The substitution of a plain, direct, unadorned style for the elaborate and musical style of the Commonwealth was a change of which the age was quite conscious, and for which many stoutly battled.

In a previous article I have traced the important and direct influence which science exerted in the simplification of English prose. [2] There I showed how consistently and emphatically the representatives of the new science from its very beginning had manifested a stylistic attitude which reached its most elaborate expression in Sprat's History of the Royal Society, and which profoundly influenced some of the writers of the day. The standard thus established was inspired by the materialistic nature of the experimental philosophy, and was dictated by the need which that philosophy felt for an accurate, plain, and clear medium of expression. Since our necessities frequently assume the guise

Reprinted by permission from Journal of English and Germanic Philology, Vol. 30 (1931), pp. 188-217.

of virtues, the scientists evolved a stylistic taste which, rebelling against all rhetorical devices, placed a premium upon plainness. These new stylistic values soon spread from the scene of their origin, and, owing to the popularity of the new science and to the representative nature of the membership of the Royal Society, were widely disseminated. It is the purpose of the present article to follow the new standard of prose as it invades an alien field, and to discuss the many and earnest efforts made to impose upon sermons the same style that had been found most serviceable to science.

Prior to the restoration of Charles II, especially in the third and fourth decades of the century, the predominating style of preaching was characterized by affectations, fanciful conceits, metaphors, similes, plays upon words, antitheses, paradoxes, and the pedantic display of Greek and Latin quotations.[3] After 1660 the scientific ideal of style — plainness, directness, clearness — steadily gained ascendency over the older manner of expression.[4] This change was materially assisted by the determined efforts of numerous stylistic reformers, the first of which appeared, as we would expect, in scientific quarters. As early as 1646 John Wilkins, in Ecclesiastes, which ran through nine editions in the seventeenth century, had advocated a plain, natural, and clear way of preaching. Some eight years later Robert Boyle found in the Bible a style pleasing to a scientist, and concluded that the plainest language was the most fitting garb for religious truth.[5] But not only in definite statements do we find evidences of a new standard for sermons. Early in the Restoration a few preachers were exemplifying in their sermons the stylistic virtues for which the scientists clamored. Tillotson, whose contact with the new science was close, drew crowded congregations by virtue of his simple, clear manner of speaking; indeed, he became so popular that his sermons began to serve as models, and to him more than to any one else has been ascribed the credit for the new kind of preaching.[6] Thus reformation in the style of religious compositions was already under way, when the attack proper on pulpit eloquence began.

Robert South, who had for some years been public orator at Oxford, fired the opening gun in a sermon preached at Christ Church, April 30, 1668, and for the next decade hardly a year passed without witnessing one or more onslaughts upon rhetorical preaching.[7] Taking as his text, Luke XXI, 15, "For I will give you a mouth and wisdom, which all your adversaries shall not be able to gainsay or resist," South interprets the expression

"a mouth and wisdom" as meaning ability of speech, which, to
suit his purpose, he analyzes into great clearness and perspicuity, an unaffected plainness and simplicity, and a suitable
zeal and fervor. By the light of these standards he inveighs
against "difficult nothings, rabbinical whimsies, and remote allusions, which no man of sense and solid reason can hear without weariness and contempt," and he maintains that only the ignorant are impressed with "highflown metaphors and allegories,
attended and set off with scraps of Greek and Latin." South obviously discovered in the Bible the manner of expression that
he wished to find, [8] for he draws his main argument from the
Apostles, who, he claims, used a plain, easy, obvious, and familiar style, in which nothing was strained or far-fetched,

> no affected scheme, or airy fancies, above the reach or
> relish of an ordinary apprehension; no, nothing of all this;
> but their grand subject was truth, and consequently above
> all these petty arts and poor additions; as not being cap-
> able of any greater lustre of advantage than to appear just
> as it is. For there is a certain majesty in plainness; as
> the proclamation of a prince never frisks it in tropes or
> find conceits, in numerous and well turned periods, but
> commands in sober, natural expressions. A substantial
> beauty, as it comes out of the hands of nature, needs
> neither paint nor patch; things never made to adorn, but
> to cover something that would be hid. [9]

This clearness of expression, he adds, made the Apostles'
preaching irresistible since the will can only be effectively
reached through reason and judgment. There is no evidence that
South was associated in any way with the scientific movement.
In fact, he actually attacked the Royal Society as being subver-
sive to the universities. [10] But the plain style advocated by him
differs in no respect from that which the scientists had pressed
and were pressing upon the world. One also senses in South an
attitude which was soon to become prevalent, namely, a natural
distaste for all verbal embellishments. South himself hardly
lived up to his ideal. [11]

Early in the following year appeared a work [12] which turned
the attack on pulpit eloquence in a direction which it pursued
until the end. The association of pedantic and rhetorical preaching with only the Puritans of Cromwell's day and the nonconformists of the Restoration was obviously too narrow. [13] In earlier

days certainly royalist ministers — witness Jeremy Taylor —
had been as guilty of eloquent preaching as the more fanatical
"men of God," and sermons generally in the first half of the
century had committed most of the stylistic sins attributed to
the nonconformists. From this association, however, the stylistic revolt acquired all the virulence characteristic of the powerful reaction against the Puritans. "Fine preaching" soon became
the rhetorical counterpart of fanatical religion; enthusiasm was
detected as quickly in the first as in the second. On the other
hand, a rational religion and a plain style were claimed by the
conforming clergy as their special possessions. [14] The author
of A Friendly Debate, Simon Patrick, destined, first as bishop
of Chichester and later of Ely, to play a worthy part in the established Church, had himself undergone a considerable stylistic change before he began to combat the style of the dissenters. [15]
That rationalism played a part in this change is evidenced by
Patrick's basing his argument squarely on the way in which the
emotions should be aroused. [16] Since the nonconformists appealed to them through the imagination and senses, they "seek
to please the itching Ears and gratifie the longings of their fancies with new-found words, affected expressions, and odd Phrases," and their audiences are affected only by pretty fancies,
fine phrases, verbal cadences, rhetorical figures, empty words,
pretty similitudes, and shreds of authors. Thus they teach many
things about spiritual truths that are nothing but the creations
of a heated imagination. The conformists, however, appealing
to the emotions only through the reason, employ a plain, proper,
and familiar style. Here appear again the stylistic values of
science, changed in no jot or title from their earlier use, though
now applied to another type of prose composition. Here also appears the rationalistic spirit which, permeating the whole period, insists upon the primacy of reason, manifests a distrust of
the imagination, and sees in language only an instrument for the
expression of intellectual concepts. [17]

The serious light in which the use of figurative language in
religious discourse, especially that of the Puritans, was viewed
becomes apparent in Samuel Parker's A Discourse of Ecclesiastical Politie, 1670. That great champion of intolerance, later
bishop of Oxford, advocates nothing less than an act of parliament "to abridge Preachers the use of fulsome and lushious Metaphors" in the belief that such measures would prevent factions and

be an effectual Cure of all our present Distempers, ... For

were Men obliged to speak Sense as well as Truth, all the
swelling Mysteries of Fanaticism would immediately sink
into flat and empty Nonsense; and they would be ashamed
of such jejune and ridiculous Stuff as their admired and
most profound Notions would appear to be, when they want
the varnish of fine Metaphors and glittering Allusions. [18]

The Discourse was not Parker's first attack upon rhetorical
compositions. Four years earlier, after he had been converted
to the experimental philosophy and had joined the Royal Society,
he had taken up cudgels in behalf of science's stylistic cause,
and had attacked the Cambridge Platonists in the same way in
which the scientists were belaboring Aristotelians and rhetorical writers. [19] He is now merely bringing to bear upon the style
of the nonconformists the same values and standards that he had
employed in behalf of science, and so it is not strange to find
him clamoring for plain, perspicuous, and intelligible terms.
The parallel between the scientific and clerical revolts in general is exact: the nonconformists correspond to the rhetorical
writers of the commonwealth, and the conformists to the experimental philosophers, while the stylistic ideal remains the same.[20]

The attack on the use of rhetoric in the pulpit received great
impetus from the publication of a book which, because of its wit,
humor, and sensational nature, achieved remarkable popularity
and ran through many editions. [21] The author, John Eachard, became master of Catherine Hall, Cambridge, in 1675, and four
years later vice-chancellor of the university. No single work
in the whole movement did so much toward bringing the problem
of style before the public or provoked so many replies. Parts of
the book are expressed in such a manner as to impugn their seriousness, but the sections dealing with style seem serious enough.
Among the causes producing contempt for the clergy, such as
poor education, slight remuneration, and unfit men, the author
emphasizes a meretricious style, which, he claims, sprang
from the neglect of the study of English. No one before him had
ever argued so earnestly for the study of the mother tongue, or
attributed such dire results to its neglect. To ignorance of the
possibilities of the English language and to reliance upon the
classics he imputes all stylistic abuses, and the latter are described in picturesque language. Though Eachard does not specifically designate the nonconformists as the object of his scorn,
they evidently are; but he had ministers of the older generation
in mind as well. [22] He introduces no new element into the charge

that had been, and was being, preferred against the former, except the emphasis upon the study of English, but he continues the attack upon the pedantic use of classical quotations, vaunting eloquence, hard words, fantastical phrases, and rhetorical devices in general. He is especially severe with "frightful metaphors" and similitudes, to find which, he says, the nonconformists

> rake Heaven and Earth, down to the bottom of the Sea, then rumble over all the Arts and Sciences, ransack all Shops and Ware-houses, spare neither Camp nor City, but that they will have them. So fond are such deceived ones of these same gay Words, that they count all Discourse empty, dull, and cloudy, unless bespangled with these glitterings. Nay, so injudicious and impudent together will they sometimes be, that the Almighty himself is often in danger of being dishonoured by these indiscreet and horrid Metaphor-Mongers: And when they thus blaspheme the God of Heaven, by such unallowed expressions, to make amends, they'll put you in an, as it were, forsooth, As I may say. [23]

The spirit of scientific rationalism is apparent in Eachard's attitude. [24] His opposition to rhetoric finds support in the fact that the latter obscures the truth, makes no appeal to the reason, and weakens the judgment. He echoes the strictures of the scientists in protesting against webs of empty speculations and useless, unprofitable, frothy expressions, and he draws upon the terms familiar to the new science in demanding that which is practical, solid, and useful expressed in plain, direct, intelligible, and common language. He is also imbued with the scientific spirit, when he contends that a luxuriant style prevents "more profitable searching into the Nature and Causes of things themselves." [25] But in nothing is the influence of the Royal Society more evident than in what he says about the proper words to be used in sermons. In this matter he only elaborates upon what Sprat had said about the virtuosi's "preferring the language of Artizans, Countrymen, and Merchants, before that of Wits and Scholars." Eachard complains that "if the Minister's words be such as the Constable uses, his Matter plain and Practical, such as come to the common Market, he may pass possibly for an Honest, Well-meaning Man, but by no means for any Scholar." Some preachers, he continues, act "As if plain Words, useful and intelligible Instructions were not as good for an Esquire, ... as for him that holds the Plough, or mends Hedges." [26] Such hostility to "hard" words finds its ultimate inspiration in those who were striving for a plain and clear medium of expression in the scientific world.

The clearest evidence, however, for the participation of science in the formulation of a standard for sermons is contained in several treatises by Joseph Glanvill. In the year following Eachard's Enquiry, when the attack on the use of rhetorical devices in religious compositions was at its height, Glanvill published his Philosophia Pia, [27] one of several attempts written during this period to reconcile science and religion. In this work he is very explicit about the influence of experimental science on sermons. It teaches men, he says, to state things clearly; to pay less regard to the niceties in religion, and more to practical and certain knowledge. "The Real Philosophy," he continues, "ends many Disputes, by taking men off unnecessary Terms of Art, which very often are the chief occasions of the Contests: If things were stated in clear and plain words, many Controversies would be ended; and the Philosophy I am recommending inclines Men to define with those that are simplest and plainest; and therefore also it very much promotes the Interests both of Truth and Peace."[28]

One cannot emphasize too much the relationship of the discussion of rhetoric to the peculiar conditions of the period which produced it. Sick of the religious controversies that had brought so much woe in their wake, men were beginning to discover in language the cause of the evil. Glanvill's sentiments had been foreshadowed by Sprat and anticipated by Parker in his proposal of a parliamentary act to abolish metaphors in order to end the distempers of the age. [29] The interpretation of rhetoric as "a cheat and imposture of an enthusiastic fancy" and the concomitant belief that the clouds raised by obscuring figures of speech were chiefly responsible for the religious factions that had rent England removed the discussion of style from a purely aesthetic and intellectual realm, and proposed it almost literally as a matter of life and death. [30] As strong as was the scientific hostility to luxuriant prose, when the spirit animating science had entered the religious world, the opposition grew much more intense. Yet after all, this spirit was only demanding for religious discourse what it had insisted upon for natural philosophy, a medium of expression that would represent real things just as they are, and thus remove controversies caused by mere fancies and the imaginative, empty, and obscuring verbosities with which they were expressed. It is not strange, then, to find Glanvill introducing the same values and employing the same phrases in formulating an ideal for sermons as had been introduced into the discussion of the proper scientific style.

Seven years later Glanvill is still harping upon the method of expressions proper to sermons. In a work written in defence of the "plain way" of preaching, he makes style a distinguishing mark between conformists and nonconformists in a manner reminiscent of Patrick's earlier distinction. The metaphors, obscure expressions, and odd schemes of speech of the dissenters, in his eyes, serve only to obscure their doctrines, "Whereas our Ministers represent the doctrine and instructions in clearness of thought and simplicity of speech."[31] He differentiates at some length between men whose learning is concerned with languages and antiquities, or with school-divinity and the spinosities of controversy, and

> another sort of learned men, whose design hath been to study things, to furnish their minds with clear and right conceptions on human nature, the manners and actions of men, to turn their thoughts, after due preparation towards practical Theology, to make parochial charges, and to exercise themselves in frequent Preaching: and these are by their learning and knowledge inabled to speak with the most judgment, propriety, and plainness. For (as I intimated before) it requires parts and understanding to be plain. He must think distinctly and clearly that would teach so: and the true useful learning is the proper instrument to inable a man for that.[32]

Glanvill's words furnish an interesting, if not significant, parallel between the conforming clergy and the Baconian philosophers. One is opposed to futile controversy over theology, the other to disputatious peripateticism; both emphasize the study of things rather than words; one observes human nature and conduct, the other, physical nature; one stresses practical theology, the other, the usefulness of the experimental philosophy; and finally, the first approves "exercise in frequent preaching," the second, the "doing" nature of the new science.

We need not go far afield to discover a possible channel through which the scientific spirit could have reached the pulpit. One of the most remarkable features of early science in England was the number of clergymen who were interested in it. Eachard comments on the number who were members of the Royal

Society, and whom he considered as capable scientists as any of
the others. [33] Glanvill also, in order to show that the Society
was not inimical to religion, points to the impressive array of
ecclesiastics who were fellows, among them the archibishops of
Canterbury and York, and the bishops of Ely, London, Rochester, Salisbury, and Winchester. [34] These men could very well
have transmitted the stylistic views of the society to their own
realm, and their influence would necessarily have been wide. In
fact, Glanvill, who figures so largely in this and my previous
article, expressly argues that the clerical members of the society were responsible for the attack on puritan rhetoric and
for the formulation of a new standard for sermons. Furthermore,
he attributes this activity of theirs directly to their training and
interest in the experimental philosophy. In an essay entitled
"Antifanatick Theologie and Free Philosophy,"[35] he borrows
Bacon's fiction of the New Atlantis, and has the Father of Solomon's House, which he identifies with the Royal Society, describe the state of religion in Bensalem. The Father gives a
most uncomplimentary picture of a religious sect, the Ataxites,
who obviously represent the Puritans, and points out how the
clerical members of Solomon's House remedied the situation.
The latter underwent a rather strange training for their profession.

> They were sensible that knowledge was still imperfect, and
> capable of further growth, and therefore they looked for-
> ward into the Moderns also, who about this time, had im-
> ployed themselves in discovering the Defects of the An-
> cients, in reviving some of their neglected Doctrines; and
> advancing them by new Thoughts and Conceptions: They
> read and consider'd all sorts of late Improvements in Ana-
> tomy, Mathematics, Natural History, and Mechanics, and
> acquainted themselves with the Experimental Philosophy
> of Solomon's House and other promoters of it. And by this
> Universal way of proceeding, They furnish'd their Minds
> with great variety of Conceptions, and rendred themselves
> more capable of judging of the Truth or likelyhood of any
> propos'd Hypothesis.... They had the felicity of clear and
> distinct thinking.

By virtue of such a training they evolved a standard for sermons
which was an exact replica of that demanded for scientific exposition. This standard Glanvill describes both negatively and
positively. "They affected," he says, "no gayness of Metaphors,

or prettiness of Similitudes: no tricks to be plaid with the words of their text," but "whereas the Ataxites had made Religion a fantastick, and unintelligible thing . . . Those Divines labour'd much to reduce it to its native plainness and simplicity . . . Laying down the genuine notions of Theology, and things relating to Faith or practice, with all possible perspicuity and plainness." And toward the end of the essay he elaborates at greater length upon the subject.

> They did not involve their discourses in needless words of Art, or subtle distinctions, but spoke in the plainest and most intelligible Terms: and distinguish'd things in the most easie and familiar manner that the matter of discourse would bear. They took this as an establish'd Rule, That unwonted words were never to be us'd, either in Pulpits, or elsewhere, when common ones would as fitly represent their meaning: and they always chose such, as the custom of speaking had rendred familiar in the subjects on which they spoke, when those were proper and expressive. . . . They affected not to ostentate Learning, by high-flown expressions, or ends of Greek, and Latin: They did not stuff their Sermons with numerous needless Quotations . . . No, their Learning . . . abundantly appeared to the intelligent, by the judgment and strength, the reason and clearness with which they spoke. [36]

Powerful though the influence of science was upon the new standard for religious discourse, it should by no means be emphasized to the exclusion of other factors. Rationalism, which was strong in the scientific movement, and which owed a great deal to Descartes, was rapidly dominating the minds of men, and appears frequently in the passages which have been discussed. More and more emphasis is laid upon the necessity of appealing to the mind through reason and clear statement. Together with the doctrine of the primacy of reason went a corresponding distrust of the imagination, which justified itself in two ways. The scientists came to view that faculty of the mind as an agent of deception, distorting, obscuring, and falsifying truth conceived of in a rationalistic manner. Hobbes, whenever he touches upon the matter, evinces such a view, and it appears frequently in those associated with the new science. [37] When morality and religion, however, were considered, the imagination underwent a moral interpretation, as well as retaining its deceptive quality.

The influence of Stoicism, so pronounced during this period, is revealed in a tendency to condemn the imagination because it is associated with passions, which are natural enemies to the ethical and rational soul of man. Sprat denounces rhetorical ornaments because they hold correspondence with the passions, the slaves of reason.[38] Casaubon refers to those who opposed eloquence because they considered the emotions closely allied to madness and distraction.[39] It is in Simon Patrick's Friendly Debate, however, that this attitude is most fully developed. Finally, as a result of the various factors involved, science, rationalism, Stoicism, there developed a definite stylistic taste that was repelled by the vanity and folly of rhetoric in all kinds of compositions, and in sermons was especially shocked at what appeared to be almost blasphemous gaudiness. The many and strong terms of condemnation, which frequently border upon vituperation, represent not only a rational judgment but also a natural revulsion. Rhetoric was no longer fashionable in polite quarters.

Another aspect of the stylistic problem, but whether as a cause or an effect of the attack on rhetoric is not easily determined, appears in a growing consciousness of the distinction between poetry and prose.[40] Prose, as a distinct type of literature, was emerging in much more definite outline; its own peculiar properties were beginning to receive attention. In the seventeenth century these properties were noted chiefly in connection with style, though content is sometimes considered. In general, poetry was related more closely to the imagination and emotions, prose to the rational mind. South thinks the style of plays and romances entirely unsuitable to a preacher;[41] and Parker is willing to consider the Cambridge Platonists poets but not philosophers.[42] James Arderne advises clergymen not "to suffer your fancy to be tempted towards following of Poetick, or Romantick writings, the latter being good for nothing, and the other best in its own measures."[43] Especially does this conception of the different provinces proper to prose and poetry appear in the defence of the figurative language used in the Bible, a defence imposed upon those who were inclined to cite the Scriptures as a model of a clear, plain style. Patrick defends David's use of rhetorical figures on the ground that "his Psalms are pieces of Divine Poetry, in which Passions are wont to be expressed much otherwise than they ought to do [be ?] in plain and familiar speech";[44] and William Sherlock explains "that there is a vast difference between Poetical Descriptions, such as the

113

Book of Canticles is, and Practical Discourse for the Government of our Lives: the first requires more Garnish and Ornament, and justifies the most mysterious flights of Fancy; the second requires a plain and simple dress, which may convey the Notions with ease and perspicuity to the mind."[45]

On the other hand, prose itself was undergoing analysis and division according to its content and purpose, and the style proper to each species was beginning to be considered. So vigorously and successfully had the scientists insisted upon an unadulterated plainness that the reformers of pulpit eloquence were moved to impose this stylistic ideal on compositions of an alien nature. Although rationalism tended to bring both science and religion to the same level, a difference in purpose, subject-matter, and the audience addressed was sure to be recognized in some quarters. The purpose of scientific discourse is to demonstrate; of sermons, to persuade and move; the material of one is concrete objects and the laws governing them; of the other, spiritual truth; and finally science addressed itself to those on a higher rational plane than is apparent in the average congregation. It should also be noted that science was primarily concerned with written discourse, and sermons with oral composition, in which rhetoric has a more natural place. [46] In view of these differences it was almost inevitable that the need of a style for sermons different from that proper to scientific experiments and observations should make itself felt.

> I can very well allow that in Philosophy [the term is generally used at this time as equivalent to science], where the Quality and Nature of things do not transcend and over match words, the less Rhetorical ornaments, providing still that the phrase be pure and easie, the better. But in Divinity, where no expressions come fully up to the Mysteries of Faith, and where the things themselves are not capable of being declared in Logical and Metaphysical Terms; Metaphors may not only be allowed, but are most accommodated to the assisting us in our conceptions of Gospel-mysteries. [47]

In somewhat the same strain Arderne says, in advocating the necessity of metaphors to make clear the obscure, "I know this is wholly rejected by some, who consider not, that the poverty of conceptions, or scarcity of words constrains, that in every sentence almost the adjectives and epithets are in strictness metaphorical."[48] In spite of the great impetus given to the idea of a plain style by the enthusiastic Baconians, there were those who, in a critical spirit, were weighing and testing its suitability to non-scientific forms of prose.

The defence of figurative language, as was to be expected, devolved largely upon the shoulders of the nonconformists, who were compelled to find some shelter in the shower of abuse cast upon them. [49] But they were sensitive enough to the spirit of the age to be very guarded in advocating the use of rhetorical devices, and to emphasize the importance of caution as much as they urged the usefulness and propriety of figures. [50] Metaphors and similitudes are to be employed only when there is need of such, when they are derived from a just analogy and founded in nature or the Scriptures, and when they are pertinent, not over-numerous, and used with prudence and reverence. When these conditions are met, rhetoric is justified by the practice of Christ and his apostles, by the recognized purpose of preaching, and by the grace, elegance, and efficacious communication of truth peculiar to it. [51] It is interesting to note that the inheritors of the puritan tradition were the chief advocates of the imaginative elements in style. Certainly the most earnest defence of the beauty and pleasure found in rhetorical compositions occurs in what is probably the most ambitious attempt on the part of the nonconformists to rehabilitate rhetoric. [52] In fact, Robert Ferguson justifies a figurative style by the critical theories of poetry current in his day, which in turn had been contaminated by rhetorical theory. [53] "I take it for granted," he says, "that as Reason gives a Discourse its strength and Nerves, so Rhetoric gives it its Colour," an idea borrowed intact from Hobbes' psychological analysis of poetry. [54] The dulce et utile underlines much that he says regarding the virtues of figurative language, and the decorum of expression is emphasized. [55]

The first argument against rhetorical preaching which Ferguson felt compelled to answer was that based upon the style of the Bible, which had been proposed as a model of plainness. In his reply he does not entirely escape obscurity and inconsistency, as was inevitable in any attempt to characterize as a whole the style of such different kinds of composition as are found in the Scriptures. [56] He emphatically states that there is hardly a single figure of speech that is not to be found in the Bible,[57] but he also discovers in it brevity, perspicuity, simplicity, and even plainness. This apparent contradiction he would explain by distinguishing between the true eloquence of the Bible and that false kind which consists of a flourish of painted words or a smooth structure of periods, and which, influencing the affections only, does not leave as lasting an impression as that produced by reason. This latter eloquence he attributes to the ancient sophists and demagogues, and he inveighs just as sternly as the conformists against empty schemes of speech, grandiloquency, bewitching smoothness, flourishes of wit, and flowers of language. In short, he objects to that type of oratory that emphasizes beauty of style irrespective of thought. [58] The majestic eloquence of Scriptures, on the other hand, is always appropriate to the thought expressed.

> There are no empty frigid phraseologies in the Bible, but where the expressions are most splendid, and lofty, there are notions and things enough to fill them out. God did not design to endite the Scripture in a pompous tumid stile, to amuse our fancies, or meerly strike to our Imaginations with the greater force, but to instruct us in a calm and sedate way; and therefore under the most stately dress of word, there always lyes a richer quarry of things and truths. [59]

In chapter II, entitled "Of the Import and Use of Scripture-Metaphors," he embarks upon a long and much needed discussion of metaphors, both as found in the Bible and as proper to sermons. [60] The purpose of the former, he points out, is not "to impregnate our minds with gawdy Phantasms, but to adjust the Mysteries of Religion to the weakness of our Capacities." [61] They are drawn from the whole field of nature, as well as from the manners and possessions of man, so that to understand them clearly one must be acquainted with natural philosophy and the customs of oriental nations. Without such knowledge, a "luxurious Fancy will be apt to frame very wild and absurd Notions out of Metaphors." [62] As regards the figures that may lawfully be used in sermons, he lays down the following rules: they must be modest, clean, easy, and common; they must "carry a due Proportion, Analogy, and Similitude to the things they are brought to illustrate"; and they must never be employed except when the preacher is thoroughly familiar with the value and use of the terms in their original sense. Of all the rules for the employment of metaphors laid down by the rhetoricians, he considers of most importance those which forbid too numerous figures and which insist upon the intelligibility of metaphors to the

116

audience addressed. Figures from classical mythology he would
ban entirely. [63] The nonconformists would not, like the scientists, sweep away all metaphors, but they imposed strict laws
upon the use of them.

As has been noted on a previous page, Ferguson acknowledges
that a plain style, while not suitable to sermons, is proper to
scientific exposition, and in other passages he draws at great
length a distinction between preaching and compositions devoted
to reasoning, argument, and demonstration. In the latter, he
claims, rhetoric has no place, since it is always accompanied
by neglect of logic, and since argument weighs more heavily
than fine language. Not only do verbal ornaments fail to convince;
they even cast suspicion on the cause for which they are employed.
"Metaphorick flourishes," he says, "may ... be useful to illustrate and brighten truth, but the naked and plain mode of disput-
ing conduceth only to the conviction and demonstration of it."[64]
Sermons, on the other hand, may avail themselves of all the
rhetorical devices which are legitimately employed in other compositions. [65]

But the nonconformists were not alone in advocating a cautious use of rhetoric in the pulpit. Several years before Ferguson's volume appeared, James Arderne had published a treatise, inspired by Eachard's Enquiry of the previous year, which
proposed to establish the proper style for sermons. [66] Advocating a diction not far removed from the ideal of science, he con-
dems archaisms, compounds, [67] and neologisms. "In short,"
he says, "chuse words, as well as you can, wholly English, and
such as are the images of your meaning, and which serve to humour the aim of the sentence whereof they are a part: and of
words thus qualified, take those which most readily offer themselves." But he fully recognizes the beauty and grace which figurative language may lend to a discourse, as well as the need
of figures to express abstract conceptions. Yet, though he considers that a bare, plain style is likely to become flat and mean,
he warns against permitting a grave and majestic one to become
inflated and bombastic. Furthermore, he lays down some of the
rules regarding the use of figures which Ferguson was later to
draw up; namely, that they should be proper, intelligible, and
not too numerous. [68] Those who upheld figurative language against
the stylistic ideal of science ransacked all the principles of rhetoric for precautions in the use of metaphors and similitudes, a
fact which bears testimony not only to other influences of the
day, but also to the deep impression which the experimental

philosophy had made upon stylistic views. [69]

Finally, we discover a defence of rhetoric in quarters where we would least expect it, in Joseph Glanvill's An Essay Concerning Preaching, 1678. The first part of the treatise reveals the same scientific values that have hitherto characterized his ideas regarding style: hostility to "hard" words; distrust of the imagination; condemnation of rhetoric, especially metaphors; and insistence upon what is plain, solid, and useful. Toward the end of the essay, however, he begins to weaken in his stand. At first, he apologizes for departing from his ideal of plainness, which is still dear to his heart, on the ground that the mob cannot appreciate it. Only the wisest, he informs us, are moved by the appeal which plainness makes to the mind; the common people have not capacity for much knowledge, for "their affections are raised by figures and earnestness and passionate representations ... so that however little you may think these, they must be heeded, and suited to the capacity, and genius of your hearers." He makes another quarter turn, when he says that, though "fullness of sense and compactness of writing are real excellencies," the spoken word is hard to follow, and thus amplifications, a certain "laxness of style," and the representation of "the same thing in different colors and lights" are necessary to sermons. At last, facing fully about, he engages in an unabashed defence of rhetorical preaching, which is a flat contradiction to the stylistic views held by him ever since he became a member of the Royal Society.

> I do not by this reprehend all Wit whatever in Preaching, nor any thing that is truly such: For true Wit is a perfection in our faculties, chiefly in the understanding and imagination; Wit in the understanding is a sagacity to find out the nature, relations, and consequences of things: Wit in the imagination, is a quickness in the phancy to give things proper Images; now the more of these in Sermons, the more judgment and spirit, and life: and without Wit of these kinds, Preaching is dull and unedifying. The Preacher should indeavour to speak sharp and quick thoughts, and to set them out in lively colours; This is proper, grave, and manly wit, but the other, that which consists in inversions of sentences, and playing with words, and the like, is vile and contemptible fooling. [70]

He issues a caution, however, against going out of the way in order to introduce rhetorical ornaments. These sentiments represent a distinctly alien element in Glanvill's conception of style, and indicate the introduction of some specific influence at this point in his career. The source of this influence is, I think, to be sought in France. [71]

The reformation of pulpit eloquence began earlier in France than in England and continued until late in the century. [72] The earliest attack on rhetorical preaching seems to have been Sirmond's Le Prédicateur, 1638, which I have not had the opportunity of examining. In 1652 Balzac, whose style, however, was by no means considered a model, published his Socrate Chrestien in which he frowned upon the use of rhetoric in religious observances and condemned rhetorical paraphrases of the Scriptures. [73] Furthermore, Port-Royal had developed a style proper to Christian humility, which Jacquinet describes as "mortifiée et pénitente," and which was free from ornamentation. [74] But the most important channel through which French influence in this matter reached England was Rapin's Réflexions sur l'Usage de l'Eloquence de ce Temps, 1672, which was translated the same year into English. [75] In it we find almost all the ideas that appear in the nonconformists and in that part of Glanvill's essay which has just been discussed. Though some of these ideas were too general to be ascribed to Rapin alone, the accumulated similarities between French and English treatises are significant. Rapin distinguishes between the true eloquence of the Bible and the false rhetoric of the sophists, with its far-fetched figures and out-of-the-way ornaments. He cautions preachers against too numerous figures and demands that metaphors be proportioned to ideas. Pointing out the large number of figures found in the Bible, he upholds rhetorical language for the ornament, grace, and force which it imparts to a discourse. For this reason, and because rhetoric is needed to move the common man, he opposes a bare and unadorned style. It is a "natural" eloquence that he approves, an eloquence in which thought is emphasized and those ornaments only are admitted which are appropriate to thought. While it is impossible to state definitely that Ferguson and Glanvill were influenced by Rapin, the evidence points that way. [76]

In general, the French, with whom the scientific movement was not so strong as with the English, left much more room for rhetoric in the simplification of prose. For the most part, their problem was to replace false eloquence with true, sophistic with rhetoric. The English, on the other hand, were imbued with a scientific spirit which impelled them to cast into the discard all rhetorical devices and ornaments and to adopt plainness for their ideal. The scientists were so intent on the actual nature of things that they resented any form of expression that did not match exactly the thing described. To them the truths of nature possessed a vivid reality which was in constant danger of being dimmed when expressed in language. Language was almost considered a necessary evil of communication. Words sank to the low estate of "marks," mere tags to be attached to things. The world has never witnessed such a thorough-going materialism, such a passion for the substantial (in its literal sense) and the matter-of-fact as characterized the mid-seventeenth century. The reformers of the pulpit brought the same spirit to religion, and strove to introduce the same exactitude in the use of words expressing moral and religious truths. Finally, the English were by nature more practical, more materialistic, more utilitarian in their philosophy, and less given to the refinements of civilization than the French. The difference between the two people is reflected in the difference between Bacon and Descartes, experimental science and mechanistic philosophy, the Royal Society and the French Academy. [77]

Needless to say, the scientific ideal of expression, with its bareness and lack of color, was hardly appropriate to artistic uses. In Defoe's works it did achieve great results, but in the prose of Temple, Addison, and Steele other stylistic elements are quite apparent. Yet science, in its aggressive attacks on the old luxuriant prose, had cleared the ground, and had, indeed, laid a foundation of clearness and directness upon which could be erected a more artistic structure. At the end of the century John Hughes proposed, as the four fundamental elements of an ideal style, propriety, perspicuity, elegance, and cadence, [78] to the first two of which the scientific movement had made a definite contribution. But though in belles lettres the plain style of the scientists underwent much improvement, in the pulpit it seems to have held its own for a considerable time, and may have been in part responsible for the desiccation of religion which disgraced the neo-classical period. In 1672 Dryden speaks as if the old method of preaching were still existent, [79] but some ten years later, according to Evelyn, it was no longer fashionable since the pulpit "is grown into a far more profitable way, of plaine and practical discourses, of which sort this Nation, or any other, never had greater plenty, or more profitable." [80] Eleven years later, Wotton, who was upholding the superiority of the moderns over the ancients, felt constrained to yield the point in eloquence because even in the pulpit "very few meet with Applause, who do not confine themselves to speak with the severity of a Philosopher."[81] And finally, Swift in A Letter to a Young Clergyman advances a standard for sermons which is exactly the same that we have been tracing. This treatise, with its many echoes of Eachard, would hardly have been out of place, had it appeared in 1670 instead of 1721.[82]

NOTES

1   "The Restoration may be taken as the era of the formation of our present style. Imagination was tempered, transports diminished, judgment corrected itself, artifice began." A. H. Welsh, Development of English Literature and Language, 1882, II, 25.

2   "Science and English Prose in the Third Quarter of the Seventeenth Century," P M L A, XLV, 977-1009.

3   See E. G. Dargan, A History of Preaching, 1912, vol. 2, pp. 146, 153. For a discussion of the style of sermons on the continent as well as in England during this period, consult J. E. Spingarn, Critical Essays of the Seventeenth Century, vol. I, pp. xxxvi-xlii. Professor G. P. Krapp discusses sermons up to and including Donne in The Rise of English Literary Prose, chap. IV. See also Fritz Pützer, Prediger des Englischen Barock, Bonn, 1929; and The Works of Symon Patrick, ed. Alex. Taylor, 1858, vol. I, pp. xcvii-ci.

4   "Pedantry, crabbed conceit, elaboration of metaphor or illustration, gave way to advanced directness, and the English language was made to show of what it was capable when it was not strained: style casting off imitation became direct and plain. During the forty years which followed the return of Charles II, English divines, in their treatment of serious themes, laid the foundation on which Addison based his mastery over the language of his day." W. H. Hutton in Cam. Hist. of Engl. Lit., VIII, 335.

5   In 1663 Meric Casaubon expressed doubt concerning the use of eloquence in the pulpit, and indicated a growing opposition to it. "I do not deny," he says, "but ardent and vehement speech is generally most plausible and powerful: yet I find that some accounted learned and judicious have avoided it, as having too much affinity, with madness and distraction." The Question, To whom it belonged Anciently to Preach, p. 29.

6   For a more extended treatment of Wilkins, Boyle, and Tillotson, see P M L A, XLV, 979, 983, 1002. Boyle's stylistic views will be fully discussed in a future article. Though Wilkins was never a popular preacher, his sermons illustrated the new style as clearly as Tillotson's. Compare William Lloyd's funeral sermon on Wilkins with Thomas Birch's description of Tillotson's style, The Life of Tillotson, 1753, pp. 22-23. Another great preacher and scientist, Isaac Barrow, illustrated the new style in his sermons, and also expressed opinions in its behalf. In a discourse entitled "Against Foolish Talking and Jesting" (found in Illustrations of the Liturgy, ed. James Brogden,3 vols., 1842) he makes "foolish talking" consist of opposite tales,plays on words, odd similitudes, startling metaphors, "in short,a manner of speaking out of the simple and plain way (such as reason teacheth and proveth things by), which ... doth affect and amuse the fancy, stirring in it some wonder, and breeding some delight thereto." (Vol. II, pp. 372-3.) However, he permits the use of "exhorbitancies of speach" when men cannot be reached by reason.

7   As will be noted on another page, Sprat had evidently, in the preceding year, meant to include sermons in his tirade against eloquence in general. History of the Royal Society, pp. 111-113.

8   Before the middle of the century not only had no suspicion been attached to the use of rhetoric in sermons, rhetorical devices had actually been advocated for religious discourses. In a work entitled Sacred Eloquence: Or the Art of Rhetoric as it is layd down in the Scripture, published in 1659, nine years after the author's death, John Prideaux, bishop of Worcester, drew up a rhetoric which defines all rhetorical terms such as tropes, metaphors, parables, similitudes and the like to be used in sermons, and which, in chapter V, recommends direct appeals to the affections of an audience. Furthermore, he takes all his numerous examples from the Bible, in which, he says, the metaphors, especially, "are eminent and numberless." Sacred eloquence he defines as "a Logicall kind of Rhetorick, to be used in Prayer, Preaching, or Conferences; to the Glory of God, and the convincing, instructing and strengthening our brethren." Instead of the Bible's justifying a plain style, to him it justified all manner of figures of speech.

9   That South had the recently deceased Jeremy Taylor in mind is apparent in what he says relative to St. Paul's manner of preaching: "Nothing here of the fringes of the northstar; nothing of the down of angels' wings, or the beautiful locks of cherubims: no starched similitude introduced with a "Thus have I seen a cloud

rolling in its airy mansion,' and the like. No, these were sub-
limities above the apostolic spirit." Some of South's ideas and
expressions argue his acquaintance with Wilkins' Ecclesiastes,
and perhaps with Boyle's Some Considerations Touching the
Style of the Holy Scriptures, and Sprat's History.

10   See John Evelyn's Diary, July 9, 1669. South, however, was
      neither ignorant of nor unfriendly toward the new science. See
      his Sermons, 1843, IV, 114-17, 206.

11   Cf. The Classic Preachers of the English Church, by J. E.
      Kempe, 1877, Chap. III. A few years later South resumed his
      attack on rhetorical embellishments in two sermons entitled A
      Discourse against long Extemporary Prayers, directed in the
      main against the dissenters.

12   A Friendly Debate Between a Conformist and a Non-Conformist.
      The Third Edition, 1669. The preface is dated Oct. 20, and the
      imprimatur Nov. 7, 1668. The popularity of the work is indica-
      ted by its reaching a fifth edition within a year of its first appear-
      ance. Baxter says that the book "was greedily read," and that it
      "did exceedingly fit the humours not only of the haters of the Non-
      conformists, but also of all the prophane despisers and deriders
      of serious Godliness." (Reliquiae Baxterianae, ed. M. Sylves-
      ter, 1696, pp. 39-43)) A Continuation or Second Part of Patrick's
      work appeared in the spring of 1669, and A Further Continuation,
      or the Third Part, dated Oct. 13, 1669, was published in answer
      to A Sober Answer to the Friendly Debate, by Philagathus (Sam-
      uel Rolls, a Presbyterian divine), the preface to which is dated
      June 1, 1669. Patrick was also attacked in An Humble Apology
      for Non-Conformists, with modest and serious reflections upon
      the Friendly Debate, by a lover of truth and peace, which he
      answered in "An Appendix to the Third Part of the Friendly De-
      bate," dated Jan. 13, 1670. In his Autobiography Patrick says
      that he was provoked to write his book by the great insolence of
      the dissenters, and that it "proved very acceptable, and had
      many editions." (See Works, ed. A. Taylor, IX, 450.)

13   The Conformist says to his opponent, "As soon as you had cast
      out of doors all that was old among us; if any fellow did but light
      upon some new and pretty fancy in Religion, or some odd unus-
      ual Expression, or perhaps some swelling words of Vanity, pres-
      ently he set up for a Preacher, and cry'd himself for a man that
      had made some new discovery." A Friendly Debate, pp. 34-35.
      Patrick was by no means responsible for first suggesting this
      aspect of Puritanism. It must have been widely noted, for five years
      earlier Butler had attributed to his hero a style characterized

123

by "hard" words, Latin and Greek quotations, and figures of
speech:

> For Rhetoric, he could not ope
> His mouth, but out there flew a trope.

See Hudibras, Part I, canto I, ll. 51-119.

14   "[The nonconformists] have found out in lieu of Moral Vertue,
a spiritual Divinity, that is made up of nothing else but certain
Trains and Schemes of effeminate Follies and illiterate enthusiasms; and instead of sober Devotion, a more spiritual and intimate way of Communion with God, that in truth, consists in little
else but meeting together in private to prate Phrases, make Faces, and rail at Carnal Reason (i. e. in their sense all sober and
sincere use of our Understanding in Spiritual Matters) whereby
they have effectually turn'd all Religion into unaccountable Fancies and Enthusiasms, drest up with pompous and empty schemes
of speech, and so embrace a few gaudy Metaphors and Allegories, instead of the substance of true and real Righteousness. And
herein lies the most material difference between the sober Chris-
tians of the Church of England and our modern Sectaries, That
we express the precepts and Duties of the Gospel in plain and
intelligible Terms, whilst they trifle them away by childish Metaphors and Allegories, ... and (what is more) the different Subdivisions among the Sects themselves are not so much distinguish'd by any real diversity of Opinions, as by variety of Phrases and Forms of Speech, that are the peculiar Shibboleths of
each Tribe." Samuel Parker, A Discourse of Ecclesiastical
Politie, 1670, pp. 74 ff.

15   Compare, for instance, the style of Mensa Mystica, 1660, with
that of the book under discussion. The former treatise contains
numerous figures of speech — comparisons, metaphors, exclamatory sentences — and in general is much warmer, more enthusiastic, more sensitive to beauty, and more imaginative than
his later work. Here is a typical example: "Our hearts must
flame with love, our minds must reek with holy thoughts, our
mouths must breeth forth praises like clouds of incense, and
our hands must be lifted up with nothing in them." (P. 47) This
is as bad as anything he reprehends in the nonconformists.

16   "I have been taught, that there are two ways to come at the Affections: One by the Senses and Imagination; and so we see people mightily affected with a Puppet-Play, with a Beggar's tone,
with a lamentable look, or anything of like nature. The other is
by Reason and Judgment; when the evidence of any Truth convincing the Mind, engages the affections to its side, and makes

them move according to its direction." Friendly Debate, p. 15.

17   See A Friendly Debate, pp. 15, 34-5, 37, 54, 85-6, 121-2, 142,
     190-1, 107. Although rationalism undoubtedly played some part
     in Patrick's stylistic attitude, the fact that his early work, com-
     posed at a time when he must have been familiar with the ra-
     tionalistic movement, by no means conformed to the standards
     here expressed, whereas later volumes, composed after the sci-
     entific attack on rhetoric had made great headway, are written
     in a much simpler style, strongly suggests that his own views
     on style as well as his practice must also have been indebted to
     the stand taken by the Royal Society. Though Patrick did not be-
     come a member of the Society, he was whole-heartedly in favor
     of the new science, as is clearly shown in his A Brief Account
     of the new Sect of Latitude-Men. Together with some reflections
     upon the New Philosophy, 1662, in which he attacks Aristotelian-
     ism and the authority of the ancients, pitting against them the
     discoveries of the moderns, particularly those indebted to the
     telescope and microscope. He fully recognizes the importance
     of these two inventions, and he also shows due appreciation of
     Boyle's experiments with the air pump, Gilbert's work in terres-
     trial magnetism, Harvey's discovery of the circulation of the
     blood, as well as of the work of Bacon, Galileo, and others. In
     emphasis upon observation and experiment, opposition to peri-
     pateticism, support of the moderns against the ancients, regard
     for the most distinguished scientists of the century, he is one
     with the experimental philosophers.

18   This proposal calls to mind the famous passage from Sprat's
     History of the Royal Society, published three years earlier, in
     which the author, considering the prevailing type of eloquence
     as injurious as international dissentions and hypocrisy in reli-
     gion, and looking upon its cure as almost impossible, advocates
     the banishing of eloquence out of all civil societies. While Sprat
     includes in his indictment "almost all arts and professions", he
     must have had sermons chiefly in mind. Needless to say, his
     attitude toward pulpit eloquence derives entirely from his scien-
     tific outlook, and furnishes another link between the stylistic
     program of science and that of the pulpit reformers.

19   A Free and Impartial Censure of the Platonick Philosophie, 1666,
     pp. 75 ff. Also see P M L A, XLV, 1001. Parker was at first
     very much impressed by the work of the Platonists, but "when I
     came to survey it more closely I soon found it was nothing else
     but words." It was the new science that had opened his eyes.

20   Cf. A Discourse of Ecclesiastical Politie, pp. 74 ff. , and A Free

and Impartial Censure, pp. 75 ff. In the following year Parker takes to task another stylistic vice which science had damned, namely, "Learned Shreds of Latin and Scholarlike Savings of ancient Poets and Philosophers." And in a letter to the author, printed at the end of the same work, Patrick, who seems to have joined forces with Parker in a common cause, apologizes for some Greek quotations on the ground that "our Antagonist makes such a noise with them." A Defence and Continuation of a Discourse of Ecclesiastical Politie, 1671, pp. 93-4, 735. The antagonist was John Owen, who will be considered later. In his Reproof to the Rehearsal Transprosed, 1673, an attack on Marvell, Parker continued his stylistic campaign with such statements as "downright English is in some Cases as good a Flower as the fairest Trope in Aristotle's Rhetorick" (p. 30). The treatise is more remarkable for its sarcastic notice of Milton's Areopagitica, concerning the style of which Parker says, "Such fustian bumbast as this past for stately wit and sence in that Age of politeness and reformation." (P. 191.) Browne, Taylor, and Milton received scant courtesy during this period.

21 The Grounds and Occasions of the Contempt of the Clergy and Religion enquir'd into; in a Letter to R. L. The treatise is dated at the end, Aug. 8, 1670. (All references are to Dr. Eachard's Works, 11th ed., 1705.) Arber has reprinted it in his English Garner. Mr. Spingarn calls Eachard "the Jeremy Collier of the corrupt rhetoric of the pulpit." Crit. Essays of the Seventeenth Cent., vol. I, p. xliv.

22 See James Arderne, Directions Concerning the Matter and Stile of Sermons, 1671, p. 1.

23 P. 38. See also pp. 24, 27, 32, 38-9, 41; and Observations upon an Answer to an Enquiry, 1671, (Dr. Eachard's Works, pp. 56, 76).

24 Eachard, though he gives us delightful caricatures of the Cartesian novice and amateur Baconian of his day, had great respect for the Royal Society, and was especially interested in the part which clergymen played in its affairs. See Some Observations upon an Answer to an Enquiry, (Dr. Eachard's Works, pp. 199 ff.).

25 See also p. 37. Cf. what Robert Boyle says about the empty phraseology of peripateticism in contrast to the new science: "But these uninstructive terms [substantial forms, real qualities, etc.] do neither oblige nor conduct a man to deeper searches into the structure of things, nor the manner of being produced and of operating one upon another." Works, ed. T. Birch, 1744, v, 43.

26   Pp. 33, 35. The stylistic attitude which science did much to
make popular appears also in A Discourse Concerning the Knowledge of Jesus Christ, 1673, by William Sherlock, rector of St.
George's, Botolph Lane, London, and later dean of St. Paul's,
of whom South said that he wrote both for and against every subject he touched upon. Sherlock manifests great grief at seeing
so many "abused with Words and Phrases, which ... signifie
nothing," and declaims against men who "argue from Fancies
and Allegories, which ... have nothing solid and substantial in
them." Since figurative language is only the "cheat and imposture of an Enthusiastic fancy," he concludes that "at this rate it
were easie to make any thing of any thing, to find out some pretty words and phrases, and illusions, types of Metaphors, to
countenance all the feats of Enthusiasm, and the more godly Romances of Popish Legends." In his eyes rhetoric is associated
with the imagination, a deceptive faculty of the mind, which per-
verts the plainest sense, and makes men "dote upon words and
phrases." See pp. 1, 55, 69-70, 81-2, 194, 254. Also consult
A Free and Impartial Inquiry into the Causes of that very great
Esteem and Honour that the Non-conforming Preachers are generally in with their Followers.... By a Lover of the Church of
England, and Unfeigned Piety, 1673.

27   This was reprinted, at the command, Glanvill says, of a person of great fame and learning, and with only slight verbal changes, as the fourth essay, entitled "The Usefulness of Philosophy
to Theology," in Essays on Several Important Subjects in Philosophy and Religion, 1676. In an earlier article I have discussed
Glanvill at length as affording the clearest example of the great
revolution which the new science was working in style. (See
P M L A, XLV, 989-998.) He had, in his earlier days, been an
enthusiastic Cartesian, as The Vanity of Dogmatizing makes
clear; but a few years later, attaching himself to the Royal Society, he became an ardent disciple of Bacon and the most unreserved supporter of the experimental philosophy. It is to be noted
that his style, when under the influence of Descartes, remained
highly rhetorical, but when he came under the discipline of the
scientists, it underwent a remarkable change toward simplicity
and directness. Some scholars have discovered Descartes' influence on the English stylistic movement in the expression
"mathematicall plainness," which Sprat employs in describing
the style demanded by the Royal Society. (See Miss Marjorie
Nicolson's interesting article, "The Early Stage of Cartesianism
in England," Stud. in Phil., XXVI, 374.) But perhaps it is not
necessary to cross the channel to find a source for these words.
There was no mean mathematical tradition in England, embrac-
ing as it did Napier, Oughtred, and Wallis, the last of whom was

127

closely associated with the Royal Society. Even though Bacon himself was no mathematician, mathematics were soon included in the general program of the Baconian philosophers. The following extract from a letter written by Dr. John Twysden to Oughtred, at some date between 1648 and 1652, shows that the stylistic quality under discussion could very well have been derived from England's own mathematicians. Speaking of Oughtred's Clavis Mathematica, Twysden says, "Neither truly did I find my expectation deceived; having with admiration often considered how it was possible (even in the hardest things of geometry) to deliver so much matter in so few words, yet with such demonstrative clearness and perspicuity: and hath often put me in mind of learned Mersennus his judgment (since dead) of it, that there was more matter comprehended in that little book than in Diophantes, and all the ancients." Correspondence of Scientific Men of the Seventeenth Century, 1841, p. 66. For an important reference to Oughtred in this respect, see Vindiciae Academiarum, 1654, pp. 20-1.

28   See Philosophia Pia, pp. 73, 90-1, 93-4; and Essays on Several Important Subjects, pp. 23, 25, 26.

29   Also consult his Reproof to the Rehearsal Transprosed, 1673, pp. 56 ff. Just as Bacon and the experimental philosophers had discovered rhetoric to be one factor in the corruption of science, so the conformists attributed the corruption of religion to rhetorical devices.

30   In the dedication to his Essay toward a real Character and a Philosophical Language, 1668, a design fostered by the Royal Society, Wilkins had pointed out, as a virtue of the language he was trying to establish, that it would "contribute much to the clearing away of some of our Modern differences in Religion, by unmasking many wild errors, that shelter themselves under the guise of affected phrases." See P M L A, XLV, 1002, note 48.

31   A Seasonable Defence of Preaching: And the Plain Way of it, 1678, p. 41.

32   See pp. 45-6. In another passage he returns to the same theme: "A man doth not shew his wit or learning by rolling in metaphors, and scattering his sentences of Greek and Latin, by abounding in high expressions, and talking in clouds, but he is then learned, when his learning has clear'd his understanding, and furnisht it with full and distinct apprehension of things; when it enables him to make hard things plain; and conceptions that were confused, distinct and orderly; and he

shews his learning by speaking good, strong, and plain sense."
P. 108.

33   Some Observations Upon an Answer to an Enquiry, pp. 119-122.
(Dr. Eachard's Works, 1705.) See also Sprat's History of the
Royal Society, p. 132.

34   Preface to Plus Ultra, 1668. See also Caroline F. Richardson's
English Preachers and Preaching, 1640-1670, Chap. IV.

35   The seventh essay in Essays on Several Important Subjects in
Philosophy and Religion, 1676. The general purpose of this essay is to show that the application of the scientific spirit to religion was responsible for the reaction against Puritanism, and
for the establishment of a rational religion. Glanvill himself was
aware that his ideas might not meet with universal approval, although he advances them with utmost sincerity. "The seventh,"
he says, "is entirely new. 'Tis a description of such a Genius
in Theology and Philosophy, as I confess I myself like; and I believe some others may. But I blame no man's different sentiment, who allows the liberty of judging that himself takes. I
have borrowed the countenance, and color of my Lord Bacons
story; of which I have given the brief contents. The essay is a
mixture of an Idea, and a disguised History." Two other essays
touch upon the same matter: the fourth, already discussed, and
the fifth, "The Agreement of Reason and Religion." Though Glanvill ignores the influence of a wider rationalism than that embodied in the scientific movement, and though he is obviously engaged in enthusiastic propaganda for the new science, there may
be some suggestion of truth in his theory that the scientific divines reformed religion in the same way as the experimental
philosophers reformed science.

36   See pp. 22, 26, 28, 31, 42, 44. If Glanvill's words were absolutely
trustworthy, it would hardly be necessary to adduce any other
evidence for science's influence on pulpit eloquence; but unfortunately, he is so intent on putting as much as possible to the
credit of the Royal Society, that he is capable of exaggerating
whatever evidence appears for his thesis, and of being blind to
the existence of other forces making for the same result. Yet
there must be some truth in what he says, for he was not such
a man as to make himself foolish with fallacious and absurd arguments.

Mention might here be made of Seth Ward, bishop of Salisbury,
who had held the Savilian professorship of astronomy for the
years 1649-61, and who had been an important member of the

group of experimental scientists which for a number of years
held weekly meetings at Oxford. In his Apology for the Mysteries, 1673, he says, "Concerning which things I shall not endeavour at a Rhetorical Harangue, but crave leave that I may be admitted to speak in a plain and humble Analytical and Didactical
way of discourse." These words reveal not only the same sentiments, but almost the same words, that had previously been expressed by scientists relative to their scientific treatises. See
P M L A, XLV, 980-1.

37   A somewhat extended discussion of the imagination is contained
in Glanvill's Vanity of Dogmatizing, chap. XI, the purpose of
which is to show how the imagination deceives. The chapter begins: "Fourthly, we erre and come short of Science, because
we are so frequently mislead by the evil conduct of our Imaginations; whose irregular strength and importunity almost perpetually abuse us. Now to make a full and clear discovery of our
Phancies deceptions; 'twill be requisite to look into the nature of
that mysterious faculty." Cf. Hobbes Leviathan, chap. II. The
whole subject of the imagination in the seventeenth century is now
being investigated by Mr. Donald Bond of Chicago University.

38   History of the Royal Society, p. 112.

39   The Question, To whom it belonged Anciently to Preach, p. 29.

40   See Miss Marjorie Nicolson's "The Early Stage of Cartesianism
in England," Stud. in Phil., XXVI, 373.

41   Sermon preached April 30, 1668.

42   A Free and Impartial Censure, p. 75.

43   Directions Concerning the Matter and Stile of Sermons, pp. 73-4.

44   A Friendly Debate, pp. 85-6.

45   A Defence and Continuation, p. 168. In the sections devoted to
style in the third book of the Rhetoric, Aristotle insists upon the
distinction between the style of poetry and that of oratory.

46   The fact, however, that thousands of sermons were published
during this period renders the simplification of their manner of
expression a very important element in the evolution of prose
style in general.

47   Robert Ferguson, The Interest of Reason, pp. 279-80. See also pp.
342-3.

48   Directions Concerning the Matter and Stile of Sermons, pp. 75-6.

49   In speaking of the attacks made upon nonconformists because of
their "lushious and fulsome metaphors," Robert Ferguson says,
"The due stating therefore the Nature and import of Metaphors,
is become not only a seasonable, but a necessary piece of service." Interest of Reason, 1675, p. 279. There is no doubt that
there was some basis for the charges preferred against the style
of the dissenters, as is evident from passages cited by their opponents from three of their number especially: Thomas Watson,
William Bridge, and John Durant. The following quotation is
more or less typical: "They say the Marygold opens and shuts
with the Sun, when the Sun shines, it opens, when the Sun with-
draws, it shuts, it opens and shuts according to the withdrawing
and shining of the Sun: and so if your comforts be true, the
more the righteousness of Christ opens before you, the more the
Sun of righteousness shines upon you, the more you will be com-
forted," etc. (William Bridge, The Freeness of the Grace and
Love of God, 1671, p. 49.) Still, one cannot help feeling that the
object of attack was really wider than the nonconformists, that
it was rhetoric in general.

50   Much that they say in this respect can be traced back as far as
Aristotle. See the Rhetoric, Book III, chaps. 2-4. Echoes of
Aristotle are rather frequent during this period, but he furnished
no argument for the plainness demanded by the scientists.

51   See John Owen's preface to Henry Lukin's An Introduction to the
Holy Scripture, 1669; and D. T.'s Hieragonisticon: or Corah's
Doom, Being an Answer to Two Letters of Enquiry into the
Grounds and Occasions of the Contempt of the Clergy and Religion, 1672, p. 148. Owen, the most prominent of the dissenters,
is evidently answering Patrick's Friendly Debate. D. T. handles
Eachard very severely, calling him names and laughing at his
advocacy of the study of English. In another work, Truth and Innocence Vindicated, 1669 (1670), written in answer to the Ecclesiastical Politie, Owen turns the tables on Parker by accusing
him of using swelling words, ambiguous terms, and rhetorical
flourishes, and by insisting upon the importance of clearness and
perspicuity in style. Owen, however, defends the nonconformists' use of rhetoric on the ground that their figures of speech
are necessary to express "Gospel Mysteries" and are found in
the Scriptures. (See pp. 19-20, 84.)

52   The Interest of Reason in Religion. With the Import and Use of
Scripture-Metaphors; ... With Reflections on several Late Writings, especially Mr. Sherlock's Discourse concerning the Knowledge of Jesus Christ, 1675.

53 For a study of the earlier contamination of poetical theory by rhetoric, see D. L. Clark's Rhetoric and Poetry in the Renaissance, 1922.

54 "Judgment begets the strength and structure, and Fancy begets the ornaments of a Poem." J.E.Spingarn, Critical Essays of the Seventeenth Century, vol. I, p. 59. In substituting "rhetoric" for "fancy," and "colours" for "ornaments," Ferguson throws into high relief the essentially rhetorical nature of Hobbes' poetic theory. Likewise, when he applies the other theories, which also belong to the rhetorical tradition, to sermons, he is only restoring to its proper realm that which had been foisted upon poetry.

55 "The strongest Arguments when delivered dryly, as they do not so delight and please, so neither do they so enlighten and instruct, as when clothed in a bright and flourishing Character. The same things nakedly and bluntly represented, do not make so great an impression, as when embellished with handsome Language. Nor is there anything more persuasive as well as delightful, than to find good words accompanying excellent Sense. And the better any subject is, the more worthy it ought to be accounted of a rich and polished, though not of a gaudy Dress. And indeed elegant expressions are impertinently bestowed, when matter and sense are not considerable. Nor is there a greater evidence of Folly in a Speaker or Writer, than to effect a loftiness of expression on a mean and petty subject. Words being manifestative of conceptions and things, ought to be proportionate to the Themes whereof we treat, and the ideas we have of them. When there is not something substantial and weighty underneath, a dazling stile serves only to amuse the Reader, and palliate the weakness of the Discourse." Pp. 256 ff.

56 This fact probably accounts for two contradictory criticisms of the Bible mentioned by Ferguson: "For as upon the one hand the Scripture is blam'd as Dull, flat and unaffecting by men of a wanton and profane wit, because of its not being adorned with the Flowers of Rhetorick; so upon the other hand, there are some who find fault with it as dark and obscure, because of the many Rhetorical Tropes and Figures which it is replenished with." Though the King James' version of the Bible has profoundly influenced English literature, there is little or no evidence that it played a part in the stylistic revolt under discussion. Robert Boyle even holds that the Bible has suffered in being translated. (See Works, ed. Birch, II, 120.) Discussions of the style of the Bible during this period are really numerous enough to justify a separate article.

57   Cf. John Prideaux, Sacred Eloquence, 1659, mentioned earlier
     in this article.

58   "The Stile of the most reputed Oratours is for the most part too
     pompous & flatulent for the subject they treat of; neither the
     Images which they form in their minds, nor the Arrangement of
     them in Words are adapted and proportioned to things ... and
     their discourses are like a load of flesh in the body of man, that
     serves to embarass it with an unprofitable weight. But to imag-
     ine so of God, or to ascribe ... great swelling words of vanity
     to him ... or to think that in the enditing the Bible, he did ...
     only feed us with gaudy phantasms, poetical Schemes, & luxur-
     iant phrases, is to impeach more than one of his perfections."
     P. 163.

59   The Interest of Reason, p. 160.

60   Ferguson admits that some of the nonconformists of the preced-
     ing age may have been guilty of the charges brought against
     them, but he would excuse them on the ground of the poor taste
     of their day. He thinks that in his own age trifling with words
     and phrases and puerile affectation of cadences were no longer
     relished. See pp. 295-6.

61   P. 342.

62   See pp. 345-7.

63   See pp. 256, 345-7, 367 ff.

64   P. 357.

65   "But as to the usage of Metaphors in Popular Sermons, and prac-
     tical Discourses, the Case is otherwise. Whatsoever is plead-
     able in their behalf upon any occasion, serves to justify the usur-
     pation of them in Discourses ad Populum and Didactical Writings.
     The Inducements and Motive of their allowance in Rhetorical
     Tracts, Orations, or whatever else doth best admit these Orna-
     ments of Eloquence, do all of them evince their agreeableness to
     the Oratory of the Pulpit." P. 358.

66   Directions Concerning the Matter and Stile of Sermons, Written
     to W. S. a young Deacon, by J. A., 1671. Arderne was at this
     time curate of St. Botolph, Aldersgate, but some years later
     became dean of Chester.

67   The mention of this verbal type is probably due to Aristotle's

having accorded it some notice. See the Rhetoric, III, iii, 1.

68 See pp. 22 ff., 43-4, 49-50, 68-70, 73-6.

69 Sherlock, who, however, in his own day enjoyed no reputation
for consistency, after he had been taken to task by Ferguson
for his advocacy of a plain style, thought it necessary to modify
his position in the following manner: "I was not so silly as to
oppose a sober use of Metaphors, no not in matters of Religion,
as Mr. Ferguson would fain insinuate; ... my quarrel with them
is, that they confound and darken the most plain and material
notions in Religion by metaphorical Descriptions." A Defence
and Continuation of a Discourse, 1675, pp. 162-3. In this last
statement, Sherlock assumes the exact attitude maintained by
the scientists.

70 An Essay Concerning Preaching, p. 71. See also pp. 55, 63.

71 It is evident that the upholders of the proper use of rhetoric in
sermons were greatly influenced, both in what they condemned
and in what they commended, by the Anti-Ciceronian movement.
We might almost go so far as to say that in the dispute between
the conformists and the nonconformists we have a clash between
Anti-Ciceronianism and the stylistic program of science. See
Professor Croll's articles on Anti-Ciceronianism in Studies in
Philology, vol. XVIII; Schelling Anniversary Papers, 1928; and
P M L A, vol. XXXIX.

72 For a treatment of the French movement see Sainte-Beuve's
Port Royal, and P. Jacquinet's Des Prédicateurs du XVIIe Siècle
avant Bossuet, 2nd. ed., 1885.

73 Discourse 6, 7. Another attack on pulpit eloquence, which I have
not seen, is Gueret's Entretiens sur l'Eloquence de la Chaire et
du Barreau, 1666. A number of years later, in 1687, Bouhours
attacked the conceits used in sermons. La Manière de Bien Penser dans les Ouvrages D'Esprit, 1687, pp. 55 ff.

74 Des Prédicateurs, p. 354.

75 Rapin's popularity in England in the sixteen seventies was considerable, owing in some degree to Rymer's translation of his
treatise on poetry, 1674.

76 The Whole Critical Works of Rapin, translated by Basil Kennet,
third ed., 1731, vol. II, pp. 1-106, passim. Mr. Spingarn refers to Voltaire's assertion, that Bourdaloue was responsible

for the transformation of English preaching, with the remark that Burnet (Suppl. to Burnet's Hist. of my own Time, ed. H. C. Foxcroft, pp. 96, 467) bears Voltaire out. But to me Burnet's words seem to point in the opposite direction. In 1664 Burnet went to France to study the manner of preaching followed there, and though he was displeased with that of the Jesuits, he liked the manner of the secular clergy. "I took a good tincture of their way — indeed more than Scotland could well bear and much more than England could endure; but I have worn off some gestures that looked too like acting, and yet the way of preaching in which I still hold is ... very like the way of the secular clergy of the Port Royal." If these words mean anything, they indicate that Burnet's French method of preaching was distinctly at odds with the ideal of simplicity which was being established in England. Furthermore, Tillotson's sermons had already illustrated the new style of preaching by the time Burnet went to France. See Critical Essays of the Seventeenth Century, ed. Spingarn, vol. I, p. xli.

77   That the English were well aware of this difference is revealed in numerous passages, but nowhere more clearly than in Sprat's History of the Royal Society. Though ostensibly apologizing for his lack of eloquence in comparison with the elegant style of Pelisson's history of the French Academy, Sprat hardly conceals a sturdy pride in his manner of expression. "I have only this to allege in my excuse; that as they undertook the advancement of the elegance of Speech, so it became their History, to have some resemblance to their enterprize: Whereas the intention of ours, being not the Artifice of Words, but a bare knowledge of things; my fault may be esteem'd the less, that I have written of Philosophers, without any ornament of Eloquence.... I hope now, it will not be thought a vain digression, if I step aside, to recommend the forming of such an Assembly as the French Academy to the Gentlemen of our Nation. I know indeed, that the English Genius is not so airy, and discursive as that of some of our neighbors, but that we generally love to have Reason set out in plain, undeceiving expressions; as much, as they to have it deliver'd with colour and beauty. And besides this, I understand well enough, that they have one great assistance to the growth of Oratory, which to us is wanting; that is, that their Nobility live commonly close together in their Cities, and ours for the most part scattered in their Country Houses.... They prefer the Pleasures of the Town; we, those of the Field: whereas it is from the frequent conversations in Cities, that the Humour, and Wit, and Variety, and Elegance of Language, are chiefly to be fetch'd." Pp. 40-41.

78 Critical Essays of the Eighteenth Century, ed. W. H. Durham, p. 80.

79 Ker, Essays of John Dryden, I, 173-4.

80 Diary, July 15, 1683. Evelyn is speaking about a sermon in the old style, which, he significantly says, was preached by "a stranger, an old man" [my italics]. The same year Patrick, perhaps taking to himself some of the glory thereof, asserts that "never did men more endeavour orderly discourse, and aim at plain, unaffected speech, than they do now in the Church of England: where good sense, in the most easy and familiar words, is now looked upon as the principal commendation of sermons." (Works, ed. A. Taylor, VI, 410.) In the following year another remarks to the same effect that the "florid strain of preaching is almost quite worn out, and is become now as ridiculous as it was once admired" (G. Burnet's preface to his translation of More's Utopia. See also his Discourse of the Pastoral Care, 1692, pp. 108-9, 111-13.)

81 Reflections upon Ancient and Modern Learning, third ed., 1705, p. 35. Wotton explains the inferiority of modern eloquence on the ground of "the Humour of the Age," which makes men suspect a trick in everything said in courts or in Parliament to move the passions, "And therefore when Men have spoken to the Point, in as few Words as the Matter will bear, it is expected they should hold their Tongues." Cf. what Locke says about rhetoric being the art of deceiving. Essay of Human Understanding, Book III, Chap. X.

82 A contrary idea of the style suitable for religious compositions is found in Hughes' essay. Though he thinks that science "requires a grave didactick Style, agreeable to the Plainness and Simplicity of Truth and Reason" and that history should also wear a plain dress, he claims that "Morality and Divinity are capable of all the Ornaments of Wit and Fancy." See p. 85. The nonconformists had, of course, made the same distinction years before.

SENECAN STYLE IN THE SEVENTEENTH CENTURY

George Williamson

As the reign of Elizabeth drew to a close, English prose style
yielded to the pressure of a new movement. The Ciceronian
movement had no sooner reached its climax in the formal periods of Hooker than the Anti-Ciceronian movement found a lead-
er in Bacon, whose terse manner of expression became the hall-
mark of style among the later essay and character writers. In
1610 Bacon wrote to Tobie Matthew: "They tell me my Latin is
turn'd Silver, and become current." By this time his English
had, in fact, taken on a Silver-Latin style and become current
among the Senecan essayists. Even Polonius was a Senecan in
theory when he observed that "brevity is the soul of wit," and
in practice when he recognized Hamlet's "points" by remarking,
"How pregnant sometimes his replies are!" But since this is
reading into Bacon and Shakespeare more than either intended,
we may well ask to what extent the English seventeenth century
was critically aware of the Senecan style.[1] To gather evidence
of such awareness, either in the theory or in the criticism of
rhetoric, will be the object of this essay.

Francis Thompson, who was sensitive to Renaissance style,
recognized Silver-Latin imitation in Browne:

> Browne was more idiomatic in structure than the Cic-
> eronian Hooker. But the admirable knitting of his senten-
> ces was not due merely to a better study of English idiom.
> He was steeped in classic models more compact and preg-
> nant than Cicero. Like his French contemporaries, he
> was influenced by the great Latin rhetoricians, Lucan,
> Ovid, and Seneca; whose rivalry it was to put an idea into
> the fewest possible words.[2]

Elsewhere I have dealt with other aspects of the Jacobean cultivation of Silver-Latin style: on the one hand, with the antithetic wit that was associated with the terse Senecan style;[3] on the
other, with the development of a cult of obscurity which produced

Reprinted by permission from Philological Quarterly, Vol. 15 (1936),
pp. 321-351.

"strong lines" after the example of Persius and Tacitus. [4] When
brevity was the soul of wit, the points of wit often became so
pregnant that "significant darkness" or "strong lines" were the
result. In short, in Jacobean times the cult of brevity in Seneca
was not unnaturally associated with the cult of obscurity in Tacitus. Enigmatic or cryptic expression, which both Chapman and
Bacon allow, reached its extreme development in the poetry of
this time under the form known as "strong lines."

At the close of the seventeenth century Shaftesbury felt that
the Senecan style still prevailed, at least so far as the essayists
were concerned. The prevailing style, in Shaftesbury's view,
derived from the Epistles of Seneca:

> He falls into the random way of miscellaneous writing,
> says everywhere great and noble things, in and out of the
> way, accidentally as words lead him (for with these he
> plays perpetually), with infinite wit, but with little or no
> coherence, without a shape or body to his work, without
> a real beginning, a middle, or an end. [5]

The great and noble things, word-play, and wit concern Shaftesbury less than Seneca's violation of unity and coherence. He remarks that whole letters or pages may be divided or combined
at pleasure; "every period, every sentence almost, is independent, and may be taken asunder, transposed, postponed, anticipated, or set in any new order, as you fancy." After this
analysis of Seneca, Shaftesbury turns to his own time:

> This is the manner of writing so much admired and im-
> itated in our age, that we have scarce the idea of any other
> model. We know little, indeed, of the difference between
> one model or character of writing and another. All runs
> to the same tune, and beats exactly one and the same mea-
> sure. Nothing, one would think, could be more tedious
> than this uniform pace. The common amble or canterbury
> is not, I am persuaded, more tiresome to a good rider
> than this see-saw of essay writers is to an able reader. [6]

Thus Shaftesbury disparages the style which not only clothed the
work of the aphoristic essayists and character-writers, but cor-
responded to the Jacobean taste for mingled wit and gravitas.
He is not struck by the aspect of this style which Professor Croll
has analyzed acutely:

SENECAN STYLE IN THE SEVENTEENTH CENTURY

> A prose-style that should adequately express this age
> must contrive, therefore, to mingle elements that in any
> other period would appear oddly contrasted. It must be at
> once ingenious and lofty, intense yet also profound, acute,
> realistic, revealing, but at the same time somewhat grave
> and mysterious. [7]

Professor Croll, however, holds that Bacon naturalized such a
style in English by imitating Tacitus rather than Seneca. But
since Shaftesbury is not unaware that Seneca combined wit and
gravity, we may leave the problem of discriminating between
Senecan and Tacitean imitation to the testimony of the time.
    Three tendencies of Anti-Ciceronian style have been associ-
ated by Professor Croll with three important names: the curt
with Lipsius, the loose with Montaigne, and the obscure with
Bacon. The curt and the loose tendencies, as Professor Croll
observes, were both Senecan in pattern; but the curt and the obscure tendencies, which he is anxious to discriminate, were
commonly confused in seventeenth-century Senecanism. And
this is not unnatural, since the peculiar quality of Tacitus is
brevity pushed to the verge of obscurity; moreover, his style
offers more likeness than difference when compared with "Seneca's own style — disconnected, pointed, antithetic, metaphorical and piquant."[8] Both differed from Cicero's polished and
flowing amplitude chiefly in the abrupt terseness and jerky movement of their sentences. For English criticism, therefore, it
will be erring on the right side to regard Senecan style in its
most obvious character — as the cultivation of sententious brevity and all the qualities that go with rhetorical sententiae. In general, the curt Senecan style is marked by a cultivation of brevity,
gravity, and point in the essay manner; its rhythm is jerky and
abrupt; in particular, the Tacitean variety is an extreme development of this style. For both Seneca and Tacitus brevity meant
Sallust, and in the seventeenth century all three were distinguished for similar qualities. To the curt Senecan style our investigation will be restricted, since the English writers of this
period were much less conscious of the loose Senecan style,
though here and there that also may be noticed.
    It is necessary to remark, however, that the curt style was
generally supplemented or relieved by the loose style. The two
were commonly intermingled in the expression of Bacon or
Browne. Both styles have been carefully analyzed by Professor
Croll in "The Baroque Style in Prose," where he has summarized

them as "the concise, serried, abrupt stile coupé, and the informal, meditative, and 'natural' loose style":

> It is necessary to repeat − once more − that in the best
> writers these two styles do not appear separately in pas-
> sages of any length, and that in most of them they inter-
> mingle in relations far too complex for description. They
> represent two sides of the seventeenth-century mind: its
> sententiousness, its penetrating wit, its Stoic intensity,
> on the one hand, and its dislike of formalism, its roving
> and self-exploring curiosity, in brief, its skeptical ten-
> dency, on the other. And these two habits of mind are gen-
> erally not separated one from the other; nor are they even
> always exactly distinguishable. [9]

The loose style was the more natural, and the curt style the
more artful, for it did have to make its "points" show. While
the loose period may suggest the Ciceronian, it avoids or breaks
the concinnitas or symmetry of structure of Cicero; while it may
adumbrate a Latin mould, it follows a more organic order of
thought. The curt style pre-empts attention before the Restoration, and the loose style predominates after, but both forms
prepare the way for modern English prose. The separation or
opposition of the curt style and the loose style distinguishes the
Restoration from the first half of the century.

I

The rise of the Anti-Ciceronian cult which marks the seventeenth century has been traced by Professor Croll to Muretus,[10]
and its dissemination to Lipsius, Montaigne, and Bacon. What
these men discovered in Seneca and Tacitus, or disliked in Cicero, characterized the new taste in style − a taste that ran to
the essay style rather than to the oratorical. In 1580 Muretus
had defended Tacitus by going so far as to praise his obscurity
and asperity of style. The passage which Professor Croll has
quoted from this excellent appraisal of Tacitus found its way
into late seventeenth-century English from the work of La Mothe
Le Vayer:

> Howsoever it be, it is no wonder if Tacitus (having im-
> itated Thucydides, and both followed Demosthenes) re-
> tained something of that roughness and austerity, which is

observed in the writings of those Two Graecians; and
which all the Ancients accounted as a virtue, so far is it
from deserving to be imputed as a fault, to him that should
propose them to himself for imitation. And as some Wines
are recommended to our palates by a little bitterness that
is in them; and as many persons find that a dusky and obscure light in Churches is most suitable to their exercise
of devotion: so others conceive the obscurity of an Author,
mixed with a little roughness of Stile, is rather to be es-
teemed than otherwise; because it disposes the mind to
attention, and elevates and transports it to notions, which
it would not arrive at in a more easy composition. [11]

Muretus, as Professor Croll remarks, "stirs the ground about
the roots of seventeenth-century style"; for the Jacobean cult of
obscurity shares this doctrine with him.

Lipsius first employed the Anti-Ciceronian style in his Quaestiones Epistolicae, which appeared just before his edition of Tacitus. The character of his new style is best described by Lipsius
himself in a letter to a friend:

I am afraid of what you will think of this work [the
Quaestiones]. For this is a different kind of writing from
my earlier style, without showiness, without luxuriance,
without the Tullian concinnities; condensed everywhere,
and I know not whether of too studied a brevity. But this
is what captivates me now. They celebrate Timanthes the
painter because there was always something more to be
understood in his works than was actually painted. I should
like this in my style. [12]

Professor Croll remarks that both the critical terms and the
style of this passage come from Seneca, but it would be hard to
show that the stylistic direction differs from that which Muretus
discovered in Tacitus. Although Lipsius, as a Stoic, was even-
tually associated with the point and brevity of Seneca, he began
by admiring the dark implications and studied ellipses of Tacitus. There is one kind of brevity which Seneca disparaged and
which was more often associated with Tacitus, and that is obscurity, obscura brevitas. Seneca approved "abruptae sententiae
et suspiciosae," of (in Lodge's words) "abrupt Sentences and
suspicious, in which more is to be understood than heard," so
long as they were not carried to the point of obscurity. Although

Seneca did not allow copia or superfluity, he did allow fluency, because it was unlabored and because it revealed personality.[13] In fact, to him fundere meant to avoid affected and labored composition, and to achieve the naturalness which he desired, but which was not without artifice.[14] It was this side of Seneca that encouraged the loose style at the same time that his cultivation of sententiae stimulated the curt style.

The difficulty of discriminating between Senecan and Tacitean imitation may be suggested by a contemporary criticism of the neo-stoic Lipsius. In Boccalini's Ragguagli di Parnasso, first translated into English in 1626, Lipsius is brought before Apollo for his idolatry of Tacitus, and Muretus is one of those who jealously indict him as follows:

> Hee now loved to discourse with no other learned man: no conversation did more agrade him: he commended no other Historian: and all with such partiality of inward affection, namely, for the elegancie of his speech, adorned more with choise conceits, than with words; for the succinctnesse of his close, nervous, and grave sententious Oratorie, cleare onely to those of best understanding, with the envy and hatred of other vertuous men of this dominion, dependents of Cicero, and of the mighty Caesarean faction, who approve it not. And did with such diligence labour to imitate him, that not onely with hatefull antonomasia, hee dared to call him his Auctor, but utterly scorning all other mens detections, he affected no other ambition, than to appeare unto the world a new Tacitus.[15]

However, Lipsius "is in the end by his Maiestie [Apollo], not only absolved, but highly commended and admired." In this trial Lipsius, the great Neo-Stoic, is specifically a Tacitean, but generally an Anti-Ciceronian. If we were to distinguish Lipsius the Tacitean from Lipsius the Senecan, we should have to distinguish where the seventeenth century often confused; furthermore, as a Tacitean he could find merit in obscurity, as a Senecan he might condone word-play. Lipsius was the standard-bearer of Senecan style, but if his Anti-Ciceronian taste culminated in an edition of Seneca (1605) it had begun with an edition of Tacitus (1574).

In 1591 the first English translation of Tacitus, the work of Sir Henry Savile, was recommended to the reader by Anthony Bacon in these words:

SENECAN STYLE IN THE SEVENTEENTH CENTURY

For Tacitus I may say without partiality, that hee hath
writen the most matter with best conceyt in fewest wordes
of anie Historiographer ancient or moderne. But he is
harde. Difficilia quae pulchra: the second reading over
will please thee more then the first, and the third then
the second.

In the second and enlarged edition of 1598 Richard Grenewey declared in his dedication that there is in Tacitus "no woord not
loaden with matter, and as himselfe speaketh of Galba, he useth
Imperatoria brevitate: which although it breed difficultie, yet
carrieth great gravitie." Thus the words of Muretus came to
partial fulfillment in recommendations to the readers of Tacitus
in English, who received the sixth edition of this work in 1640.
When Thomas Lodge revised his translation of Seneca in 1620,
he apologized to the reader for his own shortcomings:

My businesse being great, and my distractions many;
the Authour being seriously succinct, and full of Laconisme;
no wonder if in somthings my omissions may seeme such,
as some whose judgement is mounted aboue the Epicycle
of Mercurie, will find matter enough to carpe at, though
not to condemne. [16]

For Lodge Seneca was, above all, "laconic"; but W. R., in his
eulogy of Lodge, found other qualities to commend:

You are his profitable Tutor, and haue instructed him
to walke and talke in perfect English. If his matter held
not still the Romane Majestie, I should mistake him one
of Ours; he deliuers his mind so significantly and fitly.
Surely, had hee chosen any other Tongue to write in, my
affection thinkes, it had beene English; And in English, as
you haue taught him in your Translation; you expresse him
so liuely, being still the same Man in other garments ...
retaining still the natiue grauitie of his countenance....[17]

Although the praise goes to Lodge, it is for catching the qualities of Seneca, to whom Lodge becomes the "Senec-Sybill (or
rather Mercurie) of his oraculous Discourses." And thus Seneca
emerges with qualities which are difficult to distinguish from
those of Tacitus, for he too is succinct, majestic, grave, and
oraculous; moreover, Lodge's English has taught Seneca a second

143

native language, or so it seems to W. R. in Jacobean days. Whatever the origin, whether in the pregnant brevity of Seneca or in the obscure brevity of Tacitus, the virtue of difficulty suggested gravity of style to Anti-Ciceronian ears; weight rather than copia now translated the Roman majesty.

While there is evidence for saying that gravity and obscurity were more commonly associated with Tacitus, and point and ingenuity with Seneca, these qualities are not very certain differentia for writers who were celebrated for their succinctness. It is well to remember such differentia, but it is more historical to accept the general identity of the two styles as Anti-Ciceronian or fundamentally Senecan in character. In Hakewill's Apologie or Declaration of the Power and Providence of God, first published in 1627, we find important confirmation of such a view:

> Sr Henry Savill sharply censures [Tacitus] for his style, taking occasion from those words in the life of Agricola, bonum virum facile crederes magnum libenter: at te (saith he) Corneli Tacite bonum historicum facile credimus, bonum oratorem crederemus libenter, were it not for this & some other sayings of the like making: Fuit illi viro, saith Tacitus, (judging of Seneca as we may of him) ingenium amaenum, & temporibus illius auribus accommodatum: How that age was eared long or round I cannot define, but sure I am it yeelded a kinde of sophisticate eloquence and riming harmony of words; where-under was small matter in sense, when there seemed to be most in appearance, and divers instances he brings out of Tacitus.... [18]

These very interesting remarks, involving the first English translator of Tacitus, are essentially Bacon's indictment of the Senecan fashion, which we shall consider in due course. But this turning of the tables upon Tacitus, to which Hakewill subscribes, emphasizes the resemblance (even in vices) between Seneca and Tacitus as they sounded to English ears.

II

Seneca, when he spoke of style, always preferred things to words — a preference which the seventeenth century remembered to his credit. And Bacon was the first to sound the seventeenth-century preference for things rather than words. That is the burden of his attack on Ciceronian style in 1605, when he condemns the Ciceronians for hunting "more after the choiceness of the phrase, and the round and clean composition of the sentence, and the sweet falling of the clauses ... than after the weight of matter."[19] This Renaissance delight in style — "the whole inclination and bent of those times was rather towards copie than weight" — was furthered by hatred of the schoolmen, "whose writings were altogether in a differing style and form." Bacon admits the need to clothe philosophy in eloquence for civil occasions, but believes that "to the severe inquisition of truth, and the deep progress into philosophy" such a dress offers some hindrance, for it gives a premature satisfaction to the mind and quenches the desire of further search.[20]

The question of "vain words" leads Bacon to "vain matter," or the second distemper of learning, under which he attacks the schoolmen for crumbling knowledge into subtle distinctions and "vermiculate questions." Their unprofitable subtlety expressed itself in two ways: in fruitless matter and in a fruitless method of handling knowledge, splitting the "cummin seed"; "whereas indeed the strength of all sciences is, as the strength of the old man's faggot, in the bond."

> For the harmony of a science, supporting each part the other, is and ought to be the true and brief confutation and suppression of all the smaller sort of objections; but on the other side, if you take out every axiom, as the sticks of the faggot, one by one, you may quarrel with them and bend them and break them at your pleasure: so that as was said of Seneca, Verborum minutiis rerum frangit pondera [that he broke up the weight and mass of the matter by verbal points and niceties]; so a man may truly say of the schoolmen, Quaestionum minutiis scientiarum frangunt soliditatem [they broke up the solidity and coherency of the sciences by the minuteness and nicety of their questions].[21]

And thus Quintilian's criticism of Seneca, slightly misquoted, is turned by Bacon into a criticism of the schoolmen. It might be concluded that a Senecan style would make a fitting dress for a scholastic habit of mind, and we shall have occasion to recall the suggestion. But for the present this must remain a criticism of the schoolmen rather than of Seneca.

In this connection we may wonder a little at what Bacon has to say of aphorisms, especially when we remember that he certainly knew Seneca sa a master of sententiae, at which Quintilian had directed his criticism. Bacon's theory of the communication of knowledge is vital to his criticism of style, and revolves about the question of methods. The most real diversity of method concerns method as related to the use of knowledge and method as related to the progress of knowledge, or the delivery of knowledge as it may be best believed (the Magistral way), and as it may be best examined (the way of Probation). [22] Since knowledge is now delivered as it may be best believed, not as it may be best examined, "there is a kind of contract of error between the deliverer and the receiver," because "in this same anticipated and prevented knowledge, no man knoweth how he came to the knowledge which he hath obtained." This is the way of rhetoric and the oratorical style; the way of the essay style is quite different, for "knowledge that is delivered as a thread to be spun on, ought to be delivered and intimated, if it were possible, in the same method wherein it was invented; and so is it possible of knowledge induced."[23] Here we have the philosophy which underlies the organic method of the "loose" period found in the way of Probation; in the Magistral way, which merely announces the results of inquiry, one cannot see the thought grow.

This brings us to another diversity of great consequence — "the delivery of knowledge in Aphorisms, or in Methods." Here Bacon begins by condemning the practice of spinning a few axioms or observations into a solemn and formal art; "but the writing in Aphorisms hath many excellent virtues, whereto the writing in Method doth not approach."

> For first, it trieth the writer, whether he be superficial or solid: for Aphorisms, except they should be ridiculous, cannot be made but of the pith and heart of sciences; for discourse of illustration is cut off; recitals of examples are cut off; discourse of connection and order is cut off; descriptions of practice are cut off; so there remaineth nothing to fill the Aphorisms but some good quantity of observation: and therefore no man can suffice, nor in reason will attempt, to write aphorisms, but he that is sound and grounded. But in Methods,
>
> Tantum series juncturaque pollet,
> Tantum de medio sumptis accedit honoris
>
> [the arrangement and connexion and joining of the parts

has so much effect], as a man shall make a great shew of
an art, which if it were disjointed would come to little.
Secondly, Methods are more fit to win consent or belief,
but less fit to point to action; for they carry a kind of demonstration in orb or circle, one part illuminating another,
and therefore satisfy; but particulars, being dispersed, do
best agree with dispersed directions. And lastly, Aphorisms, representing a knowledge broken, do invite men to
enquire farther; whereas Methods, carrying the shew of
a total, do secure men, as if they were at furthest.[24]

If we recall the passage on the schoolmen, we must conclude
that the vice of the schoolmen becomes a virtue in the realm of
style; that aphorisms, which must be filled with "some good
quantity of observation," belong to the method of inducing knowledge; and that a Senecan style represents a knowledge broken,
and therefore avoids the "contract of error between the deliverer
and the receiver." Here methods present knowledge as it may
be best believed, and aphorisms as it may be best examined,
with a view to further inquiry. They are different styles for different purposes, and so Bacon used them. But the method of
probation is not the same as Methods of persuasion; rather, it
belongs, with Aphorisms, to induction and the Senecan style.
    Bacon wrote his severest philosophical work, the Novum Or-
ganum, in Aphorisms; but he clothed his popular Advancement
of Learning in the rhetoric of persuasion or Methods. And yet
it would be a mistake to say that "discourse of illustration,"
"discourse of connection and order," and "descriptions of practice" are always cut off in the former and never in the latter.
The habit of aphorism and the urge to persuade were too strong
in Bacon to permit single-minded devotion to one manner of expression. The chief exception to this judgment is, of course, his
early essays. They provide the best illustration of the aphorism
in which his thought seems commonly to have been formulated.
His change of style in the Essays reflects not so much a growing disapproval of Senecan style as a change from aphorisms to
methods for a particular purpose. In this instance the change
seems to have derived from his meditation on the function of
rhetoric in connection with the Stoic method in moral counsel.
In the Advancement of Learning Bacon defends rhetoric by saying that virtue must be shown "to the Imagination in lively representation":
    for to shew her to Reason only in subtilty of argument, was

147

a thing ever derided in Chrysippus and many of the Stoics; who thought to thrust virtue upon men by sharp disputations and conclusions, which have no sympathy with the will of man. [25]

But in the De Augmentis Scientiarum he declares more specifically that virtue must be shown "to the imagination in as lively representation as possible, by ornament of words":

For the method of the Stoics, who thought to thrust virtue upon men by concise and sharp maxims and conclusions, which have little sympathy with the imagination and will of man, has been justly ridiculed by Cicero. [26]

In 1623, then, Bacon condemns the method of the Stoics in moral counsel expressly because aphorisms have little imaginative appeal; then, having detected another vanity in the Senecan style, he agrees with Cicero in ridiculing the Stoic method in moral essays. That this objection was not so sharply defined for Bacon in 1605 or even in 1612 seems the plain inference from the change in his essay style, since that change really does not appear until the 1625 edition. The difference between the parallel essays of 1597 and 1612 is chiefly one of slight revision or addition; it is not so striking as the difference between the parallel essays of 1612 and 1625, for the latter can truly be said to be revised and even rewritten from the point of view of Methods. [27] Only in 1625 does the aphoristic character of the Essays appear seriously modified, if not forsaken. Aphorisms, Bacon seems to have concluded, are appropriate to philosophy or science because they "invite men to enquire farther"; they are permissible to "dispersed meditations" (his early essays) because they give "dispersed directions"; but Methods are more appropriate to moral essays because "methods are more fit to win consent or belief."

If the Advancement of Learning contained the seed of disapproval of Senecan style, the De Augmentis Scientiarum brought the full-grown plant. After his condemnation of the Ciceronian style, Bacon now adds this criticism:

Little better is that kind of stile (yet neither is that altogether exempt from vanity) which neer about the same time succeeded this Copy and superfluity of speech. The labour here is altogether, That words may be aculeate, sentences concise, and the whole contexture of the speech

> and discourse, rather rounding into it selfe, than spread
> and dilated: So that it comes to passe by this Artifice,
> that every passage seemes more witty and waighty than
> indeed it is. Such a stile as this we finde more excessive-
> ly in Seneca; more moderately in Tacitus and Plinius Se-
> cundus; and of late it hath bin very pleasing unto the eares
> of our time. And this kind of expression hath found such
> acceptance with meaner capacities, as to be a dignity and
> ornament to Learning; neverthelesse, by the more exact
> judgements, it hath bin deservedly dispised, and may be
> set down as a distemper of Learning, seeing it is nothing
> else but a hunting after words, and fine placing of them. [28]

One of "the more exact judgements," as we have seen, was Sir
Henry Savile; the "meaner capacities" with whom this kind of
expression had found such favor were, as we know, actually the
Senecan essayists and character-writers for whom Bacon had
set the example. Perhaps Bacon only perceived the dangers of
his own style when it fell into the hands of meaner talents; at
any rate, he could not be charged with the "vanity" of it, which
is what he really condemns after all. Since he prized above all
"weight of matter," it is not surprising that he should condemn
his own style when it merely disguised the lack of weight. But
to be weighty in his day it was necessary to be Senecan, and Bacon moderated rather than deserted his own Senecanism.

III

The greatest vanity of Senecan style, however, appeared in
the sermons of Bacon's friend, Bishop Lancelot Andrewes. As
we have already observed, Bacon suggested (perhaps unintention-
ally) the propriety of Senecan style to the scholastic mind: "as
was said of Seneca, Verborum minutiis rerum frangit pondera;
so a man may truly say of the schoolmen, Quaestionum minutiis
scientiarum frangunt soliditatem." Bacon fell upon the schoolmen's "digladiation about subtilities," since all their thirst for
truth proved only "fierce with dark keeping"; "in the inquiry of
the divine truth their pride inclined to leave the oracle of God's
word and to vanish in the mixture of their own inventions." [29]
The same charges were brought against preachers like Andrewes.
Bacon also remarked that in contrast to the Ciceronian the scholastic "writings were altogether in a differing style and form;
taking liberty to coin and frame new terms of art to express their

own sense and to avoid circuit of speech, without regard to the
pureness, pleasantness, and (as I may call it) lawfulness of the
phrase or word."[30] In short, the schoolmen were guilty of Senecan faults when compared with the Ciceronians. Bacon's remarks on the schoolmen contain suggestions of two charges later
brought against Andrewes's sermon style; both charges have a
curious relevance to Quintilian's criticism that Seneca broke the
weight of his matter by cultivating sententiae. One of these charges relates to Andrewes's practice of "division," of "crumbling"
his text; and the other to his "wit" or levity in serious matters.[31]
These two aspects of "rerum pondera minutissimis sententiis
fregit" are implied in Quintilian on Seneca;[32] they suggest the
propriety of the Senecan style to the scholastic mind.

Both Andrewes and Donne were not only scholastic but also
Senecan in their traits of style; they were both greatly influenced
by the church fathers who had a Senecan bent, such as Tertullian.[33] The most striking trait of "metaphysical" style, which
has a close affinity to the Senecan, is the teasing out of ideas
and figures so as to reveal their ambiguous, antithetic, or paradoxical aspects. This is present in Andrewes when he crumbles
a text to pieces; it finds a place in the criticism which Dr. Johnson directed against the "metaphysical poets"; and it is not ab-
sent from the work of the character-writers. Senecan brevity,
abruptness, and point characterize the sentences of Andrewes,
and affect those of Donne, though less obviously. The stylistic
aims once expressed by Donne are clearly Senecan:

> ... with such succinctness and brevity, as may consist
> with clearness, and perspicuity, in such manner, and
> method, as may best enlighten your understandings, and
> least encumber your memories, I shall open unto you [the
> meaning of the text].[34]

In 1710 Steele remembers Donne in connection with such aims.
Having remarked that Boccalini sentences a laconic writer, for
using three words where two would have served, to read all the
works of Guicciardini, Steele comments:

> This Guicciardini is so very prolix and circumstantial
> in his writings, that I remember our countryman, doctor
> Donne, speaking of that majestic and concise manner in
> which Moses has described the creation of the world, adds,
> 'that if such an author as Guicciardini were to have written

on such a subject, the world itself would not have been able
to have contained the books that gave the history of its
creation. '35

The "majestic and concise manner" is as brief a formulation of
Jacobean ideals as one could find; only the wit is wanting.

But before the death of George Herbert the "wit" and "division" of Andrewes, which have their analogues in Seneca, had
begun to provoke criticism. For his "country parson" Herbert
prescribes another style and method:

> The parson's method in handling of a text, consists of
> two parts: first, a plain and evident declaration of the
> meaning of the text; and secondly, some choice observa-
> tions drawn out of the whole text, as it lies entire, and
> unbroken in the Scripture itself. This he thinks natural,
> and sweet, and grave. Whereas the other way of crumb-
> ling a text into small parts, as, the person speaking, or
> spoken to, the subject, and object, and the like, hath nei-
> ther in it sweetness, nor gravity, nor variety, since the
> words apart are not Scripture, but a Dictionary, and may
> be considered alike in all the Scripture. 36

Thus Herbert anticipates the method of Tillotson and condemns
that of Andrewes, in which Donne was a lesser offender. Herbert begins his criticism of "witty" preaching in these significant words:

> By these and other means the parson procures attention;
> but the character of his sermon is holiness; he is not witty,
> or learned, or eloquent, but holy. A character, that Her-
> mogenes never dreamed of, and therefore he could give no
> precept thereof. 37

But while Herbert deplores the wit he reveals the profit to be
derived from Senecan brevity. Of course Senecan wit was not
"metaphysical" wit, but Seneca provided the chief classical model of a witty prose style.

By the time of Robert South there was something like a general disapproval of the witty preaching represented by Andrewes.
At the same time that South cultivates the Senecan qualities which
pass into Restoration style, he succumbs to some of the wit that
he condemns in Andrewes or disparages by association with

Seneca. In The Scribe Instructed, preached in 1660, South administers severe reproof to two kinds of preaching: that which sponsors "a puerile and indecent sort of levity," and that which follows a "mean, heavy, careless, and insipid way of handling things sacred," or the manner of the school of Andrewes and that of the Puritans. Of the former he declares:

> What Quintilian most discreetly says of Seneca's handling philosophy, that he did rerum pondera minutissimis sententiis frangere, break, and, as it were, emasculate the weight of his subject by little affected sentences, the same may with much more reason be applied to the practice of those, who detract from the excellency of things sacred by a comical lightness of expression: as when their prayers shall be set out in such dress, as if they did not supplicate, but compliment Almighty God; and their sermons so garnished with quibbles and trifles, as if they played with truth and immortality; and neither believed these things themselves, nor were willing that others should. [38]

Quintilian speaks to South even more pertinently about the wit of Andrewes than about that of Seneca, and South finds Quintilian relevant to the practice of "division":

> Such are wholly mistaken in the nature of wit: for true wit is a severe and manly thing. Wit in divinity is nothing else, but sacred truths suitably expressed. It is not shreds of Latin or Greek, nor a Deus dixit, and a Deus benedixit, nor those little quirks, or divisions into the ὅτι, the διότι and the καθότι, or the egress, regress, and progress, and other such stuff, (much like the style of a lease,) that can properly be called wit. For that is not wit which consists not with wisdom. [39]

South is here purging the Senecan or "differing" sermon style of its "levity" − in both of the senses in which Quintilian suggested that it was an enemy to gravitas. The standards by which South reproves this wit are obviously Restoration.

But it would be a mistake to conclude that South was not Senecan in style, or that his ideals of style were not definitely Senecan, in the better sense of brevity and plainness rather than "point." No one can overlook his clearly Senecan requirements

for style in A Discourse against Long and Extempore Prayers.[40]
His thoroughly Baconian view and an epitome of Jacobean stylistic ambitions find expression in one short paragraph:

> In fine, brevity and succinctness of speech is that,
> which, in philosophy or speculation, we call maxim, and
> first principle; in the counsels and resolves of practical
> wisdom, and the deep mysteries of religion, oracle; and
> lastly, in matters of wit, and the finenesses of imagina-
> tion, epigram. All of them, severally and in their kinds,
> the greatest and the noblest things that the mind of man
> can shew the force and dexterity of its faculties in. [41]

Here we are reminded of the advantage of "aphorisms" over
"methods," and we should not forget that "oracle" and "epigram"
led into "strong lines." It is significant that in condemning the
"vanity" of the school of Andrewes, South confuses the "metaphysical" and "Senecan" aspects of their levity; it is not less
significant that he himself remains stoutly Senecan in the plainer fashion of Bishop Hall.

Before we return to the secular prose, we should recall that
clearness or perspicuity is not a trustworthy guide to the ideals
or affinities of styles, since perspicuity is the constant of language as a vehicle of communication. It is rather the variants,
or the qualities associated with perspicuity, that give styles
their peculiar character. Thus when John Hughes tells us, in his
essay Of Style, that the qualifications of a good style are propriety, perspicuity, elegance, and cadence, it is the propriety, elegance, and cadence that are significant. When Ben Jonson likewise names perspicuity, but in connection with other qualities,
it is the other qualities that differentiate the ideals of Jonson
from those of Hughes; the difference will tell us much of the evolution of style between Jonson and Hughes. Of course an emphasis upon brevity endangers perspicuity, and obscurity flies
in the face of this constant of language; otherwise, the presence
or absence of that constant is not in itself very significant. With
this reminder, we may return to the seventeenth-century awareness of Senecan style in secular prose.

IV

Both Seneca and Tacitus were great favorites of the first half
of the seventeenth century. Seneca appealed as a moralist who

153

could put even the Christian to shame, and Tacitus rivaled Machiavelli for shrewd political wisdom. As Jonson's "New Cry" puts it, Tacitus appealed to "ripe statesmen, ripe!":

> They carry in their pockets Tacitus,
> And the Gazetti, or Gallo-Belgicus.

One of the first essayists, Robert Johnson, finds Tacitus the perfect historian and remarks his "iudiciall, but strangelie briefe sentences."[42] Seneca and Tacitus, as we have already observed, were the Jacobean models for such sentences.

But Seneca was also a model of another sort — the kind that Burton found in him. When Burton explains his own style in "Democritus to the Reader," he comments on the difference of tastes in style: "He respects matter, thou art wholly for words, he loves a loose and free style, thou art all for neat composition, strong lines, hyperboles, allegories ..."[43] To Burton the alternatives are the "loose" style, which respects matter, and the "neat" style, which employs strong lines; for both of which Seneca provided a model. Respecting matter rather than words, Burton calls upon Seneca to support his "extemporean style":

> Besides, it was the observation of the wise Seneca, when you see a fellow careful about his words, and neat in his speech, know this for a certainty, that man's mind is busied about toys, there's no solidity in him. Non est ornamentum virile concinnitas.[44]

The seventeenth century did not forget this other side of Seneca, but his "curt" style attracted more attention. Somewhat later a more elaborate Latin mould engaged the attention of Browne and Milton; it cannot be called loose in quite the same sense that Burton is loose, for it endeavored to suggest concinnitas.

In 1615 when Nicholas Breton, a belated Elizabethan, wrote Characters upon Essaies, he dedicated his work to Bacon, but it was a feeble imitation. Nevertheless, it received significant praise in the eulogistic verse of I. B. "In Laudem Operis":

> I herein finde few words, great worth involve:
> A Lipsian stile, terse Phrase....

But the praise was not significant enough for a modern editor,[45] who explains "Lipsian" by the note "lip salve, flattering speech."

SENECAN STYLE IN THE SEVENTEENTH CENTURY

A "Lipsian stile, terse Phrase," refers of course to the Senecan style of Justus Lipsius. Less flattering is another reference to Lipsian style which appears in John Earle's character of "A selfe-conceited Man" as set forth in 1628:

> His tenent is always singular, and aloofe from the vulgar as hee can, from which you must not hope to wrest him. He ha's an excellent humor, for an Heretique, and in these dayes made the first Arminian. He prefers Ramus before Aristotle, & Paracelsus before Galen, and whosoever with most Paradox is commended & Lipsius his hopping stile, before either Tully or Quintilian. 46

In later editions the Lipsian passage is deleted. Earle must have realized either that this style had become too common to be a paradox or that his own style made the paradox invidious. At any rate, Earle shows us that the abrupt or "hopping" style of Lipsius was the smart fashion as opposed to the correct Ciceronian. These two references to Lipsius give us the cardinal features of the Senecan style as it seemed to the seventeenth century: it was terse in phrase and abrupt in movement.

Owen Feltham, who bears the clear imprint of Baconian imitation, speaks of style in his essay "Of Preaching," which was added to his Resolves in 1628. His preferences in style are plainly Senecan:

> A man can never speak too well, where he speaks not too obscure. Long and distended clauses, are both tedious to the ear, and difficult for their retaining. A sentence well couched, takes both the sense and the understanding. I love not those cart-rope speeches, that are longer than the memory of man can fathom. . . . The weighty lines men find upon the stage, I am persuaded, have been the lures, to draw away the pulpit-followers. 47

Sententious but not obscure, such is the good style; apparently the pulpit had not been Senecan enough. Feltham feels that besides the advantage of action, the stage has the benefit of a "more compassed language: the dulcia sermonis, moulded into curious phrase." Echoing the opinion that action is "the chiefest part of an Orator," Feltham adds:

And this is Seneca's opinion: Fit words are better than

fine ones. I like not those that are injudiciously made, but
such as be expressively significant; that lead the mind to
something, besides the naked term. [48]

But judgment is necessary for depth: as "Saint Augustine says,
Tully was admired more for his tongue, than his mind." And
yet studied language is not altogether vain, for "he that reads
the Fathers, shall find them, as if written with a crisped pen."
Fit words do not preclude study, but rather enjoin it. "He pro-
digals a mine of excellency," says Feltham, "that lavishes a
terse oration to an aproned auditory"; but if the orator must
have judgment, still a terse oration was a mine of excellency
to Feltham.

If we have any doubt of Feltham's Senecanism, Thomas Randolph sets it at rest. His Conceited Peddler (1630), which W. C.
Hazlitt calls "a shrewd satire on the follies and vices of the
age," makes much of "points" and of "a sovereign box of cere-
brum" produced by alchemy, "the fire being blown with the long-
winded blast of a Ciceronian sentence, and the whole confection
boiled from a pottle to a pint in the pipkin of Seneca."[49] Of
course "points" were the favorite form of Senecan wit, and the
brevity of Seneca appeared by contrast with Ciceronian length.
Randolph shows that for his age the Senecan and the Ciceronian
were the two poles between which style turned. His verses "To
Master Feltham on his book of Resolves" place Feltham accordingly: "Nor doth the cinnamon-bark deserve less praise":

> I mean, the style being pure, and strong and round;
> Not long, but pithy; being short-breath'd, but sound,
> Such as the grave, acute, wise Seneca sings —
> That best of tutors to the worst of kings.
> Not long and empty; lofty, but not proud;
> Subtle, but sweet; high, but without a cloud.
> Well-settled, full of nerves — in brief 'tis such,
> That in a little hath comprised much. [50]

Little could be added to this character of Senecan style, for such
it appeared to that age; pithy, short-breathed, grave, acute, and
nervous — such was Seneca and such Feltham. "Round," here
and elsewhere, seems to acquire an Anti-Ciceronian significance
if we recall Wats's translation of Bacon on Senecan style: "The
labour here is altogether, That words may be aculeate, sentences concise, and the whole contexture of the speech and discourse,

rather rounding into it selfe, than spread and dilated." The Senecan style was concise and "round" rather than "spread and dilated" like the Ciceronian; in Bacon's Latin, "oratio denique
potius versa quam fusa." Jonson, following Vives, gives a similar significance to "round":

> The next thing to the stature, is the figure and feature
> in Language: that is, whether it be round, and streight,
> which consists of short and succinct Periods, numerous,
> and polished, or square and firme, which is to have equall
> and strong parts, everywhere answerable, and weighed.[51]

Here "round" goes with short and succinct periods, while
"square" goes with concinnitas or symmetry of structure.

Jonson pauses in his Discoveries (1641) to condemn all the
essayists,[52] but a few pages later he eulogizes Bacon:

> Yet there hapn'd, in my time, one noble Speaker, who
> was full of gravity in his speaking. His language (where
> hee could spare, or pass by a jest) was nobly censorious.
> No man ever spake more neatly, more pressly, more
> weightily, or suffer'd lesse emptinesse, lesse idlenesse,
> in what hee utter'd. No member of his speech, but con-
> sisted of his owne graces. His hearers could not cough,
> or looke aside from him, without losse.[53]

Of course, Jonson is speaking of Bacon as an orator, but it was
for speaking thus "prestly" that Cicero condemned the Stoics.[54]
For Jonson, however, Bacon may "stand as the mark and acme
of our language," and of the style which Jonson favored.

Much of his most personal stylistic doctrine Jonson draws
from Seneca's famous Epistles (114, 115) and from similar matter in Vives's De Ratione Dicendi. Out of Vives comes his summary of the varieties of succinct style:

> A strict and succinct style is that, where you can take
> away nothing without losse, and that losse to be manifest.
> The briefe style is that which expresseth much in little.
> The concise style, which expresseth not enough, but leaves
> somewhat to bee understood. The abrupt style, which hath
> many breaches, and doth not seeme to end, but fall.[55]

Against this passage Jonson sets the names Tacitus, The Laconic,

Suetonius, Seneca and Fabianus; Vives refers to Seneca for the
remark that Fabianus inclines to the abrupt style but Cicero
ends everything. Jonson does not borrow intact one of Vives's
most Senecan comments: "Venustissimae sunt periodi, quae
fiunt vel ex antithetis, vel acutè concluso argumento." While
Jonson echoes Bacon's words on Ciceronian style, he removes
their sting. [56] However, when Jonson writes on epistolary style,
his remarks are thoroughly Senecan. These remarks present
his most complete statement on style, and although apparently
drawn from John Hoskins's Directions for Speech and Style, [57]
are parallel to the requirements laid down in the Epistolica
Institutio of Justus Lipsius.

In the Lipsian scheme five qualities were necessary: brevitas, perspicuitas, simplicitas, venustas, and decentia. These
are subsumed under four heads by Hoskins, whose statement
of the Lipsian doctrine is retailed by Jonson. [58] "The first is
brevity":

> Brevity is attained in matter, by avoiding idle Comple-
> ments, Prefaces, Protestations, Parentheses, superflu-
> ous circuit of figures, and digressions: In the composi-
> tion, by omitting Conjunctions (Not onely; But also; Both
> the one, and the other, whereby it commeth to passe) and
> such like idle Particles, that have no great business in a
> serious Letter, but breaking of sentences; as often times
> a short journey is made long, by unnecessary baits. [59]

Remembering that Jonson on epistolary style was merely the
public voice of Hoskins, we may say that Jonson particularizes
the means by which the disjunctive or disconnected Senecan
style was achieved. [60] But he remembers that Quintilian says
"there is a briefnesse of the parts sometimes, that makes the
whole long"; and comments thus: "This is the fault of some
Latine Writers, within these last hundred years, of my reading,
and perhaps Seneca may be appeacht of it; I accuse him not."
"The next property of Epistolarie style is Perspicuity," and
with this Jonson combines "Plainenesse," which is simplicitas
in Lipsius. Following Lipsius, who quotes Seneca's wish that
his epistles might be "illaboratus et facilis," Jonson counsels
informality or "a diligent kind of negligence." The third quality
is vigor or "Life and Quickness"; Lipsius says, "Venustatem
appello; cum sermo totus alacer, vivus, erectus est." Here
Lipsius names and Jonson suggests the "argutae sententiae" of

Senecan style. The last quality, the decentia of Lipsius, becomes discretio, "respect to discerne," or propriety in Jonson.
In all these matters, however, Jonson was merely repeating
Hoskins, who noted with some disapproval the new tendency
toward a "sententious" or Senecan style.

But his hierarchy of stylistic qualities, with brevity heading
the list, is Senecan; and perspicuity, being a constant in communication, is less significant than vigor, which receives a
Senecan definition. Although Jonson is given to quoting Quintilian, his own practice shows that Senecan doctrine was more persuasive in moulding his style. [61]

The "English Seneca," Bishop Hall, was criticized by the
eighteenth century because "he abounds rather too much with
antitheses and witty turns";[62] but his Senecanism had already
been criticized by Milton. In the Smectymnuan controversy Hall
referred to his own style in his Answer to Smectymnuus's Vindication: "In the sequel, my words, which were never yet taxed
for an offensive superfluity, shall be very few; and such as, to
your greater wonder, I shall be beholden for, to my kind adversaries." While defending the authors of Smectymnuus in his
Apology, Milton declares that Hall's design was "with quips and
snapping adages to vapour them out," and that he could not endure that they "should thus lie at the mercy of a coy flirting
style; to be girded with frumps and curtal gibes, by one who
makes sentences by the statute, as if all above three inches
long were confiscate."[63] Although his opponent was anonymous
(Hall's son?), Milton was here answering Bishop Hall directly,
and criticizing his style for its Senecan traits. Milton returns
to the attack in a stronger vein when he declares that the Re-
monstrant

> sobs me out half-a-dozen phthisical mottoes, wherever
> he had them, hopping short in the measure of convulsion-
> fits; in which labour the agony of his wit having escaped
> narrowly, instead of well-sized periods, he greets us
> with a quantity of thumb-ring posies.[64]

Milton, who believed in well-sized periods, thus condemns
"Lipsius his hopping style" and "this tormentor of semicolons."

Milton's own taste comes out more clearly in a later statement about the clerks of the university who are to be ministers:

> How few among them that know to write or speak in a
> pure style; much less to distinguish the ideas and various

159

> kinds of style in Latin barbarous, and oft not without sol-
> ecisms, declaiming in rugged and miscellaneous gear
> blown together by the four winds, and in their choice pre-
> ferring the gay rankness of Apuleius, Arnobius, or any
> modern fustianist, before the native Latinisms of Cicero.[65]

Here is clear disapproval of the "modern fustianist," who was
commonly an Anti-Ciceronian. In 1622 Archbishop Abbot, in a
letter to All Souls College, had found fault with the general deterioration of Latin style at Oxford: "The style of your letter
is somewhat abrupt and harsh, and doth rather express an affected brevity than the old Ciceronian oratory. And I am sorry
to hear that this new way of writing is not only become the fault
of the College, but of the University itself."[66] Likewise, to Milton the humanist a pure style meant Cicero, and neither "the
knotty Africanisms, the pampered metaphors, the intricate and
involved sentences of the fathers,"[67] nor the Senecan style condemned by Abbot. As a humanist Milton scorned not only those
who confused "the ideas and various kinds of style in Latin barbarous," but also those who introduced Senecan style into English prose.

The Latin mould of Milton's style is so obvious that we may
pause to consider the contemporary awareness of such a mould
in English. In "A Discourse of Languages" Richard Flecknoe
attributes the variations of English style "to the severall Inclinations and Dispositions of Princes and of Times":

> That of our Ancestors having been plain and simple:
> That of Queen Elizabeths dayes, flaunting and pufted like
> her Apparell: That of King Jame's, Regis ad exemplum,
> inclining much to the Learned and Erudite, as (if you ob-
> serve it) in the late Kings dayes, the Queen having a mayne
> ascendancy and predominance in the Court, the French
> style with the Courtyers was chiefly in vogue and Fashion.[68]

Flecknoe goes on to say that the inclination of the times has cor-
rupted their metaphors with military terms; "much of the Chican
having likewise entred for its part, even to the Scripture style
amongst the common Rabble, who are our Rabbies now, and
Gypsies cant it in the Hebrew phrase." The consequence of all
this appears in another passage:

> For the differencing of Stiles (to go on with this matter,

160

since we have begun) wee may divide them into the Vulgar, or that of the Time, and the Learned and Erudite:
which he, who writes for Fame and lasting, should principally affect: It bearing Translation best, being cast in
the Latine mould, which never varies: whilst that of the
Time changes perpetually, according to the various hu-
mors of the Time. [69]

Those who would write for posterity must now write, not in Latin, but in the learned and erudite style which is cast in the Latin mould. Since the Jacobean style was of this persuasion, we
might expect that a Jacobean writer would offer a suitable model; and in the refinement of English no name stood higher than
that of Bacon at this time. In 1644 the writer of Vindex Angli-
cus tells us that "the renowned Lord Bacon taught us to speak
the terms of art in our own language";[70] in 1650 Dr. Walter
Charleton links Browne with Bacon in the "Carmination or refinement of English";[71] and in 1653 S.S. (probably Samuel Sheppard) praises Bacon for being "so succinct, elaborate, and sententious" that the best foreign wits think it the highest honor to
translate him into their native languages. [72] If Bacon set a popular example in his Essays, he set a more learned example in
his Advancement of Learning; for his terms of art carried from
Jonson to Browne, and his period supplied an Anti-Ciceronian
but Latin mould for more elaborate writing.
    Sir Thomas Browne seems to have been of Flecknoe's mind
when he explained why he wrote the Pseudodoxia Epidemica in
English rather than Latin, and how the "paradoxology" of his
subject sometimes carried him into "expressions beyond mere
English apprehensions":

    And, indeed, if elegancy still proceedeth, and English
    pens maintain that stream we have of late observed to flow
    from many, we shall, within few years, be fain to learn
    Latin to understand English, and a work will prove of equal
    facility in either. Nor have we addressed our pen or style
    unto the people, (whom books do not redress, and [who]
    are this way incapable of reduction,) but unto the knowing
    and leading part of learning. [73]

Thus, in Milton's time, Browne suggests that there was an unusual effort to cast English into a Latin mould, or to bring Latin terms into English, at least when a writer was not addressing

the vulgar. But where Browne went to extremes in the terms of art, Milton went to extremes in the Latin mould, setting his Latin constructions against the idiom of the "loose" period in English. This more elaborate Latin mould, which suggested concinnitas, was the result of an effort to stem the idiomatic current of the time.

In 1654 Richard Whitlock, in his preface to Zootomia, declared that Plutarch's discourses most invite imitation for the form, and are not behind any for matter, "if mixt sometimes with those Mucrones Sermonum, Enlivening Touches of Seneca full of smart Fancy, solid sense and accurate reason." The wit of Seneca was for Whitlock still a desirable addition to the essay; but "Exactness of writing on any Subject in Poetick heights of Fancy, or Rhetoricall Descants of Application," he left to others:

> For my own part I may say, as Lipsius in his Epistle; Rationem meam scribendi scire vis ? fundo, non scribo, nec id nisi in Calore & interno quodam Impetu, haud aliter quam Poetae. Would you know (saith he) my manner of writing ? it is a kind of voluntary Tiding of, not Pumping for; Notions flowing, not forced; like Poets unconstrained Heats and Raptures: such is mine, rather a running Discourse than a Grave-paced Exactnes.... 74

Fundere, if we remember, was the aim of Seneca's "loose" style; and Lipsius here echoes Seneca no less than when he subscribed to the curt style in his Quaestiones. But Whitlock's subscription to this aim suggests that the loose rather than the curt style was proving congenial to the essay as the product of "a mind thinking." Informality is the effect of this style and the aim of the personal essay.

If Whitlock suggests that the loose style is to triumph in the Restoration, Thomas Blount's Academie of Eloquence shows that the curt style still has some life before it. This rhetoric, which adopts almost in full the Directions of Hoskins and borrows considerably from Bacon, ran through five editions between 1654 and 1684; in fact, no other rhetoric of that time seems to have been quite so popular. If we examine a passage in the Academie on sententiae (borrowed with some modernization from Hoskins), we shall discover notwithstanding that the ideal form of the curt style is seriously threatened:

Sententia, if it be well used, is a Figure; if ill and too
much, a Style, of which none that write humorously and
factiously, can be clear in these days, when there are so
many Schismes of Eloquence. We study now-a-days according to the predominancy of Criticall fancies. Whilst Moral
Philosophy was in request, it was rudeness, not to be sententious; whilst Mathematics were of late in vogue, all
similitudes came from Lines, Circles and Angles; But
now that Mars is predominant, we must recruit our wits,
and give our words a new Quarter. [75]

The sententia, which is still acceptable as a figure, is no longer quite approved when used so much as to make a style, although it is still popular in certain kinds of writing. Its association with moral philosophy, and so with the moral essay, is
specified. But this wariness toward the pure form of the curt
style does not prevent Blount, any more than it prevented Hoskins, from retailing Senecan instructions for an epistolary style.
Blount, who repeats the instructions of Hoskins and Jonson,
begins with their opening remark on the fashion of this style:
"Now for Fashion, it consists in four qualities of your Style.
The first is Brevity."[76] As a sample of Blount's borrowing, let
me quote the passage which I have already cited from Jonson:

Brevity is attain'd upon the matter, by avoiding idle
complements, prefaces, protestations, long Parentheses,
supplications, wanton circuits of Figures, and digressions,
by composition, omitting conjunctions, Not onely but also,
the one and the other, whereby it comes to passe, etc. and
such like particles, that have no great business in a serious Letter; By breaking off sentences; as oftentimes a
short journey is made long by many baits. [77]

"Omitting conjunctions" and "breaking off sentences" are precise phrases with which to describe the disconnected "curt period" that Professor Croll has analyzed. Blount, however, looks
ahead when he adds a remark that is much more explicit than
any similar idea in Jonson, not to mention Hoskins:

Under this Notion somewhat may be said of Periods,
which ought not to bee too long, nor yet too short, QUO
MAGIS VIRTUS, EO MAGIS MEDIETAS. All virtue consists

163

in a certain Geometrical mediocrity, equally distant from excess and default.

Again reflecting his time, Blount quotes Longinus in support of another requirement which suggests that the reign of abruptness is over: "There ought likewise to be a speciall regard had to the cadence of the words, that the whole contexture of the Period may yeeld a certain kind of harmony to the ear."[78]
But the next requirement carries Blount back to the text of Hoskins and Jonson: "The next property of Epistolary Style, is, Perspicuity, which is not seldom endangered by the former quality."[79] "Under this vertue," echoes Blount, "may come Plainness, which is, not to be too curious in the order," but to use "a diligent kind of negligence."[80] Blount likewise frowns upon "perfumed moding terms," but goes beyond Hoskins and Jonson by referring explicitly to Seneca:

> Besides, a vain curiosity of words hath so scandalized some Philosophers, that Seneca (in one of his epistles) says, Had it been possible to make himself understood by signes, he would rather serve himself of them, then of discourse, to the end he might the better avoid all manner of affectation.[81]

Blount's third and fourth qualities are identical with those of Hoskins and Jonson, the third being "Life" or "Vigor," and the fourth "Respect" or Propriety.[82] Thus Blount fulfills the promise of his Epistle Dedicatory "with some particular Instructions and Rules premised, for the better attaining to a Pen-perfection." As this Senecan scheme of style passed from Hoskins and Jonson to Blount it received important though slight alterations; and the Academie of Eloquence, perhaps because of this modification, renewed the life of Senecan ideals in the early days of the Royal Society — a fact which cannot be without significance.

V

In conclusion, we may attempt to place the curt Senecan style by comparing the stylistic aims expressed by Jonson, Blount, Glanvill, and Hughes. In these aims we shall find a simple graph or outline of the evolution of prose style during the century.
Jonson and Blount both advocate brevity, perspicuity (and

plainness), vigor, and propriety; but Blount adds the requirements of cadence and medium length in the period. By placing
brevity first, both testify to the reign of the terse Senecan style;
but by advancing cadence and "mediocrity" in the period, Blount
looks beyond that style. In the quality of plainness, which Jonson and Blount place under the head of perspicuity, we find the
aim of style which becomes dominant after the reign of brevity.

Joseph Glanvill has as good a right as any to speak for the
plain style, and his general theme is that "plainness is for ever
the best eloquence." After such works as Sprat's History of the
Royal Society (1667), Eachard's Grounds and Occasions of the
Contempt of the Clergy (1670), and Arderne's Directions concerning the Matter and Stile of Sermons (1671), Glanvill gave
vigorous expression to the doctrine of plainness in An Essay
concerning Preaching and A Seasonable Defence of Preaching:
And the Plain Way of it," both published in 1678. Plainness is
the watchword at this time, and Glanvill would have sermon
style plain, natural, adequate, familiar but not mean; "obvious"
rather than "Cryptick." Glanvill knew what the terse Senecan
style was, for he had practiced it; hence the significance of his
remarks on wit. While "some Sermons lose their efficacy and
force by being too full, and close," he would not go so far as
"what M. Cowley saith of Wit in Poetry,"

Rather than all be Wit, let none be there.

Associating wit with "closeness," he concludes that the right
course is to seek a mean between prolixity and brevity. [83] For
Glanvill, who would not be dull, the "proper, grave, and manly
wit" is still "sharp, and quick thoughts" set out in lively colours;[84] his wit still comes under the head of "vigor" or "life."

But Glanvill emphasizes Blount's new requirement of a mean
between prolixity and brevity, and he elevates the rather subordinate plainness of Jonson and Blount to first place in the
hierarchy of style. With Glanvill the reign of brevity has definitely given way to the reign of plainness; and plainness, "the
best Character of Speech," is not "Bluntness," but rather a
simplicity in which there are no "words without sense." Of the
other qualities specified by Jonson and Blount, vigor outweighs propriety with Glanvill. If he believes that the wit
which consists in "playing with words" is "vile and contemptible fooling," he points out that "there is a vice in Preaching quite opposite to this, and that is a certain road-dulness,

and want of wit," which only philosophy will cure.[85]

In 1698 John Hughes is much more concerned that a man's learning be "polite"; the philosopher is now to be saved from the "Rust of the Academy" by "Polite Learning," which gives the mind a "free Air and genteel Motion." "In a Word," says Hughes, "it adds the Gentleman to the Scholar";[86] and Henry Felton soon found Dryden too much the scholar.[87] The qualifications of a good style are now these four: propriety, perspicuity, elegance, and cadence. "Propriety of Words, the first Qualification of a good Style," is to be learned from the "most correct Writers" and "People of Fashion."[88] As usual, perspicuity is necessary rather than significant: "Little need be said of the second Qualification, viz. Perspicuity. If your Thoughts be not clear, 'tis impossible your Words shou'd, and consequently you can't be understood."[89] For Hughes "Elegance of Thought is what we commonly call Wit," or "Curiosa Felicitas";[90] for Jonson it came under the head of "Life" or "Vigor." Cadence is "a sort of musical Delight" in the periods, but this had been anticipated by Blount. In Hughes the plainness of Glanvill gives way to propriety as the quality of prime importance. Elegance comes from the gentleman and may be called "ease"; it is the genteel and proper "Motion" of a polite mind.

The style which discovers a mean between brevity and prolixity was suggested in Blount, established in Glanvill, and maintained in Hughes; it developed out of the loose "unexpected" period of Seneca rather than out of the formal "expected" period of Cicero. To Henry Felton at the beginning of the eighteenth century a just style was threatened by obscurity from two directions: either by laboring to be concise, or by running into a "Prodigality of Words." Of course, Jonson had been aware of this, but he had, nevertheless, emphasized brevity. Studying to be concise produced "close contracted Periods," which were now outlawed; on the other hand, there could be no return to the copiousness that Bacon had condemned in the Ciceronians. Moreover, since the terse Senecan style often produced a tissue of epigrams, Shaftesbury could object that "every period, every sentence almost, is independent, and may be taken asunder, transposed, postponed, anticipated, or set in any new order, as you fancy." But the neo-classical impulse to order modified this "random way of miscellaneous writing" just as the neo-classical regard for "ease" rebuked what Hobbes had called "the ambitious obscurity of expressing more then is perfectly conceived, or perfect conception in fewer words then it requires."

NOTES

1   M. W. Croll's excellent studies of "Attic" or Senecan prose afford but a partial answer to this question; see Studies in Philology, vol. XVIII; Schelling Anniversary Papers, 1923; P M L A,
vol. XXXIX; and Studies in English Philology, 1929. For the
claim of science in the formation of seventeenth-century prose
see the articles by R. F. Jones, P M L A, vol. XLV; Journal
of English and Germanic Philology, vols. XXX and XXXI.

2   Works (London, 1913), III, 166-67. On the significance of Jacobean translation from Silver Latin see H. B. Lathrop, Translations from the Classics into English from Caxton to Chapman,
1477-1620 (Madison, 1933), chap. IV, especially pp. 235, 244,
252, 304.

3   See "The Rhetorical Pattern of Neo-Classical Wit," Modern
Philology, XXXIII (1935), 60-67.

4   See "Strong Lines," English Studies, XVIII (1936), 152-59.
Two versions of the same Horatian warning describe the nature
and the name of these lines. First in Jonson's translation of
Horace's Art of Poetry:

>   Myself for shortness labour, and I grow
>   Obscure. This, striving to run smooth, and flow,
>   Hath neither soul nor sinews.

Second in Soame's translation of Boileau's Art of Poetry:

>   A verse was weak, you turn it much too strong,
>   And grow obscure for fear you should be long.

5   Characteristics, ed. J. M. Robertson (London, 1900), II, 170.

6   Ibid., p. 171. This "see-saw" suggests the antithetic wit of the
Senecan essayists.

7   "Attic Prose: Lipsius, Montaigne, Bacon," Schelling Anniversary Papers (New York, 1923), p. 142.

8   J. W. Duff, A Literary History of Rome in the Silver Age (London, 1927), p. 198; cf. pp. 228-29 and 593 ff. See Montaigne's
account of the "sharpe and witty fashion [d'une façon poinctue et
subtile]" of Tacitus: "He draweth somewhat neare to Senecas
writing. I deeme Tacitus, more sinnowy, Seneca more sharpe"
(Essayes [Everyman ed.], III, 180). "Il ne retire pas mal à

l'escrire de Seneque: il me semble plus charnu; Seneque plus aigu."

9   Studies in English Philology, ed. Malone and Ruud (Minneapolis, 1929), pp. 452-53. Croll describes four marks of the curt style: "first, studied brevity of members; second, the hovering, imaginative order; third, asymmetry; and fourth, the omission of the ordinary syntactic ligatures" (ibid., p. 435); the loose style is differentiated by its relaxed syntactic ligatures, its "linked" or "trailing" period, and its "natural" order (ibid., pp. 440-53).

10   "Muret and the History of 'Attic' Prose," P M L A, XXXIX (1924), 254-309.

11· Notitia Historicorum Selectorum, translated by W. D. (William Davenant), Oxford, 1678, pp. 217-18. Cf. Croll, P M L A, XXXIX, 300.

12   Quoted by Croll, Schelling Anniversary Papers, p. 122.

13   See Epistles 114, 59, 100. Cf. F. I. Merchant, "Seneca the Philosopher and his Theory of Style," American Journal of Philology, XXVI (1905), 57 ff.

14   See Epistles 75 and 115.

15   The New-found Politicke, translated by Florio, W. Vaughan, and Another (London, 1626), p. 15 (Part I, Rag. 86). J. G. Robertson (The Genesis of Romantic Theory, p. 246) seems to think the 1656 translation by Henry, Earl of Monmouth, the first in English; but Monmouth claims only to have made the first complete English version.

16   Workes of Seneca (London, 1620), sig. b1r.

17   Ibid., sigs. b2r- b2v.

18   London, 1635, p. 285.

19   Philosophical Works, ed. J. M. Robertson (London, 1905), p. 54.

20   Ibid., p. 55.

21   Ibid., pp. 55-56. In the essay "Of Seeming Wise" Bacon attributes this quotation to A. Gellius and applies it to those who "are never without a difference, and commonly by amusing men with a subtilty blanch the matter."

22   Ibid., p. 124.

23   Ibid., p. 124.

24   Ibid., p. 125.

25   Ibid., p. 128.

26   Ibid., p. 536.

27   See E. Arber's Harmony of the Essays (London, 1871) for par-
     allel versions. Bacon's attitude toward rhetoric and Stoic meth-
     od should be added to the explanation of his change of style in
     R. S. Crane's article on the Essays, Schelling Anniversary
     Papers (New York, 1923), pp. 98 ff.

28   Advancement and Proficience of Learning, translated by Gilbert
     Wats (Oxford, 1640), p. 29; cf. Works, ed. cit., p. 55 n.

29   Works, ed. cit., p. 56.

30   Ibid., p. 54.

31   See W. F. Mitchell, English Pulpit Oratory (London, 1932),
     pp. 351-65, "The Attack on the 'Metaphysicals'."

32   Quintilian, Institutiones Oratoriae, X. 1.

33   On the Senecan cult in sermon style see W. F. Mitchell, op. cit.,
     items indexed under "Senecan" and "Tertullian."

34   Works, ed. Alford (1839), VI, 146; quoted by Mitchell, op.cit.,
     p. 191.

35   Tatler, No. 264, December 16, 1710. Cf. Donne, ed. Alford,
     IV, 491.

36   Works (London, 1836), I, 17-18. The Priest to the Temple was
     first printed in 1652. Herbert, it may be recalled, had acted as
     Latin scribe for Bacon.

37   Ibid., pp. 15-16. The witty preacher used his "pyrotechnics" to
     procure attention.

38   Sermons (Oxford, 1842), II, 359.

39   Ibid.

40   Ibid., I, 334-56.

41   Ibid., p. 388. South, like Donne, praises the style of Genesis for its brevity; unlike Donne, he refers to Longinus in this connection.

42   Essaies, or Rather Imperfect Offers (London, 1601), "Of Histories."

43   Anatomy of Melancholy (Bohn ed.), I, '25.

44   Ibid., pp. 30-31.

45   Ursula Kentish-Wright (ed.), A Mad World My Masters and Other Prose Works (London, 1929), I, 151.

46   Micro-cosmographie (London, 1628), "Character 12." Note that a love of paradox goes with a Senecan style.

47   Resolves (Temple Classics ed.), p. 62. "In the development of English style," says Joseph Jacobs, "the decisive and critical moment is the introduction of the easy short sentence" (Howell's Familiar Letters [London, 1892], I, lxi). But the curt style brought premeditated shortness rather than extemporary ease; cf. Howell's emphasis on brevity in his first letter.

48   Ibid., p. 63.

49   Works, ed. W. C. Hazlitt (London, 1875), I, 40 and 44.

50   Ibid., II, 575. This passage clearly suggests the pattern of Denham's apostrophe to the Thames; cf. "The Rhetorical Pattern of Neo-Classical Wit," Modern Philology, XXXIII (1935), 77.

51   Discoveries, ed. M. Castelain (Paris, 1906), pp. 105 and 106 n.

52   Ibid., p. 39.

53   Ibid., p. 47. Bacon, like Seneca, was nobly censorious "where he could spare, or pass by a jest."

54   Cf. Brutus, XXXI.

55   Ibid., pp. 100-01. Quintilian (X. i. 106) says that "from Demosthenes nothing can be taken away, to Cicero nothing can be added."

56   Ibid., pp. 108-109.

57   Edited from manuscript by Hoyt H. Hudson (Princeton, 1935). Although the Directions (1599 ?) was not printed under Hoskins's

name, it was given to the public partially by Jonson and almost completely by Blount. The section "For Penning of Letters," which Hoskins adapted from Lipsius, is found almost verbatim in Jonson, and with some modification in Blount, whose version will be discussed later.

58   Op. cit., pp. 112-16.

59   Ibid., p. 113.

60   Suetonius records Caligula's contempt for Seneca's style as "sand minus mortar" (Cal., LIII).

61   See Dryden's character of Jonson in the Essay of Dramatic Poesy: "If there was any fault in his language, 'twas that he weaved it too closely and laboriously, in his serious plays: perhaps too, he did a little too much Romanize our tongue, leaving the words which he translated almost as much Latin as he found them: wherein, though he learnedly followed the idiom of their language, he did not enough comply with the idiom of ours.

62   Cf. W. F. Mitchell, op. cit., p. 367.

63   Prose Works (Bohn ed.), III, 99.

64   Ibid., p. 135. This passage does not refer directly to Hall, but it repeats the charges already made against his style.

65   Ibid., p. 155.

66   Quoted from the Archives of All Souls by Montagu Burrows in his edition of The Register of the Visitors of the University of Oxford, 1647 to 1658 (Camden Society, 1881), p. xcvii.

67   Prose Works, II, 388. The effect of academic Latin composition upon English prose is often neglected in modern accounts of 17th century style. Both Lipsius and Muretus were read in the schools.

68   Miscellania (London, 1653), p. 77.

69   Ibid., p. 78.

70   Harleian Miscellany (London, 1810), V, 431.

71   Epistle Dedicatory to Helmont's Ternary of Paradoxes (London, 1650), sig. clr.

72   Paradoxes or Encomions (London, 1653), p. 10.

73   Works, ed. S. Wilkin (Bohn ed.), I, 3.

74   Zootomia (London, 1654), sig. a5r.

75   Academie of Eloquence (London, 1654), p. 34. Cf. Hoskins, op. cit., pp. 38-40. Although Hoskins retailed Senecan doctrine, he was critical of it; and Blount adapted this criticism to his own time. Jonson borrowed some of this dispraise, which is more discordant in him.

76   Ibid., p. 142; cf. Discoveries, ed. cit., p. 112.

77   Ibid., p. 143; cf. Discoveries, p. 113.

78   Ibid., pp. 143-44.

79   Ibid., p. 144; cf. Discoveries, p. 114.

80   Ibid., p. 145; cf. Discoveries, p. 115.

81   Ibid., pp. 145-46; cf. Discoveries, p. 116. John Wilkins's Essay towards a Real Character and a Philosophical Language (1668) was an effort in this direction.

82   Ibid., p. 146; cf. Discoveries, p. 116.

83   An Essay concerning Preaching (London, 1678), p. 63. This is not, to be sure, his first word on the plain style, but it is one of the best statements of that style.

84   Ibid., p. 72. Cowley had also said that wit is not "the dry chips of short lung'd Seneca."

85   Ibid., pp. 72-73.

86   "Of Style," Critical Essays of the Eighteenth Century, ed. W. H. Durham (New Haven, 1915), p. 79.

87   A Dissertation on Reading the Classics and Forming a Just Style (London, 1715), pp. 64-65. See pp. 92-93 for a condemnation of the close, contracted style of sententious writers.

88   Hughes, op. cit., p. 80.

89   Ibid., p. 81.

90   Ibid., p. 82.

COUPLET VERSE

BEN JONSON AND THE CLASSICAL SCHOOL

Felix E. Schelling

"The words, classical and romantic, although, like
many other critical expressions, sometimes abused by
those who have understood them vaguely or too absolutely, yet define two real tendencies in the history of art and
literature. *** The 'classic' comes to us out of the cool
and quiet of other times, as the measure of what a long experience has shown will at least never displease us. And
in the classical literature of Greece and Rome, as in the
classics of the last century, the essentially classical element is that quality of order in beauty, which they possess,
indeed, to a pre-eminent degree. *** It is the addition of
strangeness to beauty, that constitutes the romantic character in art; and the desire of beauty being a fixed element
in every artistic organisation, it is the addition of curiosity to this desire of beauty that constitutes the romantic
temper."[1]

These are the words of that rare interpreter of the "House
Beautiful," the late Mr. Walter Pater, and may serve us as a
fitting position whence to depart in a search for the origin of
some of those elements which combined to produce the many and
noteworthy changes that came over English literature during the
seventeenth century.

Without entering here into definitions and distinctions which
have been much aired and not a little abused, it is well to notice
that these terms are not necessarily hostile to each other or
even mutually exclusive. Classicism and Romanticism are tendencies rather than opposed methods in art. Literature has always partaken of both, although one may dominate in one age,
the other in another. It may be surmised that in the ebb and flow
of these elements consists the life of literature, and that in the
absolute triumph of either lies its destruction: for death may
come to art no less from freedom run to licence than from the
riveted fetters of absolute convention. In a sense every 'classic'

Reprinted by permission from Publications of the Modern Language
Association, Vol. 13 (1898), pp. 221-249.

has once contained within it the 'romantic,' has once moved by its novelty and appealed to curiosity. If the romantic temper is more concerned with the choice of subject, as has sometimes been affirmed, there may be even a finer art in novelty of treatment; nor may novelty be denied although it consist but in the change from romantic excesses grown common and hence distasteful. Be this as it may, the classic temper studies the past, the romantic temper neglects it. The romantic temper is empirical; in its successful experiments it leads us forward, as did Wordsworth, Shelley and Browning, and creates new precedents on which to found the classics of the future. It is revulsion from the failures of romantic art that brings us trooping back to the classics with Matthew Arnold who felt that he could "find the only sure guidance, the only solid footing among the ancients."[2]

The history of English literature since the Renaissance exhibits three periods of unusual interest in the models of the past, three notable returns to the classics as they were understood in each age, with a possible fourth period of interest yet to come and widely presaged in our many retranslations of Greek and Roman authors and in the poetry of Matthew Arnold and the late Mr. William Morris. With this last we have nothing to do; an important name is identified with each of the other three: Sir Philip Sidney, whose classicism was concerned with externals, and soon overwhelmed with the flood of romanticism on which he was himself "the first fair freight;" Ben Jonson, whose classicism came alike by nature and by study; Pope, who long after stands for the culmination of a movement which, losing its aims and substituting too often mere form for living principle, is none the less worthy of a greater respect and consideration than has been usually accorded it at the hands of the critics of our century.

That minor contemporaries of Sidney like Ascham, Webbe, and Gabriel Harvey should look to classic example for the salvation of English letters is little to be wondered. Their education demanded it, and contemporary literature offered nothing. Save Chaucer, there was not an English poet that a scholar dared to name with the mighty dead of "insolent Greece or haughty Rome;" and Chaucer was antiquated to the Elizabethan, who might love to archaize in the pastoral lingo of Hobbinol and Cuddy, but who was likely to leave unread what he could not readily conform to his own time and place. The classicism of Sidney is that of his age, and shows itself mainly in two characteristics: the reaffirmation of ancient aesthetic theory, in which the Defense of Poesy far outweighs all similar contemporary work, and

in metrical experiments in English verse modelled on classical
prosody. In the former Sidney was the companion of Gascoigne,
James VI, William Webbe, and George Puttenham; in the latter,
of Harvey, Stanihurst, Abraham Fraunce, and Spenser himself.
If Sidney's sapphics and asclepiads stand as a warning to the
temerity of venturesome youth, it must be remembered that our
own contemporaries have not ceased from theorizing upon such
metres nor indeed from imitating them. Such turning to the classics as Sidney's and Spenser's is purely empirical and due less
to any deep seated conviction on the subject than to a contemplation of the dead level of contemporary literary achievement.
Sidney's Defense was directly called forth by Gosson's attack
upon poetry in his School of Abuse, and Sidney's own practice of
classical metres went hand in hand with experiments in the Italian sonnet, the canzone and the sestine, many specimens of
which are to be found in Astrophel and Stella, and the Arcadia.
Lastly, it would be difficult to find a work farther removed from
classical ideals than the famous Arcadia itself, the story of
which vies with the Faerie Queene in rambling involution and
elaborated episode, the style of which is ornate and florid, though
often very beautiful, the essence of which, in a word, is novelty,
the touchstone of romantic art.

Vastly in contrast with this superficial imitation of classical
verse is the classicism of Ben Jonson, from his character as
a man and a scholar, and in its relation to his environment. Between Sidney, dead in the year 1586, and Jonson beginning his
career but a year or two short of the next century, a great literature had sprung up, which up to the end of the reign of Elizabeth and, without the domain of the drama, was dominated by
the overwhelming influence of Spenser. It would be difficult to
find a contrast more marked than that which exists between Spenser and Jonson. As the qualities of these two poets in their contrasts are at the very root of our subject, they must be considered in some detail.

What may be called the manner of Spenser – i.e., Spenser's
way of imitating and interpreting nature artistically by means
of poetic expression – may be summarized as consisting of a sensuous love of beauty, involving a power of elaborated pictorial
representation, a use of classical imagery for decorative effect,
a fondness for melody of sound, a flowing sweetness, naturalness
and continuousness of diction, amounting to diffuseness at times,
the diffuseness of a fragrant, beautiful, flowering vine. We may
say of the poets that employ this manner that they are worshipers

of beauty rather than students of beauty's laws; ornate in their expression of the type, dwelling on detail in thought and image lovingly elaborated and sweetly prolonged. To such artists it is no matter if a play have five acts or twenty-five, if an epic ever come to an end, or if consistency of parts exist. Rapt in the joy of gentle onward motion, in the elevation of pure, poetic thought, even the subject seems to be of small import, if it but furnish the channel in which the bright limpid liquid continues musically to flow. Drayton, who, besides pastorals after the manner of his master, Spenserized the enormous Polyolbion; the allegorical Fletchers, Giles and Phineas; George Wither and William Browne in their beautiful later pastorals; Milton himself in his earliest poetry, though somewhat restrained by a chaster taste than was Spenser's and by a spirit in closer touch with the classics: these are some of the multitude of followers and imitators of Spenser.

If now we will turn to the poetry of Ben Jonson, more especially his lyrical verse, the first thing we note is a sense of form, not merely in detail and transition, like the "links ... bright and even" of The Faerie Queene, but a sense of the entire poem in its relation to its parts. This sense involves brevity and condensity of expression, a feeling on the part of the poet that the effect may be spoiled by a word too much – a feeling which no true Spenserian ever knew. It is thus that Jonson writes in courtly compliment to his patroness Lucy, Countess of Bedford:

> This morning timely rapt with holy fire,
> I thought to form unto my zealous Muse,
> What kind of creature I should most desire,
> To honor, serve, and love, as poets use.
> I meant to make her fair, and free, and wise,
> Of greatest blood, and yet more good than great;
> I meant the day-star should not brighter rise,
> Nor lend like influence from his lucent seat.
> I meant she should be courteous, facile, sweet,
> Hating that solemn vice of greatness, pride;
> I meant each softest virtue there should meet,
> Fit in that softer bosom to reside.
> Only a learnèd and a manly soul
> I purposed her; that should, with even powers,
> The rock, the spindle, and the shears control
> Of Destiny, and spin her own free hours.
> Such when I meant to feign and wished to see,
> My Muse bade Bedford write, and that was she. [3]

BEN JONSON AND THE CLASSICAL SCHOOL

About such poetry as this there is a sense of finish rather than of elaboration. It is less continuous than complete; more concentrated, less diffuse; chaste rather than florid; controlled, and yet not always less spontaneous; reserved, and yet not always less natural. There are other things in the Jonsonian manner. It retained classical allusion less for the sake of embellishment than as an atmosphere — to borrow a term from the nomenclature of art. Its drafts upon ancient mythology become allusive, and the effects produced by Horace, Catullus or Anacreon are essayed in reproduction under English conditions. Not less eager in the pursuit of beauty than the Spenserian, the manner of Jonson seeks to realize her perfections by means of constructive excellence, not by entranced passion. It concerns itself with choiceness of diction, selectiveness in style, with the repression of wandering ideas and loosely conceived figures, in a word the manner of Jonson involves classicality. Sidney's return to the ancients has been called empirical; the classicism of Jonson may be termed assimilative.

It is a commonplace of the history of literature that Jonson literally dominated the age in which he lived. But it is not so generally understood just why this was true in the face of the unexampled popularity of Shakespeare's plays and the frequent failure of Jonson's own, and with the existence of strong poetical counter-influences which seemed more typical of the spirit of the time than Jonson's own. It is notable that it is the egotists, like Byron and Rousseau, that often most strongly impress themselves upon their own times; they are, in Ben Jonson's well known words, "of an age;" those who have mastered themselves and risen, as did Shakespeare, above his own environment while still sharing it, move in larger circles, and influence the world "for all time." Shakespeare was not literary, Jonson was abundantly so. Despite Shakespeare's popular success, Jonson had with him the weight of the court and the learned. Thus it came about that Shakespeare enjoyed the greatest pecuniary return derived from literature, directly or indirectly, until the days of Sir Walter Scott; whilst Jonson, dependent on patronage, often almost in want, achieved a reputation and an influence in literature altogether unsurpassed up to his time. There was only one poet who shared even in part this literary supremacy of Jonson, and that poet was John Donne. To Donne, especially to the Marinist in him, must be granted the credit — if credit it be — of delaying for more than a generation the natural revulsion of English literature back to classicism and restraint. This is not the place in which to discuss the interesting relations of Jonson and Donne. Except for a certain rhetorical and dialectical address, which might be referred to a study of the ancients, the poetry of Donne is marked by its disregard of conventions, by its extraordinary originality of thought and expression, by that rare quality of poetic insight that justifies Jonson's enthusiastic claim that "John Donne [was] the first poet in the world in some things."[4] Not less significant on the other hand are Jonson's contrasted remarks to Drummond on the same topic: "That Donne's Anniversary [in which true womanhood is idealized if not deified] was profane and full of blasphemies," and "that Donne, for not keeping of accent, deserved hanging."[5] The classicist has always regarded the romanticist thus, nor have the retorts been more courteous, as witness the well known lines of Keats' Sleep and Poetry in which the age of classicism is described as "a schism nurtured by foppery and barbarism."[6]

Thus we find Spenser and Jonson standing as exponents respectively of the expansive or romantic movement and the repressive or classical spirit. In a different line of distinction Donne is equally in contrast with Spenser, as the intensive, or subjective artist. Both of these latter are romanticists in that each seeks to produce the effect demanded of art by means of an appeal to the sense of novelty; but Spenser's romanticism is that of selection, which chooses from the outer world the fitting and the pleasing, and constructs it into a permanent artistic joy. Donne's is the romanticism of insight, which, looking inward, descries the subtle relations of things and transmutes them into poetry with a sudden and unexpected flood of light. Between Jonson and Donne there is the kinship of intellectuality; between Spenser and Donne the kinship of romanticism; between Spenser and Jonson the kinship of the poet's joy in beauty. Spenser is the most objective and therefore allegorical and mystical; Donne is the most subjective and the most spiritual; Jonson, the most artistic and therefore the most logical.

But not only did Jonson dominate his age and stand for the classical ideal in the midst of current Spenserianism, Marinism, and other popular modes, it was this position of Jonson, defended as it was in theory as well as exemplified in his work, that directed the course which English literature was to take for a century and a half after his death. There are few subjects in the history of English literature attended with greater difficulty than the attempt to explain how the lapse of a century in time should have transformed the literature of England from the traits which

178

characterized it in the reign of Queen Elizabeth to those which
came to prevail under the rule of Queen Anne. The salient characteristics of the two ages are much too well known to call for
a word here. Few readers, moreover, are unfamiliar with the
more usual theories on this subject: how one critic believes
that Edmund Waller invented the new poetry by a spontaneous
exercise of his own cleverness;[7] how another demands that this
responsibility be fixed upon George Sandys. [8] How some think
that "classicism" was an importation from France, which came
into England in the luggage of the fascinating Frenchwoman, who
afterwards became the Duchess of Portsmouth; and how still
others suppose that the whole thing was really in the air, to be
caught by infection by anyone who did not draw apart and live
out of the literary miasma as did Milton. [9] It may not be unnecessary to add that some of these theorists place the beginning
and end of "classicism" in the definite and peculiar construction
of a certain species of English decasyllabic verse; and that even
when they escape this, the "heroic" or "Popean couplet" has
always usurped an undue share of consideration.

The conservative reaction which triumphed with the Restoration has been so "hardly entreated" and so bitterly scorned that
there is much temptation to attempt a justification. Imaginative
literature did lose in the change, and enormously; but if the imagination, and with it the power that produces poetry, became
for a time all but extinct, the understanding, or power which
arranges, correlates, expounds and explains, went through a
course of development which has brought with it in the end nothing but gain to the literature considered as a whole.

If the reader will consider the three great names, Ben Jonson, finishing his work about 1635, John Dryden, at the height
of his fame fifty years later, and Alexander Pope, with nearly
ten years of literary activity before him a century after Jonson's
death, he will notice certain marked differences in a general
resemblance in the range, subject-matter and diction of the
works of these three. The plays of Jonson, despite the restrictive character of his genius, exemplify nearly the whole spacious
field of Elizabethan drama, with an added success in the development of the masque, which is Jonson's own. Jonson is the first
poet that gave to occasional verse that variety of subject, that
power and finish, which made it, for nearly two centuries, the
most important form of poetical expression. The works of Jonson are pervaded with satire, criticism and translation, though
all appear less in set form than as applied to original work.

Finally Jonson's lyrics maintain the diversity, beauty and orig-inality which distinguishes this species of poetry in his favored age.

If we will turn now to Dryden, we still find a wide range in subject, although limitations are discoverable in the character of his dramas and of his lyrics. If we except his operas and those pseudo-dramatic aberrations in which he adapted the work of Shakespeare and Milton, Dryden writes only two kinds of plays, the Heroic Drama and the Comedy of Manners; whilst his lyrics, excepting the two odes for Saint Cecilia's Day and some perfunc-tory religious poems, are wholly amatory in the narrow and vi-tiated sense in which that term was employed in the time of Charles II. The strongest element of Dryden's work is occasion-al verse; and he makes a new departure, showing the tendency of the time, in the development of what may be called occasional prose: the preface and dedicatory epistle. Satire takes form in the translation of Juvenal and in the author's own brilliant orig-inal satires, translation becomes Dryden's most lucrative liter-ary employment, and criticism is the very element in which he lives. Lastly, we turn to Pope. Here are no plays and very few lyrics, scarcely one which is not an applied poem. Occasional verse, satire, criticism, and translation have usurped the whole field. There was no need that Pope should write his criticism in prose, as did Dryden; for verse had become in his hands essen-tially a medium for the expression of that species of thought which we in this century associate with the prose form. The verse of Pope was a medium more happily fitted for the expres-sion of the thought of Pope, where rhetorical brilliancy and tell-ing antithesis rather than precision of thought was demanded, than any prose that could possibly have been devised.

It has often been affirmed that England has the greater poetry, whilst France possesses the superior prose; and in the confusion or distinction of the two species of literature this difference has been explained.[10] Poetry must be governed by the imagination, it must not only see and imitate nature, it must transform what it sees, converting the actual into the terms of the ideal: if it does much beside, it is less poetry. On the other hand, prose is a matter of the understanding, to call in as helps whatever other faculty you will, but to be ruled and governed by the intelligence alone, to the end that the object may be realized as it actually is. With this distinction before us, when passion, real or simu-lated, when imagination, genuine or forced, takes the reins from the understanding, the product may become poetry, or enthusiasm,

or rhapsody; it certainly ceases to be prose, good, bad or indifferent. So, likewise, when the understanding supplants imagination, we have also a product, which, whatever its form or the
wealth of rhetoric bestowed upon it, is alien to poetry. This is
to be interpreted into no criticism of the many English literary
products, which have the power to run and to fly; we could not
spare one of the great pages of Carlyle, or of Mr. Ruskin; and
yet it may well be doubted if, on the whole, the French have not
been somewhat the gainers from the care with which they have
customarily, and until lately, kept their prose and their poetry
sundered.

Up to this point it has been our endeavor to establish the si-
multaneous existence of the restrictive as well as the romantic
element in our literature as early as the reign of Elizabeth, to
show the relation of the one to the other in the stretch of years
that elapsed from her reign to that of Queen Anne, and to exemplify the relation of Jonson (who is claimed to be the exponent of the classical spirit) to his immediate contemporaries and
to his two most typical successors. Let us now examine some
of the reasons which may be urged for placing Jonson in so
prominent a position.

In Ben Jonson we have the earliest example of the interesting
series of English literary men who have had definite theories
about literature. Dryden, Pope, and Wordsworth were such,
each potent in moulding the taste of his own age, and, with it,
the course which literature was to take in times to come. It is
notorious that the attitude of Jonson towards the prevalent literary taste of his age was far from conciliatory. He despised the
popular judgment with an arrogance unparalleled in the annals
of literature, although he constantly professed himself solicitous
of the favorable opinion of the judicious. Jonson was a great
moralist in his way, and "of all styles he loved most to be named
Honest;"[11] but he was likewise an artist, and many of his current criticisms of his contemporaries: his strictures on Shakespeare for his anachronisms, on Sidney for making all the characters of the Arcadia speak like gentlemen and gentlewomen, his
objection to the obscurity and irregular versification of Donne,
are referable to an outraged aesthetic sense. [12] This position
was altogether conscious, the position of the professional man
who has a theory to oppose to the amateurishness and eclecticism abundantly exemplified in contemporary work; and Jonson
must have felt toward the glittering, multiform literature of Elizabeth much what Matthew Arnold suffered "amid the bewildering

confusion of our times" and might well have exclaimed with him,
"I seemed to myself to find the only sure guidance, the only solid footing, among the ancients. They, at any rate, knew what
they wanted in Art, and we do not. It is this uncertainty which
is disheartening."13

The theories which Ben Jonson held about literature were
from the first those of the classicist. He believed in the criticism of Horace and in the rhetoric of Quintilian;14 in the sanction
of classical usage for history, oratory, and poetry. He believed
that English Drama should follow the example of the vetus comoe-
dia,15 and that an English ode should be modelled faithfully on the
structural niceties of Pindar. Despite all this, Jonson's theories
about literature were not only, in the main, reasonable and consistent, they were often surprisingly liberal. Thus he could
laugh, as he did, in a well known passage of the prologue to
Every Man in His Humour, at the absurdities of contemporary
stage realism which,

> with three rusty swords,
> And help of some few foot-and-half-foot words,
> Fight over York and Lancaster's long jars;
> And in the tiring-house bring wounds to scars;16

and yet declare, as to that fetish of the supine classicist, the
three unities, that "we [English playwrights] should enjoy the
same licence or free power to illustrate and heighten our invention as they [the ancients] did; and not be tied to those strict and
regular forms which the niceness of a few, who are nothing but
form, would thrust upon us."17 He could affirm that "Spenser's
stanzas pleased him not, nor his matter;"18 and yet tell Drummond that "for a heroic poem there was no such ground as King
Arthur's fiction" (i.e. the legends concerning King Arthur). 19
He censured the pastoralists for their unreality, and yet he had
by heart passages of the Shepherds' Calendar20 and showed how
to write a true pastoral drama in the Sad Shepherd; he mocked
the sonneteers, 21 especially Daniel, 22 in his satirical plays,
for their sugared sweetness and frivolity, but wrote himself
some of the finest lyrics of his age. The catholicity of Jonson's
taste in its sympathy included the philosophy and eloquence of
Lord Bacon, the divinity of Hooker, the historical and antiquarian enquiries of Camden and Selden, the classical scholarship
of Chapman and the poetry of such diverse men as Spenser, Father
Southwell, Donne, Sandys, Herrick, Carew, and his lesser "sons."23

BEN JONSON AND THE CLASSICAL SCHOOL

The characteristics of Jonson as the exponent of the conservative spirit in literature in an age conspicuous for its passionate love of novelty are somewhat these: an unusual acquaintance
with the literature of Greece and Rome, a holding of "the prose
writers and poets of antiquity," to employ the happy phrase of
the late Mr. John Addington Symonds, "in solution in his spacious memory," and a marvelous ability to pour them "plasti-
cally forth into the mould of thought;"[24] a keen appreciation of
the principles which lie at the root of classical literature with
an intelligent recognition and a liberal interpretation of those
principles in their adaptation to the needs of contemporary English conditions. The rhetorician in Jonson was alike his distinction and his greatest limitation. It was this which gave him an
ever-present sense of an inspiring design, whether it was in the
construction of a complete play or in the selection and ordering
of the words of a single clause. These more general characteristics of the classicist will be recognized at once as Jonson's;
but even the specific qualities that mark the coming age of English classicism are his. We have already remarked Jonson's
fondness for satire and criticism, and his exceeding use of that
species of applied poetry called occasional verse. Restriction
in the range of subject is always attended by a corresponding
restriction in style and form, and we are prepared to find in Jonson's occasional verse a strong tendency to precise and pointed
antithetical diction, and a somewhat conventionalized and restricted metrical form. If we will look at Jonson's prose we
shall find other "notes" only less marked of the coming classical supremacy, in his slightly Latinized vocabulary and in his
occasional preference for abstract over concrete expression.
Take the following from the <u>Discoveries</u>: "There is a difference between mooting and pleading; between fencing and fighting.
To make arguments in my study and to confute them, is easy;
where I answer myself, not an adversary. So I can see whole
volumes despatched by the umbractical doctors on all sides. . . .
but indeed I would no more choose a rhetorician for reigning in
a school, than I would a pilot for rowing in a pond."[25] And again;
"When a virtuous man is raised, it brings gladness to his friends,
grief to his enemies and glory to his posterity. Nay, his honors
are a great part of the honor of the times; when by this means
he is grown to active men an example, to the slothful a spur, to
the envious a punishment."[26]
Besides Jonson's several strictures on cross rimes, the stanzas of Spenser, the alexandrine of Drayton, English hexameters

and sonnets, the very first entry of the Conversations with Drummond tells us of a projected epic with the added information "it
is all in couplets for he detested all other rimes."[27] A little below Jonson tells of his having written against Campion's and
Daniel's well-known treatises on versification to prove "couplets to be the bravest sort of verses, especially when they are
broken like hexameters," i. e., exhibit a regular caesural pause.[28]

The non-dramatic verse of Jonson was grouped by the author
under the headings Epigrams and The Forest, both published in
the Folio of 1616, and Underwoods, miscellaneous poems of the
collected edition of 1640. Aside from his strictly lyrical verse
in which Jonson shared the metrical inventiveness and variety
of his age, the decasyllabic rimed couplet is all but his constant
measure. For epistles, elegies, and epigrams, some two hundred poems, he seldom uses any other verse, and he employs
this verse in translation and sometimes even for lyric purposes.
In Jonson's hands the decasyllabic couplet became the habitual
measure for occasional verse, and, sanctioned by his usage, remained such for a hundred and fifty years. But not only did Jonson's theory and practise coincide in his overwhelming preference for this particular form of verse, but the decasyllabic
couplet as practised by Jonson exemplifies all the characteristics which, in greater emphasis, came in time to distinguish the
manner and versification of Waller and Dryden. Moreover, the
practice of no other poet exemplifies like characteristics to anything approaching the same extent until we pass beyond the accession of Charles I.

In an examination of the versification of several Elizabethan
and later poets[29] for the purpose of establishing the truth of this
proposition, several things are to be noted. Spenser's use of the
couplet, despite the early date of his only example (Mother Hub-
berd's Tale) and his conscious imitation in it of Chaucer, was
found to stand as a very fair representative of the use of this
metre by those who followed Spenser in other particulars of style
and versification. Spenser's use of the couplet has therefore
been employed as representative here. Thus although a certain
rigidity of manner, that caused him all but to give up run-on
couplets and lines, distinguishes the couplets of Drayton, and
although Chapman shows a greater freedom and variety in the
same respects, both these poets, with many others, their contemporaries, may be said to use the couplet in a manner in general resembling that of Spenser, and to group with him in not
making a strong medial caesura a characteristic of their use of

this verse. As we are not concerned with these poets in this discussion except so far as the determination that Spenser is representative of them, the figures which establish this point may be relegated to the note below. [30]

In the case of Jonson a consideration of the length of his career and the variety of his practice demanded a wider range from which to judge. The passages chosen range from 1603 to 1631, and include almost every species of poetry which Jonson wrote in this verse. Sandys exhibited an unexpected diversity of manner, although within a well defined range. The poem Deo Optimo Maximo is the only original poem of any length by Sandys: it has been considered with two translations. Lastly, the passages from Waller, Dryden, and Pope will be seen to take into consideration both the earlier and the later manner of each.

The points considered in this enquiry are (1) the number of the run-on couplets; (2) the number of run-on lines; (3) the character of the line as to internal caesura, especially in the contrast which exists between the continuous line (i.e., one in which there is no internal caesura) and that exhibiting an internal caesura so placed as to produce the effect of splitting the line into two halves. This last results when the rhetorical pause occurs after the second stressed syllable or after either of the syllables following. This tendency to split the decasyllabic line into two is a notorious feature in the versification of the Popean School; as well as of Waller and Dryden. It is scarcely less marked in the verse of Jonson. The following table gives the average of all the passages examined and for each author:

	Spenser, 1591.	Sandys, 1636-1641.	Jonson, 1603-1631.	Waller, 1660-1680.	Dryden, 1660-1687.	Pope, 1713-1732.
Run-on Couplets..........	5.	5.	4.4	3.5	.6	0.
Run-on Lines.............	19.5	22.6	21.8	12.5	7.6	5.5
Lines which show no Medial Caesura...........	59.	47.	26.	36.	36.3	21.
Lines showing a caesura after the fourth, fifth and sixth syllables......	35.	40.	55.2	56.	53.	67.5
Lines showing a caesura after the fourth, fifth, sixth and seventh syllables....	35.5	44.6	64.4	58.5	55.	71.

The following features appear: —

1. As to the run-on couplets, Jonson shows, with Sandys and Spenser, the earlier freedom, and shows it to about the same degree. But Waller shows it too, and his proportion in this respect (3.5) is far nearer to Jonson's (4.4) than to Dryden's (which is only .6). Pope gave up the run-on couplet. 2. As to run-on lines, Sandys exhibits a slightly larger proportion than Jonson or Spenser, but their averages (Spenser, 19.5, Sandys, 22.6, Jonson, 21.8) are substantially the same. It may be noted that Jonson's average in run-on couplets and verses falls in his Epigrams very nearly to that of Dryden in The Hind and the Panther; the former showing eleven run-on lines and the latter nine; both having two run-on couplets. But nearly the same is true of Sandys' Paraphrase of the Psalm LXXIII, in which there is but one run-on couplet and eleven run-on lines. On the other hand Sandys' freest verse in these respects, the Paraphrase of Job, surpasses the utmost freedom of Jonson. Thus as to run-on couplets and run-on lines, the test places Spenser, Sandys and Jonson in one group, with Waller and Jonson showing averages which dwindle to the stricter manner of Pope in these respects. It may be remarked in passing that it is a mistake to consider that the Elizabethans often practised the couplet with the freedom, not to say licence, that characterizes its nineteenth-century use in the hands of such poets as Keats.

Now if these passages be considered with reference to the occurrence of a medial caesura and the contrasted non-occurrence of any caesura within the lines, they fall at once into two groups, (1) that of Spenser and Sandys, whose manner is continuous and whose use of the internal caesura is correspondingly infrequent;[31] and (2) that of Jonson, Waller, Dryden and Pope, whose manner is characterized by shorter clauses, inversions and interpolations, which breaks up continuity and prevailingly places the internal caesura within the range of the fourth and seventh syllables of the verse, positions which tend to break the verse into two halves. The proportion of lines in which no medial caesura occurs is largest in Spenser, 59 being the average; Sandys' average is 47. Sandys' Paraphrase of Psalm LXXIII shows the highest number of continuous lines, 63; Pope's Essay on Man the smallest, 17. Jonson's average is but 26, showing a smaller average number of continuous lines than either Waller or Dryden, and approaching Pope's average, which is but 21.

The proportion of lines, which show a rhetorical pause or caesura after the second accent, after the arsis of the third foot, and after the third accent, hence producing the general effect of cutting the verse into two halves, are smallest in Spenser and Sandys, their averages being respectively 35 and 40 to each 100 lines. In Jonson the average of these lines rises to 55.2, which is greater than Dryden's 53; and nearly that of Waller, 56. It is interesting to note that Jonson's fondness for a pause after the arsis of the fourth foot (seventh syllable of the verse), which is shared by Pope, brings the averages of these two, by including that caesura with the count already taken of the caesuras of the three preceding feet, up to 64.4 per cent. for Jonson and 71 per cent. for Pope. In the use of this feminine caesura and the corresponding caesura of the previous foot (that after the third arsis), Jonson's verse is more like that of Pope than is Dryden's, whose preference is for the masculine caesura, i.e., that after an accented syllable. It is not in the least here assumed that the versification of Jonson, Dryden, and Pope is all reducible to a single definition; but it is claimed that the characteristics of the versification of Jonson's couplets are of the type which, developed through Dryden and Waller, led on logically to the culmination of that type in Pope; and that no possible development of the couplet of Sandys and Spenser could have led to a similar result.

Examination has been made into the versification of this group of poets, not because peculiar store is set upon such matters, but because of the mistakes which have arisen in consequence of the obiter dicta of Dryden and of Pope. It was sufficient for the subsequent "historians" of English literature to know that in the rough draft of an outline of the course of English literature, communicated by Pope to Warburton, and preserved by Ruffhead, the great poet made Sandys in his Paraphrase of Job one of the originals of Waller in versification; the thing is copied forever after. [32] More important is the classical manner with its crisp diction, its set figures, its parallel constructions, its contrasted clauses, its inversions. Without pursuing this subject into minute detail, the following passages may be well compared.

In 1660 Dryden wrote thus:

> And welcome now, great monarch, to your own,
> Behold th'approaching cliffs of Albion:
> It is no longer motion cheats your view,
> As you meet it, the land approacheth you.

> The land returns, and in the white it wears,
> The marks of patience and sorrow bears.
> But you, whose goodness your descent doth show
> Your heavenly parentage, and earthly too,
> By that same mildness, which your father's crown
> Before did ravish, shall secure your own. [33]

In obvious further development of the same manner, Pope writes some seventy-five years later:

> To thee, the world its present homage pays,
> The harvest early, but mature the praise;
> Great friend of liberty! In kings a name
> Above all Greek, above all Roman fame:
> Whose word is truth, as sacred as revered
> As heav'n's own oracles from altars heard.
> Wonder of kings! like whom to mortal eyes
> None e'er has risen, and none e'er shall rise. [34]

Sandys wrote as follows in 1638, the year after the death of Jonson:

> The Muse, who from your influence took her birth,
> First wandered through the many-peopled earth;
> Next sung the change of things, disclosed th'unknown,
> Then to a nobler shape transformed her own;
> Fetched from Engaddi spice, from Jewry balm,
> And bound her brows with Idumaean palm;
> Now old, hath her last voyage made, and brought
> To royal harbor this her sacred fraught:
> Who to her King bequeaths the wealth of Kings,
> And dying, her own epicedium sings. [35]

But Jonson had written thus, near the beginning of the reign of James:

> Who would not be thy subject James, t'obey
> A prince that rules by example more than sway?
> Whose manners draw more than thy power constrain,
> And in this short time of thy happiest reign,
> Hast purged thy realms, as we have now no cause
> Left us for fear, but first our crimes, then laws.
> Like aids 'gainst treason who hath found before"
> And than in them how could we know God more?

> First thou preservèd wert, our Lord to be,
> And since, the whole land was preserv'd in thee. [36]

These four passages meet on the common ground of royal panegyric, and may be regarded as typical of the manner of each poet, and as abundantly upholding the conclusions already reached with respect to their versification.

If now we consider rhetorical structure and remember how true it is of the style of Pope that it is built upon antithesis and parallel construction, word against word, clause against clause, verse against verse, paragraph against paragraph, and what is more important, thought against thought, we shall find an interesting result. There is nothing antithetical in the prevailing style of Sandys, either in his translation — except so far as Hebrew parallelism may easily account for it — or in his original verse. On the other hand Jonson knew the value of antithetical construction and used it with intelligence and frequency, though not, as did later writers, almost to the exclusion of all other rhetorical devices. In the passages from Dryden and Pope quoted above, this characteristic appears as prevailingly in both poets; but the quotation from Jonson also exemplifies antithetical construction in all its subtlety. The prince and his subject are contrasted; the prince rules, the subject obeys. The prince rules by example more than by sway; his manners draw more than his powers constrain. The subject fears his own crimes more than the prince's laws; and in the end the prince is preserved to be king, and his subjects are preserved in him; which last antithesis involves "conceit" as it often continued to do in Dryden as witness "the approaching cliffs of Albion" in the passage cited above.

The epigram of Jonson to King James, from which the lines above are taken, was written in 1604. The Panegyric on the same Sovereign's accession, written in the previous year and the earliest extended piece of Jonson's writing in couplets, shows beyond any cavil the beginnings of those qualities which, developed, differentiate the couplet of Dryden and Pope from others' usage of the same measure, and it displays what is more important, a treatment and mode of dealing with material, a diction and style which equally determine its kinship. [37]

An examination of Jonson's use of the couplet through successive years exhibits less advance towards the later regularity than might have been supposed, and it can hardly be affirmed that Jonson was any more rhetorically constructive in his later writings than in those composed when his classical theories were

new and strong upon him. We cannot expect the laws which govern organic growth to coincide with those controlling constructive ingenuity; a house is built, a tree grows, and the conscious
and self-controlled development of such a man as Jonson is alien
to the subtle and harmonious unfolding of a genius like Shakespeare's. What we do find in Jonson's use of the devices of the
later classicists is a full recognition of their actual value, and
an application of each to the special needs and requirements of
the work which he may have in hand. Thus he employed the couplet for epigram and epistle alike, but used it with greater terseness and more in accord with later usage in the former, feeling
that fluency and a somewhat negligent manner at times were fitting to epistolary style. The latter can be found in any of the
Epistles. No better specimen of Jonson's antithetical manner
could be found than the fine epigram to Edward Allen: —

> If Rome so great, and in her wisest age,
> Fear'd not to boast the glories of her stage,
> As skilful Roscius, and grave AEsop, men,
> Yet crown'd with honors, as with riches, then;
> Who had no less a trumpet of their name,
> Than Cicero, whose every breath was fame:
> How can so great example die in me,
> That, Allen, I should pause to publish thee?
> Who both their graces in thyself hast more
> Out-stript, than they did all that went before:
> And present worth in all dost so contract,
> As others speak, but only thou dost act.
> Wear this renown. 'Tis just, that who did give
> So many poets life, by one should live. [38]

The liberality of Jonson's spirit, despite his own strong preferences, caused him likewise to admit into his practice forms
which theoretically he disapproved. He had the sanction of Catullus and Tibullus for his lyrics, but he even stooped to write a
few sonnets, to bits of pastoral in the prevailing mode like a
Nymph's Passion, and to concetti after the manner of the Mari-
nists, like the dainty trifle, That Women are but Men's Shadows.
This eclecticism of practice in the great classical theorist combined with the strong influence of Donne's subtle novelty of treatment and the older romantic influence of Spenser, perpetuated
in men like Drayton, Drummond and the later Spenserians, de-
layed the incoming tide of classicism, which setting in, none the

less, about the time of the accession of Charles I, became the
chief current until after the Restoration, and reached its full
when Milton, the last of the Elizabethans, died.

Nothing could more strongly exemplify this eclecticism in the
practice of Jonson than the fact that two such diverse men as
Robert Herrick and Edmund Waller were alike his poetical
"sons." Herrick, the man, has a naïve and engaging personality,
which is choice, though not more sterling than the solid worth
of Ben Jonson himself; whilst the frank Paganism of Herrick, the
poet, and his joy in the fleeting beauties of nature are things
apart from Jonson's courtly and prevailingly ethical appraise-
ment of the world. Notwithstanding, Herrick had his priceless
lyrical gift of Jonson, though he surpassed his master in it. Unhappily for his fame, he inherited also Jonson's occasional gross-
ness of thought, his fondness for the obscenities of Martial, and
he surpassed his master in this as well. Waller's debt to Jonson is also two-fold: in the lyric, which he impoverished and
conventionalized, and in occasional verse, for which he possessed
a peculiar talent, and which he freed of the weight of Jonson's
learning, his moral earnestness and strenuousness of style, cod-
ifying the result into a system which was to give laws to generations of poets to come. Waller was a man, the essence of whose
character was time-serving, to whom ideals were nothing, but
to whom immediate worldly success, whether in social life or
letters, was much; a man whose very unoriginality and easy
adaptability made him precisely the person to fill what Mr. Gosse
deftly calls the post of "Coryphaeus of the long procession of the
commonplace." The instinct of his followers was right in singling Waller out for that position of historical eminence, not because, as a boy, he sat down and deliberately resolved on a new
species of poetry, but because he chose out with unerring precision just those qualities of thought, form and diction which appealed to the people of his age, and wrote and re-wrote his poetry
in conformity therewith. In Carew, Waller found the quintes-
sence of vers de société, and "reformed" it of its excessive
laces and falling-bands to congruity with the greater formality
which governed the costume of the succeeding century. Lastly,
in Jonson he found an increasing love of that regularity of rhythm
which results from a general correspondence of length of phrase
with length of measure, amongst much with which he was in little
sympathy, a minute attention to the niceties of expression, a
kind of spruce antithetical diction, and a versification of a con-
structiveness suited to the epigrammatic form in which the

thought was often cast. In Sandys, Fairfax, Drummond and some others, he found a smoothness and sweetness of diction, in which these poets departed measurably from their immediate contemporaries and preserved something of the mellifluousness of the Spenserians. With almost feminine tact Waller applied these things to his unoriginal but carefully chosen subject-matter, and in their union wrought his success.

The real value of the following age of repression consisted in its recognition of the place that the understanding must hold — not only in the production of prose — but in the production of every form of enduring art. It endeavored to establish a standard by which to judge, and failed, less because of the inherent weakness of the restrictive ideal, than because the very excess of the imaginative age preceding drove the classicists to a greater recoil and made them content with the correction of abuse instead of solicitous to found their reaction upon a sure foundation. The essential cause of this great change in the literature of England, above all question of foreign origin, precocious inventiveness of individual poets, artificial and "classical heroic couplets," lies in the gradual increase of the understanding as a regulative force in the newer literature, the consequent rise of a well-ordered prose, and the equally consequent suppression for several decades of that free play of the imagination which is the vitalizing atmosphere of poetry.

Making due allowance for the existence of many concurrent forces, English and foreign, which made for the coming age of repression, but which it is not within the province of this paper to discuss, it has been the endeavor of this enquiry to establish the following points: —

1. That the position of Ben Jonson was such as to give a sanction and authority to his opinions and practise above any man of his age.

2. That Jonson's theories were those of the classicist from the first, though put forward and defended with a liberality of spirit and a sense of the need of the adaptation of ancient canons of art to changed English conditions, that warrant the use of the term, assimilative classicism, as applied to these theories.

3. That the practice of Jonson as exemplified in his works exhibits all the "notes" of this assimilative classicism; amongst them in subject, a preference for applied poetry over pure poetry, as exemplified in his liking for satire, epigram, translation and occasional verse; in treatment, a sense of design and construction, repressiveness and selectiveness, a feeling for

BEN JONSON AND THE CLASSICAL SCHOOL

brevity and condensity, a sense of finish, and the allusiveness of the scholar; in diction, qualities distinctive of the coming "classical" age, such as care in the choice of words, a slightly Latinized vocabulary, the employment of a spruce, antithetical style, and the use of parallel construction and epigram; in versification, a preference for the decasyllabic couplet and the writing of it in a manner, which is distinguishable from the continuous manner of Spenser, but which contains all the distinctive characteristics which, developed, led on to the later use of this measure by Waller, Dryden and Pope.

4. That these theories and practices of Jonson are traceable in his work from the first, and in their range, consistency, and intensity antedate similar theories and practise in the works of any other English writer.

From all this is derived the conclusion that there is not a trait which came to prevail in the poetry of the new classic school as practised by Waller and Dryden, and later by Pope, which is not directly traceable to the influence or to the example of Ben Jonson. We cannot but view with renewed respect a genius so overmastering that it became not only the arbiter of its own age, but gave laws which afforded sanction and precedent to generations of successors.

NOTES

1   Walter Pater, Appreciations, "Postscript," p. 253 f.

2   Preface to Arnold's Poems, ed. 1854.

3   Epigrams, No. LXXVI, Fol. 1640, i, 22.

4   Jonson's Conversations with Drummond, Shakespeare Society, 1842, p. 8.

5   Ibid., p. 3.

6   Poems by John Keats, ed. Bates, 1896, p. 59.

7   Gosse, Eighteenth-Century Literature, p. 2.

8   Henry Wood, "Beginnings of the 'Classical' Heroic Couplet in England:" "At all events it was Sandys, and not Waller, who at the beginning of the third decade of the century, first of all Englishmen, made a uniform practice of writing in heroic couplets

which are, on the whole, in accord with the French rule, and which, for exactness of construction, and for harmonious versification, go far towards satisfying the demands of the later 'classical' school in England."—American Journal of Philology, XI, p. 73.

9   Gosse, From Shakespeare to Pope, p. 19.

10   See in general Matthew Arnold's essay on "The Literary Influence of Academies."

11   Jonson's Conversations with Drummond, as above, p. 37.

12   Ibid., pp. 16, 2, and 3.

13   Preface to Matthew Arnold's Poems, ed. 1854.

14   See the many passages of the Discoveries which are no more than translations of the Institutes, and the weight given to the theories of Horace in the same book.

15   Prologue to Every Man out of his Humour, Fol. 1640, i, 74.

16   Ibid., i, 5.

17   Ibid., i, 74.

18   Conversations, as above, p. 2.

19   Ibid., p. 10.

20   Ibid., p. 9.

21   Ibid., p. 4.

22   See especially on this topic The War of the Theatres by J. H. Penniman, Publications of the University of Pennsylvania, Series in Philology, Literature and Archaeology, Vol. IV, No. 3, pp. 24-30, 53, 54.

23   See the Conversations, as above, passim.

24   Ben Jonson, English Worthies, p. 52.

25   Discoveries, ed. Schelling, p. 16. Cf. also, "In her indagations often times new scents put her by, and she takes in errors into her by the same conduits she doth truths." — Ibid., p. 28.

26   Ibid., 42.

27   Ibid., pp. 2, 4, and 1.

28   Ibid., p. 2.

29   As to versification, the following passages have been considered
      as typical, one hundred lines in each case:

1591, Spenser:	(a)	Mother Hubberd's Tale, lines 1-100, Riv. Ed., p. 99.
	(b)	" " " " 977-1077, p. 133.
1593, Marlowe,		Hero and Leander, Sestiad I, lines 1-100, ed. Bohn, p. 157.
1598, Drayton,		Rosamond to Henry II, England's Heroical Epistles, ed. Drayton, 1619, p. 105.
1600, Chapman,		Hero and Leander, Sestiad VI, last 100 lines, as above, p. 226.
1603, Jonson:	(a)	A Panegyry on the Happy entrance of James our Sovereign to his first high session of Parliament in this Kingdom. Ed. 1640, i, 87.
1612	(b)	To Penshurst, pr. in Fol. of 1616, ed. Bohn, p. 347.
1616	(c)	The first XVII Epigrams and four lines of XVIII, excepting Epig. VIII, which is not in couplets, and Epig. XII, which has a peculiar movement, due to its subject, and is hence not a fair example, ibid., pp. 283-88.
1623	(d)	An Execration on Vulcan, p. 461.
1631	(e)	Elegy on Lady Winton, p. 552.
1636, Sandys:	(a)	Psalm LXXIII. Library of Old Authors, Sandys, II, p. 204.
1638	(b)	Paraphrase upon the Book of Job, ibid., I, 1.
1641	(c)	Deo Optimo Maximo, ibid., II, 403.
1660, Waller:	(a)	To the King, ed. Drury, p. 163.
1678-80	(b)	On the Duke of Monmouth's Expedition, 1678, 48 lines. On the Earl of Roscommon's Translation of Horace, 1680, 52 lines, ed. Drury, pp. 212 and 214.
1660, Dryden:	(a)	Astraea Redux, Globe ed., p. 8.
1687	(b)	Hind and the Panther, ib., p. 171.
1693	(c)	Epistle to Sir Godfrey Kneller, ib., p. 264.
1713, Pope:	(a)	Windsor Forest, Chandos ed., p. 95.
1732	(b)	Essay on Man, Epistle IV, lines 19-110, ibid., p. 218.

30   This table may be compared with that of the text, p. 185.
      The count is made upon the passages mentioned in the note pre-
      ceding this, and the averages of Spenser and Sandys are repeated

from the other table for convenience of comparison. It will be noted that Sandys corresponds to Drayton in his use of the continuous line, and to Marlowe in the frequency of the medial caesura, whilst his freedom in the run-on line exceeds even that of Chapman.

	Spenser, 1591.	Marlowe, 1593.	Drayton, 1598.	Chapman, 1600.	Sandys.
Run-on Couplets	5	2	1	12	5
Run-on Lines	19.5	11	4	28	22.6
Continuous Lines	59	51	46	55	47
Lines showing a Medial Caesura	35	40	44	38	40

31 See note above.

32 See Ruffhead's Life of Pope, 1769, p. 410 seq.; also Pope, Amer. ed., 1854, I, clvi.

33 Astraea Redux, Dryden, Globe ed., p. 14.

34 First Epistle of the Second Book of Horace, To Augustus, 1737, Pope, Chandos ed., p. 313.

35 Dedication of A Paraphrase upon Job. Sandys, ed. Library of Old Authors, I, lxxix.

36 Epigram XXXV, To King James, fol. 1641, I, p. 12.

37 I add some typical instances of Jonson's use of this structure out of the scores that can be culled from his pages. These will be seen to involve nearly all the mannerisms afterwards carried to so artificial a degree of refinement by Pope himself, and to hinge, all of them, on a pointed, condensed and antithetical way of putting things.

Call'st a book good or bad as it doth sell. Epigram 3.
And I a poet here, no herald am. Epig. 8.
He that dares damn himself, dares more than fight. Epig. 16.
Blaspheme God greatly, or some poor hind beat. Epig. 28.
Look not upon thy dangers, but our fears. Epig. 51.
At once thou mak'st me happy and unmak'st. Epig. 55.
And hoodwinked for a man, embrace a post. Epig. 58.
Active in's brains and passive in his bones. Epig. 68.
And no less wise than skilfull in the laws. Epig. 74, p. 21.
The ports of Death are sins, of Life, good deeds. Epig. 80, p. 23.
In making thy friends books, and thy books friends. Epig. 86, p. 24.
That dares not write things false, nor hide things true. Epig. 95.

And study conscience more than thou wouldst fame. Epig. 98.
Truth might spend all her voice, fame all her art. Epig. 106.
And first to know thine own state, then the state's. Epig. 109.
He wrote with the same spirit that he fought. Epig. 110.
They murder him again that envy thee. Epig. 111.
Til thou canst find the best choose the least ill. Epig. 119.

And in their error's maze, thine own way know,
Which is to live to conscience not to show. Ibid.

That strives his manners should precede his wit. Epig. 121, p. 39.
Outdance the babion, or outboast the brave. Epig. 130, p. 41.
Men love thee not for this, they laugh at thee. Ibid.
The learned have no more privilege than the lay. Epig. 132, p. 42.
For fame with breath soon kindled, soon blown out. Ibid.

In place of scutcheons, that should deck thy hearse,
Take better ornaments, my tears and verse. Epig. 27, p. 10.

Believe it, Guilty, if you lose your shame,
I'll lose my modesty, and tell your name. Epig. 38, p. 13.

That we thy loss might know, and thou our love,
Great heav'n did well, to give ill fame free wing. Epig. 51, p. 15.

Nay ask you how the day goes in your ear
Keep a star-chamber sentence close twelve days
And whisper what a proclamation says. Epig. 92, p. 26.

It is the fair acceptance, Sir, creates
The entertainment perfect, not the cates. Epig. 101, p. 30.

And did not shame it by our actions then
No more than I dare now do with my pen. Epig. 108, p. 34.

Thou rather striv'st the matter to possess
The elements of honor than the dress. Epig. 109, p. 34.

I modestly quit that, and think to write
Next morn an ode; thou mak'st a song e'er night. Epig. 112, p. 35.

                    I pity thy ill luck
That both for wit and sense so oft doth pluck. Ibid.

But blood not minds, but minds did blood adorn,
And to live great, was better than great born. Epig. 116, p. 37.

Who sees a soul in such a body set
Might love the treasure for the cabinet. Epig. 125, p. 39.

38   Epigram LXXXIX, fol. 1640, I, p. 25.

THE DEVELOPMENT OF THE RHETORIC AND METRE OF THE HEROIC COUPLET, ESPECIALLY IN 1625-1645

Ruth C. Wallerstein

The purpose of this paper is to point out certain elements in the development of the rhetoric of the "classical" pentameter couplet in the middle seventeenth century and to show how the development of this rhetoric is bound up with the establishment of its formal metrical pattern. The rhetoric and metre interacted and helped to shape each other into the integral form which we know in Dryden and Pope. The paper proceeds as follows: After defining the tendencies of metrical and rhetorical form in the early closed couplet, which derives from the elegiac distich, I shall trace the marked development of this form during the first quarter of the seventeenth century, when the pentameter couplet of some sort won great popularity and became the recognized form for familiar verse such as Donne's letters, and for the steadily increasing output of reflective and occasional verse, critical, complimentary, or topical. Then I shall show in detail how the couplet became almost prescriptively associated with the verse of definition and with occasional verse, and as it became thus established, it gained strength in its distinctive form in the twenty years from 1625 on. In order to show how this final form took shape, I shall analyse the couplet in detail in two separate groups of minor occasional verse; namely, the laudatory poems which accompanied the volumes of George Sandys, 1636-40, and the occasional verse in a minor volume of 1646, the Men-Miracles of Martin Lluelyn, both that written by Lluelyn himself and that written for his volume. The first of these I choose because the work of Sandys himself is important in the history of the couplet, and chiefly because the laudatory verse includes that of Falkland, of whose literary circle at Great Tew Waller was a member; the second, because it is significant to see to what point the couplet had developed in some very minor writers by the time Waller and Denham were reaching maturity. And finally, I shall compare the occasional poems with the verse of Waller and Denham. Thus we can form an idea how far the couplet had taken shape in minor poets, as well as

Reprinted by permission from Publications of the Modern Language Association, Vol. 50 (1935), pp. 166-209.

in Waller and Denham, and how far the general effort and the general literary taste helped in the shaping of it.

The closed couplet originated as a naturalization of the Latin elegiac distich, the single largest influence being that of Ovid. Beginning with Nicholas Grimald's contribution to Tottel's Miscellany in 1557,[1] we can trace a continuous direct influence of the distich on the English form; in Grimald in 1557, with translations from Ovid, Martial, and the neo-Latin epigrammatists; in Marlowe's translation of Ovid's Amores, 1587-88 (?);[2] in Thomas Heywood's translations of Ovid's Heroides, XVI and XVII, and of The Art of Love, 1596[3] — these all direct translations; and in 1597 in Hall's Virgidemiarium, which owes much to the distich in the Latin satiric epigram,[4] and again in Drayton's Heroicall Epistles, which is modelled on the Heroides of Ovid.[5]

Drayton's work demands special treatment with the coming of the couplet into dominance at the turn of the century. Here we must define what the couplet achieved at its inception among the other men we have listed. They show no coherent advance, but were all aiming at the same effect under the same influence. Perhaps Grimald is the most purposive of them. In sixteen sets of his occasional verse and epigrams, giving a fair body of continuous couplets, 97 per cent of the couplets are end-stopped; the lines have masculine rhymes on strongly accented syllables; and balance and antithesis are frequent.[6] All these qualities are suggested by the originals, but balance and antithesis, both in Grimald and in others, exceed that in their originals.[7] But the balance and contrast are present in Grimald more often in possible idea than in explicit form; and where present in actual syntax, they are primarily the decorative balance and antithesis so almost universally pervasive in Renaissance literature, neo-Latin and vernacular, verse and prose. One or two examples are:

> But of the deed, throughout the life, the shame
> Endures, defacying you with fowl defame.

> Hereto heap vp vndaunted heed, stiff hart,
> And all the rest; eche spouse can tell a part.

> To rid my wo, and pull these pangs away.

> Measure forbids vnmeasurable prayse.

Yet this balance had certain design to suggest for the future development of the couplet; and we may note several cases where the balance, such as it is, depends on the double adjective:

> But pleasant ayr in quiet countrie sought.
> . . . .
> Thee, Nero stern, rigor extreem did kill. [8]

The presence of balance and antithesis thus ties up with the significance of the end-stopping and the formation of pattern in the couplet; for in defining the classical couplet we imply by the term not merely that there shall be a distinct pause, but that the two lines shall form an organic and distinct unit of thought. In these early couplets, the sentences are so unfolded as to give a rhetorical separateness to each two-line unit. But as yet these couplets have not consistently anything like the syntactical distinctness, or anything like the terse completed thought that marks the fully developed couplet.

The same thing is true of the metrical form. The basic element of the two-line pattern is made neat by firm rhymes, and there is a tendency to divide the line by medial pause, but no distinctive rhythms or patterns. The structure of the balance is not specifically related to anything in the structure of the line. But the presence of the pause is structurally important for both metre and rhetoric. For the tendency toward such a pause sometimes helps to give form to both elements by relating the rhetoric to an elaboration of the two-line metrical pattern into lines or half-lines. And thus, though there is no principle of pause either rhetorical or metrical, Grimald, for instance, sometimes strikes into so definite a form and rhythm as,

> But my good syre gaue, with soft woords, releef:
> And clokes, with outward chere, his inward greef:

In the realization of this tendency, the development of the rhetoric and of the metrical form help to further each other; but there is as yet nothing like the completeness of mutual pattern which they finally attained. And the couplet still lacks, except by occasional accident, any distinct organic musical form.

1. THE TURN OF THE CENTURY: THE DEFINITE FORM ESTABLISHED
In the first quarter of the new century the closed couplet in

its distinctive rhetoric developed rapidly as a mode of continuous verse and at the same time took on a new type of line movement. [9] This growth is marked by the rise and increase of the
explicitly sententious and didactic element in poetry, an increase
abundantly shown not only by tables of contents of the old collections of the poets of the period, but by study of the contemporary
manuscript collections and commonplace books. In the development of couplet music and elaboration of the rhetoric three men
call for consideration – Drayton, Fairfax, and Ben Jonson.
Drayton in his England's Heroicall Epistles, 1597, wrote narrative couplets. Fairfax, in his translation of Tasso's Gerusalemme, 1600, wrote narrative in ottava rima; yet through Waller, the movement of his stanzas, in both rhetoric and musical
pattern, contributed significantly to the development of the couplet. In both, this development owes much to the prevalence in
their narrative of reflective, moralizing, and sententious elements. In Drayton we find, especially in passages where rhetoric and sentiment prevail, an analytical balance and antithesis
marked by alliteration, related to the movement of line and half-
line, emphasized by balanced musical patterns. In him these
developments are sporadic. Fairfax is more sententious than
Drayton; and in him such elements are more frequent and hit
upon with more steady success. They still do not form, however,
the warp and woof of his verse. In the occasional work and epigrams of Ben Jonson, from about 1600 to 1630, with his style
definitely formed by 1603, we have a large body of couplets specifically devoted to the purpose of reflective and satiric verse
and shaped up by a conscious master. He is by far the most important of the three. In defining his work we shall rely heavily
on Professor Felix E. Schelling's article on Ben Jonson and the
Classical School. [10]

We take up Drayton first. Professor Schelling in his article
on Jonson shows that in many respects, if studied by an analysis
according to the standard tests of the proportions of run-on couplets, run-on lines, over-flowing lines, and medial caesura, Drayton in his use of the couplet looks back to the school of Spenser
rather than forward to the classical school. This is true particularly in the respect that he does not use the medial caesura,
"although a certain rigidity of manner ... caused him almost to
give up the run-on couplets and lines."[11] But, as we have already seen, a strong conscious impetus to the couplet would be
given to Drayton by Ovid, whom he was imitating. We find in
him, where sentiment and reflection prevail, a very marked

elaboration of rhetoric and metrical pattern as compared with
the simple forms of Grimald.

It may be noted as a principle of method in making this examination that the study of the proportion of lines with medial
caesura to those without, or the proportion of lines and couplets
with parallelism and antithesis to those without, does not tell
the whole story. Even though couplets with a striking and characteristic new couplet movement and rhythm do not form the
prevailing pattern of Drayton's Heroicall Epistles, the presence
in the poem of a good number of such couplets, emerging with
a clear emphasis in a general pattern of end-stopped couplets,
might serve as a very influential model to later writers. It
will be remembered how large a part of the seventeenth and
eighteenth-century discussion and imitation of Denham's much
admired "strong" couplets centres around two couplets. As Professor Schelling's statistics are readily available, I do not here
give any proportional figures, but turn to a detailed consideration of some striking lines, using for study "Rosamond to Henry" and "Queen Isabel to Mortimer."

The most important trait of their form is, of course, the development of the thought in couplet sentiments. In this Drayton
but takes the basic element of the form already developed. In
comparison with Grimald, however, not only does he use a sharp
rhetorical pause, but his two-line units coincide with more complete sentiments. In addition to this more incisive syntax, balanced pairs of lines and balanced half-lines are common enough
to give color to the whole. The origin of this balance is various.
Word-play and conceit upon the pros and cons of an idea or feeling are common devices of Renaissance literature, particularly
of the literature that expresses the set and self-conscious analysis of a sentimental situation. They are frequent, to name only
one example, in the Rime of Petrarch. And where, as here in
Drayton's poem, this word-play and conceit are cast into the
couplet mould, it is natural that they should incline to a sharp
rhetorical balance expressed in a pattern of line set against line,
of half-line set against half-line. Such lines as the following at
once strike the eye and mind:

> Punish my fault, or pitie mine estate;
> Reade it for loue, if not for loue, for hate. [12]

> As this pure ground whereon these letters stand
> So pure was I ere stained by thy hand. [13]

> Lights on the ground, themselues doe lessen farre
> But in the ayre, each small sparke seemes a starre[14]

> Fatall my birth, vnfortunate my life,
> Vnkinde my children, most vnkind my wife. [15]

> What doth auaile vs to be Princes heires,
> When we can boast, our birth is only theirs ?[16]

The letters italicized in these examples show alliteration definitely parallel to the balance and emphasizing it.

Then there is the matter of metrical pattern, perhaps even
more important. Strong and great verse, it is recognized, must
have not only firm and unmistakable pattern, but rich variation
from that pattern, harmoniously subdued, but still so insistent
and so organically melodious as to suggest counter-pattern.
Professor P. F. Baum states with great clarity this principle. [17]
Now if we examine further into the aesthetics of established pattern and variation in verse, we find in large stanzas, in blank
verse, or in run-on couplets that, where a number of lines form
the unit of perception and give the design, there is room for ample and subtle variation from pattern in the individual line;
whereas if the unit of perception be limited to two lines, the pattern, to be firmly kept, must be more sharply and formally perceptible in the two individual lines on which the sense of design
depends. This law of the relation of secondary-pattern to basic
design is illustrated in the seventeenth-century emphasis on the
need for smoothness in the couplet, and in the consequent evening out of the beat of its pentameters. In the second place, the
counter-patterns may, in verse of large units such as the long
stanza, blank verse, and the run-on couplet, move with a good
bit of sweep and may themselves employ large melodic units in
their phrasing. Mr. Baum points out the successively varied
secondary-patterns of four-beat or other patterns against the
five-beat patterns in the lines of Paradise Lost; Mr. Johannes
Andersen points out very interestingly that in Paradise Lost,
by his use of the caesura combining with the run-on line, Milton
frequently puts a second iambic pentameter pattern across the
span of the first. [18] And we may note Chaucer's use of the same
device; out of the four run-on lines in the first paragraph of the
Prologue, three yield, with the pauses, beautiful pentameter lines.

But with the closed couplet, if we are to have vigorous music,
these counter-patterns must find new patterns designed within

the confines of the couplet pattern itself. Looking in detail at Drayton's verses in the light of this aesthetic principle, we find in many lines and couplets just such metrical patterns emerging. The colorlessness of other couplets reaffirms the need of this secondary design. We shall consider first the general effect of the first two paragraphs (eighteen lines) of "Rosamond to Henry" and the first paragraph (sixteen lines) of "Queen Isabel to Mortimer," and then we shall examine certain outstanding lines and effects throughout these epistles.

1 If yet thine eies (great <u>Henry</u>) may endure
2 These tainted lines, d<u>rawn wi</u>th a hand impure,
3. (Which fain would blush, but feare keeps blushes back,
4 And therefore suited in dispairing black,
5 This in loues name, O that these lips might crave.
6 But that Sweete name (vile I) prophaned haue;
7 Punish my fault, or pitie mine estate;
8 Reade it for loue, if not for loue, for hate.
9 If with my shame mine eies thou fain wouldst feed,
10 Heere let them surfeit, of my shame to reede.
11 This scribled paper which I send to thee,
12 If noted rightly, doth resemble mee;
13 As this pure ground, whereon these letters stand,
14 So pure was I, ere stained by thy hand;
15 Ere I was blotted with this foule offence,
16 So cleere and spotlesse was my innocence:
17 Now like these marks which taint this hatefull scroule,
18 Such the blacke sinnes which spot my leprous soule.

1 Though such sweet comfort comes not now from her
2 As Englands Queene hath sent to <u>Mortimer</u>.
3 Yet what that wants, which might <u>my po</u>wer approue,
4 If lines can bring this shall supply with loue.
5 Me thinks affliction should not fright me so,
6 Nor should resume these sundry shapes of woe;
7 But when I faine would finde the cause of this,
8 Thy absence shewes me where the errour is.
9 Oft when I think of thy departing hence,
10 Sad sorrow then possesseth eu'ry sence:
11 But finding thy deere blood preseru'd thereby,
12 And in thy life, my long-wisht liberty,
13 With that sweet thought myself I only please
14 Amidst my griefe, which sometimes gives me ease;

15 Thus doe extreamest ills a ioy possesse,
16 And one woe makes another woe seeme lesse.

The variations from the norm of the verse are few, not sufficient to produce counter-patterns or melodic phrases. Most
common are trochaic substitution in the first or third foot (first
foot, seven times: R. to H., 7, 8, 10, 17, 18; I. to M. 9, 15;
third foot three times: R. to H., 2; I. to M., 2, 4.); and the
line of four main beats with one light beat on a preposition (which
occurs four times in the thirty-four lines: R. to H., 4, 7, 10, 14.).
In these cases (all except line 7 in I. to M.) the variation gives
a weak pattern rather than a contrasting pattern, for it is musically perfectly casual or accidental and, on the other hand, has
no relation to the rhetorical rhythm of the line as distinct from
the metrical rhythm. It registers, therefore, simply as a failure to complete the full rhythmic motion. Moreover, it is so
infrequent that we can have no sense of contrast arising from
the shift of this light or suppressed beat from line to line. Only
two lines have two variations: R. to H., 7 and 10, which combine a trochaic substituion with a light beat. The lines are, lastly, very largely monosyllabic and dissyllabic, and there is, accordingly, very little variation by secondary stress.

A few lines call, however, for special comment. In line 6,
R. to H., which scans perfectly regularly, the metrical pattern
and the rhetorical patter of antithesis in sweet and vile pull so
strongly in different ways that they almost cancel each other out.

     *   `   *   ´   * ´   * ´ * ´
But that sweet name (vile I) prophaned have;

Name and I lose their antithesis, which tries to assert itself in
sweet and vile by forcing the words into prominence in the metrical pattern and which thus leaves two weak hovers in succession over sweet name and vile I.   Line 7 offers a striking contrast. First, the rhetorical antithesis is strongly stated in
verb-object parallels; second, this rhetoric is underscored by
a strong caesura and by alliteration; third, the metrical pattern
still further marks the rhetoric.

        ´ * *   ´ ´ * ´ * *   *   ´
Punish my fault, or pitie mine estate;

The trochaic substitution in the first place and the suppressed
beat in the fourth, combining with the caesura, give a distinct

new pattern offering in itself both repetition (in the design of unstressed syllables included within the stressed) and variation (in the number of unstressed syllables). Here is a distinct case in which Drayton designs a counter-pattern within the scope of the main pattern. It is the product not of rhetoric, nor of metre, but of the two working upon each other. The secondary-pattern does not weaken but rather gives strength and firmness to Drayton's usually languid pentameter line. It is first vigorous music and then effective rhetoric. — Lines 17 and 18 again offer something of the same strength derived from the same source.

Now like these marks which taint this hateful scroule,

Such the black sinnes which spot my leprous soule.

In these lines the parallel rhetorical and syntactical elements repeat metrical and rhythmical pattern, and this balance in turn selects certain elements of the metrical pattern for emphasis and thereby gives energy to the music of the line. By contrast lines 15 and 16 in I. to M. show blurred rhetoric and casual metre. Other outstanding passages in the poems deserve comment. In R. to H. lines 25 and 26, we find again rhetorical parallelism with contrast between the two lines sustained by alliteration and by a distinct metrical emphasis on the outstanding elements of the contrast.

Lights on the ground themselves do lessen farre,

But in the ayre, each small sparke seemes a starre.

Notable are the trochaic substitution in the key word light and the strengthening of lessen by alliteration in line one; in line two the cluster of beats; and in the two lines together the rhythmic and syntactic parallelism of the second, third, and fourth syllables. A little later in the same poem comes the line:

My lookes should be the index to my fault;

Here the suppressed beat makes a single strong phrase of index to my fault, ´ * * * ´, and brings out the rhetorical emphasis of the subject and its complement. In such a line as

Here in the garden wrought by curious hands,

the trochaic substitution of the first place in the opening phrase is repeated in effect in the second phrase by the feminine cae- sura, which causes that phrase likewise to begin with a beat and sets up a secondary pattern; and thus the line is made vigorous by a syncopation that moves with the rhetoric. In the lines from I. to M. :

> ´   *   *   ´   *   /(*) *   ´   *   ´
> What doth auaile us to be Princes Heires,
>
> ´   *   *   ´ /   *   ´   *   *   ´
> When we can boast, our birth is only theirs ?

the suppressed beat with the caesura in the first line puts the peak of the metrical variation on the rhetorical key words avail and Princes heires. In the second line the key words which par- allel the first line are marked out by alliteration. Here in the first line we note again that the supressed beat is not casual but forms an integral element in the patterning of the line, operating with the caesura to divide it into a two-part counter-pattern to the pentameter design. Here too the supressed beat is compen- sated by the caesural pause or hover, and hence the time move- ment of the line is maintained. The same element of pattern marks more continuously the fine lines beginning:

> *   `   *   ´   *   ´   *   ´   *   ´
> That after all this feareful massacre,
>
> *   ´   *   ´   * / ´ */ ´   *   ´
> The fall of Beauchamp, Lacy, Lancaster,
>
> *   ´ *   ´   *   ´   *   (*) *   ´
> Another faithlesse fauorite should arise,
>
> *   ´   *   ´   * (*)   * ´ *   `
> To cloude the sunne of our Nobilities ?
>
> *   ´   *   ´ *   ´ *   *   ´   ´
> And glory'd I in Gauestons great fall,
>
> *   ´   *   ´   *   (*)   *   ´   *   ´
> That now a Spenser should succeede in all ?

In lines 5 and 6 the peak of metrical emphasis is thrown upon the antithetic element in the two contrasting lines, — first, by the shift of beat at the end; second, once more by the suppressed beat, stressing Gaveston and Spenser. The lines beginning — "When minions heads must wear our monarks crowns," very strongly reminiscent in rhetoric of Henry VI, have a line move- ment like that of Shakespeare's early blank verse rather than a couplet movement. And yet the balance of the two half-lines in

the adjective- (or possessive-) noun, adjective-noun arrangement anticipates the double adjective half-line movement later
so characteristic of the Popean couplet.

One last example I wish to take from the "Epistle of Henry
to Rosamond"because it offers so interesting a definition both
positive and negative of what Drayton was feeling for. In the
couplet:[19]

´ * * ´ /* ´ * ` * ´

Fatall my birth, vnfortunate my life,

* ´ * ´ * / ´ * ´ * ´

Vnkinde my children, most vnkinde my wife;

the first line is strong both metrically and rhetorically, the
second insignificant. In the first, the two half-lines have patterns distinct and interplaying. These patterns are created first
by the beat shift in fatall giving the pattern ´ * * ` and by the
very secondary stress on the fourth syllable of unfortunate,
which, working with the alliteration, gives the repeated but varying pattern (*) ´ * ` * ´; and secondly by the rhythmic repetition
in my birth and my life. Again the metric and rhythmic forms
underscore the rhetorical. In the second line, on the contrary,
the half-lines have no sort of distinct metrical or rhythmical
pattern to sustain either by parallel or by contrast the rhetorical pattern, and the most which gains whatever point of emphasis is gained through rhythmic movement, by beginning the second element of the line after a feminine caesura, is rhetorically
the weak point of the line. Thus rhetorical and metrical design
obliterate each other.

Drayton's Heroicall Epistles, then, are written at their average pace in a series of end-stopped couplets with masculine endings, which incline to rhetorical statement, and which are marked
by new elements of possible design, but which remain defective
and colorless in rhetoric and languid in metre. Among these
average lines, however, are other lines and passages strikingly
vigorous both in music and in expression. These passages,
though sporadic, show certain definite principles of technique.
The rhetorical structure uses either line or half-line as the
rhetorical unit element, balancing exactly the syntactic elements, either large or small, so as to give completeness of
form to the rhetorical balance and contrast. And this arrangement gives structural form to the music of the couplet by using
the same line and line of the end-stopped lines within the couplet, or the same two half-lines given by the medial caesura, to

form within the pentameter line new <u>metrical</u> unit-elements.
That is, they shift the regular iambic pentameter rhythm in
such a way as to gain within the compass of the couplet a fresh
distinct musical design or counter-pattern suspended in the
main pattern. To secure these new designs they turn such devices as the trochee or the suppressed stress into integral elements of pattern, obviating casual variation. Clearly these designs we thus trace are of the formal order. The rhetorical
movement which defines endstopped couplet, line, and caesura
serves as the framework or oak panelling within which the metrical design is worked out and vice-versa.

Within the new structure Drayton suggests roughly a number
of possible designs. But in fact, of the 184 lines of "Rosamond"
only about 6 per cent have well-formed counter-pattern and of
the 164 lines of "Isabel" only 11 per cent. Around these counter-
patterns, too, the remainder of the line is often rough. To Fairfax's Tasso (1600), which Waller named to Dryden as the model
for his own style, the new verse-movement owes an important
advance in smoothness and fixity of purpose. Fairfax has less
energy than the best of Drayton, but he creates a line and two-
line movement much more even in its tension and much more
obvious. His poem has a more sententious and generalized tone
than that of Drayton, and consequently the frequency of lines and
pairs of lines built on co-ordinated parallelism and phrases with
secondary-pattern is higher. Indeed, it is no longer sporadic
but standard for sententious passages. He suggests fewer patterns than Drayton, but he perfects the few he does realize, and
he gives to the line rhythm as a whole a smooth, evened, neat
flow against which the line and half-line designs stand out clearly.

The Tasso is, like its original, in <u>ottava rima</u>, and we look
first to the concluding two rhymed lines for a succession of couplets that might give the pattern of the heroic couplet.[20] These
lines often summarize a special point reached by a whole stanza,
or describe a figure applicable to the whole stanza somewhat as
the Alexandrine does in Spenser. Moreover, as to musical quality in relation to the whole stanza, they are remarkable, in sharp
contrast to the swelling music of Spenser, for their low-pitched
evenness of texture.

> So if with drought endangered be their grain,
> Poor plowmen joy when thunders promise rain.[21]

But such summarizing couplets are not predominant or characteristic and are rarely distinct from the movement of the stanza

as a whole. The closed line is the rule with him, not in general a closed line created by strong rhetoric in the line units, but the end-stopped lines of the metrical beginner whose basic need is to secure the primary metrical form. Then considering the thought periods built up on these metrical closed lines we find that a two line units prevails not only in the final couplet, but throughout. If we divide the first fifteen stanzas into their thought-units and represent the number of lines in each unit by a digit, with sub-division where there is a longer unit composed of two distinct lesser ones, they run thus:

$$\text{I: } 4 \& 4; \text{ II.} \frac{4}{2 \& 2} \& \frac{4}{2 \& 2}; \text{ III. } \frac{4}{2 \& 2} \frac{4}{3 \& 1}; \text{ IV: } 4 \& \frac{4}{2 \& 2};$$

$$\text{V:} \frac{6}{2 \& 2 \& 2} \& 2; \text{ VI: } 2 \& 2 \& 2; \text{ VII. } 2 \& 6; \text{ VIII. } 2 \& 4 \& 2;$$

$$\text{IX. } 2 \& 2 \& 2 \& 2; \text{ X: } 2 \& 2 \& 2 \& 2; \text{ XI. } 2 \& 2 \& 2 \& 2; \text{ XII: } 4 \&$$
$$1\frac{1}{2} . \& 2\frac{1}{2}; \text{ XIII: } 2 \& 2 \& 2 \& 2; \text{ XIV: } 2 \& 2 \& 2 \& 2; \text{ XV:} \frac{4}{2 \& 2} \& 4.$$

In this movement the rhyme words have no distinct importance, and the final rhymed couplet has generally nothing to define its two-line movement more sharply than that of the ab, ab, "couplets." Stanza nine is typical.[22]

> In Baldwin next he spied another thought,
> Whom spirits proud to vain ambition move:
> Tancred he saw his life's joy set at naught,
> So woe-begone was he with pains of love;
> Boemond the conquered folk of Antioch brought,
> The gentle yoke of Christian rule to prove:
> He taught them laws, statutes, and customs new,
> Arts, crafts, obedience, and religion true.

If we compare Fairfax with his original, we find in this stanza of Tasso a distinct two-line movement in lines 1-2 and 3-4, but not in the second half of the stanza.[23] A second important fact is that, although Fairfax follows Tasso closely in general stanza movement, his lines are end-stopped; whereas in Tasso the run-on line is highly characteristic. In this Spenser's movement is the one that is like Tasso's. Thus in Fairfax the two-line thought-movement is composed again and again of two equal elements or units of pattern, and hence the simple "couplet" effect is by this second fact also made very much sharper in him.

> giá non lasciammo i dolci pegni, e 'l nido
> nativo noi (se'l credo mio non erra)
> ne la vita esponemmo al mare infido
> ed a i perigli di lontana guerra,
> per acquistar di breve suono un grido
> vulgare, e posseder barbara terra:
> che proposto ci avremmo angusto e scarso
> premio, e in danno de l'alme il sangue sparso. [24]

> "But not for this our homes we first forsook,
> And from our native soil have marched so far:
> Nor us to dangerous seas have we betook,
> Exposed to hazard of so far sought war,
> Of glory vain to gain an idle smook,
> And lands possess that wild and barbarous are:
> That for our conquest were too mean a prey,
> To shed our bloods, to work our souls' decay. [25]

In rhetoric the style of Tasso is marked by compressed energy and by sharply defined statement which sometimes uses contrast and balance.

> opre nostre non giá, ma del Ciel dono
> furo, [26]

> a la fatica invitti, al cibo parchi: [27]

> mostra in fresco vigor chiome canute: [28]

Fairfax makes this contrast and balance more explicitly verbal.

> By Heaven's mere grace, not by our prowess done: [29]

> On diet spare, untired with labor long: [30]

> His looks were gray, yet was his courage green, [31]

And he underlines this explicitness by the epigrammatic effect of line pattern as is shown in line five of the twenty-second

stanza quoted above. He sacrifices the energy and narrative zest
of Tasso, but creates on his own score a certain sententious
quality that is his distinctive note. Further he often uses balance
and contrast where it is not in his original.

> Usa a temprar ne' caldi alberghi il verno,
> And pass cold days in baths and houses hot, [32]

> O più bel di maniere e di sembianti,
> O più eccelso ed intrepido di core.

> With majesty his noble countenance shone,
> High were his thoughts, his heart was bold in fight,[33]

> Ove rinovi il prisco onor de gli avi,
> O mostri al men, ch'a la virt latina
> O nulla manca, o sol le disciplina,

> So to revive the Romans' old renown,
> Or prove at least to all of wiser thought,
> Their hearts were fertile land although unwrought.[34]

This is often a merely verbal balance, as in line 2 of the ninth
stanza already cited, the original of which reads, "ch' a l'umane
grandezze intento aspira:" or on stanza 16, line 6:

> tu al fin de l'opra i neghittosi affreta,
> Comfort the feeble, and confirm the strong.

Yet it strongly increases the epigrammatic effect of his poem.
To this increase in rhetoricalness of expression, Fairfax adds
an explicitness of sentiment which must have been particularly
interesting to Waller. Thus line 6 of stanza nine contains an
explicit sentiment not expressed in the original. The same is
true of stanza sixty-four, lines 6-8 just cited, and of stanza
twenty-two as a whole. As we have suggested in the example of
stanza fifty-three, [35] Fairfax increases the whole sententious
tone by moulding all his rhetorical effects to the pattern of the
single line. This practice further tends to create the line with
a medial caesura as a common type. With particular frequency,
we find the last line of the stanza built on parallelism and divided by the caesura.

The general movement of Fairfax is a very even one, as a

result in a large measure of its monosyllabic and dissyllabic
quality. In the sixty-four lines of the first eight stanzas, there
are two monosyllabic lines; eighteen lines contain only one word
other than a monosyllable; thirty-three lines contain only two
words other than a monosyllable, of which twenty-six contain
two dissyllables; ;in all there are eleven trisyllables, mostly
verbs in ed, and one word of four syllables. So prevailing a use
of monosyllables just relieved with dissyllables gives, in the
nature of verse music, beats of very equal value and irons out
the line. This evening process is strengthened by the rhymes,
which are masculine. Moreover, of the one hundred and twenty
rhyme words in the first fifteen stanzas, ninety-nine are monosyllables and nineteen dissyllables.

There is distinct patterning between the half-lines of the sort
we have seen in Drayton. A frequent type of pattern is the syllabic parallel made identical with the rhetorical parallel, which
is sometimes strengthened by alliteration.

His fellows late shall be his subjects now. [36]

Comfort the feeble and confirm the strong[37]

On every footman and on every knight. [38]

Few golden hairs to deck his ivory chin. [39]

Here more definitely than in Drayton the pattern is often further
emphasized by the suppressed medial beat, as in the first example above, and very markedly the third example, where the balance is deliberately made to sustain the whole structure and almost the substance of the line. A common extension is the balanced antithesis with reversed order.

$$\overset{1\qquad 2}{\text{And pass cold days in}}\ \overline{\overset{2}{\text{baths and houses}}}\ \overset{1}{\text{hot}}[40]$$

$$\overset{1}{\text{High were his thoughts,}}\ \overset{2}{\text{his heart was}}\ \overline{\overset{2}{\text{bold in flight}}}\overset{1}{!}[41]$$

$$\overset{1\quad 2}{\text{In diet spare, untired}}\ \overline{\overset{2}{\text{with labor}}}\ \overset{1}{\text{long.}}[42]$$

More subtle variations are less common in Fairfax than in Drayton. But we may note the clustered beats in stanza 26, line 33.

By Heaven's mere grace, not by our prowess done:

and the trochaic substitution with alliteration in the fourth line of stanza forty-five, "High were his thoughts, his heart was bold in fight."

Thus Fairfax's Tasso, though not written in couplets, made a distinct contribution to the development of the heroic couplet. The development of its form seems to result in large measure from interest in the sententious and in generalized reflection, which impels him to seek and find a rhetoric and a music to harmonize with it. Nor was his the only case in which such an interest contributed to the development of the couplet style. This suggests a stream of possible influence, kindred to Fairfax's, which deserves further study. There was in the sixteenth and seventeenth centuries a great deal of translation of poetry, and it is possible that two factors on the very work of translation, operating hand in hand with the general interest in moral sentiment, tended to accelerate this development toward the didactic and the generalized reflection. A translator has before him a concentrated expression which exhibits as a whole an organic reality and scope of meaning larger than the sum of its parts. Thus it is natural that as a translator, in his endeavor to get this whole, he should, in seizing the concept or expression which he is to translate, state it to himself in more explicit and logically complete terms than the original. The original gathers much in one creative flash; any other statement seems tenuous beside that flash and accordingly tends to explain itself in order to gain completeness. This fact produces in translations a tendency to paraphrase and to sententious generalization. Indeed, the theory of paraphrase came to be specifically discussed[43]; but the tendency was operative long before the theory. The point is illustrated by the opening lines of the Second Day of the First Week of Sylvester's Du Bartas.

Tous ces doctes esprits, dont la voix flateresse
Change Hecube en Heleine, & Faustine en Lucresse:
Qui d' vn nain, d' vn bastard, d' vn archerot sans yeux
Font, non vn dieutelet, ains le maistre des dieux.[44]

Those learned spirits whose wits applyed wrong,
With wanton Charms of their inchanting song,
Make of an olde, foul, frantike Hecuba,
A wondrous, fresh fair witty Helena:
Of lewd Faustina, (that loose Emperess)
A chaste Lucretia, loathing wantonness:

> Of a blinde Bowe-Boy, of a Dwarf, a Bastard,
> No petty Godling, but the Gods great Master;[45]

It is also seen in Drummond's translation of Tasso's O vaga
tortorella.

> Misera vedovella,
> Tu sovra il nudo ramo
> A pié del secco tronco io la richiamo.
> Ma l' aura solo e 'l vento
> Risponde mormorando al mio lamento.[46]

> Unhappie widow'd Dove,
> While all about do sing,
> I at the Roote, thou on the Branche above,
> Even wearie with our Mones the gaudie Spring.
> Yet these our plaints we do not spend in vaine,
> Sith sighing Zephyres answer vs again.[47]

Innumerable other examples might be given.

In the case of the English translations, in the second place,
where the writer keeps to the metrical pattern of his original,
but where English words have fewer syllables than Greek or Latin or Italian, the pattern must be filled out, and the explicitness in sentiment or in form of statement we have just spoken
of thus becomes the material for the necessary amplification.
The passages from Fairfax already considered bear witness to
this fact, or, to take only one other example, the first line of
Drummond's translation of Marino's sonnet to night.

> O del Silenzio figlio, e della Notte,[48]
> Sleepe, Silence Child, sweet Father of soft Rest.[49]

It is perhaps a virtue in Fairfax at this stage of the couplet
development that he should be so obvious and so simple and
thereby so insistent on the new verse and rhetorical structure.
But the simplicity and sameness of his line structure hardly allow for energetic forward movement or larger design even had
he not been confined to occasional reflective lines and couplets
scattered through narrative verse. When we turn to Ben Jonson,
we come to a master craftsman deliberately evolving a style for
continuous occasional and reflective verse. In him balance and
contrast are the instruments of analytical definition with a steady

forward drive of thought; and on these forms he builds up, on
the simple basic units we have defined, a verse-movement with
the sublety and variety necessary to scope and progression.

Professor Schelling in the article already referred to has so
fully defined the position of Ben Jonson as the founder of "classicism" as a whole that I shall for the most part simply summarize his argument and refer the reader to his article for more
ample consideration. As to substance, Mr. Schelling points out,
Jonson was the first poet to give occasional verse that variety,
and that power and finish, which made it for nearly two centuries the most important form of poetical expression. As to style,
drawing his conclusions from several tables, Mr. Schelling
shows that in the matter of run-on couplets, Jonson falls somewhat nearer than Spenser and Sandys to Dryden and Pope, though
not so near as Waller to these masters; and in the matter of medial caesura, Jonson, Waller, Dryden, and Pope fall into one
group. In regard to the caesura, Jonson had a distinct theory
that "couplets be the bravest sort of verses, especially when
they are broken like hexameters";[50] i.e., exhibit a regular
caesural pause. Next Mr. Schelling states that although Pope
names Sandys's Paraphrase upon Job as one of the sources of
Waller's versification, more significant in the formation of Waller's style is the classical manner, with the crisp diction, set
figures, parallel constructions, contrasted clauses, and inversions, all of which he found in Jonson. Jonson uses the couplet
in the epigram tersely, in the epistle more fluently.

We have already seen how bound together are the "classical
manner" or rhetoric of the couplet and its characteristic musical form. It is essential to our study to go into Jonson's musical form, which Professor Schelling does not touch upon. The
relation between the rhetoric and the musical pattern we may
see by a glance at epigram XXV, To King James[51] which Professor Schelling especially notes as characteristic of Jonson's
rhetoric and at the lines on Shakespeare.[52] In the epigram the
first two lines contain double parallelism; first between the two
lines; then between the two halves of the second line.

> Who would not be thy subject, // James t' obey
> A Prince that rules by example, // more than sway ?

In the first line, the key words of the parallel receive emphasis
by position just before the caesura and at the close in the rhyme
word. In the second line the antithetic words receive the same

emphasis. The third catches up and states more explicitly the idea of the preceding line.

> Whose <u>manners draw,</u> // more than thy <u>powers constrain,</u>

This development is focused by being carried on a sharper musical pattern; not only do the key words of the antithesis come on

caesura and rhyme, but they repeat musical pattern, manners´ *//

draw, powers constrain with reversal of verbal rhythm in the

   1   1   2

repetition to give variety. The effect of the three lines taken together is akin to that achieved in musical composition when a composer tries out and suggests the melodic phrase with variations before he states it fully. The result is important. For in it Jonson not only uses the terse and epigrammatic power of the couplet, but also supplies forward movement beyond the couplet. Within the closed couplet, the half-line becomes the basic unit of design, and patterns built up on these half-lines preserve and give definition to the couplet form even when the actual stop at line-end and couplet-end is for the moment slight. This form is highly characteristic of Jonson's music and seems to have exerted a strong influence on Falkland and Denham. In the next line the balance of the adjective-noun rhetoric is given musical emphasis again by caesura and end position and then by clustered beats and clustered unstressed syllables, secured through the trochaic foot in the third place.

> And in this short time of thy happiest reign,

The whole of the lines on Shakespeare offers interesting patterns, both musical and rhetorical. Lines 7-12 are typical and will serve our study.

> For silliest ignorance on these may light,
> Which, when it sounds at best, but echoes right;
> Or blind affection, which doth ne'er advance
> The truth, but gropes, and urgeth all by chance;
> Or crafty malice might pretend this praise,
> And think to ruin, where it seemed to raise.

These three couplets contain three parallel clauses beautifully

varied. Each of the three begins with the subject: "silliest ignorance," "blind affection," "crafty malice"; and in each the
adjective contains the germ of the idea of the whole. In each
this idea is developed by antithesis. But among the three the detail of the rhetoric and the music varies. The first couplet states
the antithesis in the second line, not sharply, but still using the
two half-lines to make the contrast. The second couplet sharp-
ens the rhetoric: <u>gropes</u> reiterates <u>blind</u> more distinctly than
the idea is formally pursued in the preceding couplet, and the
antithesis is more explicit. In this couplet the first line is run-
on. The consequent loss of sharpness in line-pattern, however,
is more than compensated by the effect of the antithetic <u>truth</u>
and <u>chance</u> at the beginning and end of their line. More, the run-
on line in the middle of the three couplets saves the balanced
movement of the whole from monotony. The third couplet is
completely definite in both rhetoric and musical pattern. The
whole idea is stated in the first line, and with rhetorical sharpness underscored by musical secondary-pattern, * ´ * ´ * (*)
* ´ * ´ . Finally, the antithesis already defined in "pretend this
praise," and underscored by the secondary-pattern and by alliteration, is completed by the perfectly balanced syntax and musical phrase of the second line:

   *   ´ * ´ *// (*)   *   ´   * ´
And think to ruin, where it seems to raise.

Thus again Jonson builds up to a musical and a rhetorical climax
that are mutual. His strength lies in the fact that the perfected
pattern of half-line, couplet, balance, antithesis, repeated musical phrase, is always suggested, but actually realized only
often enough to create form without imposing rigidity. Although
such effects are not as continuous in him as they are in later
men, they are what give character to his couplets.

2. THE RELATION OF WALLER AND THE SANDYS GROUP.
THE COUPLET OF SANDYS AND THE SANDYS COMPLIMEN-
TARY VERSE

The dates of Waller's work and of that of Sandys and of the
Sandys complimentary verse overlap. And doubtless these poets
influenced each other, as the following analysis of dates will
show. Waller was an intimate of the Falkland circle at Great
Tew, where he presumably showed his verse and would be likely to have read that of Sandys and Falkland even before publication.

THE DEVELOPMENT OF THE HEROIC COUPLET

Sandys's Ovid was probably first published in 1626, though written in part by 1623;[53] the second edition revised came out in 1632. I have not seen the first edition, and my comment will therefore be based on the second edition. As to the relation of the two editions, Hooper in his edition of Sandys says that the alteration is not great; the first lines which he quotes from the original edition suggest that the changes were in the direction of smoothness. Thus "Of formes, to other bodies changed, I sing," becomes "Of bodies changed to other shapes I sing."[54] The Paraphrase upon the Psalms was published in 1636, the Paraphrase upon Job in 1638, and Christ's Passion in 1640. These give the dates of both Sandys and Falkland, for the last three volumes all contain complimentary poems by Falkland.

Waller's first collected publication, including most of the occasional verse we are to consider, came in 1645. But much of the verse was written and read many years before. The poems of Waller that we shall consider are: Of the danger His Majesty (being Prince) escaped in the road at St. Andrews, Of His Majesty's receiving the news of the Duke of Buckingham's death, Upon His Majesty's repairing of St. Paul's, At Penshurst (While in the park I sing), The battle of the Summer Islands, A Panegyric to my Lord Protector. The first occasion of the St. Andrews poem was 1623, and Mr. Thorn Drury inclined to place it at that date.[55] Mr. Henry Wood has shown, however, that the lines containing the reference to Henrietta Maria at least cannot have been written before early in 1625.[56] The occasion of the Buckingham poem was 1628, of the St. Paul's poem 1633. The lines on Penshurst were written during the Sacharissa episode, 1635-39; The battle of the Summer Islands is placed by tradition at the close of that episode, that is, late 1639 or after, although the late Professor Alden 1638.[57] The Cromwell lines were written in 1652 or 1654.

The style of the poems offers some further evidence as to dates. Although these poems are written in the closed couplet, only the St. Andrews poem in some lines, To Penshurst in some lines, The Summer Islands and the Cromwell poem are distinguished by strongly developed contrast and balance and by such distinctive music as we have previously defined. The following table is interesting to study. Although due allowance must be made for different effects aimed at in different poems, the figures in columns 2, 3, and 4, especially the last two, taken in conjunction with the general rhetorical qualities of the poems, suggest that the St. Andrews poem may have been revised when

Waller's style was maturing, some years after it was first written, and while Waller was part of the circle at Great Tew. Thus no priority can be assigned, and we must, as we have already said, think of the work of Sandys, Waller, and Falkland as interactive.

	% closed couplets	% closed first line	% caesura	% medial caesura
St. Andrews (1623 ?)	84.75	61.2	61.2	53.53
Buckingham (1628)	89.47	58.	52.6	42.1
St. Paul's ll. 1-26 (1633)	77.	46.15	42.3	42.3
Penshurst (1635-39)	66.67	25.	66.67	54.16
Summer Is. (ca.1639)	89.18	73.	74.32	64.86
Cromwell (1652-54)	95.75	70.21	66.	52.66

We shall take up first Sandys and the Sandys volumes. In the work of Sandys himself we return to narrative verse and directly to the roots of the closed couplet in the Latin elegiac distich. In the complimentary verse of his volumes we see, in the verse of one distinguished writer and a number of minor versifiers, the first standardization of the couplet in occasional verse. In the detailed study of the relation of Sandys's Metamorphosis to Ovid we shall see that Sandys in his whole verse and not merely in sententious passages, with a deliberate technique translated the rhetoric of Ovid into forms suited to the idiom of English speech and built upon the structure of the closed and epigrammatic couplet. He shows an advance over Drayton then in a system of closed couplets with prevailingly closed lines and medial caesura. And much more completely than Drayton, and more simply, obviously, and constantly than Jonson, he moves his rhetorical expression in close lock-step with the metrical units. In the development of this style he is highly original, for although he found in Ovid many suggestions for this rhetoric and design, what is in Ovid a general method of thought, Sandys has stylized into a pattern of rhetorical and musical expression. In music, he is less fertile in patterns than Ben Jonson, but makes these patterns the basic pattern of his verse; and as compared to Drayton's narrative, he shows a gain in evenness.

The Paraphrase upon Job has fewer closed couplets and fewer rhetorical lines than the Ovid. Its style varies widely with the substance of particular passages, the passages of general reflection such as the wail of Job's wife in Chapter II, or Job's own lament in Chapter III containing a large number of terse epigrammatic lines and more balance and contrast, together with more medial caesura and more metrical design within the line and couplet, than do narrative passages. Professor Schelling suggests in his article on Jonson that there is no more antithesis than would naturally arise from the metrical parallelism of the Hebrew; but so far as one can gauge by the Authorized Version or the Vulgate – the Latin form which Sandys appears to have translated I have not seen –Sandys has increased the antithesis and made it more external and explicit, just as he did with his Ovid. And for us the important fact is that the antithesis is there, with all that it implies of both rhetorical and metrical structure. In a somewhat low-pitched style, it is the outstanding characteristic, and is more emphatic than would appear in any table of the proportion of lines with parallelism or antithesis. The types of pattern are less varied than in the Ovid, and in their often purely formal development they carry on and enlarge the technique of Fairfax.

In the translation of Ovid's Metamorphoses, we shall consider as typical passages the introduction and the incident of Apollo and Daphne. Here we must deal, we have already said, not merely with the character of Sandys's style, but with his relation to his source. His translation keeps close to its text; thus the first twenty lines of Ovid are rendered in the first eighteen of Sandys, and in general each of Sandys's couplets renders approximately the two corresponding lines in Ovid. Occasionally but not commonly, Sandys expands by floriate decoration, as in the account of the winds:

> His quoque non passim mundi fabricator habendum
> aera permisit; vix nunc obsistitur illis,
> cum sua quisque regat diverso flamina tractu,
> quin lanient mundum; tanta est discordia fratrum.
> Eurus ad Auroram Nabataeaque regna recessit
> Persidaque et radiis iuga subdita matutinis

> Yet not permitted every way to blow;
> Who hardly now to teare the World refraine
> (So Brothers jarre!) though they divided raigne,
> To Persis and Sabbaea, Eurus flies;
> Whose gums perfume the blushing Mornes up-rise:[59]

221

Occasionally he fills out with a general, intellectualized, abstract expression inclined toward periphrasis.

> Quae, diversa locis, partim sorbentur ab ipsa,
> In mare perveniunt partim campoque recepta
> liberioris aquae pro ripis litora pulsant.[60]

> Of these not few Earth's thirsty jawes devour:
> The rest, their streams into the Ocean poure;
> When, in that liquid plaine with freer waue,
> The foamie cliffes, instead of Banks, they lave:[61]

This expansion is also not common. He is in general more literal.

Sandys's couplets are closed and rhetorical in structure. Of forty-one couplets in a characteristic passage of the Daphne episode, thirty-seven are strongly end-stopped; moreover twenty-six first lines are stopped, or sixty-three lines in all out of eighty-two. Of balance and antithesis there are seven instances where line balances line; five more where there is balance within a couplet although not in line parallels; nine very sharply defined instances of balance and contrast within a line, and a number of further instances of implicit antithesis.

How is this style related to the original? The style of Ovid is rhetorical and balanced and in that characteristic had much to suggest to Sandys, but the character of its rhetoric in relation to the form of its line is somewhat different from that of Sandys. In the description of the origin of the world, where Ovid describes how the distinct elements take their places, he inclines to closed lines, and in naming the antithetic pairs of elements he balances the elements in antithetic half-lines. Here Sandys follows him closely.

> Nulli sua forma manebat,
> obstabatque aliis aliud, quia corpore in uno
> frigida pugnabant calidis, umentia siccis,
> mollia cum duris, sine pondere, habentia pondus.[62]

> No certaine forme to any one assign'd:
> This, that resists. For, in one body joyn'd,
> The Cold and Hot, The Drie and Humid fight;
> The Soft and Hard, the Heavie with the Light.[63]

Often, however, the Latin style characteristically halves the

line musically by caesura and then binds the two halves together
by noun-adjective or noun-verb phrase or phrases suspended
between the halves (often, because of inflectional endings, with
rhyme effect).

> Nec nova crescendo reparabat cornua Phoebe,
> nec circumfuso pendebat in aere tellus. 64

This type of balance is unsuited to the idiom of English, since
English is an analytical and not an inflectional language, and in
its place Sandys substitutes the balance of separated half-line
units with antithesis.

> Nor waxing Phoebe fill'd her wained hornes:
> Nor hung the self-poiz'd Earth in thin Ayre plac'd;65

In lines 44 and 45 of the description of the shaping of the earth,
Ovid gives rapidity to his narrative by the four staccato phrases of the four parallel half-lines.

> Iussit et (1) extendi campos, (2) subsidere valles,
> (3) fronde tegi silvas, (4) lapidosos surgere montes,66

The rhetoric is further enhanced by a suggestion of cross-line
parallel in verbal rhythm between the active and passive verbs,
an arrangement which makes the two lines parallel each other,
and this effect is again increased by the antithesis of units two
and four. Sandys cannot, because of the English verb-forms,
use the actives and passives for balance; instead, he shifts the
phrases in these two lines, with the result that he makes the
antithesis more obvious.

> Bid's Trees increase to Woods, the Plaines extend,
> The rocky Mountaynes rise, the Vales descend. 67

Through these passages, explicit contrast is characteristic of
Sandys's translation. For this contrast certain suggestions lie
in the original, but not nearly so many nor such obvious instances. Finally whereas Ovid, though he tends to the line unit, uses
the run-on line frequently, Sandys very definitely uses the stopped
line. In general where Ovid uses two, three, or four line periods, Sandys levels these first to line units and then to couplet
units. One further example, with the passages already cited,

will make this very clear.

> Principio terram, ne non aequalis ab omni
> parte foret, magni speciem glomeravit in orbis. 68

> First, least the Earth vnequall should appeare,
> He turn'd it round, in figure of a Spheare;69

A few further examples from the Daphne episode will show, in a different type of material, the same insistence upon antithesis, the same line-movement.

> Primus amor Phoebi Daphne Peneia, quem non
> fors ignara dedit, sed saeva Cupidinis ira.
> . . . .
> "quid" que "tibi, lascive puer, cum fortibus armis ?"
> dixerat: "ista decent umeros gestamina nostros,
> . . . .
>   "quantoque animalia cedunt
> cuncta deo, tanto minor est tua gloria nostra."
> . . . .
> ille quidem obsequitur, sed te decor iste quod optas
> esse vetat, votoque tuo tua forma repugnat:70

> <u>Peneian</u> Daphne was his first belou'd,
> <u>Not</u> Chance, but <u>Cupid's</u> wrath that fury mou'd.
> . . . .
> And said: Lasciuious Boy, how ill agree
> Thou and these Armes! too Manly far for thee.
> . . . .
> So farre as Gods exceed all earthlie powr's:
> So much thy glorie is exceld by ours.
> . . . .
> But thee, thy excellencie countermands:
> And thy owne beautie thy desire with-stands. 71

In the development of the couplet melodies, the chief contribution of Sandys's Ovid is his evenness, varied by the shift of caesura. Of other counter-pattern, we find occasionally such emphasis as is given by parallel phrase rhythm:

> Nor <u>waxing Phoebe</u> fill'd her <u>wained hornes</u>:

When in that liquid Plaine with freer wave,

This emphasis is sometimes strengthened by alliteration; sometimes, but rarely, there is a pattern between line and half-line through varied beat, as in

Bright Constellations, and faire-figured Gods. [72]

a line in which the effect of the polysyllables (uncommon in Sandys) increases that of the varied beat. Of the suppressed beat there is very little effective use.

In the Paraphrase upon Job, as we have suggested, the balances and contrasts are worked out in a few very obvious and very definite patterns. Sandys frequently states a thought or action in two parallel elements or defines a thought by contrast, with detailed balance of the contrasting units.

> Th' invited sisters with their graces blest
> Their festivals, and were themselves a feast. [73]
> . . . .
> Shot through the spheres, and stood before His throne. [74]
> . . . .
>   much people won
> From Thy strict rule to my indulgent reign; [75]
> . . . .
> "Is this the purchase of thy innocence ?
> O fool, thy piety is thy offence.
> He whom thou serv'st hath us all bereft,
> Our children slain, and thee to torments left. . . . [76]
>
> Else had I an eternal requiem kept,
> And in the arms of peace forever slept:
> With kings and princes rank'd, who. lofty frames
> In deserts raised, t' immortalize their names;
> Who made the wealth of provinces their prey;
> In death as mighty, and as rich as they; [77]

Another type of parallelism is the more purely verbal sort in which the line is built on the double adjective structure.

> Three beauteous daughters and sev'n hopeful boys [78]

225

With <u>sober</u> banquets and <u>unpurchas'd</u> food.
. . . .
Like <u>sweet</u> perfumes from <u>golden</u> censers rise;
. . . .
From <u>bleating</u> flocks <u>unblemish'd</u> fatlings chose, [79]

I   In the development of rhythm, the <u>Job</u> stands about with the
Ovid, although there is more variation and perhaps somewhat
more frequent realization of pattern in the variation. But perhaps it just misses pattern as often as it achieves it. Thus in
"Affected virtue more, vice more abhorr'd."[80] <u>vice</u>, by force
of the antithesis and alliteration, tries to take the <u>stress</u> and
make the pattern, but as the second <u>more</u> is also part of the contrast, the normal line pattern prevails, and metre blurs rhetoric. In the line

Sev'n thousand broad-tail'd sheep graz'd on his downs;[81]

the clustered beat in <u>broad-tailed</u> is lost because casual, and
the line really compels a sing-song reading by the violation of
normal word-rhythm; as does also the slightly wrenched accent
of <u>un-purchased</u> in the line.

$$* \quad ´ \quad * \quad ´ \quad * \quad (*) \quad * \quad ´ \quad * \qquad ´$$
With sober banquets and un<u>pur</u>chas'd food.

although in this line the structural parallel gains metrical emphasis from the suppressed beat. Sandys is less casual than
Drayton and more vigorously even, but his chief metrical
strength here as in the Ovid lies in the emphatic units of verbal
parallel repeated in two halves of a divided line.

Sandys's <u>Paraphrase upon the Psalms</u> and his Ovid were both
dedicated to the King, with dedicatory verse in heroic couplets.
The verse in the first volume is end-stopped, but with little rhetoric; that in the second decidedly end-stopped in line and couplet, and with medial caesura. A few lines will show the rhetorical quality.

Iove, whose transcendent Acts the Poets sing
By men made more then Man, is found a King:
Whose Thunder and Ineuitable Flame,
His Iustice and maiestick Awe proclaime:[82]

We come now to the occasional verse which accompanied the

Sandys volumes. The <u>Paraphrase upon the Psalms</u> has two sets of commendatory verse, one in closed couplets by Falkland, and one in alternate rhyming tetrameters and dimeters by Dudley Digges. There are nine sets of commendatory verse prefixed to the <u>Paraphrase upon Job</u> of which six are in closed couplets, one by Falkland, one by Henry King, one by Dudley Digges, one by Francis Wiatt, one by Henry Rainsford, and one anonymous; one by Carew in run-on couplets; one by Waller in lyric measure; one by Wintour Grant in heroic quatrain; and one in triplets by Sidney Godolphin. And finally, there is another poem by Falkland prefixed to <u>Christ's Passion.</u>

Of these thirteen poems, the most important are the three by Falkland, the first of seventy-four couplets written by 1636, the second twenty-two couplets written by 1638, the third of fifty-four written in 1639 or 1640, one hundred and fifty couplets in all. They are bold, vigorous, and artistically mature work. Their balance and contrast are much less simple than the rhetoric in most of the work we have been looking at with the exception of Jonson; they are the incisive instrument of definition. As compared with the 6-11 per cent in Drayton, about 50 per cent of his lines show counter-pattern; and there is a continuous forward movement of the verses. He is free of his pattern.

First as to the formal outlines of his couplet. In the whole body of verse, 82 per cent of the couplets are end-stopped. In the first 104 lines of the poem on the Psalms, [83] 90.4 per cent of the couplets are closed, 51.9 per cent of the first lines are closed, 62.5 per cent of the lines have caesuras, and 52.9 per cent medial caesuras. But the figures, once more, reveal little. We must look at the deeper aspects of form to see the true power of Falkland's verse. Let us note first the terse energy of the expression, the tough, condensed, penetrating wit of the images, to which line and couplet frame add cleanliness of outline.

> And need I say more than my thoughts indite,
> Nothing were easier then not to write;
> . . . .
>
> And more a wonder, scorns at large to show
> What were indifferent if true or no:
> . . . .
>
> Doth each land's laws, belief, beginnings show;
> Which of the natives but the curious know:
> . . . .

> What state than theirs can more unhappy be,
> Threaten'd with hell, and sure of poverty?
> . . . .
>
> Business and war, ill midwives to produce
> The happy offspring of so sweet a Muse:

The energetic condensed definition flashes upon us in balance and contrast in line after line. The variety in forms of these balances and contrasts is remarkable, and all are clear-cut and sure. Amid the variety, certain types are repeated, as the line with complete parallel of syntax marked by repetition of words and scored by medial caesura.

> Where Theseus govern'd, and where Plato taught;
> . . . .
>
> Owes all her arts and her civility,
> . . . .
>
> Whom the west damns, and whom the east devours.
> . . . .
>
> . .   whatsoever most they raise
> In private, that they most in throngs dispraise.

This complete balance of syntax is varied, as in the last example, by the form in which the contrast is suspended in the whole couplet, instead of being equally poised in two half-lines, a form which is strengthened by focusing the antithesis in the two rhyme words; and again in other cases it is varied by stating the contrast in two brief elements pivoting sharply around a grammatical center.

> Their fortunes not more slavish than their souls
> . . . .
>
> Though scarce a part; yet to be all doth claim
> . . . .
>
> Or thinks it fit we should not leave obtain
> To learn with pleasure what we act with pain.

THE DEVELOPMENT OF THE HEROIC COUPLET

The modes are so varied that instead of a sense of monotony
arising from the oft-repeated balance and contrast, there springs
up a sense of design that gives forward movement. Just as great
verse must always suggest its pattern, yet avoid rigidity, so it
is manifest as we read over these illustrations that a rhetoric
of this sort, which is to give intellectual order and not a mere
formal verbal pattern, must likewise have constant design moving in constant variety.

Besides this variation of parallelism, another source of continuous movement in Falkland is the way in which the second
line grows out of the first and often completes the contrast begun by it, yet does this without blurring the independent terse
vigor of each separate line. Thus,

> We know that town is but with fishers fraught
> Where Theseus governed and where Plato taught.
> . . . .
> Lie now distress'd between two enemy pow'rs
> Whom the west damns and whom the east devours.

> What state than theirs can more unhappy be,
> Threaten'd with hell and sure of poverty?

Contrast between line and line is present in illustrations already
given. Falkland makes each individual phrase, half-line, or line,
terse and finished and yet constructs each with a periodic forward drive to the larger unit of line or couplet. So too he has
the art of finished and epigrammatic couplets which, however,
in their turn do not break the whole apart into two-line units of
thought, but are integral elements in a larger whole. The balance and contrast building steadily up to larger units of thought
are well illustrated in the following passages:

> That spring of knowledge to which Italy
> Owes all her arts and her civility,
> In vice and barbarism supinely rolls,
> Their fortunes not more slavish than their souls.

> Next Ovid called me; which, though I admire
> For equalling the author's quick'ning fire,
> And his pure phrase; yet more, remem'bring it
> Was by a mind so much distracted writ:
> Business and war, ill mid-wives to produce
> The happy offspring of so sweet a muse:

In the second passage it is interesting to note how the couplet is, for the moment, lost, but how the general pattern is sustained by the half-line movement, and how this form of variation adds to the forward drive. Another interesting example of the same movement is found in the following from the lines prefatory to <u>Christ's Passion</u>. [84]

> Ulysses, if we trust the <u>Grecian</u> song,
> Travell'd not far, but was a prisoner long,
> To that by tempest forc'd; nor did his voice
> Relate his fate: his travels were his choice,
> All all these numerous realms, return'd again,
> Anew he travell'd over with his pen,

In melodic handling Falkland shows the same power. The secondary patterns which we have seen in Drayton and Sandys, present in them, however, infrequently and uncertainly, are in him sustained and sure. A few types of pattern will illustrate this. For suppressed beat giving metrical balance to parallel elements,

> * ´ * ´ * (*) * ´ * ´
> A lofty poet and a deep divine
>
> * ´ * ´ * (*) * ´ * ´
> Correct an author and uphold a state[85]
>
> * ´ * ´ * (*) * ´ * ´
> To learn with p̲leasure what we act with p̲ain [86]
>
> * ´ * ´ * (*) * ´ * ´
> The happy offspring of so sweet a muse[87]

It will be noted here and anywhere that we look that Falkland's repetition is close enough to make constant pattern and yet not exact enough to dull pattern to monotony.

> ´ * ´ * ´ * ´
> learn with p̲leasure   act with p̲ain
>
> * ´ * ´ * * ´ * ´
> Where Theseus govern'd where Plato taught

A slight shift to secure clustered beat is also well handled by him.

> ` ´ \* ´ \* \* ´ ´ \* `
> Sharp-sighted Envy and blind Ignorance:
>
> * * ´ * ´ *
> The small beginning of the Turkish Kings,
>
> * * ´ ´
> And their large growth, show us that diff'rent things[88]

Common is the trochaic inversion in the first place by virtue
of which both the balanced elements start with a strong beat

> Nothing were easier than not to write
>
> Threat'nd with hell and sure of poverty[89]
>   2   1   1   1   1   3

In the last example the variety secured both in the phrase as a
whole and between word-rhythms in the two balanced elements
is notable. Finally, Falkland uses rhyme very pithily, a fact
which needs no further illustration than that supplied in the couplets already quoted. Each of these devices gains firmness and
interest because while some one of them is always present, they
are yet constantly varied and juxtaposed in new ways. The reader may refer to almost any continous passage to illustrate this
fact more fully. In sum, Falkland has less smoothness than
Waller or than Denham, but he has both in basic pattern and in
secondary-pattern a full and unflagging hold of the closed couplet design and of the integration of its rhetoric and music, and
rapid energy and freedom.

The other commendatory couplets, though they have not so
much to say as Falkland, or anything like his firm mastery of
design, show that the essential form of the reflective couplet is
well established by this date. The first, unsigned, lines upon
Job have less vigor and variety than Falkland's verse but the
use of balance, of line and half-line units, of counter-pattern,
is clearly established, as a few lines will show.

> Even I (no yielding matter) who till then
> Am chief of sinners and the worst of men,
> (Though it be hard a soul's health to procure,
> Unless the patient do assist the cure)
> Suffer a rape by virtue, whilst thy lines
> Destroy my old, and build me new designs. [90]

King's couplets have many more run-on lines and much less
definite neatness in balance and contrast than these. They often,
when they come close to the characteristic couplet rhetoric, yet
just miss or just refrain from it. But it is evident that they tend
to clothe their clear-cut distinctness of definition in neat rhetorical and metrical patterns.

> Or in this service that 'twas my intent
> T' exclude your person from your argument.
>
> . . . .
>
> Whose choice acquits you from the common sin
> Of such who finish worse than they begin.[91]

Dudley Digges has not distinction, but in him too the formed
couplet of Falkland is seen to be well established. Of his twenty
couplets, sixteen are closed and almost all have balance and
contrast, for which they often employ the epigrammatic single
stopped line and frequently the half-line, half-line balance. He
has less variety of detail of pattern within the couplet than Falkland and less strength in the whole because many lines lack distinctive form. He also lacks continuity. But where his thought
is clearly focused and succinct it falls into just such couplets
and lines as we have been describing.

Francis Wiatt also writes in closed couplets. He is less succinct even than Digges, and to secure the couplet he sometimes
slurs his syntax.

> Thy living works since oft have pass'd the test,
> And every last (to wonder) prov'd the best.[92]

He also rarely succeeds in single epigrammatic lines. Metrically he is characterless, and not either smooth or strong. But,
once more, it is clear that he aims throughout at the couplet we
have defined, and the passages which strike us as strongest are
those in which he achieves it.

Henry Rainsford's eighteen lines are the last in closed couplets with balance and antithesis. They are, however, hardly reflective verse, but merely an argument of the volume. Being
such, it is notable that they too are invaded by balance and antithesis.[93]

3. WALLER AND DENHAM

Of Waller we may take the St. Andrews lines, the Buckingham
lines, the lines on St. Paul's, To Penshurst, and the Cromwell
panegyric as representative of Waller both in the type of subject
for which they were used and in his style from its beginning till
the time it had reached its maturity and was widely enough known
to exert its full influence. Denham is adequately represented by
Cooper's Hill, his chief work, and that in which he had most to

say. Waller's "smoothness" is on the whole an evenness of tension beyond what we have seen in any one else. Floating on the level surface of this, his rhetorical and musical patterns are the perfection and systematization of the basically simple and formal units created by Fairfax and Sandys. His development is the progress of this systematization until the whole ground is filled with design. In his mature work, as in Falkland's verse, 50 per cent of the lines have perfected counter-pattern. His basic line rhythm is smooth and even. For counter-pattern he depends principally on the play of line, half-line, couplet, with the variation of melody found in the varied length and phrasing of half-lines, a variation produced by the shifting caesura, together with the indivisibility of the line into two equal halves, which causes the two-beat half to play against the three beat. Some slight further musical pattern results from the increased emphasis upon the balanced words. More subtle melodic phrasing and variation than this are rare. Musically, Waller has nothing like the scope and force of design of Falkland. In rhetorical design he is somewhat richer and more varied than in metrical mode, but still he is monotonous and has nothing like the fecundity and range of Falkland. Of Jonson's neat and flexible phrase he seems to have learned much; of his boldness and scope nothing. Of Falkland's secret of perfectly establishing the closed couplet in the reader's ear and then varying this basic unit itself while still suggesting it firmly in the half-lines, he is not possessed. The secret is Denham's. So much of Denham's mature work in Cooper's Hill is descriptive or narrative that percentage figures are not useful. In the sententious and reflective passages the classical couplet in both music and syntax strides forward on the bold and keen-edged lines laid down by Jonson and Falkland. He is "strong" because more subtle and more free than Waller.

The first three of Waller's poems may be grouped together without much differentiation. Their oft-noted smoothness is dependent first upon the almost constant repetition of the twenty-syllable unit in the closed couplet, and upon the prevalent repetition of the half-line pattern with medial caesura (an element present also in Drayton and Sandys, and typical of Jonson and Falkland) and upon the flexible syllabization[94] and the little variation in stress. All this is sustained in a way not quite found in any previous case we have been considering, by the unemphatic, direct, smooth-flowing, conversational ease of the expression, deliberate and perfectly neatly defined, which makes every word duly weighty, though it prevents any word from attaining a thrilling emphasis. This type of expression is truly the base in which the color of the melody is mixed. More condensation of feeling, more rapidity of movement from concept to concept, would create points of energy in the rhetoric which must sweep the music with them. But Waller's music has no such impetuosity. It finds its emphasis rather in the just neatness of its analysis. And this in turn seeks its own becoming decoration in metrical patterns which are low-pitched, but very neat and definite. The perceptions, which are without emotional shade or complexity, fall into simply moulded syntax that easily leaves neat, balanced centers of thought to form the centers of interest in line and half-line. Indeed, in these three poems on the whole the balances and antitheses are as simple in expression and in musical pattern as those of Sandys and Drayton, though the effect is stronger because more sustained.

> He rent the crown / from vanquished Henry's head,
> Raised the White Rose, / and trampled on the Red;
> Till love, / triumphing o'er the victor's pride,
> Brought Mars and Warrick / to the conquered side;
> . . . .
> Proud with the burden / of so brave a charge,
> . . . .
> These surges ruin, / those our safety bring.
> . . . .
> But that their wonder / did divert their care. [95]
>
> At once it threatens / and obliges Heaven!
> . . . .
> To frame no new church, / but the old refine; [96]

A very common form of rhetoric is the mere verbal balance we have already noted in Sandys and Fairfax. This is the line built on two centers in the double-substantive-adjective.

> With the sweet sound of this harmonious lay
> . . . .
> On the smooth back of silver Thames to ride
> . . . .
> The hated relics of confounded Troy;
> . . . .
> And dear remembrance of that fatal glance, [97]

These simple turns are much more common in the St. Andrew's lines than in the other two. The reader will observe how the last two examples emphasize thought and structure by the suppressed beat. Metrical variation is, however, rare in these early poems. The whole tone is so low-pitched that the balance itself rises to the force of emphasis, as a bit of red paint here and there might pick out certain lines in a set of smooth silver whorls without adding any new element of form. The lines which are balanced stand out distinctly, but on the whole the lines do not form notable units, and most of the couplets are closed by sheer pause for intellectual breath, rather than by an organic structure. Then too the couplets stand apart and rarely build up a continuous effect of style, though the narrative moves forward with ease.

The lines to Penshurst are less reflective in substance than these first three and more pensive. Yet in these lines the style is more terse, and Waller builds a simple but definitive syntactic structure more organically constructed on the pattern of half-line, line, and couplet than in the earlier poems. For this reason he is also able to mass his units to a larger whole.

> a) While in the park I sing, b) the listening deer
> c) Attend my passion, and forget to fear.
> a) When to the beeches I report my flame,
> b) They c) bow their heads, as if they felt the same.
> b) To gods appealing, a) when I reach their bowers
>   With loud complaints, c) they answer me in showers.
>   To thee a wild and cruel soul is given,
>   More deaf than trees, and prouder than the heaven![98]

Numbers "a," "b," and "c" suggest the repeated elements in the first three couplets and their variation. In the third couplet there is also a parallelism of elements between the two first half-lines and the two second. Couplet four catches up and applies the ideas of the first three, thereby securing forward movement; further, it emphasizes the fact that it gathers up the meaning, in that it makes an explicit statement of the parallelism which the other lines only suggest, and shapes this statement to an epigram. As to musical pattern, the first six lines have half-line movement with the caesura varied in position to 6, 5, 5, 4, 5, 4. Line 2 creates secondary-pattern by the suppressed beat between the parallel units. Then in couplet 4, the unbroken first line, with its double key-elements in the center, <u>wild</u> and

cruel, forms a pattern with the emphatic half-lines of the second line into which the key thought spreads. Line 8 sets syntactical variation against metrical variation in repetition.

$$\overline{\text{More deaf than trees}}\ \text{and}\ \overline{\text{prouder than the heaven}}!$$
$$\quad 1 \quad\ 1 \qquad 1 \qquad\qquad\quad 2 \qquad\quad 1 \qquad 2$$

This is richer in design and ampler in movement than anything
in the earlier three poems.

In The battle of the Summer Islands Waller exploits to the
full this ampler skill. The lines and half-lines are distinct units,
and there is much cross-patterning between the lines. Lines 31
and 32 of Canto I offer an interesting example of variation worked
up into greater complexity of pattern.

> Such is the mould, that the blest tenant feeds
> On precious fruits, and pays his rent in weeds. [99]

Here for repetition the order of balanced parts in verb, preposition, object is repeated, but for variation the rhyme falls first
on part "a" and then on part "c," thus giving an effect of trans-
position which is further enlarged by syllabic weight.

$$\quad\ a \quad\ b \qquad\quad c \qquad\qquad\quad a \qquad\quad b \quad\ c$$
$$\text{feeds on}\ \overline{\text{precious fruit}};\ \overline{\text{pays his rent}}\ \text{in weeds}$$
$$\quad\ 1 \quad\ 1 \qquad\quad 3 \qquad\qquad\quad 3 \qquad\quad 1 \quad\ 1$$

In general by inversion and by other kindred sharpenings of outline, Waller in this poem achieves more strength and variation
of the sort we find in Falkland. Lines 42-45 will give a further
example.

> Ripe fruits and blossoms on the same trees live;
> At once they promise what at once they give.
> So sweet the air, so moderate the clime,
> None sickly lives, or dies before his time.

The chief technical metrical variation is the suppressed beat
falling after caesura and compensated by caesural pause, which
leaves the parallel elements very distinct, or which in one case
moulds a phrase into an organic unit by leaving the first and
last beats very emphatic.

236

The prince of trees! is fuel to their fires;[100]

But in the sixteen typical lines beginning "Bermuda walled with rocks," there are only three instances of this variation. In the same lines there are two examples of the trochaic first beat, one example of trochaic beat after caesura, and one instance of suspended beat in line 10.

On the rich shore, of ambergris is found.

This last seems to strengthen the effect of the suspended rhetoric. These metrical variations altogether are of the sort used by Drayton and Sandys and established by Falkland. They are less frequent than in Falkland, and hence they give to the whole less sustained energy of design, but they are handled very deftly and neatly.

The Cromwell poem is more vigorously reflective in substance than any of the other poems of Waller we are considering except the St. Andrews lines, and also stronger in style and music. It is almost wholly in end-stopped couplets, an effect greatly sharpened by the quatrain arrangement with full period at the end of every quatrain but one; the lines, too, are very sharply closed, and the medial caesura a fixed rule; the table on page 220, indicating caesura in 66 per cent of the lines, takes account only of very heavy pauses; there is some pause in practically every line, usually medial. In mode of development the definition proceeds almost wholly in terms of moral sentiment and epigram, and there is hardly a line without balance or balance and contrast. These devices are artfully used to give the forward movement sometimes lacking in Waller's earlier work. The two couplets of the quatrain are integrated; the first may give a figure which is applied in the second, or the second expands and particularizes a general truth stated in the first. The dance of the balanced phrases of repetition is varied by cross-patterning between phrases and from line to line.

> a, 1) Your drooping country 2) torn with civil hate,
> b, 1) Restored by you, 2) is made a glorious state;
> c, 1) The seat of empire, 2) where the Irish come,
> d, 1) And the unwilling Scotch, 2) to fetch their doom.[101]

Here line "a" parallels line "b" as a whole. Half-line "a, 2" explains "a, 1," "b, 2" explains "b, 1"; but "a, 2" also crosses to "b, 1" and "b, 2" crosses to "a, 1." "C, 1" as an appositive gathers up "b, 2." Then the cross-patterning of idea is repeated between "c, 1" and "d, 2,"'and "c, 2" and "d, 1."

The influence of Waller and Denham, as Mr. T. H. Banks points out in his edition of Denham, [102] was interactive. To this interaction, as we have seen, should be added that of other poets writing contemporaneously. Denham's style, like Waller's, was a gradual growth. Mr. Banks states[103] that the original version (1636) of Denham's Virgil abounds in run-on lines. One example which he cites indicates how the development of the closed couplet and of the antithetic rhetoric went hand in hand. "Timeo Danaos et dona ferentes" was translated in 1636, "The Grecians most when bringing gifts I fear." But in 1653 this was revised to, "Their swords less danger carry than their gifts." Cooper's Hill was written in 1643, although the famous Thames lines were not added until 1655. [104] But Denham's manner is pretty well formed in even the early version of On the Earl of Strafford's Tryal and Death though less chiseled than later. [105] If, as seems natural, we may suppose that poem written just after the event in 1641, Denham had the technique in hand by 1641.

To examine Cooper's Hill in some detail we may select a few outstanding passages, lines 1-88, lines 125-134, and the Thames lines. [106] He has more run-on lines than Waller, not because of less fixity of aim and method but because he is, like Falkland, more free of his technique. The half-line is the basic unit of design, through which the couplet may be always suggested so that it may also be formally broken. We have noted in Waller the occasional play of an unbroken line against a line with two sharply marked halves. Denham sometimes extends this form to give the unbroken line effect in the end of one line and the beginning of the next, [107] instead of line by line, an effect used twice in the first lines.

> Which did never dream
> Upon Parnassus, // Nor did tast the stream
> Of Helicon; //

The effect is the stronger because the two syncopated lines (end-stopped, if I may use the phrase) are themselves balanced; and yet we feel the basic original pattern very distinctly because the two rhyme words, the true line ends, are strongly emphasized in being the centers of the balanced phrases. Line 7 is again run on. Here the parallel structure bridges the line, but a new

metrical parallelism in a new stopped line effect, arises in the
two tetrameter units thus created.

> Parnassus stands; // if I can be to thee
> A Poet, // thou Parnassus art to me.

The variety is carried further by inversion. Lines 11 and 12
have more regularized balance, but 11 in the two halves, 12
within the second half. Such variation in the particular form of
balance is common, although simple half-line parallelism is
also frequent. Of further melodic phrase, we find in the parallel

          *   ´ *   ´ * ´

phrases Upon Parnassus and in Helicon reversal of metrical
pattern in the two names thus balanced. In lines 4 and 5 there is
inversion; in 4 suppressed beat and repeated-varied pattern;
and in 5, repeated-varied pattern:

     ´   *   * ´ *   *   ´ *   ´
> Those made not Poets, but the Poets those,

   * *   ´   ´   *   ´   *   ´   *   ´
> And as Courts make not Kings, but Kings the Court

                                           ´   *   ´

In 11 the parallel repeats the pattern exactly, untrac't ways,

   ´   ´

and aery paths; but 12, continuing the same parallel, varies the

       *   ´ *   * ´

phrase, in my fancy: than my eye.
     Lines 125-134 are more regular in their form of balance, with
almost exact balance in lines 128, 129, 130, 132, 134, strengthened by alliteration; yet with caesura and varied stress, no two
lines are alike. Line 130 emphasizes the antithesis by the suppressed medial beat and the repeated initial heavy beat in both
phrases, and then introduces variation by the alliteration in-
verted from adjective to noun, an alliteration which further
marks off the beginning and end of the phrase and ties together
what other devices have separated.
     I would not rashly endeavor to explain the secret of the
Thames lines where Dryden refrained. Yet certain points are
worth noting. In line 190 the two balanced elements are set off
by the suppressed beat and the secondary stress.

       *   ´ * ´   * // (*) * `   *   ´
> My great example, as it is my theme

Lines 190 and 192 have sharp caesuras and distinctly molded

half-lines; line 191, set between these, doubles the effect by four almost distinct quarter-lines.

> Though deep, // yet clear; // though gentle // yet not dull

Lines 191 and 192 both contain two balanced halves within which there is again balanced antithesis; but in this reiterated design, 191 repeats syntax exactly, 192 inverts it. The lines are also rich in metrical variety. In 191 the second half-line repeats the pattern of the first but doubles the proportion,

$$\acute{\ }\quad *\quad \acute{\ }\quad \acute{\ }\quad *\quad \grave{\ }\quad *\quad \acute{\ }$$

deep yet clear   gentle yet not dull
$\overline{1}$ 1   2 $\overline{2}$

and binds the whole together by initial-final alliteration; 192 offers the same kind of repetition with variation, but dies down to the smaller pattern where 191 rises to the larger.

$$\acute{\ }\quad *\quad *\quad \acute{\ }\quad (*\quad *\quad *)\quad \acute{\ }\quad *\quad \acute{\ }$$

Strong without rage, without o'erflowing full

Put the two lines together, and you get a swelling and receding wave.

$$(*)\ \acute{\ }\ *\ \acute{\ }\ /\ (*)\ \grave{\ }\ *\ \grave{\ }\ *\ \grave{\ }$$
$$\acute{\ }\ *\ *\ \acute{\ }\ /\ (*\ *\ *)\ \grave{\ }\ *\ \grave{\ }$$

Denham's substance and expression have more boldness and edge than Waller's. A similar sweep is given to his form, too, by these devices and elements of form, although in truth they do not explain his music any more than a course in harmony accounts for Purcell.

One more little collection of occasional verse written at about the same date will show, finally, how widely the couplet had established itself by this time. In 1646, the year after Waller's first volume, and between the two versions of Cooper's Hill, appeared Men-miracles with other Poemes by M. LL. St. of Ch.Ch. in Oxon.[108] Lluelyn's chief power in this sort of verse lies in the intellectual vigor of his condensed definitions and sententious observations, and his form accordingly is fittingly that of the couplet we have now defined, with balance and contrast built on the two halves of the divided line, and with frequent metrical shift that gives emphasis to the essential point of the analysis. The best lines are perhaps these from the Elegie on the Death of Sir Horatio Vere.

> Valour's not borne of Nature, but the Will,
> They only conquer that with Judgement kill.
> . . . .
> The mind, not the tough flesh was his defence,
> He lost the feare of Wounds, but not the Sence;[109]

They show maturity in the variety with which they use the formula. Another interesting example is his Elegie. On the death of Master H. C.

> As Clouds of Incense 'bove the Altars come,
> Yet all those Clouds lay treasur'd up ith' Gumme.
> . . . .
> So was thy life, it might gaine breadth, and rise,
> And purchase more Extent, but not more prise.
> Good parts in Youth and Manhood are the same,
> They're the same Picture in a smaller frame.[110]

Metaphysical in its analysis of its thought through scientific image, this poem is in form classical; epigrammatic and terse in statement, with balance and contrast as its instruments of definition, phrased in closed couplets.

The work which accompanies Lluelyn's verse shows even more emphatically how widely the couplet was established. His poems were introduced, as was customary, by sets of complimentary verse, seven in number, from his friends, men unknown to us, and presumably very minor authors. Of these seven poems, five are in closed couplets. One, by J. F., is so assured in its form that it is worth illustrating at some length. Indeed, one wonders whether Denham had not seen it between 1642 and 1655.

> A poet's then exact in every part
> That is borne one from Nature, nurst by Art.
> Whose happy mixture both of skill and fate,
> Makes the most suddaine thought Elaborate.
> Whose easie straines a flowing sense doth fit,
> Unforc'd expression, and unravisht wit.
> Words Fill'd with equall subject such as brings
> To chosen Language high and chosen Things.
> Harsh reason cleare as day, as smooth as steepe.
> Glide here like Rivers, even still though deepe.
> . . . .

> Those wretched soules, whose Cold and Hunger writes,
> That in their Inke-hornes weare their Appetites.
> Whose labours still ride Post, and for their Toile,
> Receive the Hackney hire, a groate a Mile. [111]

This verse lacks even tension between unstressed syllable and
beat; but it is terse and pungent, and it uses line and medial
pause and pithy rhyme very effectively to give sharp emphasis
to its balance and contrast. The placing of the pause is, too,
skilfully varied. It is classical, also, in the force given to each
syllable by the terse beat of the half-line units in the couplet.
Note particularly the sixth couplet of those cited. This musical
definiteness is as apparent as the weight of meaning given to
each word by the epigrammatic compression. Then both in this
couplet and in the following one, the way in which the second
line grows out of the first into a stinging lash-tip is remarkable.
And this effect again is dependent on the condensed definiteness
of the couplet form with its neat regular parts tied together in
organic formality. As was plain in Waller, the inevitable rhetorical weight of the words, too, in such a style focuses the
sharpest beat of the music on the balancing elements. This work
of an unknown J. F. in 1646, thus, at its best, contemporaneously with the mature work of Waller and Denham, speaks with almost the weight of Dryden; speaks so chiefly as the result of a
steady process of growth since Tottel's Miscellany, through the
mastered technique of the didactic and satiric couplet.
  I put down my pen to read with a class the close of Lycidas.

> In solemn troops, and sweet Societies
> That sing, and singing in their glory move,...

The difference here is not that between skilled poets and a supreme musician. Nor is it merely one of technique. It is a difference of modes, of the fundamental nature of the experience
aimed at. Melodic phrasing in verse is, in the very nature of
the case, conditioned by syntactic development; but even if we
could secure with the terse and formalized epigram of this poetry the liquid flow of Milton's music, or with the Miltonic period,
the neat tunes of Waller, we should experience from the result
a psychological confusion. The effects which we have described
sprang from no mere loss of skill or failure of musical ideas.
Even those who feel most keenly the narrowing of horizons, and
the loss of emotional power in the music of this period will feel,

too, that the new expression and the new metrical form have as much an organic imaginative harmony with the substance they embody as has the sublimity of Milton's music with his vision. The Greeks, with their lucid sense of fact, recognized, without explaining, the absolutely fundamental differences in aesthetic and ethical effect of the several modes of music. So here we see the formal mode changing with the change in spirit. It was because they were artists that these craftsmen strove, consciously and unconsciously, as they formed a new standard of expression, to create new metrical designs both technically realizable within the new medium and aesthetically harmonious with its meaning.

NOTES

1   See G. P. Shannon, "Nicholas Grimald's Heroic Couplet and the Latin Elegiac distich," P M L A, XLV (1930). 532-542. My quotations follow the text of Hyder Rollins.

2   See C. E. Knowlton, "The origin of the Closed Couplet in English," The Nation, XCIX (July 30, 1914), 134. Professor H. B. Lathrop, of the University of Wisconsin, has pointed out to me also how closely Marlowe's couplets preserve the couplet units of his original.

3   See J. S. P. Tatlock, "The Origin of the Closed Couplet in England," The Nation, XCVIII (April 9, 1914) 390 and A. M. Clark, "Thomas Heywood's Art of Love Lost and Found," The Library, Fourth Series, III, 210-222; Transactions of the Bibliographical Society, Second Series, III (1923).

4   See Knowlton, op. cit.

5   See Tatlock, op. cit., — I do not know of any discussion of the elegiac distich as found in the Greek and Latin and neo-Latin epigrams upon the form of the English epigram in pentameter as a whole, and then more particularly in the work of Ben Jonson, and from his time on through the first half of the seventeenth century. But that influence is obviously very great.

6   For valuable tables and comparisons with other poets, see Shannon's article.

7   See the articles already cited, especially Shannon's and Tatlock's. Shannon points out, on the distich as a model for the

couplet, that half of the hexameters and all the pentameters in the lines from which Grimald translates end in monosyllables or dissyllables, and the pentameter, moreover, gives a strong analogy for the masculine ending.

8 In both instances the italicized adjectives are in Grimald's originals, as Shannon notes.

9 The importance of certain men and works has been so widely noted, in general terms, in the commentaries, that I cite no individual comments unless they have suggested particular points.

10 P M L A, XIII (1898), 221-249.

11 Ibid., p. 237. — The article is full of valuable tables and of essential definitions.

12 Michaell Draiton, Esquire, Poems, Printed for the Spenser Society (Manchester, 1888), Part I, p. 170.

13 Idem.

14 Idem.

15 Ibid., p. 178.

16 Ibid., p. 204.

17 Paull Franklin Baum, The Principles of English Versification. (Cambridge, 1924), pp. 18-19. — As Professor Schelling reminds me, syncopation as used by Mr. Baum is not syncopation in the strict musical sense; and I shall, accordingly, in referring to this aspect of verse use the term counter-pattern or secondary-pattern.

18 For example:
                          Wherefore do I assume
These royalties, // and not refuse to reign,
Refusing to accept as great a share
Of hazard as of honour, due alike
To him who reigns, // and so much to him due
Of hazard more, // as he above the rest
High honour'd sits ?// Go therefor mighty Powers,
Terror of Heav'n, // though fall'n;// intend at home,
While here shall be our home, // what best may ease
The present misery, // and render Hell
More Tolerable://   (P. L. 2, 450 et seq.)

Johannes C. Andersen, The Laws of Verse (Cambridge, 1928), p. 122.

19   Op. cit., p. 198.

20   Any previous study that I have seen has merely noted the statement of Waller and referred to the epigrammatic nature of some of Fairfax's concluding couplets.

21   Edward Fairfax, Jerusalem Delivered, ed. Henry Morley, Revised edition (London, n.d.) p. 17.

22   Ibid., p. 3.

23   For so general a comparison as this, the question of variations in Tasso's text and of the relation of Fairfax's work to them seems unimportant.

24   Torquato Tasso Gerusalemme Liberata (Opere, v. 2) a cura di Luigi Bontigli (Bari, 1930), Canto I, stz. 22, p. 6.

25   Fairfax, Jerusalem Delivered, Canto I, stz. 22, p. 6.

26   Tasso, Canto I, stz. 26, l. 3.

27   Ibid., Canto I, stz. 50, l. 6.

28   Ibid., Canto I, stz. 53, l. 6.

29   Fairfax, Canto I, stz. 26, l. 3.

30   Ibid., Canto I, stz., 50, l. 6.

31   Ibid., Canto I, stz. 53, l. 6.

32   Tasso and Fairfax, Canto I, stz. 42, l. 5.

33   Ibid., Canto I, stz. 45. ll. 3-4.

34   Ibid., Canto I, stz. 64, ll. 6-8.

35   See p. 211.

36   Fairfax, Canto I, stz. 12, l. 6.

37   Ibid., stz. 16, l. 6.

38   Ibid., stz. 35, 1. 8.

39   Ibid., stz. 60, 1. 8.

40   Ibid., stz. 42, 1. 6.

41   Ibid., stz. 45, 1. 4.

42   Ibid., stz. 50, 1. 6.

43   See the whole seventeenth-century discussion of the theory of paraphrase in translation and the many works which are distinctly conceived of and titled paraphrases.

44   G. de Saluste, Sr. Du Bartas, Les OEuvres Poetiques et Chrestiennes, (à Geneve; M. DC. XXXII.), p. 31.

45   Du Bartas. His Devine Weekes and Workes Translated: ... by Joshua Sylvester. Now thirdly corrected and augm. (London, 1611), p. 24.

46   Torquato Tasso, Le Rime, a cura di Angelo Solerti (Bologna, 1898), II, 439.

47   William Drummond of Hawthornden, The Poetical Works, with a Cypresse Grove, ed. L. E. Kastner (Edinburgh and London, 1913), I, 30.

48   Giambattista Marino, Poesie Varie, a cura di Benedetto Croce (Bari, 1913), p. 104.

49   Drummond, op. cit., I, 7. – I have considered the effects of these tendencies in the work of Drummond in an article on Drummond of Hawthornden, P M L A, XLVIII, 1090-1107.

50   Quoted by Professor Schelling from Discoveries, ed. Schelling, p. 28.

51   Ben Jonson, Poems (London, 1910), p. 294. – Italics in quotation are mine.

52   Ibid., p. 398.

53   On the dates of Sandys's Ovid, see George Sandys, The Poetical Works, with an Introduction and Notes by the Rev. Richard Hooper (London, 1872) I, xxvii.

54   Ibid., Introduction, p. xxxiv.

55   Edmund Waller, The Poems, ed. G. Thorn Drury (London, n.d.), Intro. p. lxxiv.

56   Henry Wood, "The Beginning of the Classical Heroic Couplet," A J P, XI (1890), 554-579.

57   Raymond M. Alden, English Verse (New York) 1903, p. 187.

58   Ovid, Metamorphoses, with an English Translation by Frank Justus Miller (London and New York, 1916), Book I, ll. 57-62, 6.

59   Ovid's Metamorphosis. Englished Mythologiz'd and Represented in figures by G. S. (Oxford, 1632), p. 3. – The italics are mine.

60   Ovid, op. cit., ll. 40-43, p. 4.

61   Sandys, op. cit., p. 3.

62   Ovid, op. cit., ll. 17-20. p. 2.

63   Sandys, op. cit., p. 3.

64   Ovid, op. cit., ll. 11-12, p. 2.

65   Sandys, op. cit., p. 3. – Italics mine.

66   Ovid, op. cit., p. 4. – Italics and figures mine.

67   Sandys, op. cit., p. 3. – Italics mine.

68   Ovid, op. cit., ll. 34-35, p. 4.

69   Sandys, op. cit., p. 3.

70   Ovid, op. cit., ll. 452-453, 456-457, 464-465, 488-489, pp. 34 and 36.

71   Sandys, op. cit., pp. 10-11.

72   Ibid., p. 3.

73   Sandys, ed. Hooper, Vol. I, A Paraphrase upon Job, Chap. II, p. 2.

74   Idem. Italics in these quotations mine.

75 Idem.

76 Ibid., Chap. II, p. 6.

77 Ibid., Chap. III, p. 8.

78 Ibid., Chap. I, p. 1.

79 Ibid., p. 2. — The double-adjective-substantive line is in itself no new thing; indeed it is common in Spenser. It is differentiated here, however, both by substance and form. Spenser's adjectives are either directly sensuous adjectives or qualifying adjectives of sentiment, in either case wrought into his picture as a whole. These adjectives, on the other hand, incline to become words of intellectual or sententious definition, or in some cases hardly more than empty adjectives or fillers. And on the formal side, the end-stopped line, and even more when it is joined with the medial caesura, throws them into a perspective and gives them an insistent balance which they did not have in the run-on line of Spenser.

80 Ibid., p. 1.

81 Idem.

82 Sandys, Ovid, etc., "A Panegyricke to the King."

83 Falkland, "To my noble Friend, Mr. George Sandys, upon his Excellent Paraphrase of the Psalms," in Sandys, ed. Hooper, I, 83-87.

84 Falkland, "To the Author," in Sandys, ed. Hooper, II, 412-415.

85 Falkland, "To My Noble Friend, Mr. George Sandys," Ibid., I, 83-87.

86 Idem.

87 Idem.

88 Idem.

89 Idem.

90 "To my noble Friend Mr. Sandys, Upon His Job ...," in Sandys, ed. Hooper, pp. lxxxv-lxxxviii.

91 Henry King, "To My Much Honoured Friend Mr. George San-
    dys," ibid., pp. xc-xciv.

92 Francis Wiatt, "To My Honoured Kinsman Mr. George Sandys,
    On His Admirable Paraphrases." ibid., pp. c-ciii.

93 Waller's lines to Sandys are in lyric measure and so they must
    not be compared with the others. But in neat rhetoric, succinct-
    ness, and strong rhymes they surpass all the others except
    Falkland, and in smoothness they excel him. Obviously in mak-
    ing a study of this sort, we must keep to the body of material
    which can be defined in common terms, namely, poems in pen-
    tameter in two line units. But we have seen how much the de-
    velopment of the special and distinctive music of the closed coup-
    let depends upon the formation of a rhetoric lucid in expression,
    and of a verse-system even in texture, and one which uses small
    elements as the basic units of its design. The lyric measures of
    Ben Jonson, Waller, and Sandys may well have been as influen-
    tial upon the metrics of their successors as were their couplets.
    We can here only suggest that a study of this lyric verse must
    form part of any complete history of the heroic couplet in the
    seventeenth century.

94 On this point of flexible syllabization, see the anonymous pre-
    face to the edition of 1690 conveniently available in Alden's
    English Verse. See also the discussion of this preface by Canon
    Beeching in "A Note upon Waller's Distich" in An English Mis-
    cellany Presented to Dr. Furnival (Oxford, 1901), pp. 4-9. Wal-
    ler has, in fact, fewer monosyllables than Spenser, but much
    less variation as to syllabization in successive lines.

95 Waller, op. cit., I, 2, 4, "Of the Danger ..." ll. 15-18; 40;
    72; 78.

96 Ibid., I, 18, "Upon His Majesty's repairing of Paul's," l. 56.

97 Ibid., I, 2-5, "Of the Danger," ll. 34; 62; 88; 101. Italics mine.

98 Ibid., I, 64, "At Penshurst," ll. 1-8. — If the reader wishes to
    see both how far formalization had progressed, and how purely
    formal Waller is, he may compare this with Grimald's "The
    Lover asketh pardon of his dere ..." from Beza (Tottel, ed.
    Rollins, I, 94), which may have been in Waller's memory.

99 Waller, op. cit., I, 66 ff.

100 Ibid., l. 12.

101 Waller, op. cit., I, 10, "Panegyric to My Lord Protector,"
     ll. 13-16.

102 John Denham, Poetical Works, ed. T. H. Banks Jr., (New
     Haven, 1928), p. 35.

103 Ibid., pp. 43-44.

104 Ibid., p. 52.

105 Ibid., p. 153-154.

106 Ibid., pp. 63-87.

107 Compare this with the examples of counter-pattern from Milton
     and Chaucer ante p. 203 and note 11.

108 This M. LL. is Martin Lluelyn. His volume contains among oth-
     er things, ranging from comic folksongs to religious lyrics, a
     number of occasional poems and elegies. Of these the majority
     of the occasional poems and all the elegies are in closed coup-
     lets. It is not remarkable poetry – not at all Lluelyn's greatest –
     but it is firm and clear-cut in movement, and it takes the clas-
     sical couplet for granted.

109 Lluelyn, op. cit., p. 122. – Italics in the original.

110 Ibid., p. 126. – Italics in the original.

111 Ibid., sig. A 5 verso. – Italics in the original.

THE SATIRIC GENRE

A NOTE IN DEFENCE OF SATIRE

Louis I. Bredvold

The purpose of this paper is to reopen the question of the nature of satire and to make some suggestions towards the answer. In the current standard treatises on laughter and the comic spirit satire appears as the least attractive and the least defensible of the many manifestations of the comic spirit, — if, indeed, it can be defended at all. No one cares to champion anything so ignoble and ill-mannered and negative. And it is not difficult to understand why this should be so, in view of the orientation and general tendency of modern theory regarding the nature of the comic. The psychologists and estheticians who have studied laughter and the comic spirit have quite properly insisted that in their "pure" states they are innocent, even though they may be corrective; laughter is related to the play instinct, for instance, and the pure comic spirit is an enjoyable perception of mere incongruity, a free play of the intelligence without malice — as Meredith described it in his classic treatise. But in satire, they observe, the comic spirit is contaminated, if not obscured, by something foreign to its nature; in the place of hearty and wholesome laughter we get the sneer of malignity. Moreover, they derive conclusions distinctly unfavorable to satire from their historical study both of the theories of the comic and of its manifestation in literature. The earlier theories assumed that laughter is derisive or vindictive, and the possibility of neutral or sympathetic laughter is a discovery of modern times. It is a commonplace also to observe that the scope of our humanitarian feelings has been greatly extended even since the Renaissance, and that we consequently no longer laugh at such unfortunates as cripples and idiots; and with this advance in civilization, which no one surely would sacrifice, the derisive laughter of some Renaissance comedy appears vulgar and brutal. Such a reflection naturally makes us rather uneasy regarding the ethics of satire. On the other hand, one of the most charming and civilizing developments in modern feeling is that of humor, which joins sentiment and sympathy with the comic spirit and thus reconciles it

Reprinted by permission from English Literary History, Vol. 7 (1940), pp. 253-264.

with humanitarianism;[1] this is admirable, this keep, the other banish. We can measure our progress against Hobbes' classic statement of the mistaken theory of derisive laughter:

> Sudden glory is the passion which maketh those Grimaces called Laughter, and is caused either by some sudden act of their own, that pleaseth them; or by the apprehension of some deformed thing in another, by comparison whereof they suddenly applaud themselves. And it is incident most to them, that are conscious of the fewest abilities in themselves; who are forced to keep themselves in their own favour, by observing the imperfections of other men. And therefore much laughter at the defects of others, is a signe of Pusillanimity. For of great minds, one of the proper workes is, to help and free others from scorn; and compare themselves onely with the most able. [2]

The modern theorist has an easy triumph over Hobbes, who could not understand the very common phenomenon of innocent laughter nor conceive of the pure comic spirit, and who so dogmatically asserted that all laughter is derisive. But perhaps the modern theorist goes wrong in turn in his assumption that, in the course of his refutation of the derision theory, he has by implication dealt adequately with the nature of satire.

It is evident, however, that the lover of good satire is now put to it to defend his taste; new difficulties have arisen from an important group of historical and theoretical considerations which must in the main be accepted. For, although much great satire can probably be read only with a grave countenance and a pain in the heart, nevertheless all satire is related to laughter through the common element of the comic, and any sound theory of it must be adjusted to our theories of the comic and of laughter. The apologist must accordingly begin by acknowledging that derisive laughter is now regarded as a survival of our earlier barbarism which it is not honorable to cultivate. And if derisive laughter is no longer defensible, how can anyone extenuate the derision of satire, which, being of the same nature, must fall under the same condemnation? It is therefore not surprising that so little attention is given to satire in modern discussions of the comic spirit, and that this little is so unsympathetic.

It may be helpful at this point to sketch in outline the alternatives usually taken by modern theorists of satire. It is not easy, and perhaps sometimes not fair, to reduce their casual and often

paradoxical comments to consistent systems, but it seems possible to distinguish three general types of theories either implicit or explicit in current discussion of the comic; the first
is a direct condemnation of satire, and the second and third,
which attempt to defend it, curiously begin by accepting uncri-
tically the first.

According to the first of our theories, the pleasure we derive from satire may be explained frankly as a perversion of
the emotions, an indulgence in cruelty, a Schadenfreude. Of
course, if satire is a form of sadism, there is little to be said
for it except that it is valuable clinical material for medical
study. This unpleasant theory is not often expounded at length
or pressed to its logical conclusion. It would involve us in the
absurdity of condemning as corrupt a great body of literature
which has been enjoyed by good men in all ages; it would be a
ridiculous indictment of some of the Hebrew prophets and Dr.
Johnson and Burke and Carlyle, as well as of Pope and Swift.
It usually lurks in the background, as an unexamined but indis-
putable axiom, its full enormity covered or softened by considerations of a more edifying character.

For it is the basic concession against which two other current theories attempt to erect the defence that satire is pardonable because it may be the instrument of moral and social reform. These theories begin by subscribing to the psychology of
the Schadenfreude, of the laughter of derision, as the correct
explanation of all shades of satire, from the light and gay to the
malignantly bitter. The cruelty is admitted, but the application
of whips and scorpions, it is added, is a necessary and wholesome corrective; like Hamlet, we must "be cruel only to be
kind." On this fundamental principle one may proceed to vindicate satire in two ways.

A correction may be effected in the victim of the satire. This
seems to be a very general hope, but a vague one, and plausible
only if it is left vague. Although we frequently read about the
satirist standing over the prostrate form of his victim, this picture seldom corresponds to any known historical fact. We have
no evidence that corrupt politicians or hypocrites ever read the
satires directed against them, or that, reading, their hearts
are purified or their habits changed. The mere notion that literary satire accomplishes such a reformation is so preposterous
as to be itself a specimen of the comic, and was so treated by Swift
in a two-edged passage in that prefatory letter by Captain Gulliver
which he added to the Faulkner edition of Gulliver's Travels in 1735:

253

> I do in the next place complain of my own great want
> of judgement, in being prevailed upon by the entreaties
> and false reasonings of you and some others, very much
> against my own opinion, to suffer my travels to be pub-
> lished. Pray bring to your mind how often I desired you
> to consider, when you insisted on the motive of public
> good; that the Yahoos were a species of animals utterly
> incapable of amendment by precepts or examples: and so
> it hath proved; for instead of seeing a full stop put to all
> abuses and corruptions, at least in this little island, as I
> had reason to expect: behold, after above six months warn-
> ing, [3] I cannot learn that my book hath produced one single
> effect according to my intentions.... And it must be owned
> that seven months were a sufficient time to correct every
> vice and folly to which Yahoos are subject, if their natures
> had been capable of the least disposition to virtue or wisdom.

We can all agree, and Swift doubtless would, that satire ought
to accomplish more than it does; but Swift knew better than to
expect in seven months to see "judges learned and honest; plead-
ers upright and modest, with some tincture of common sense;
the young nobility's education entirely changed; the physicians
banished; the female Yahoos abounding in virtue, honour, truth
and good sense," and other such wholesale reforms. He had observed long before that satire is popular because every man applies it to his neighbor.

More credible is the second theory that satire is useful because it stirs up public opinion against malefactors, and thus
prepares the way for effective social action against evils. This
may be called the publicist function of satire. It would be easy
to multiply evidence of its essential truth; revolutionists find
"songs of hate" indispensable for their purpose; political satires, such as Swift's Drapier's Letters, have checked the
courses of governments; poets, novelists, and artists have added momentum to many a great reform movement. But even with
this element of truth in it, this theory is inadequate because it
does not touch the heart of the problem; it is concerned with
accidental effects rather than with the essential nature of satire;
it is not even relevant to much great satire. Only an extraneous
interest would impel a reader to hasten to historical works to
discover whether Juvenal purified Rome and Dr. Johnson reformed London. We certainly read the satires of past ages, even
those which had an influence on history, for some other reason

than their historical or sociological importance.

The real weakness of both of these theories in defence of satire is that they are essentially sociological; they rely ultimately on some sort of statistical evidence — always a suspicious tendency in any theory of literary values. A theory of literature must first state with some precision the nature of the experience of the reader who enjoys it, and then inquire what implications of this experience appear necessary to the reader himself. If satire has any beneficent effects, they should be discoverable in this experience; and it is obvious enough that our enjoyment and our approval of satire are both integral parts of this experience, whereas all theories about the social utility of satire must in their very nature be derivative. We are therefore obliged to return to a further examination of the first theory we have described, the premise of the others.

As we have seen, satire is usually explained as that experience of the comic which is accompanied by a feeling of derision, of Schadenfreude; and it has been condoned, so far as possible, by the reflection that it often issues in social or moral reform. But the whole case is prejudicated by the iteration among our theorists of the word "derision," which is assumed to be the precise equivalent of satire. This term has not been a favorite with the satirists themselves; Juvenal did not say fecit irrisio versum, nor did Swift write in the epitaph he proposed for himself that he had gone ubi saeva irrisio cor ulterius lacerare nequit. The substitution debases them both; had they written so, they would have left us curious, but cold. The word they used was indignatio, which is nobler and touches deep sympathies within us. And the profound distinction between derision and indignation, which current theories either ignore or obscure, may be the clue to a more authentic explanation of our enjoyment of satire.

We must recognize that there are many kinds and shades of satire, and that some of these, lampoons for instance, may express nothing but derision. But personal abuse is satire of low order, unless neutralized by brilliant style and the gaiety of the comic spirit. Lampoons and libels are adequately explained by the derision theory, or, if they are witty enough, as Dryden suggested, to be enjoyed even by their victims, they would come under the theory of the vis comica, which need not be expounded again here. These ramifications of the subject have received abundant treatment elsewhere. We must limit our inquiry to the satire that arouses indignation, and to the possible alternative that it offers to the derision theory.

Derision and indignation cannot be absolutely opposed to one another; they are blended in our experience. Without disparagement there can be no satire. There is something like derision also in our indignation, but it is part of a larger complex and qualified by other elements; it may be better called contempt. On the other hand, what we usually call derision is incompatible with indignation. Derision is ridicule with an implication of our own superiority to its application; it is a cruel personal triumph, and deserves the condemnation it has received from Hobbes down to the present. Indignation is also directed against comic incongruities in our fellow-men, and implies, as truly as derision, a sense of our own superiority; but it includes also, by one of the marvels of our moral chemistry, a judgment which our moral integrity obliges us to make. We may laugh with mere derision at the failures of some incompetent bungler whose boasts may have bored or irritated us; but if we are worthy citizens we must feel a different kind of joy when an incompetent bungler is defeated for public office; we must rejoice at his defeat, lest we become unworthy in our own eyes. Derision, like envy, may be a mere personal feeling of a not very honorable kind; as it is essentially selfish, and unchecked by any ethical element, it may even turn brutally on victims of misfortune, such as a cripple or an old woman carrying a heavy burden. Indignation differs from derision in all these respects. It is an indictment, and as such appeals to some sort of categorical imperative, to what is right and just. It springs from some over-individual principle within us, not merely from our ego. Its harshness is not cruelty, but a judgment against the avoidable errors, vices, and absurdities of life. We could feel indignation in the presence of a cripple only if we believed that his misfortune was the consequence of his own viciousness. For indignation is a judgment, not only of an individual, but against him. It is more than a perception of comic incongruity; it is a reproach addressed to some responsible individual who has deviated from a right and reasonable standard. Inanimate things and animals may be perceived as comic, but satire can be applied only to human beings, and only in situations for which they can be assumed responsible.

We often speak, too, of the anger and malice of the satirist. But we must distinguish between the simple and instinctive forms of these feelings and their very limited and specialized character when they become associated with indignation. The anger of

256

the cheated horse-trader who vows revenge is one thing; the
anger of a just God is another, and more likely to help us understand the nature of indignation. Irrascibility and churlishness
are not sufficient for satire, though they may inspire mockery
of a low kind. Malice and anger, like derision, may be either
noble or ignoble, depending on the circumstances; and we must
guard against the tendency of such words to carry over into our
theory of satire certain meanings and connotations which, however applicable they may be in our other experience, are irre-
concilable with the nature of indignation.

Indignation is distinguished from a merely personal feeling
of resentment or desire for retaliation by the fact that its core
is a judgment, an affirmation of some standard which we as
good men cannot refuse to sustain. We must distinguish it on the
other hand from the judgment involved in the pure comic, which
is an intellectual perception of incongruity. All authorities seem
to agree that laughter, whether derisive, neutral, or sympathetic, is a great corrective of human conduct; but its characteristic judgment is based on other than moral grounds, and its issue is merriment rather than condemnation. It may be the
laughter of the mind at the incongruities of our civilization, as
in Meredith; but Falstaff, the master comedian, is never more
agreeably funny than when he mocks at old father antick the law.
Laughter is a kind of play, which we may enjoy either by itself
or in combination with a number of other feelings. Satiric indignation is aroused when we discover the incongruity of the comic in a situation which our moral judgment also condemns as
unworthy, as indignus. It is this combination of the moral judgment with the comic experience which gives satire its distinctive character.

These propositions are of course not advanced here for the
first time; they are in fact commonplaces. But they seem always to have been taken hold of by the wrong handle and their
real significance discounted in favor of the derision theory. Max
Eastman devotes a brief paragraph to one of the mistaken methods of "compensating for the inadequacy" of the "ungracious
theory" of Hobbes; this method, he says, "was to mix a little
feeling of the justice of one's scorn, a little moral complacence,
into the comic emotion."[4] That is, in order to conceal the real
cruelty of our derisive laughter, we mask it with hypocrisy. On
this theory the satire of indignation would be doubly vicious.
Sully begins with a commendable concession regarding the ethical element in satire, but as his exposition progresses it

deteriorates in the direction of a pure theory of derision.

> The distinguishing note of satire is the angry one of re-
> probation. Here vices and follies are no longer set before
> us as a diverting spectacle, but emphasis is laid on their
> moral indignity. The satirist is at the point of view of the
> moral judge; only, instead of the calmness of the judge, he
> has something of the fierce attitude of the prosecutor who
> aims at exposing and denouncing the turpitude of an offence.
> This being so, we see that laughter enters into satire
> as an expression of contempt and as an instrument of pun-
> ishment. It assumes its most pungent and most dreaded
> form, ridicule or derision.... It is clear that the mirth-
> ful spirit when it thus lends itself to the purpose of dam-
> aging attack becomes modified to the point of transforma-
> tion. To laugh with Juvenal or with Swift is to feel more
> of a bitter malignity than of gaiety. We may say that satire
> takes us back to the brutal laughter of the savage standing
> over his prostrate foe. Or we may describe the laughter
> as a feeling of "sudden glory" deeply tinged by the domi-
> nant angry attitude of the laugher. [5]

It is instructive to observe how the "note of reprobation" here
changes into derision, thence into "bitter malignity," even as
the judge in the end turns out to be a brutal savage. Such a conclusion is inevitable if we first accept the derision theory in its
usual form, as do Eastman and Sully, and assume that derision
is the same constant and unchanged component in the satire of
Juvenal and Swift as in the jubilation of the savage victor or of
Paris, who "laughed sweetly" when he had pierced the foot of
Diomedes with an arrow. [6] In this assumption lies the error.
Against it we propose the theory that the derision of good satire
is qualified and modified by the moral judgment which is combined with it in one act and one feeling, and that it is thus transformed and elevated into indignation, a state of mind of which
the judge need not be ashamed and which is certainly more characteristic of him than of the brutal savage.

We have said that the moral judgment in our experience of
indignation is felt as over-individual, as a categorical imperative; we are not thereby committed to any inference that there
can be no wrong-headed satire, or that indignant men must be
infallible. All men are liable to error in judgment, although
this charge is not the one most frequently leveled against satirists.

A NOTE IN DEFENCE OF SATIRE

But such doubt and hesitancy is excluded from our enjoyment
of satire; whatever we may think of the categorical imperative
in our more reflective moments, we acknowledge its validity
when we are indignant. We are indignant only because what actually is falls so far short of what it ought to be, and for the
moment at least we are committed to an unreserved moral idealism. We have passed the weighing and balancing stage; our indignation only increases if anyone else begins to question our
judgment. It is a popular non sequitur in our era to berate the
wickedness of the world and then add in bitterness of spirit that
there is no good. If we are seriously to believe in ethical "relativity" in its vulgar form, if we deny any imperative force to
any moral principle, we must be more complacent; for how can
we then berate wickedness, or how can it be judged to be wickedness ? The saeva indignatio is a negation of such negation.
The whole art of satire rests on the assumption of the moral
sympathy and agreement of the reader with the writer. For, as
Hazlitt has said, ridicule "does not contain or attempt a formal
proof" of truth,

> but owes its power of conviction to the bare suggestion
> of it, so that if the thing when once hinted is not clear in
> itself, the satire fails of its effect and falls to the ground....
> Before we can laugh at a thing, its absurdity must at least
> be open and palpable to common apprehension. Ridicule is
> necessarily built on certain supposed facts, whether true
> or false, and on their inconsistency with certain acknow-
> ledged maxims, whether right or wrong. It is, therefore,
> a fair test, if not of philosophical or abstract truth, at
> least of what is truth according to public opinion and com-
> mon sense; for it can only expose to instantaneous contempt
> that which is condemned by public opinion, and is hostile
> to the common sense of mankind. [7]

Hazlitt's statement, however, does not cut deep enough; for
though the satirist counts on the quick understanding and assent
of the reader, even to the extent of saying the opposite of what
he means, as in irony, his appeal is to a higher authority than
the court of public opinion. He is more than likely to believe
that his readers are only a minority, a saving remnant; but he
will never have peace of mind until all honest men are of his
opinion.
It is after all the honest man, the man who is at least potentially

reasonable − rationis capax − , who can read satire with any enjoyment; for him it is written, even when the rhetoric of direct
address suggests the great improbability of wisdom crying out
in the streets and iniquity patiently lending an ear. His goodness,
which as things go in this world is in all likelihood normally languid, is activated through his sympathetic response to the innu-
endo of the satirist. And it is the nature of his enjoyment, rather
than historical or sociological evidence that satire has actually
been productive of good results, that must in the last analysis
disclose whatever principles of justification may be advanced
in defence of this genre. These principles we have sought for
in the implications of indignation, the characteristic emotion
which satire arouses in good men. And indignation, as we have
seen, involves a moral judgment or condemnation; the writer
and reader must have in common not only an antipathy towards
the iniquity in question, but a conviction that there are valid
universal principles upon which a condemnation may be based.
Common parlance supports this contention. The expression
"moral indignation," or "righteous indignation," comes readily
to the lips of us all, not because there is need to distinguish one
kind of indignation from another, but merely for emphasis. We
mean to assert that our feelings are noble and impersonal; we
are not merely yearning for retaliation, − we rather imply that
we have no desire for retaliation; we are appealing to the eternal
verities and on that basis demand the assent of our hearers to
our judgment and their sympathetic participation in our anger.
Those who hesitate must in their turn become the objects of our
scorn; they betray the fact that they do not belong to the free-
masonry of satire, the invisible church − not to speak it profane-
ly − of good men. We may experience only a deferred satisfaction from the severity of the cleansing and cauterizing effect of
satire − for, pace Swift, every man capable of honest confession
must have had some smarting of that kind; but our immediate
exhilaration comes from the tone-restoring exercise of our slug-
gish moral muscles. We are summoned from our indifference
and quiescence; our latent energies awake and assume definite
direction and character. We participate in the communion of
those men − few though they may be − for whom things matter,
and with them we share the faith in the validity of universal principles. The judgment at the core of the feeling of indignation involves a conviction regarding righteousness; indignation is the
emotional realization of righteousness and all great satirists,
as has always been observed, have been moralists. Though their

picture of mankind has been anything but cheerful, they have not yielded to the ultimate cynicism, the derision which is directed against the very concept of the good. For in the true satirist, derision is limited and tempered by moral idealism.

NOTES

1   Max Eastman calls it the "discovery of benign humor." See his Sense of Humor (New York, 1922), Part 2, chap. 5.

2   Eastman, op. cit., p. 139. Eastman devotes a chapter to the illustration and refutation of the "derision theory." For other criticisms of it, see James Sully, An Essay on the Theory of Laughter (London, 1902), pp. 120 ff.; J. C. Gregory, The Nature of Laughter (New York, 1924), pp. 16 ff.; and Samuel S. Seward, Jr., The Paradox of the Ludicrous (Stanford, 1930), pp. 89-90.

3   Swift assigned to this letter the fictitious date of April 2, 1727.

4   Eastman, op. cit., p. 141.

5   Sully, op. cit., pp. 380-381.

6   Iliad, 11, 378.

7   English Comic Writers. Works, ed. Waller and Glover (London, 1903), 8, 20.

THE STRUCTURAL DESIGN OF THE FORMAL VERSE SATIRE

Mary Claire Randolph

The word "formal" in the phrase "formal verse satire" implies that the genre has some specific vertebrate form or architectural design despite its apparently loose-meshed, casually
discursive surface. So far as I now know, there exists in English no study which considers what the general aspects of that
structural pattern may be. Should an alertly critical reader or
student set out to discover how a formal verse satire should be
made he could find nothing or next to nothing within the range of
English scholarship to help him to recognize and appreciate the
satirical patterns of Horace, Persius, or Juvenal; DuBellay,
Régnier, or Boileau; or Donne or Pope or Edward Young. The
following condensed treatment, by no means exhaustive, attempts
to synthesize available information concerning the form of the
formal verse satire. [1]

It is generally agreed that the formal verse satire is the only species or genre within the wide area of the genus Satire to
have any sort of identifiable crystallized form or framework.
Fluid and elusive as mercury, the Satiric Spirit almost refuses
to be bound by any rigid tenets but easily flows into and fuses
itself (especially in periods when it encounters episcopal and
legal opposition) with other essentially or even temporarily congenial genres – comedy, beast fable, prose narrative, etc. [2]
Formal verse satire itself, brittle, fragile, and unstable for
all its core of pattern, easily drifts and fades before stern,
organized opposition on spins itself out into brief, ephemeral
by-products: dare-devil lampoons, pasquils, political libels, invective, goliardic ballads and street-songs, fly-by-night pamph-
lets and corantos. This fugitive character of the genre and our
long uncertainty as to its ancient origins and terminology have
combined to discourage investigations into form, a point always
neglected in any theorizing about the genre.

The precise pattern and plan of Latin satura has long been
a puzzle to classical scholars. Once its deceptively simple ex-
terior is penetrated, an intricate honeycomb of allusion and

Reprinted by permission from Philological Quarterly, Vol. 21 (1942),
pp. 368-384.

inheritance appears. Reduced to simplest terms, the extensive scholarship on the subject[3] resolves into these conclusions: the formal verse satire, as composed by Lucilius, Horace, Persius, and Juvenal, was evidently bi-partite in structure,[4] that is, some specific vice or folly, selected for attack, was turned about on all its sides in Part A (if one may arbitrarily call it so) in something of the way premises are turned about in the octave of a sonnet; and its opposing virtue was recommended in Part B.[5] The arraignment in Part A of the specific vice or folly was clearly a process of intellection whereby a mode of dialectic was employed to view the various facets of the subject through the opaque media of plebeian folk proverb, Oriental beast fable, dramatic vignette, chriea-like anecdote, rationalized myth, Socratic dialogue, and so on. Thus, a vice was laid open to the light by a sophisticated exegetical process, almost labyrinthine, in which practically every known Hellenic literary form was employed. Formal verse satire consequently has an astonishing array of affiliations and relationships with a myriad phases of world culture since there is almost nothing that cannot appropriately be poured into its quasi-dramatic mould, as the name satura indicates. On the score of literary organism alone, it owes specific debts to ancient repetitive incantation,[6] the Old Comedy (in fact, to all of the Greek comic genres), the Theophrastian character,[7] the Bionean diatribe, the Socratic or Platonic dialogue, all "frame" literature, and all gnomic or wisdom literature.

Various scholars have attempted to show that the formal verse satire of the Augustan period owes all or nearly all of the multiple aspects of its deceptively intricate structure to various inchoate Greek forms.[8] Certain theorists have argued that it is most nearly like the Bionean diatribe, which came closer to achieving crystallized fixity of pattern than any other satiric type before Lucilius.[9] This Cynic diatribe was a short conversational disquisition, addressed to an imaginary listener or even to an entire company, autobiographical and highly informal in character, arranged sometimes in letter form, on a single ethical thesis or theme, arraigning a single vice and commending the opposing virtue, packed with extremely personal illustrative anecdotes, animal similes, allegorical personifications, realistic little mime-like scenes or vignettes, reflective soliloquy, citations from and parodies of older writers, witty and caustic comparisons, maxims and sententiae, strong contrasts, clever metaphors, and excessively coarse jests and colloquialisms.

Attractively gay and spirited and extremely various in content, rhymed and designedly quotable, these diatribes of Bion were very popular and served as influential, easily remembered pieces of philosophic propaganda. They were written in a variety of verse-forms: scazons or choliambics (reserved usually for the severest abuse), dactylic hexameters, elegiacs, iambic trimeters, and tetrameters, trochaic tetrameters, and sotadean measures. The Bionean diatribe thus seems in its jocular exegetical character and in its heterogeneous materials as well as in its dichotomous pattern very like formal verse satire.

Other scholars, the French Paul Lejay, for instance, see in the extremely variable architectural design of the Aristophanic comedy (i.e., Prologos; Parados; Proagon; Agon; Parabasis, and Exodos) a plan broadly comparable to the similarly variable structure of the Horatian satire.[10] Lejay experimentally sets the comic Prologos against satiric prologue; the comic Agon against the satirical exegesis or dialectical exposition of a vice; and the comic Exodos against the satiric conclusion or exhortation to the opposing virtue. In each of Horace's first four Satires, Lejay finds three of the five major elements of the Aristophanic comedy; and, after similar though less successful analyses of the remaining Satires, he concludes: "Nous pouvons dire que ses satires ont des vestiges certains d'une influence technique de la comedie ancienne, plus exactement de la comedie aristophanienne, en ce genre la seule donc nous connaissions la structure."[11]

Whatever the genesis of the classical satura and whatever its salient contributing factors, the usual structure of formal verse satire seems to be this: An outer shell-like framework encloses the entire piece; more likely than not a combative hollow man or interlocutor, an Adversarius, who may be identified by name and occupation or who may remain shadowy and anonymous, serves as whip and spur to the Satirist, now baiting him with a question, now thrusting in a barbed rejoinder calculated to draw out from him fresh comment and anecdote concerning the vice in question. Sometimes this second figure is only a straw decoy who utters no word but simply listens throughout the Satirist's monologue; sometimes he is a pessimistic, hard-headed Mentor; again he is an annoyingly irrational person who early detaches himself from a crowd and draws near the Satirist; very rarely is he such a one as can cleverly turn the tables on the Satirist himself. The background against which these two talk is ever so lightly sketched in; perhaps it is only half suggested or possibly only barely intimated, but it is nearly always there. Not infrequently it is a moving panoramic background – a street, a royal court, another journey to Brundisium – some setting wherein people pass by and thus provide a steady stream of type-figures on whom the Satirist can comment to the Adversarius. Altogether, then, we have the minimum essentials for the quasi-dramatic genre that formal verse satire is: two actors or participants, a Satirist and his Adversarius; a setting of sorts; and a thesis to be argued.

Within this outer frame lies the satire itself wherein, in what has been called Part A, some irrational behavior of Man, either foolish or vicious, is turned about on a pivot and its various sides and facets mercilessly exposed and illumined by a wide variety of lively exegetical device. When the conversation begins abruptly and jerkily, as it usually does, and continues elliptically, broken and interrupted here and there, throughout the whole elaborate, studied rhetorical apparatus, frequently without either Satirist or Adversarius being clearly identified as the speaker, the uninitiated reader is apt to feel thoroughly lost. One of the most common editorial and critical accusations against formal verse satire is that its lack of clarifying guide-words and transitions results in extreme confusion of dialogue. What we have now perhaps lost sight of is the fact that classical satire, as it was descended from oral genres, was still in Augustan Rome designed to be recited in public arcade or forum and was probably energetically dramatized as the speaker gave his lines.

To illustrate his thesis, win his case, and move his audience to thought and perhaps to psychological action, the Satirist utilizes miniature dramas, sententious proverbs and quotable maxims, compressed beast fables (often reduced to animal metaphors), brief sermons, sharp debates, series of vignettes, swiftly sketched but painstakingly built up satiric "characters" or portraits, figure-processions, little fictions and apologues, visions, apostrophes and invocations to abstractions – anything and everything to push his argument forward to its philosophical and psychological conclusions in much the same manner as events might push action forward to a dénouement in drama or fiction. In addition to these structural devices, an innumerable variety of purely rhetorical devices is employed to give point, compactness, speed, climax, contrast, surprise, and a score more of the special effects so necessary to good satire. Holding these varied materials together internally is the unifying thesis-thread or core of argument, while the outer frame serves as external enclosure for the entire piece. Thus, whatever simplicity and nonchalance formal satire seems to have is only an assumed simplicity of verbal surface beneath which there exists a skilfully evolved and delicately convoluted development of dialectical argument. The method employed in satire thus connects it with formal dialectic, psychology, and medicine; the end in view, the correction of folly and vice by persuasion to rational behavior, connects it with all didactic literature and with the organized forces of religion and law; while the miscellaneous illustrative materials utilized connect it with all the daily activities of man.

In practice, the negative portion of the formal satire has always outweighed the positive portion, as it must in any satire, formal or informal, verse or prose, since, paradoxically, in the very act of presenting the negative or destructive side of human behavior the satirist is establishing a positive foundation on which he can base his specific recommendation to virtue. [12] Sometimes there is a transition followed by a direct admonition to virtue or rational behavior couched in plain words. Often the admonition to virtue, never psychologically pleasing at best, is only implied throughout Part A or perhaps cleverly introduced by way of quotable proverb and maxim throughout that portion. But it is there, it must be there, spoken or unspoken, if the piece is to be more than mere virulence and fleeting invective. Now, this positive side of satire toward which the whole exegetical and rhetorical procedure is pointed is usually a dogma of a rationalistic philosophy since the essential function of Satire is ever by Ridicule to recall Man from the by-ways of Unreason to the base line of Reason, that is, to present Rational Man as the norm or standard. [13] In any age, Satire never fails to assume the colorations of the dominant rationalistic philosophy of that period: in antiquity, Cynicism and Stoicism; in the Middle Ages, Scholasticism; in the Renaissance, Humanism; and in the neo-classic period, Cartesianism. In antiquity the standard or Rational Man was the vir bonus, the tranquil, ideal citizen of the Roman commonwealth whose ideal was the Golden Mean and who preferred the quiet life "at Ulubrae;" in the Renaissance, Rational Man is the Sidneian humanist described in the courtesy books of the period; and in the Age of Enlightenment, he is the honnête homme.

It would thus be possible, if a satirist so chose, to build each satire around an essential dogma of a chosen philosophy, and,

in a whole cluster of ten or a dozen satires, to present a pragmatic exegesis of that single philosophy. Persius did essentially that for Stoicism, although it is but rarely that a satirist is
so closely identified with any single system of thought as is Persius. It would also be possible to select a single broad thesis
and to write a group of satires on various aspects of that single
thesis as Edward Young did in his seven satires, Love of Fame,
the Universal Passion (1725-1728). In any case, whatever the
plan, the positive rational mode of procedure advocated or un-
mistakably implied in a satire will be the precise opposite of
the vice or folly ridiculed; as in the mediaeval morality plays
with which formal satire has obvious generic sympathy, the Virtue will oppose the Vice, or more accurately, specific Reason
will oppose specific Unreason.

Two further points concerning form should be noted in connection with classical satire. The first concerns the still unset-
tled question of the satiric epistle. Horace wrote two books of
Epistles, 19 in the first, 2 in the second, the first book of which
appears in every way to be satires, save for title and an added
freedom of conversation justified by the fact that the satirist
writes informally to friends. The now familiar and unresolved
question is posed: may formal verse satires properly be written in letter form ?[14] Various satirists have solved the question
for themselves by writing a cluster of satiric "epistles" supple-
menting their satires exactly as Horace had done. In France,
Boileau wrote 12 Epîtres (1669-98), distinct supplements to his
12 Satires (1660-1711); and his very competent predecessor in
the genre, Mathurin Régnier, wrote 16 Satires (1608), all in the
form of familiar letters, besides three additional épîtres. In
England, Alexander Pope, besides brilliantly adapting nearly
one third of the Satires, Epistles, and Odes of Horace, wrote
four original formal verse satires in the epistolary form, the
Moral Essays (1731-35), like Horace's Epistles, so similar to
formal satires as to be so considered, though not so titled.

The second point concerns the one set form to be encountered
in formal verse satire, the satirist's apologia pro satura sua
which he seems bound to write sooner or later, and for which
there is now a considerable tradition. Lucius R. Shero[15] has
analyzed the framework and content of the Latin apologia, i.e.,
the remaining fragments of Lucilius XXX; Horace II, i; Persius
I; and Juvenal I, and finds this common pattern: a dissuading
Interlocutor or friendly Monitor warns the satirist to be prudent,
to transfer his talents and efforts before it is too late to a safer,

more popular genre, epic, for instance, or the exceedingly profitable panegyric. The satirist vehemently replies that his passion for satire cannot be restrained, that he must discharge his
spleen when provocation evokes it, and that he but follows inex-
pertly in the Lucilian tradition and writes for sympathetic, understanding folk, cognizant of the demands of that tradition.
The Interlocutor's pleas are highly stylized and so are the satirist's rebuttals. At the close, the satirist usually makes some
polite concession to the Interlocutor; he may, for instance, agree
to write only of the dead or of persons without political power.
In a way, these stock-in-trade debates are not unlike the mediaeval debates between the body and soul wherein the soul or
Muse dissuades and the body persists. Modern apologiae of this
pattern, simultaneously defining and defending satire, are frequent, e.g., Régnier's XII ("Régnier apologiste de soi-même");
Boileau's famous IX ("A son Esprit"); and Pope's An Epistle to
Dr. Arbuthnot. [16] Swift's Verses on the Death of Dr. Swift (1731)
is an adaptation of the traditional apologia to the Dean's own
ironic method.

In England very little serious attention, critical or otherwise,
has ever been paid the baffling subject of the form proper to a
formal verse satire. It has never been the way of the English
critical mind, as it is the way of the French, to busy itself primarily with questions of literary form any more than it is the
way of the English creative mind to hinder itself seriously with
the strict limitations imposed by certain literary forms; in fact,
the native English temperament, inherently opposed to strict
schematization and antipathetic to formal moulds of any sort,
has always tended to regard the formal verse satire as an artificial genre transplanted from the Mediterranean. The Englishman's taste for moral perfection, however, has always been as
lively as his feeling for highly stylized form has been inert; and
so he has been constantly drawn to satire because of its moral
purpose. That fact accounts for the Englishman's early and continued admiration of Juvenalian saeva indignatio, his swift elevation of Juvenal as the "prynce of all" among the Latin satirists,
his own constant and wearisome emphasis on the moral mission
of satire, and his reiterated intent in the Renaissance to scourge
and flay, the more fiercely the better. Among the scores of ca-
ual, informal critical statements having to do with verse satire
from 1509 to 1692/3, there is not one, so far as I have been able
to discover, that has to do with form.

In France, on the other hand, a very great deal, relatively

speaking, had always been made of the question of satiric form.
At a time when English satirists were marshalling their victims
pell-mell into Cock Lorell's Bote and many another such capa-
cious craft, the French had carefully divided contemporary society into three strata for the satirists' convenience: noblesse,
église, labeur, each with specific degrees, hierarchies, and
vices propres. The satirist began with the noblesse, cited the
conventional faults, and leisurely pursued his way downward,
utilizing prescribed transitions, until he arrived at the lowest
division of labeur. [17] Highly stylized, geometrically air-tight
patterns were devised for half a dozen small, preliminary satiric forms which served as forerunners to the first formal verse
satires of DuBellay and Régnier. Nothing like them was ever
devised in England, although one occasionally finds some fleeting mention of the French patterns, particularly among the
Scotch. Among the pages of the fifteenth- and sixteenth-century
rhétoriqueurs appear neatly worked out instructions for the
making of the blason;[18] the Provençal sirventois; the completely mechanized fatras which admitted of being a fatras simple or
double (with a reversed pattern in the second group of lines),
possible (coherent) or impossible (incoherent);[19] and the satan-
ically clever coq-à-l'âne. [20] Although in England there were
"comicall satyres," satirical characters in verse, satirical
epigrams, and "gulling" sonnets with stings in their specially
appended tail verses, there are not, early or late, any such rigorously set and prescribed forms as these of the French rhétoriqueurs.

If the Renaissance English satirist thought at all critically
of form in connection with verse satire, he left no printed expression of his thoughts. But certain elementary points in connection with the satires of Horace, Persius, and Juvenal were
immediately visible to him; indeed, he could hardly escape them.
The English satirist noted, for instance, that the ancients had
seemingly written their satires in clusters of varying numbers,
groupings which were further subdivided into "books." What he
perhaps did not know was that the classical satires were primarily intended to be recited aloud and that no "book" (libellus)
of the ancient form could have contained many more than a thousand lines; consequently, satires had to be preserved in groups
or "books" containing approximately that many lines. He noted
that Lucilius had reputedly written 30 books of satires; that Horace had written 18 satires, grouped into two books, 10 in Book
I, 8 in Book II; as well as two books of epistles; that Persius

wrote a cluster of 6 satires, prefaced by what appears to be a prologue of 14 choliambics; and that Juvenal wrote 16 satires preserved in 5 "sets" or books with Satire I often regarded as preface to the entire number. English Renaissance satirists obediently took their cue from this classical precedent and wrote similar clusters of satires, sometimes grouping them arbitrarily into "books" with short prologues, sometimes not, apparently according to whim. Donne, for instance, wrote a cluster of 5 satires, perhaps more; Lodge, 4, although he declared himself to have written a whole centon; Hall, 35, the largest collection of satires in the Renaissance, which he chose to break up into three books of "toothlesse" and three of "bytyng" satires; Rankins, 7: Marston, 11, numbered consecutively through three books, called The Scourge of Villanie, besides another group of 5, simply called "Satyres." Seven became an extremely popular number in the early seventeenth century because of the Seven Deadly Sins and the seven planets which presumably regulated human fortunes and human behavior. For new editions Renaissance satirists casually added new satires to their original groupings or eked out slender volumes with satirical epigrams, practices which indicate that the original arrangement had been arbitrarily determined, perhaps by the printer, at the outset.

When the English satirist looked at the lengths of the Latin satires, he found them widely variant. Juvenal's Sixth Satire, for instance, contains 661 lines, and is twice the length of any of his other satires (the Fourth has only 173 lines); and Persius' longest satire, the Fifth (191 lines), immediately follows his shortest, the Fourth (52 lines). Finding no special rule in evidence, the Renaissance measured his own pieces by rule of thumb, sometimes extending his "epigrammes" into satires or shortening his "satyres" until they approached a brevity consonant with the theory of epigram.

Classical tradition had taught Renaissance English satirists that formal satire was in direct descent from the Old Comedy and from the Greek satyr-play and should therefore be quasi-dramatic in character. The long persisting lexicographical error connecting English "satyre" with Greek satyros (δάτυϱος) instead of Latin satura (a myth dissipated by Casaubon in his De Satyrica, Book I) was responsible for the current popular notion that satire should be loose-jointed, crudely devised, and obscurely and harshly worded, a supposition hardly calculated to foster critical investigation into classical Latin form. Still, whatever else they may not have known about the form, Renaissance

and early seventeenth-century satirists were certain of the principle that the genre was a semi-dramatic one held together by
the figure of the Narrator-Satirist and became extremely clever
at devising and reviving dramatic devices to give life and color
to what might have been forthright, unadorned imprecation
against vice. So far as verse form was concerned, the English
satirist early noted that the classical satires were monometric
and gradually and naturally, without much critical ado, fixed on
his own iambic pentameter with its "grappling-hooks" of rhyme.

From observation and study of the classical satires, then,
the English Renaissance satirist learned these elementary things
about form: that satires were usually written in clusters of in-
determinate number, sometimes introduced by separate prologue
or preface; that their lengths were extremely variable; and that
they were semi-dramatic and monometric. Those Latin satires
dealing directly with satiric theory, Horace's Fourth and Tenth,
Book I, and the First, Book II; Persius' Prologue and his First
Satire (the Fifth perhaps incidentally); and Juvenal's First Satire,
concerned themselves chiefly with spirit, tone, and ethics, and
not at all with form. So far as one can now tell, the English
verse satirist of the Renaissance must have decided that the architectural pattern was his own to make and that only the tone,
direction, and general external outline of the genre had been
marked out for him by the ancients.

John Dryden was the first and he remains almost the only
English man of letters to have considered critically the matter
of the architectural pattern of formal verse satire and then only
in 1692/3 when England's first period of verse satire was long
gone by and a second and greater one even then under way. It is
the latter portion of Dryden's A Discourse on the Original and
Progress of Satire (1692/3), perhaps the most generally neglected and inadequately edited major critical essay in our literature, plus the extremely interesting headnotes or "Arguments"
to the translations of Persius and Juvenal, which show that Dryden's chief interest at this time was the form proper to formal
verse satire. Possibly roused by the bold Bolevian experimenta-
tions in the larger aspects of satiric form going on across the
Channel,[21] Dryden's interest was fostered by his extensive use
of Isaac Casaubon's learned introductory essay of nearly 300
pages, De Satyrica Graecorum Poesi et Romanorum Satira as
well as Casaubon's copious notes to his great Paris edition of
Persius (1605). Dryden says in the Discourse:

> I will tell you ... how a modern satire should be made....
> please ... observe, that Persius, the least in dignity of
> all the three, has notwithstanding been the first, who has
> discovered to us this important secret, in the designing
> of a perfect satire, that it ought only to treat of one sub-
> ject; to be confined to one particular theme; or, at least,
> to one principally. If other vices occur in the manage-
> ment of the chief, they should only be transiently lashed,
> and not be insisted on, so as to make the design double...
> In general all virtues are everywhere to be praised and
> recommended to practice; and all vices to be reprehended,
> and made either odious or ridiculous; or else there is a
> fundamental error in the whole design. [22]

Thus, according to Dryden, one vice and one alone must be
the subject of a formal verse satire. If any other vices enter
into the design, they must be logical subdivisions of the one
chief vice. Dryden immediately compares this precept of unity
of design in a satire to unity of action in a drama, a comparison
not infrequently echoed here and there in the eighteenth century
and even extended to include the unities of place and time. Casaubon had carefully brought the principles of Aristotle's Poetics
to bear on satire throughout his essay, e.g., in Book II, Chap.
III; and Dryden follows Casaubon in remarking that since Horace knew the rules of unity as they applied to drama, he should
have applied them to his satires;

> As in a ... tragi-comedy, there is to be but one main de-
> sign: and, though, there be an underplot, or second walk
> of comical characters and adventures, yet they are subser-
> vient to the chief fable, carried along under it, and help-
> ing to it: so that the drama may not seem a monster with
> two heads.... It is certain, that the divine wit of Horace
> was not ignorant of this rule, — that a play, though it con-
> sists of many parts, must yet be one in the action, and
> must drive on the accomplishment of one design; ... yet he
> seems not so much to mind it in his satires, may of them
> consisting of more arguments than one; and the second
> without dependence on the first. [23]

Dryden rejects the very plausible argument that satura, as
it signifies etymologically a variety of fruits and grains, may
properly imply a miscellaneous assortment of literary materials,

unless, he specifies, the miscellaneous materials all fall logically under one single, broad heading, so that the variety may
be ordered and organized variety. Juvenal, Persius, and Boileau, he notes, have all confined themselves to unity of design
in the single satire and have allowed their finished groups of
satires to provide the variety traditionally implied in the generic term satura. Moreover, Dryden argues, if the satirist insists on variety, he can illustrate these subordinate branches of
the major vice with sufficient examples to provide color and
change and avoid monotony. [24]

A further point, included in this neo-Aristotelian rule for unity of design within a satire, is that a satirist must offer one
single positive precept of moral virtue to balance his attack on
the one particular vice. "He is," says Dryden, "chiefly to in-
culcate one virtue and insist on that."[25] If he has subdivided the
chief vice into component parts, then he must offer corresponding minor precepts of moral virtue which will be logical subdivisions of the major precept. Thus, for every vice, major and
minor, there must be a precisely corresponding precept of
virtue.

But this is not all of Dryden's formula. He sees clearly, as
did Persius, that a satirist's entire collection of satires could,
if carefully planned, present a unified, practical exegesis of
the essential dogmas of some particular rationalistic philosophy:

> Herein then it is, that Persius has excelled both Juvenal
> and Horace. He sticks to his own philosophy; he shifts not
> sides, like Horace, who is sometimes an Epicurean, some-
> times a Stoic, sometimes an Eclectic, as his present humour
> leads him ... Persius is every where the same; true to
> the dogmas of his master ... His kind of philosophy is one,
> which is the Stoic; and every satire is a comment on one
> particular dogma of that sect, unless we will except the
> first, which is against bad writers; and yet even there he
> forgets not the precepts of the Porch. [26]

The eleven headnotes to the satires translated by Dryden
are visible evidence that he had striven to put his theory of bi-
partite form to immediate, pragmatic use. In every instance
he tries to discover and state exactly what vice has been the
satirist's special target of attack. If there are subordinate
vices or tangential subtopics, Dryden notes carefully how they
logically fall into proper place under the main heading. He takes

273

pains to point out "artful" transitions from Part A to Part B and to note and to phrase carefully the constructive precept to virtue or philosophic dogma offered and stressed by the satirist. Some of the satires very obviously present difficult problems; and occasionally Dryden has to admit outright that Part B, the precept to virtue, is only implied or that the needful transition is blurred or missing altogether. [27]

This concept of symmetrical, interlocking pattern for a formal verse satire which Dryden has outlined in the latter portion of the Discourse and attempted to apply in his headnotes is as stiffly geometric in its contrasting parts as the most severely formal eighteenth-century garden. The basic suggestions for it came both directly and indirectly from the pages of Casaubon's 1605 edition of Persius, specifically from the essay, De Satyrica ..., Book II, Chapters III, IV, and V, as well as from certain of the notes. [28] It will be noted that in large outline Dryden's theory of formal satire coincides very well with the theory of form earlier described in this paper.

But the Drydenian formula for the making of a "modern satire" was too mechanically cut-and-dried for any satirist to put to actual use, and so it seems to have been as generally overlooked in the poet's own time as later. Ranking English men of letters, however, even in England's greatest age of satire, wrote very few original formal verse satires. Dryden himself wrote none; Swift, Gay, Addison, Steele, and Arbuthnot wrote none; only Edward Young and Alexander Pope, in company with a certain few of the lesser poets, wrote any formal verse satires that could properly be termed original. Add to these the five formal Satyres of John Donne, and one has England's chief original contributions to the genre. Not one of the half dozen or so great English satires, it must be noted, is a formal verse satire. But if English satirists did not themselves create great numbers of original formal verse satires, they so admired the clusters of classical satires that they paid constant, careful lip-tribute to them as the great ancient patterns; they studied and imitated them; they paraphrased and adapted them, altering locale and names in Bolevian fashion; and they translated and edited them — but in actual creative practice they chose to go their own English ways. The formal verse satires of the neoclassical period would be almost negligible in number were it not for the large body of translations and adaptations of Horace, Persius, and Juvenal.

Various reasons suggest themselves in explanation of the

FORMAL VERSE SATIRE

English critical neglect of the form of this particular literary genre. Obviously the architectural design or structure of formal verse satire has never been clearly defined or generally understood at any time. Dryden is apparently the only critic in English literature who has come reasonably close to an apprehension of the basic structure of the genre and then only by the aid of Casaubon's suggestions. Even now when twentieth-century classical scholars (mentioned in the footnotes to this paper) have investigated various aspects of the architectural pattern of classical Latin satire, no one of them, so far as I know, has synthesized their scattered materials into anything like a connected, detailed analysis of the form. Thus, it may be that English satirists generally have not clearly recognized and perceived the structure of the genre and have warily preferred to confine themselves to translations and adaptations of the classical patterns. It seems rather more likely, however, that the paucity of original formal verse satire in England may be explicable as one result of the staunch resistance of British temperament to the rigorous schematization and regimented formalism of certain phases of neo-classicism. Formal verse satire is designed with greater syllogistic precision than the sonnet, and its intellectual demands on both writer and reader are specialized, multiple, and stringent. Englishmen have varied the sonnet and the ode forms to suit themselves; in the case of the formal verse satire, however, they have been content, for the most part, with score on score of "adaptations." As a form, formal verse satire was never to be a leading genre in English literature; but its peculiar spirit and temper were to pervade and animate nearly every literary genre in England for a hundred years and more.[29]

NOTES

1 It has not been possible within the range of this article to describe or list the scores of devices, both rhetorical and structural, and traditional generic conventions contributory to the form.

2 Censorship has always affected the theory and practice of satire: made it cautiously recommend veiling allegory, fable, subterfuges, keys, and obscurity of diction; seek other channels of expression; or take refuge in minor forms. Satire has had a long battle with the law from the time of the Roman Twelve Tables to the present day when increasing numbers of political cartoonists, the modern approximation of the verse satirists, have been fined and imprisoned.

3   Important studies bearing on form are: H. Nettleship, "The
     Original Form of the Roman Satura," (originally written, 1878),
     Lectures and Essays (2nd. ser., Oxford, 1895), pp. 24-43;
     G. L. Hendrickson, "The Dramatic Satura and the Old Comedy
     at Rome," Amer. Jour. of Philology, XV (1894), 1-30; H. M.
     Hopkins, "Dramatic Satura in Relation to Book Satura and the
     Fabula Togata," Proceedings of the American Philological So-
     ciety, XXXI (1900), 1-51; G. L. Hendrickson, "Satura, the
     Genesis of a Literary Form," Classical Philology, VII (1912),
     177-89; C. Knapp, "The Sceptical Assault on the Roman Tradi-
     tion concerning the Dramatic Satura," Amer. Jour. of Philology,
     XXXIII (1912), 125ff. (Knapp makes a grievous error when he
     asserts that to Horace comedy and satire were convertible
     terms); R. J. E. Tiddy, "Satura and Satire," English Literature
     and the Classics, ed. G. S. Gordon (Oxford, 1912), pp. 196-227;
     A. L. Wheeler, "Satura as a Generic Term," Classical Philology,
     VII (1912), 457-77; J. W. D. Ingersoll, "Roman Satire. Its Early
     Name ?" Classical Philology, VII (1912), 59-65; B. L. Ullman,
     "Satura and Satire," Classical Philology, VIII (1913), 173-94;
     and "The Present Status of the Satura Question," Studies in Phil-
     ology, XVII (1920), 379-401; and G. L. Hendrickson, "Satira tota
     nostra est," Classical Philology, XXII (1927), 46-60.

4   The fact has long been recognized that formal verse satire as a
     poetic form breaks sharply into two markedly disproportionate
     divisions – thesis and antithesis, destruction and construction,
     black and white – with the latter portion being ever the weaker
     and less striking of the two. Augustin G. C. Cartault in his Etude
     sur les Satires d'Horace (Paris, 1899), p. 347, proposed a
     grouping of the materials of the Satires into ideas of destruction
     and construction for study purposes (see Oscar E. Nybakken,
     An Analytical Study of Horace's Ideas [Iowa City, Iowa, 1937],
     p. 12).

5   In simple outline, this is not unlike the form of the ancient beast
     fable with its attached moral or unlike the bestiary tale with its
     appended significatio.

6   If the beginnings of Greek satire were not so completely lost to
     us, we should probably discover that the satirist in a less so-
     phisticated age was akin to the magician, prophet, soothsayer,
     juggler, and buffoon with the sorcerer's power to wreak enor-
     mous destruction, as in early Germanic, early Irish, and early
     Arabic literatures. See F. N. Robinson, "Satirists and Enchant-
     ers in Early Irish Literature," Studies in the History of Reli-
     gions (New York, 1912), pp. 95-130; and Mary Claire Randolph,
     "Celtic Smiths and Satirists: Partners in Sorcery," E L H, VIII

(1941), 184-97; "The Medical Concept in English Renaissance
Satiric Theory: Its Possible Relationships and Implications,"
Studies in Philology, XXXVIII (1941), 127-59; and "Female Sa-
tirists of Ancient Ireland," S F Q, VI (1942), 75-87.

7 Character-portraiture, the delineation of types by means of fo-
cus on the individual, is ever a forerunner or concomitant of
satire. Theophrastian characters preceded classical satire; mediaeval type-portraiture preceded the gallery of satirical characters in Chaucer's Prologue (ca. 1387); vast quantities of such
pictorial writing, e.g., The Ship of Fools (1509) and its numerous progeny, preceded Elizabethan formal satire; and the seventeenth-century characters were preliminary to the "timeless
engravings" of Achitophel, Atticus, Sporus, and Atossa. Satiric
efforts in the plastic arts and in portrait-painting, especially
caricature, not infrequently flourish in an era of literary satire,
e.g., Hogarth's serial "Progresses," Marriage à la Mode, Gin
Alley, etc. See Thomas Wright, History of Caricature and Grotesque in Literature and Art (London, 1839), and F. G. Stephens,
Catalogue of Prints and Drawings in the British Museum (London, 1870-1879, 4 vols.), I.

8 See Paul Lejay's Introduction (pp. vii-xxxii) to Horace's Satires
(Paris, 1911); George Converse Fiske, Lucilius and Horace:
A Study in the Classical Theory of Imitation (Madison, 1920),
Chaps. II and III; Mary A. Grant, The Ancient Rhetorical Theories of the Laughable: The Greek Rhetoricians and Cicero
(Madison, 1924), pp. 7-100; the numerous articles by J. Geff-
cken, George L. Hendrickson, and B. L. Ullman; and Nicola Terzaghi's recent work, Per la storia della satira (Turin, 1932),
for extended research in the Hellenic backgrounds of Roman
satire.

9 Terzaghi, op. cit., Part I, "Della Diatriba alla Satira," pp. 7-
51. See also M. R. Heinze, De Horatio Bionis imitatore (Bonn,
1899); Lejay, op. cit., pp. xv-xvi; and Archibald Y. Campbell,
Horace: A New Interpretation (London, 1924), pp. 154-56.

10 Op. cit., pp. xlvii-lxxv.

11 Ibid., p. lx.

12 The satiric picture, being negative, is usually heightened to increase the impact of the positive precept. Exaggeration downward, always preserving verisimilitude, however, is regarded
as a legitimate artifice of the satirist. Precisely how much satiric exaggeration this side falsehood is justifiable is almost

indeterminable. Swift, of course, uses exaggeration downward until it has passed the line of verisimilitude into the realm of the false and thence beyond into the regions of Fantasia.

13   See C. W. Mendell, "Satire as Popular Philosophy," Classical Philology, XV (1920), 138-57. Mendell regards the satiric form as a sort of dilute, shortened, versified Platonic dialogue, a metrical descendant of the popular philosophic essay, a genre from the field of ethics, concerned with the science of behavior. See also B. L. Ullman, "Q. Horatius Flaccus, Ph.D., Professor of Ethics," Classical Journal, XIII (1917), 258-66; and J. Tate, "Horace and the Moral Function of Poetry," Classical Quarterly, XXII (1928), 65-72.

14   See G. L. Hendrickson, "Are the Letters of Horace Satires?" American Jour. of Philology, XVIII (1897), 313-24. The satires in Juvenal's last two books (IV and V) are really epistolary moral essays, each addressed to a friend, lacking dialogue, and almost lacking dramatization.

15   "The Satirist's Apologia," Classical Studies, Series II, University of Wisconsin Studies (Madison, 1922), 148-67. From its inception as a genre, satire has been apologetic and on the defensive, even occasionally regarded as outside the pale of respectability in some periods, but ever justifying its sometimes questionable means by its impeccable, never-to-be-questioned ends. An outcast from Parnassus and under the protection of no Muse, Satire has ever eaten humble-pie and bowed to its betters.

16   In the 419-line dialogue, Arbuthnot the Adversarius speaks approximately a dozen lines, the usual proportion for the second figure. Pope's Epistle closely follows its Horatian model (II, i), but the whole piece has been pitched to a higher, sharper tone than in Horace, Boileau, or Swift.

17   Henry Guy, Histoire de la Poésie française au moyen-âge (Paris, 1910), pp. 69-70.

18   The blason was an exquisitely figured small satiric pattern, lavish in its detail, utilizing flowers, precious stones, parts of the feminine body, medicine, geography, politics, practically everything for subject matter, and concluding in some startling fashion. The blason had a tremendous vogue for a time. See Thomas Sebillet, Art Poétique Françoys, 1548, Chapitre X, "Du Blason, et de la définition, et déscription" (Gaiffe edition, Paris, 1910), pp. 169-73.

19   Bauldet Herenc, Le Doctrinal de la Seconde Rhétorique (Lang-
lois, III), and Jean Molinet, L'art de Rhétorique vulgaire (Paris, 1493), quoted by Warner F. Patterson, Three Centuries of
French Poetic Theory (Ann Arbor, 1935, 2 vols.), I, 123-24;
148-49.

20   The four coqs-à-l'âne of Clément Marot (written 1535-36) are
regarded as the most important predecessors of the formal
verse satire in France. An agile cock (the satirist) holds a
touch-and-go conversation with a stolid donkey (the Adversarius and in this instance the partial butt of the satire). The absurdity of the situation is its very essence: the Aesopic cock,
deliberately speaking illogically and disjointedly, outwits the
donkey with sprightly enigmas. The term in French satire
means a hodge-podge composition in octosyllabic verse without
proper transitions or connections, without any evident logic,
jumping from one subject to another, the general confusion serv-
ing to conceal partially much sharp criticism not infrequently
uncouth and vulgar. See my note, "The French Coq-à-l'âne as
a Satiric Form," N. & Q, CLXXI (1941), 100-2.

21   Boileau, technician first and moralist afterward, had broken
Juvenal's Third Satire (on city noises, filth, traffic, thieves,
etc.) into two parts, expanding them into his own full-fledged
First ("Adieux d'un poète à la ville de Paris") and Sixth ("Em-
barras de Paris") Satires, and had similarly broken the conventionally stylized classical apologia into two parts, his own Seventh ("Le Genre satirique") and Ninth ("A son Esprit") Satires.
Besides changing settings and names from Rome to Paris and
adapting the Latin satires in other significant ways, he had
chosen to unify his own pieces by writing the greater part of
them around various aspects of a single thesis, a propaganda
thesis — the inept writer and his output of mediocre or bad literature. (It has been noted that Joseph Hall may have had some
such idea a century and a half earlier.)

22   The Works of John Dryden, ed. Sir Walter Scott and George
Saintsbury (Edinburgh, 1882-1893, 18 vols.), XIII, 109; 112.

23   Ibid., pp. 109-10.

24   Ibid., pp. 110-11.

25   Loc. cit.

26   Works, ed. Scott-Saintsbury, XIII, 204; 111-12. See the "Argument" to the First Satire of Persius, op. cit., XIII, 213.

27   <u>Ibid.</u>, pp. 124, 135, 154, 214, 249.

28   I hope to show in detail in a later paper the extent of Dryden's dependence on Casaubon, both directly by his own use of Casaubon's great edition of Persius and indirectly by his reliance on Dacier's neat summary of Book I of the Huguenot editor's work. English scholars have erred in their failure to investigate the relationships existing between the Continental scholars, particularly those at Leyden, and the seventeenth-century satirists.

29   Since writing this paper, I have read and wish to note Professor Elizabeth H. Haight's urbane and competent volume, <u>The Roman Use of Anecdotes in Cicero, Livy, and the Satirists</u> (New York, 1940), an investigation into one aspect of the structure of the formal verse satire which is closely linked with much that I have said here.

THEORY AND GENERAL IDEAS

"DISTRUST" OF IMAGINATION IN ENGLISH NEO-CLASSICISM

Donald F. Bond

The neo-classical movement in England has been variously appreciated. Fuller study of the major figures and chief genres of the late seventeenth and eighteenth centuries has resulted in a better understanding of the literature produced during this period. As yet, however, comparatively little investigation has been made into the aesthetic and critical doctrines of neo-classicism.[1] These find expression in the numerous contemporary treatises devoted to belles-lettres, music, the pictorial arts, architecture, and gardening.[2] One aspect of neo-classical theory in particular deserves attention: its view of the imagination as an element in literary composition.

The indubitably rationalistic character of the neo-classical movement has led to rather extreme statements about "repression" and "distrust" of imagination. "Fancy, provided she knows her place, is tolerated; but Imagination is kept well at a distance; a flight is perdition, a conceit at best danger."[3] These words of Saintsbury are of a generation ago, yet more recent critics have likewise stressed this view. Even such a penetrating critic as Mr. A. S. P. Woodhouse, for example,[4] speaks of "the reduction of imagination to mere 'imaging' and its function to the adornment of actual fact or of reason's concepts, in strict subordination to judgment."[5] A recent German critic makes an even more derogatory statement of the neo-classical attitude toward poetic composition.

Man sieht in ihm nicht mehr die freie Schöpfung, sondern lediglich die regelnde Darstellung des Seienden, oder die Nachahmung der antiken Vorbilder, in denen jene Regelung schon vollzogen ist. Der Dichter muss vor allem vergleichen, abstrahieren, ordnen.[6]

But neo-classical theory is not so unqualifiedly hostile to the free play of imagination. The majority opinion, one may say at once, is that in the composition of poetry there are two essential

Reprinted by permission from Philological Quarterly, Vol. 14 (1935), pp. 54-69.

elements – imagination, to give to a poem life and spirit; and judgment, by which the poet exercises discrimination in the selection of material.[7] Undue stress upon either is deplored. Nor must we be misled by the frequent reproaches directed against the mischiefs of an "unbridled imagination" in ethical matters. We must distinguish between the warnings which seventeenth-century moralists direct against the free exercise of imagination (resulting in idle day-dreaming, "castles in Spain," or perhaps melancholic delusions) and the opinions which literary critics hold of this faculty. Furthermore, neo-classical "distrust" of imagination is in large part concerned not with criticism of imaginative literature (tragedy, epic, lyric poetry, etc.) at all, but with criticism of intellectual literature (eloquence, philosophy, science, etc.). The present study attempts to assemble characteristic "hostile" criticisms of the imagination from the literary criticism of the late seventeenth and early eighteenth centuries, and to assess as fairly as possible the degree of "distrust" with which neo-classicists regarded the imagination, first in intellectual literature and then in imaginative literature proper.[8]

I

The seventeenth century, as has often been noted, was a period of reform in prose style. The origin and meaning of this movement toward simplicity and plainness of utterance have been variously interpreted, but the resultant effects upon the prestige of the imagination are clear. An age which held scientific truth as the great goal to be attained in prose would quite naturally regard with some suspicion a faculty traditionally allied with the senses and passions and devoted primarily to the making of images.[9] We should be careful, warns one writer, "lest Imaginations (which are the Offsprings of Fancy, and do oft misrepresent the Thing) do delude us, or the Equivocation of Words draw us aside, and make us deviate from those Genuine and Nature instill'd Notions."[10] And the endeavor to achieve a style of "Mathematical plainness"[11] for the attainment of such truth would not presuppose a favorable attitude toward a faculty long regarded as the foundation of wit and metaphor. "The proper work of man," says Isaac Barrow, "the grand drift of human life, is to follow reason, (that noble spark kindled in us from heaven ...) not to sooth fancy, that brutish, shallow, and giddy power, able to perform nothing worthy much regard."[12]

"DISTRUST" OF IMAGINATION

The objection to an ornate style was, of course, not new. The Elizabethan age had witnessed the objections of men like Nashe to the frequent use of ink-horn terms, "the ingrafted ouerflow of some kil-cow conceit, that ouercloyeth their imagination ..."[13], or of those who, with Bacon, protested against the Ciceronian imitators, those who "began to hunt more after wordes than matter, and more after the choisenesse of the Phrase, and the round and cleane composition of the sentence, and the sweet falling of the clauses, and the varying and illustration of their workes with tropes and figures, then after the weight of matter, worth of subiect, soundnesse of argument, life of inuention, or depth of iudgement."[14]

Imagination, we find critics saying, tempts the writer to a round-about way of expression, to a style overladen with images. Truth needs not the ornamentation of a fanciful or metaphorical style.

> How many excellent discourses are tortured, wrested, and pinched in, and obscured through curiosity of penning, hidden allusions, forced phrases, uncouth Epithites, with other deformities of plaine speaking; your own eares and eyes may be sufficient judges.... Good speech (make the most on't) is but the garment of truth: and she is so glorious within, she needs no outward decking: yet if [s]he do appear in a rayment of needle-work, it's but for a more majestick comelinesse, not gawdy gaynesse. Truth is like our first Parents, most beautifull when naked.... [15]

The greatest virtues, this Puritan preacher goes on to declare, are "perspicuity" and "method." "I must alwaies think they know not what they say, who so speake, as others know not what they meane."[16] This great fault, of obscurity, is that which Rapin finds in the style of Thucydides, which is "choaked with the multitude and force of his Images."[17]

Figures of speech, the products of wit, "whose purlews are chiefely words, as matter is of wisdome,"[18] are moreover unsuitable for serious writing because they "rather exhibit the mask or shadow of Truth, than discover its real and substantial Beauty to us ..."[19]

> Now to Discourse of the Natures of Things in Metaphors and Allegories is nothing else but to sport and trifle with empty words, because these Schems do not express the

Natures of Things, but only their Similitudes and Resemblances, for Metaphors are only words, which properly signifying one thing, are apply'd to signifie another by reason of some Resemblance between them. When therefore any thing is express'd by a Metaphor or Allegory, the thing it self is not expressed, but only some similitude observ'd or made by Fancy.... All those Theories in Philosophie which are expressed only in metaphorical Termes, are not real Truths, but the meer Products of Imagination, dress'd up (like Childrens babies) in a few spangled empty words.... Thus their wanton & luxuriant fancies climbing up into the Bed of Reason, do not only defile it by unchast and illegitimate Embraces, but instead of real conceptions and notices of Things, impregnate the mind with nothing but Ayerie and Subventaneous Phantasmes. [20]

Here we may see the force of the psychological objection to the imagination, which is capable of making only "corporeal images," in contrast to the abstract reasoning of the intellect. The fantastic power of the soul, says Cudworth, is never willingly idle, so that when the intellect is busy with "Abstracted Intellections and Contemplations," fancy is also busy in "making some kind of Apish Imitations, counterfeit Iconisms, Symbolical Adumbrations and Resemblances of those Intellectual Cogitations of Sensible and Corporeal things." [21] Hence, he continues, "in Speech, Metaphors and Allegories do so exceedingly please, because they highly gratify this Phantastical Power of Passive and Corporeal Cogitation in the Soul, and seem thereby also something to raise and refresh the Mind it self, otherwise lazy and ready to faint and be tired by over-long abstracted Cogitations ..." [22]

Metaphors were "at first, no doubt, an admirable Instrument in the hands of Wise Men, when they were onely employ'd to describe Goodness, Honesty, Obedience, in larger, fairer and more moving Images; to represent Truth, cloth'd with Bodies; and to bring Knowledg back again to our very sense, from whence it was at first deriv'd to our understandings." [23] Ideally they are, as Bouhours said, "comme ces voiles transparens, qui laissent voir ce qu'ils couvrent; ou comme des habits de masque sous lesquels on reconnoist la personne qui est déguisée" [24]; their justification is the two-fold one of making an abstract truth more clear and palpable, and of making it more agreeable to the mind.

Its beauty appears at first sight, and there is required
no labour of thought to examine what truth or reason there
is in it. The mind, without looking any further, rests satisfied with the agreeableness of the picture and the gaiety
of the fancy. And it is a kind of affront to go about to examine it, by the severe rules of truth and good reason.... [25]

But inasmuch as they are formed as "apish Imitations" by
the fantastic part of the soul, they inherit a share of the distrust with which the imagination had been regarded by Platonic
and Stoic thinkers, — by the former for its deceptive qualities
and its inability to attain to abstract truth, by the latter for its
power of stirring up the passions to revolt. Hence we find Sprat
saying that "they are in open defiance against Reason, professing not to hold much correspondence with that, but with its
Slaves, the Passions; they give the mind a motion too changeable
and bewitching to consist with right practice."[26] "A luxurious
Fancy," writes another, "will be apt to frame very wild and
absurd Notions out of Metaphors, if the Understanding be not
furnished with a knowledg of the qualities, operations, and use
of those things from which they are drawn."[27]
Such a style can only be suitable where pleasure rather than
truth is the end. And the pleasure derived is that of a tour de
force, "like that of seeing rope-dancers, where people take a
pleasure in seeing men in danger of their lives,"[28] "the Antick
Quickness and Preternatural Agility of Dancers, and Buffoons,
and Posture-men." [29] Certainly in serious writing it has little
place. "If we would speak of things as they are, we must allow
that all the art of rhetoric, besides order and clearness; all the
artificial and figurative application of words eloquence hath invented, are for nothing else but to insinuate wrong ideas, move
the passions, and thereby mislead the judgment; and so indeed
are perfect cheats ..."[30] It gains "more credit and applause
with the generality of People, than that more difficult and trou-
blesome, which after much labour and study presents us with
the very truth of things drawn from their Causes, and delivers
the same in distinct and plain expressions."[31]

II

In criticism of poetry, on the other hand, we find less insistence upon a controlled imagination, less discussion of the dangers
inherent in the free play of fancy. There is general agreement

that both imagination and judgment are essential. Nowhere is there the implication that imagination is not the stuff of poetry, much less that the poet could dispense with this faculty altogether. Poetry is, as Cowley said, "the Picture of ... things and persons imagined." [32] There are, it is true, certain ill effects which are at times ascribed to an overabundance of imagination.

In the first place, we find doubts expressed as to the value of poetry which appeals only to – or is inspired solely by – fancy. [33] The poet must instruct as well as please. Failure to remember this, says Shadwell, "makes him of as little use to Mankind as a Fidler or Dancing Master, who delights the fancy onely, without improving the Judgement. Horace, the best judge of Poetry, found other business for a Poet." [34] The greatest poetry, according to John Norris, "where equal address is made to the Judgment and the Imagination, and where Beauty and Strength go hand in hand," degenerates, like music, when it comes "down to light, frothy stuff, consisting either of mad extravagant Rants, or slight Witticisms, and little amorous Conceits ..." [35] Blackmore is equally severe. "They are Men of little Genius, of mean and poor Design, that imploy their Wit for no higher Purpose than to please the Imagination of vain and wanton People." [36]

Allied to this is the objection to poetry altogether, compounded as it is of imagination. This view was current of course among the Puritans, those

> Who since themselves miss'd it,
> Will damn all Wit;
> Such dull grim Judges, were it in their Power,
> Would leave nor Heav'n a Star, nor Earth a Flower! [37]

But it may also be regarded as a part of the large current of rationalism which pervades the period. [38] There are many who disparage imagination on the ground that it has to do only with the surfaces of things, and that it fails in the perception of higher, spiritual matters. To a certain extent this attitude is reflected in the rationalistic objection to poetry. As a popular courtesy book of the time puts it:

> If we respect only the Senses, and their Pleasures, the Imagination, and its Charms, the Passions and their Motions; a good Poet, I confess, is really inestimable; because amongst the other Pleasures of the Mind, the Talent

of <u>Poetry</u> is the most exquisite, especially to Persons
of a delicate Fancy.

But if we will guide our selves by our Reason and its
Decisions, this Quality becomes on a sudden contemptible;
the pretended Charms and Excellencies of a <u>Poets</u> Wit
being like those dull heavy Beauties we look on with Indifference.[39]

Since the poet appeals to the imagination rather than to the intellect he "must be as much, if not more, imploy'd in the search
of Words, and their Measure, than the nature of Things.... He
must therefore strain himself to humour a strong Imagination
rather than consult just and good Reason, and rather aim at lively Representations, than right and solid Judgment."[40]

We find others urging the view that the poet should not depend upon his imagination but should base his poetry upon the
solid foundation of learning. He must have a knowledge of arts
and sciences and must practice the labor of the file. "To such
a Poet as would aim at those noble effects, no knowledg of Morality, or the nature and course of humane actions and accidents
must be wanting: he must be well versed in History, he must
be acquainted with the progress of nature, in what she brings
to pass, he must be deficient in no part of Logick, Rhetorick,
or Grammar; in a word, he must be consummate in all arts and
Sciences, if he will be excellent in his way."[41] Those who pretend to write "out of the treasonous mint of their owne imaginations," without the necessary background of learning, produce
nothing more than "Ixion's issue."[42] "For hee that with meerely
a naturall veine, and a little vanity of nature ... writes without
other grounds of solid learning than the best of these vngrounded
rimers vnderstand or aime at, what does he more than imbrace
assembled cloudes with Ixion, and beget only Monsters?"[43]

All these expressions reveal a somewhat supercilious and
patronizing attitude toward imagination and imaginative literature generally. More extensive and, I believe, more significant
are the criticisms which point to specific ill results from the
poet's imagination. In these, the necessity for imagination working in harmony with judgment is assumed: the evils remarked
upon are those resulting from too great license of imagination.
They are: a lack of selectiveness and a lack of probability.

The poet who trusts to fancy without judgment, says Rapin,
will be led into endless digressions, like "those Travellers, who
upon a long Journey are diverted and stopt by every little Thing."[44]

Such was the case with Homer, who "is continually hurried away with the Impetuosity and Violence of his Imagination, to which he lets himself loose without the least Discretion."[45] If the poet needs invention, "a Capacity to discover abundantly all that may be said upon any propos'd Subject," he needs equally the faculty of judgment. "A good Judgment chuses and picks, it stops not at every thing presented by the Imagination, but discerns and discriminates betwixt what is fit to be said, and what is fit to be pass'd ... "[46]

Neo-classical criticism of older poets often turns upon this point of lack of selectiveness, over-abundance of imagery. Lucan and Statius, Dryden notes, were "men of an unbounded imagination, but who often wanted the poise of judgment."[47] And Ovid, despite his general merit, had such imagination "that he often writ too pointedly for his subject, and made his persons speak more eloquently than the violence of their passion would admit: so that he is frequently witty out of season; leaving the imitation of Nature, and the cooler dictates of his judgment, for the false applause of Fancy."[48] Similarly Claudian is criticized by Addison for carrying his description of the destructive work of the giants to ridiculous excess. "It is visible to every judicious Reader, that such Ideas savour more of Burlesque than of the Sublime. They proceed from a Wantonness of Imagination, and rather divert the Mind than astonish it."[49] Addison then proceeds to show how Milton treated the same situation, but by uniting imagination with judgment attained "the full Majesty of Homer ... improved by the Imagination of Claudian, without its Puerilities."[50]

In more recent times it is the metaphysical poets who seem to exhibit most prominently this lack of judgment.

> Great Cowley then (a mighty genius) wrote,
> O'er-run with wit, and lavish of his thought:
> He turns too closely on the reader press:
> He more had pleas'd us, had he pleas'd us less.[51]

So wrote Addison in 1694. Although Cowley's first biographer thought that he had the necessary balance of judgment,[52] neoclassical critics point to Cowley as the prime example of a poet whose fancy flowed too freely. He had, says Welsted, "so luxuriant a Fancy, that I can compare him to nothing more properly than a too rich Soil, which breeds Flowers and Weeds promiscuously, and exerts it self with so great an Exuberance, that at

length it becomes Barren thro' its Fertility ..."[53]
The following passage from Applebee's Journal (June 3, 1732)
illustrates the continuance of this attitude in the early eighteenth
century.

> Mr. Addison observes, that the Redundancy of Mr. Cow-
> ley's Wit has done him more Harm, than the Deficiency of
> it has done other Poets. Nor was this the Fault of Mr. Cow-
> ley alone, but of all the Authors of that Age. They were
> not only inspir'd, but transported with the Furor Poeticus.
> They gave the Reins to their Imagination, and swept all
> that could be said on a Subject with a Drag-Net; conse-
> quently a multitude of good and bad Thoughts, Sentiments
> and Allegories, were crowded into the same Piece.[54]

Hence the necessity for rules, which are merely the formulation of such laws as antiquity had discovered to be more valuable in the production of good work. Dennis justifies them on
the assumption that the art of poetry, like any other art, requires constant "practice" for perfection.

> Rules are necessary even in all the inferiour Arts, as
> in Painting and Musick. If any one should pretend to draw
> a Picture without having ever been taught, or without know-
> ing or practising any thing of Perspective or Proportion,
> but should pretend to succeed alone by the natural force of
> his Fancy, that man would certainly be esteem'd a very
> Impudent and Impertinent person.[55]

Without rules, says Gildon, "all must be governed by unruly
Fancy, and Poetry becomes the land of Confusion, which is, in
Reality, the Kingdom of Beauty, Order, and Harmony."[56]
Without the check imposed by judgment through the rules the
poet may be led equally astray into the production of "loose Im-
ages, and loose Sentiments."

> When the Imagination and Invention are so busy, Reason
> and Judgment are seldom allowed Time enough to examine
> the Justness of a Sentiment, and the Conclusiveness of an
> Argument. Many of our own Poets, the most celebrated
> for their Ingenuity, have been very incorrect and injudi-
> cious, as well as irreligious and immoral, in their Senti-
> ments. They seem to have studied rather to say fine things

289

than just ones, and have often shewn their Fancy at the
Expence of their Understanding, which is buying Reputation at a very extravagant Price. [57]

The imagination, which is the source of all that is fruitful in
poetry, needs thus the check of judgment, so that the poet will
not be betrayed into over-luxuriance. It is on this account that
Dryden justifies his preference for rhyme. "The great easiness
of blank verse renders the poet too luxuriant; he is tempted to
say many things, which might better be omitted, or at least shut
up in fewer words ..." Some say that rhyme "is only an embroi-
dery of sense, to make that which is ordinary in itself pass for
excellent with less examination. But certainly, that which most
regulates the fancy, and gives the judgment its busiest employment, is like to bring forth the richest and clearest thoughts." [58]
But a more serious charge against the imagination is that it
is apt to lead the poet away from the pursuit of nature, into the
improbable and unnatural, tempting him, as Rapin says, "rather
to speak things Wittily, than Naturally." [59] The neo-classicists,
interested as they were in combatting the stylistic excesses of
the metaphysical poets and in setting up a standard of taste which
should contain the elements of universality, quite naturally demanded that imagination should not be allowed complete license,
but that it should work in combination with judgment. While imagination was felt to be the life-giving power in poetry, it contains too many elements of change and subjectivity to furnish the
sole criterion for literary excellence. "But whatever is meant
by Fancy, this we must agree in, that it cannot be good and
right, any farther than it is conformable to Reason, and follows
it close; nor can a Man be said to have a good Fancy, but when
he loves nothing but what is True, Natural, and Just." [60] Both
the precept and the example of the ancients "show the ridiculous
Absurdities one is apt to fall into, who follows only his Fancy;
for though Poesie be the effect of Fancy, yet if this Fancy be
not regulated, 'tis a meer Caprice, not capable of producing any
thing reasonable." [61]
Such a disregard for the "nature of things" in poetry is comparable to a similar disregard in religion on the part of the dissenters. The eccentricities of the metaphysical poets were indeed associated, in the minds of the severer neo-classical critics,
with the contemporary vagaries of the Puritan enthusiasts. Like
the religious fanatics, such poets would let their imaginations
run wild, and would pretend that poetry "is never to be school'd

and disciplin'd by Reason; Poetry, say they, is blind inspiration, is pure enthusiasm, is rapture and rage all over."[62] But
fancy, Rymer insists, is too subjective and changeable to be a
guiding force, without any control whatever.

> Fancy, I think, in Poetry, is like Faith in Religion: it
> makes far discoveries, and soars above reason, but never
> clashes or runs against it. Fancy leaps and frisks, and
> away she's gone, whilst reason rattles the chains and fol-
> lows after. Reason must consent and ratify what-ever by
> fancy is attempted in its absence, or else 'tis all null and
> void in law. However, in the contrivance and oeconomy of
> a Play, reason is always principally to be consulted. Those
> who object against reason are the Fanaticks in Poetry, and
> are never to be sav'd by their good works.[63]

> > But,when you lay tradition wholly by,
> > And on the private spirit alone rely,
> > You turn fanatics in your poetry.

(Poetical works, ed. G.R.Noyes [Boston, 1909], p. 84).

Nature itself shows that wit or fancy is not a faculty superior
to judgment. Some men speak, remarks Shadwell, "as if judgment were a less thing than wit. But certainly it was meant otherwise by nature, who subjected wit to the government of judgment.... In fancy mad men equal if not excel all others...."[64]
The writings of the early peoples, those who follow their fancy
without the discipline of judgment, illustrate this. "Fancy with
them is predominant, is wild, vast, and unbridled, o're which
their judgment has little command or authority: hence their
conceptions are monstrous, and have nothing of exactness,noth-
ing of resemblance or proportion."[65] Rymer makes a similar
criticism of Spenser.

> He had a large spirit, a sharp judgment, and a Genius
> for Heroic Poesie, perhaps above any that ever writ since
> Virgil. But our misfortune is, he wanted a true Idea, and
> lost himself by following an unfaithful guide. Though besides
> Homer and Virgil he had read Tasso, yet he rather suf-
> fer'd himself to be misled by Ariosto; with whom blindly
> rambling on marvellous Adventures, he makes no Con-
> science of Probability. All is fanciful and chimerical,

without any uniformity, without any foundation in truth.... [66]

> Old Spenser next, warm'd with poetick rage,
> In ancient tales amus'd a barb'rous age;
> An age that yet uncultivate and rude,
> Where-e'er the poet's fancy led, pursu'd
> Thro' pathless fields, and unfrequented floods,
> To dens of dragons, and enchanted woods.

(Miscellaneous Works, ed. Guthkelch, I, 31.) One may compare Sir Richard Blackmore's comment, in his preface to Prince Arthur (1695): "But Ariosto and Spencer, however great Wits ... are hurried on with a boundless, impetuous Fancy over Hill and Dale, till they are both lost in a Wood of Allegories, − Allegories so wild, unnatural, and extravagant, as greatly displease the Reader. This way of writing mightily offends in this Age...." (Spingarn, III, 238.)

This antithesis between "wit's false mirror" and "Nature's light," as Pope later put it, is often used in judging the worth and permanent value of a writer. One of the points The Rehearsal makes against Bayes is his fondness for taking material from his own fancy, rather than from Nature. "I despise your Jonson and Beaumont, that borrowed all they writ from Nature: I am for fetching it purely out of my own fancy, I."[67] In conceiving a tragic character, says Rymer, "a Poet is not to leave his reason, and blindly abandon himself to follow fancy, for then his fancy might be monstrous, might be singular, and please no body's maggot but his own; but reason is to be his guide, reason is common to all people, and can never carry him from what is Natural."[68] This is one of the excellences of the great writers of antiquity, and one of the reasons why they retain their wide appeal. The poets, according to the classical critics, should be allowed considerable liberty in their selection of material, "provided their Draughts and their Models be fram'd and govern'd by the nature of things; they must not joyn Serpents with Doves, nor Tygers with Lambs; that is, they must not couple Contraries, and show impossible Chimaeras. This is all the Caution Horace gives either to Poets or Painters; he exempts nothing that is natural from the imitation of Art, nor does he set any thing out of the reach of Fancy that is within the bounds of Truth."[69]
Even in works of avowed wit, Addison points out, "there is a kind of Nature that is to be observed ... and a certain Regularity

of Thought which must discover the Writer to be a Man of Sense,
at the same time that he appears altogether given up to Caprice ..."[70] In another essay he quotes Bouhours and Boileau,
who have shown "That it is impossible for any Thought to be
beautiful which is not just, and has not its Foundation in the Nature of Things: That the Basis of all Wit is Truth; and that no
Thought can be valuable, of which good Sense is not the Ground-
work."[71]

That this conception of art was never wholly lost sight of
throughout the eighteenth century is perfectly true,[72] but it per-
sisted with decreasing emphasis. The great exception to this
ideal was Shakespeare, and, it is to be noted, even his "irregu-
larities" were fitted into this mould by some of the neo-classical critics. "His Imaginations," says Dennis, "were often as
just, as they were bold and strong."[73] But it was the recognition of a new field outside and beyond nature, which Shakespeare
had entered in A midsummer-night's dream and The tempest,
a fairyland where imagination has complete freedom to move,
without the balancing power of judgment, that was to prove in
the eighteenth century an important factor in the apotheosis of
the imagination. But at the height of the neo-classical period
the prevailing attitude is that expressed by Henry Felton: "Our
Thoughts must be conformable to the Matter and Subject that
lye before us, but we have full Liberty to range, provided we
can command our Fancy, and bring it home to the Purpose."[74]

It is quite correct, then, to say that the neo-classical critics
did see certain disadvantages in the uncontrolled imagination.
The traditional association of this image-making faculty with
the non-rational part of man's soul and the contrast − often assumed, if not explicitly stated − between its transitory, subjective nature and eternal, unchanging reason, were bound to find
expression in critical opinion. Yet, even so, we may observe
that most of the severe judgments have to do with the dangers
of an unbridled imagination in prose, where exactness and unadorned truth are the aims. As to poetry, those who insist most
rigidly on its utilitarian nature are likely to disparage imagination, if not all imaginative writing; but for the most part the
criticism of imagination in poetry is that it tempts the poet to
overabundance of expression and "unnatural" imagery. Neo-
classical doctrine here, as in other fields of thought, warns
against lack of balance and control. Nowhere is there the implication that poetry should be devoid of fancy or that it should be
purely the product of cold reason. If neo-classical critics had

little regard for poetry which was purely a "flight of fancy," neither did they recognize an art which ruled imagination out or held it in strict subordination.

NOTES

1   There has been, as yet, no comprehensive study of neo-classical theory in England comparable to that of M. René Bray, La formation de la doctrine classique en France (Paris, 1927).

2   The publication of Prof. J. W. Draper's bibliography (Eighteenth century English aesthetics: a bibliography) (Heidelberg, 1931) has revealed how much the eighteenth century produced in the way of specific criticism to these various art forms. Cf. also the additions to Draper: R. S. C[rane] in Modern philology, XXIX (1931), 251-52; R. D. Havens in Modern language notes, XLVII (1932), 118-20; William D. Templeman, "Contributions to the bibliography of eighteenth-century aesthetics," Modern philology, XXX (1933), 309-16.

3   George Saintsbury, A short history of English literature (1898), p. 565.

4.   "Collins and the creative imagination: a study in the criticial background of his odes (1746)," Studies in English by members of University College, Toronto (Toronto, 1931), pp. 59-130.

5   Ibid., p. 77.

6   Hans Thüme, Beiträge zur Geschichte des Geniebegriffs in England (Halle, 1927), p. 44.

7   Without imagination, writes Sir William Temple, "all Poetry is flat and languishing; without the succors of Judgment 'tis wild and extravagant...." (Miscellanies, ii [1690], in J. E. Spingarn, Critical essays of the seventeenth century [Oxford, 1908-09], III, 81). This collection is referred to hereafter as Spingarn.

8   For valuable criticism in the preparation of this paper I am indebted to Prof. R. S. Crane. To Prof. George Sherburn and to Prof. R. F. Jones (who first turned my attention to the subject) I am also grateful for many helpful suggestions.

9   For the psychological background the following may be consulted: Murray W. Bundy, The theory of imagination in classical and mediaeval thought (Urbana, Ill., 1927); and Ruth L. Anderson, Elizabethan psychology and Shakespeare's plays (Iowa City, 1927).

10   J. S[ergeant], The method to science (1696), p. 6. "I that am
too simple or too serious," writes Samuel Parker, "to be ca-
jol'd with the frenzies of a bold and ungovern'd Imagination cannot be perswaded to think the Quaintest plays and sportings of
wit to be any true and real knowledge" (A free and impartial
censure of the Platonick philosophie (Oxford, 1666), p. 73). In
bibliographical references London may be assumed to be the
place of publication unless otherwise noted.

11   Thomas Sprat, History of the Royal-Society (1667), in Spingarn,
II, 118.

12   Isaac Barrow (d. 1677), Sermon xiv, "Against foolish talking
and jesting," Theological works (Oxford, 1830), I, 410.

13   Preface to Greene's Menaphon (1589), in Works of Thomas
Nashe, ed. R. B. McKerrow (1905), III, 311-12.

14   Advancement of learning (1605), in Spingarn, I, 2.

15   William Pemble (d. 1623), "Vindiciae gratiae: a plea for grace,"
in Workes (4th ed., Oxford, 1659), p. 11.

16   Ibid.

17   Whole critical works (1706), I, 274.

18   Richard Flecknoe, Miscellania (1653), p. 99.

19   Franciscus M. Van Helmont, The spirit of diseases (1694),
Sig. A3^V.

20   Samuel Parker, Censvre of the Platonick philosophie, pp. 75-76.

21   Ralph Cudworth, A treatise concerning eternal and immutable
morality (1731), pp. 144-45.

22   Ibid., p. 145.

23   Sprat, History of the Royal-Society, in Spingarn, II, 116.

24   Manière de bien penser (2nd ed., Amsterdam, 1692), pp. 16-17.
The comparison is commonly traced to Cicero, De oratore,
book iii.

25   Locke, Essay concerning human understanding (1690), II, xi, 2.

26   Spingarn, II, 116-17.

27   Robert Ferguson, The interest of reason in religion; with the import and use of Scripture-metaphors (1675), pp. 346-47. Cf. also Father Malebranche his treatise concerning the search after truth (trans. T. Taylor; 2nd ed., 1700), pp. 90-99; and George Stubbes, A dialogue in the manner of Plato, on the superiority of the pleasures of the understanding to the pleasures of the senses (1734), pp. 52-54.

28   John Constable, Reflections upon accuracy of style (1731), p. 20.

29   Peter Browne, The procedure, extent, and limits of human understanding (1728), p. 399.

30   Locke, Essay, III, x, 34.

31   F. M. Van Helmont, The spirit of diseases (1694). Sig. A3^V. There were of course other elements in the attack upon metaphors. Prof. R. F. Jones (P M L A, XLV [1930], 977-1009; J E G P, XXX [1931], 188-217; ibid., XXXI [1932], 315-31) has shown the influence of the scientists in the reformation of prose style. Another element, I think, is to be found in the reaction of Restoration writers to the "Republick words" of the Puritan divines and statesmen. Jasper Mayne, in the epistle dedicatory to his Part of Lucian made English (Oxford, 1664), ridicules the efforts of the "self-conceited Preacher" to "goe up buskin'd into the Pulpit, and there in a Tragicall stile, and voyce as Cothurnall, entertain his Hearers with a Romantick showre of words...." (Sig. A3^V). We have succeeded, he says, "a canting Generation of men, whose Rhetorick was as rude, & mechanick as their persons...." Such "defile the English Tongue with their Republick words, which are most immusicall to the Eare, and scarce significant to a Monarchicall understanding.... Coyned, & minted by those Seditious, Rump Grammarians, who did put their own impressions to the Kings Silver, and so committed Treason against their Prince, and their own rude stamp and sense to their Goth and Vandall words; and so committed Treason against His good people" (Sig. A4). Samuel Parker thinks the "childish Metaphors and Allegories" characteristic of the dissenters, who "will not talk of Religion but in barbarous and uncouth Similitudes...." (A discourse of ecclesiastical politie [1670], p. 75). He goes so far as to say that "the different Subdivisions among the Sects themselves are not so much distinguish'd by any real diversity of Opinions, as by variety of Phrases and Forms of Speech, that are the peculiar Shibboleths of each Tribe" (ibid.). Much the same kind of ridicule is cast

later upon the enthusiasts. Cf. e.g., James Lowde, A discourse concerning the nature of man.... (1694), pp. 34-36.

32 Preface to Poems (1656), in Spingarn, II, 85.

33 The terms "fancy" and "imagination" were used interchangeably throughout the seventeenth and eighteenth centuries.

34 Preface to The humorists (1671), in Spingarn, II, 153. For similar views in France, see René Bray, La formation de la doctrine classique en France, pp. 63-84.

35 Preface to A collection of miscellanies: consisting of poems, essays, discourses, and letters occasionally written by John Norris. M. A. (Oxford, 1687), Sig. A4ᵛ.

36 Preface to Prince Arthur (1695), in Spingarn, III, 229.

37 E. Nevill, "To the memory of Mr. William Cartwright," prefixed to Cartwright's Comedies (1651), Sig. ****ᵛ.

38 Poetry originally, remarks Senault, was in the service of virtue and encouraged mortals to glorious enterprise. "But men who corrupt the best things, did at last abuse Poetry; and did unjustly submit her unto their Passions, who had reformed them by her advice. This innocent art which had always courted vertue, is become a slave to vice" (Of the use of passions, trans. H. Cary [1649], p. 169).

39 Henry Barker, The polite gentleman; or, reflections upon the several kinds of wit ... Done out of French (1700), p. 80.

40 Ibid., pp. 82-83.

41 Sir Kenelm Digby, Of bodies, and of mans soul ... (1669), part ii, p. 36 (originally published at Paris in 1644). "'Tis a high presumption," writes Davenant, "to entertain a Nation (who are a Poets standing Guest, and require Monarchicall respect) with hasty provisions; as if a Poet might imitate the familiar dispatch of Faulkoners, mount his Pegasus, unhood his Muse, and with a few flights boast he hath provided a feast for a Prince" (Preface to Gondibert [1650], in Spingarn, II, 24). "T. P. baronet" in a commendatory poem prefixed to Cartwright's Comedies (1651) writes:

> "No, his learn'd Phansie still was full of Light,
> First study'd how, and then began to write...."

Even Temple argues that "tho' Invention be the Mother of Poetry, yet this Child is like all others born naked, and must be Nourished with Care, Cloathed with Exactness and Elegance, Educated with Industry, Instructed with Art, Improved by Application, Corrected with Severity, and Accomplished with Labour and with Time, before it Arrives at any great Perfection or Growth" (Miscellanea, ii [1690], in Spingarn, III, 80).

42   Henry Reynolds, Mythomystes ... (1632), in Spingarn, I, 145.

43   Ibid., I, 148. Cf. also Davenant, Preface to Gondibert (1650), in Spingarn, II, 24-25; Sir Robert Howard, Preface to Four new plays (1665), in Spingarn, II, 102; A. Blackwall, An introduction to the classics (1718), pp. 7-8.

44   Whole critical works (1706), I, 153.

45   Ibid. "Tout ce qui est excessif," remarks Eudoxe in Bouhours' Manière de bien penser (2nd ed., Amsterdam, 1692), pp. 22-23, "est vicieux, jusqu'à la vertu, qui cesse d'estre vertu dés qu'elle va aux extrémitez, & qu'elle ne garde point de mesure."

46   Bernard Lamy, The art of speaking: written in French by Messieurs du Port Royal.... Rendred into English (2nd ed., 1708), p. 213.

47   Preface to The state of innocence (1677), in Ker, I, 184. Cf. also Rapin, Whole critical works, I, 170.

48   Dryden, Preface to Ovid's Epistles, translated by several hands (1680), in Ker, I, 233-34.

49   Spectator 333 (March 22, 1712).

50   Ibid. Cf. also Shaftesbury, Second characters (1712), ed. B. Rand (Cambridge, 1914), pp. 143-44; Charles Gildon, Complete art of poetry (1718), I, 97; Bezaleel Morrice, An essay on the poets (1721), p. 19; Alexander Forbes, Lord Pitsligo, Essays moral and philosophical ... (1734), pp. 42-43; an anonymous letter in Dodsley's Museum, III (March 28, 1747), 9; Johnson, Rambler 86 (Jan. 12, 1751); Monthly Review, XIV (June, 1756), 529n.; John Ogilvie, Poems on several subjects (1762), I, xii-xiii; Monthly Review, XXVIII (Feb., 1763), 148; Owen Ruffhead, Life of Alexander Pope (1769), pp. 458-60; Percival Stockdale, An inquiry into the nature, and genuine laws of poetry ... (1778) pp. 5-11, 28-29.

51 Addison, "An account of the greatest English poets," in Miscellaneous Works, ed. Guthkelch (1914), I, 32. For Cowley's reputation at this time see A. H. Nethercot, "The reputation of Abraham Cowley (1660-1800)," P M L A, XXXVIII (1923), 588-641.

52 "His Fancy," says Sprat, "flow'd with great speed, and therefore it was very fortunate to him that his Judgment was equal
to manage it." Although his invention was "powerful and large,"
it seemed "all to arise out of the Nature of the subject, and to
be just fitted for the thing of which he speaks" (An account of
the life and writings of Mr. Abraham Cowley (1668), in Spingarn,
II, 130.)

53 Leonard Welsted, "Remarks on Longinus," appended to The
Works of Dionysius Longinus, on the sublime ... (1712), pp.
170-71.

54 "A critique on English poets" (quoted in Gentleman's magazine,
II (June, 1732), 787). One may note that this is simply a caveat
against the abuse of imagination: "The two great Excellencies
of a Poet are the Fire of his Imagination, and the Sweetness of
his Stile ..." (ibid., p. 786).

55 Advancement and reformation of modern poetry (1701), Epistle
dedicatory, Sig. [A8r-v].

56 Complete art of poetry (1718), I, 91. Fancy is frequently referred to as the element in poetry which most objects to such
discipline. Hildebrand Jacob writes: "There is a Kind of native
Liberty in Fancy, which abhors the Chain of Rules, and Manage-
ment of Art; yet it is not in human Nature to perfect any Thing
without some Labour, and Patience ..." (Works [1735], p. 415).
Cf. also the ironic praise of Samuel Johnson (author of Hurloth-
rumbo) in Philip Skelton, The candid reader (1744), p. 30:
"Rules ... were made only for little and narrow Spirits. They
are mere Leading-strings for infant Imaginations, which would
tumble and grovel on the Earth without them...."

57 Weekly miscellany (Sept. 28, 1734), quoted in Gentleman's
magazine, IV (Sept., 1734), 499.

58 The rival ladies (1664), Epistle dedicatory, in Ker, I, 8. Cf.
Neander's observation in the Essay of dramatic poesy (1668):
"Judgment is indeed the master-workman in a play; but he re-
quires many subordinate hands, many tools to his assistance.
And verse I affirm to be one of these; 'tis a rule and line by
which he keeps his building compact and even, which otherwise

lawless imagination would raise either irregularly or loosely"
(Ker, I, 107).

59   Whole critical works, II, 172.

60   Henry Barker, The polite gentleman (1700), p. 129. Poems
"born from a flash of fancy," writes Gildon, "and applauded by
fancy alone, when that was spent, vanish'd of a sudden away into forgetfulness, as all things must do, which are the product
of fancy without judgment ..." (The laws of poetry [1721], p.20).

61   Rapin, Whole critical works, II, 146. For later expressions cf.
James Arbuckle, Hibernicus's letters (1729), I, 60; Hume, "Of
simplicity and refinement in writing" (1741); Gentleman's magazine, XII (1742), 364-65, 479; William Melmoth, Fitz-osborne's
letters (1748), p. 30; Richard Hurd, Commentary on Horace's
Ars poetica, in Works (1811), I, 31; The world, No. 26 (June
28, 1753), No. 117 (March 27, 1755); Lord Kames, Elements
of criticism (1762), III, 74-83; Monthly review, XXVIII (Feb.,
1763), 146; etc.

62   Thomas Rymer, The tragedies of the last age (1678), in Spingarn, II, 185. "Inspiration," according to Davenant, is "a dangerous word which many have of late successfully us'd ..."
(Preface to Gondibert, in Spingarn, II, 25).

63   Tragedies of the last age, in Spingarn, II, 185. Dryden, in the
same year, makes a similar comparison, in the prologue to
Oedipus.

64   Preface to The humorists (1671), in Spingarn, II, 159.

65   Rymer, preface to translation of Rapin's Reflections on Aristotle's treatise of poesie (1674), in Spingarn, II, 165.

66   Ibid. (Spingarn, II, 167-68.) Addison's lines on Spenser, in his
"Account of the greatest English poets" (1694) reflect this attitude.

67   II, i, 78.

68   The tragedies of the last age, in Spingarn, II, 192. This, it will
be remembered, is the argument of the bee in the famous apo-
logue in The battle of the books.

69   R. Wolseley, Preface to Valentinian (1685), in Spingarn, III,
18. Cf. Hobbes, Answer to Davenant (1650): "Beyond the actual

works of nature a Poet may now go; but beyond the conceived
possibility of nature, never" (Spingarn, II, 62).

70   Spectator 35 (April 10, 1711).

71   Spectator 62 (May 11, 1711).

72   Cf. e.g., Johnson, Ramblers 4, 36, 92; John Brown, Essays
      on the Characteristics (1751), pp. 17-18; John Gilbert Cooper,
      Letters concerning taste (3rd ed., 1757), pp. 67-68; John Gor-
      don, Occasional thoughts on the study and character of classical
      authors ... (1762), pp. 85-87; Kames, Elements of criticism
      (1762), I, 282; Monthly review, XXVI (Jan., 1762), 41-42;
      Owen Ruffhead, Life of Pope (1769), p. 440; Percival Stockdale,
      Inquiry into the nature, and genuine laws of poetry (1778), p.4.

73   An essay on the genius and writings of Shakespear (1712), p.2.

74   A dissertation on reading the classics, and forming a just style
      (1713), pp. 84-85.

THE TENDENCY TOWARD PLATONISM IN NEO-CLASSICAL ESTHETICS

Louis I. Bredvold

It is a matter of common observation that we can to-day recapture only with great difficulty the authentic esthetic experience of the Neo-Classical age. We do our thinking under a different set of current theories and presuppositions, and our feelings have had an education of a different character; without careful study we are likely to attach wholly false meanings even to the terminology of Neo-Classical criticism. Even when we enjoy the art, we are in danger of misinterpreting and falsifying it. We can see everywhere in the modern imitations of Colonial architecture that its beauty has been badly contaminated by a more modern enthusiasm over quaintness, picturesqueness, and sentimental antiquarianism. The legitimacy of these adaptations in our day is not in question here, but whatever beauty they have is not truly Neo-Classical. The Colonial builders were traditionally not interested in quaintness and oddities, but in perfection and symmetry of design, in pleasing proportion, in beauty of geometrical purity. In one of the more popular and authoritative English builders' manuals of the eighteenth century one may read, for instance, that a door or window may be either two or two and one-sixth diameters high; that to raise the pitch or slope of a pediment with grace and beauty, divide the width given into nine equal parts, two of which will then be its perpendicular height; in building a steeple, we learn, if with a square base, make the height four times the diameter, if with an octagonal base, make it eight times the side of the octagon; even the vane at the top has its arithmetical relation to the proportions of the steeple; "the length of the said vane is equal to two thirds of one side of the octagon at bottom, being divided into three parts, one for its point, or dart, and two for its tail."[1] Such were the Palladian recipes which produced the charming beauty of Colonial architecture. Every student of the Neo-Classical age is familiar with similar rules for the various types of literature as well as with mathematical computations of the proportions of the perfect human figure.

Reprinted by permission from English Literary History, Vol. 1 (1934), pp. 91-119.

PLATONISM IN NEO-CLASSICAL ESTHETICS

Our difficulty with these esthetic formulas arises very largely from the fact that we tend to approach them with presuppositions quite the opposite from those of their promulgators. We
say that these "rules" are merely traditional and mechanical;
their formulators regarded them as rational and inspired truth.
To understand this theory — and, what is of main importance,
to appreciate the art produced under it — we must discover and
formulate the presuppositions which made it possible to think of
Neo-Classical theory as rational and significant. We must re-
state the Neo-Classical ideology in order to recapture the esthetic experience which that age sought to express in all the
various arts.

Such a comprehensive study is obviously beyond the scope of
a paper; my purpose here is only to make a very small contribution toward it. I hope to indicate the affinity of the Neo-Classical conception of beauty to the esthetics and metaphysics of
the Platonic — or, more definitely, the Neo-Platonic — tradition
as it had been developed and modified through the centuries. A
complete history even of this subject would require a volume;
but perhaps a brief study of certain moments in the history of
Neo-Classicism, when its theory merged with Platonism, may
be useful in giving us some insight into the characteristic enthusiasm and idealism which guided the creative activity of the
whole age.[2]

I

The Platonism with which we are to be concerned is the doctrine of the ideality of Beauty, a doctrine better formulated by
his followers than by Plato. For Plato, in a famous passage in
The Republic, condemned art as a mere imitation of actuality,
which is in turn a mere copy of the reality of the Ideas; art therefore, he argued, is an imitation twice removed from the Real.
Nevertheless Plato was a lover of beauty; and his disciples easily amended his theory by declaring that an artistic creation is
a copy, not of the actual world, but of the Idea itself, and a more
perfect copy than actuality. Beauty, so Plotinus taught, is an
emanation from the Divine Reality. A beautiful object, said Proclus, is fabricated according to an eternal paradigm; in so far
as a statue is beautiful, it partakes of the presence of a divine
nature. Proclus, as we shall see, was frequently appealed to
by the Neo-Classical theorists of beauty. A passage in Cicero's
Orator, however, became for the eighteenth century perhaps its

most important authority for the Platonic theory of beauty. Cicero explained that he sought to portray in his orator an ideal type, such an orator as had probably never existed. He asked himself, he said, not who had been the perfect orator, but wherein that perfection consists which nothing can excel and which appears only partially and imperfectly in any particular oration. "I lay down this principle," he said,

> that no beauty can be found in any art which can equal this perfect beauty of which the other is only, as it were, a copy or image. This perfect beauty is not to be perceived by the eye or the ear or any sense; it can be comprehended only in thought and imagination. Thus as regards the statues of Phidias, than which we have seen nothing more perfect, and those paintings I have mentioned, we may nevertheless conceive of something more perfect. When Phidias undertook a statue of Jupiter or Minerva, he did not select a model and follow it strictly, but in his mind he had an extraordinary ideal type of beauty; this he contemplated, on this he fixed his mind, and to rendering this he directed his skill and hand. For, as in the arts of sculpture and painting there is something perfect and excellent which is not perceived by the eye but which is derived from an ideal image in the mind, so we perceive the true type of eloquence in our minds and not with our ears. These types of things the weighty author and master Plato called ideas; they do not, according to Plato, arise occasionally in our minds, but are ever present and inherent in reason and intelligence; everything else springs up, dies, flows, disappears, and never remains long in one condition. Whatever is to be studied rationally and methodically must therefore be discussed with reference to that ultimate form and type which gives it its character.[3]

Somewhat less in the spirit of Plato is the statement by Seneca in Epistle LXV. After discussing Aristotle's four causes, he continues:

> To these four Plato adds a fifth cause, – the pattern which he himself calls the "idea"; for it is this that the artist gazed upon when he created the work which he had decided to carry out. Now it makes no difference whether he has his pattern outside himself, that he may direct his

glance to it, or within himself, conceived and placed
there by himself. God has within himself these patterns
of all things, and his mind comprehends the harmonies
and the measures of the whole totality of things which are
to be carried out; he is filled with these shapes which Plato calls the "ideas," — imperishable, unchangeable, not
subject to decay. And therefore, though men die, humanity
itself, or the idea of man, according to which man is
moulded, lasts on, and though men toil and perish, it suf-
fers no change. Accordingly, there are five causes, as
Plato says: the material, the agent, the make-up, the
model, and the end in view. Last comes the result of all
these. Just as in the case of the statue, — to go back to the
figure with which we began, — the material is the bronze,
the agent is the artist, the make-up is the form which is
adapted to the material, the model is the pattern imitated
by the agent, the end in view is the purpose in the maker's
mind, and, finally, the result of all these is the statue
itself. [4]

Seneca's notion that the artist's model may be regarded as an
Idea in Plato's sense evidently assumed that the artist may find
a model which he can copy without deviation. Seneca certainly
was aware of the transcendental nature of Plato's conception of
Ideas, which he expounded in Epistle LVIII. But even in that
epistle he speaks of the Idea as the actual object imitated by the
artist: "When the artist desired to reproduce Vergil in colours
he would gaze upon Vergil himself. The 'idea' was Vergil's outward appearance, and this was the pattern of the intended work. "[5]
Nevertheless, it is significant that Seneca regarded his exposition of the Idea as genuinely Platonic, for a multitude of parallels to his thought and phrasing can be culled from later ages
down to the eighteenth century.
    These passages from Cicero and Seneca not only illustrate
the Platonic theory of ideal beauty, a theory fully formulated in
antiquity and inherited by the Renaissance and Neo-Classicism
from venerated authorities; they also suggest how variously this
theory could develop without losing its root contact with the Platonic tradition. To be called truly Platonic the theory should, as
in Cicero, assume the eternal reality of the Idea. But the phraseology of Platonism was often used, as in Seneca, to express an
esthetic idealism without any real commitment regarding the
Platonic metaphysics. In such cases the Idea became merely the

conception in the artist's mind, not an eternal and transcendental reality. But even when the Idea was thus reduced in metaphysical significance, it still remained a symbol of the corrective and selective principle in art, and retained always some of the glamour of the more genuine Platonic idealism.

It was of course to be expected that these Platonic theories should have a wide currency in the Renaissance.[6] They were accessible in Medieval as well as ancient authorities,[7] and with the revival of Platonism they enjoyed their popularity along with all the other forms of Platonic enthusiasm. The conception of the Idea as the source of beauty was particularly serviceable to the theorists of painting in an age when that art was predominantly ideal in tendency. Giuliano Goselini, in a sonnet prefatory to Lomazzo's Trattato dell' arte de la Pittura (1584), disparaged the accomplished technician who imitates actuality even to deception; the true artist derives his beauty from another source:

> Agguagliò si costui l' alma Natura,
>> Tanta daua à i colori, e forza, e vita;
>> Ch' ella dal suo pennel vinta, e schernita
>> Gli occhi à lui tolse, ah tropporea ventura.
> Ma con la vista interna hà la Pittura,
>> In così chiara, e vera historia ordita;
>> Ch' ella n'è in pregio assai maggior salita,
>> Et ei la tolta luce homai non cura.
> Da i cieli, e da le stelle il moto, e' i lumi,
>> E da la prima Idea tragge le forme
>> Del disegnar, del colorire à l'Arte.
> E come orbo ei discenda, e per quali orme
>> Da l'Empireo à gli Abissi, e gli altri allumi,
>> Lettor qui impara in dotte, illustri carte.

It could not be more forcibly stated than in this typically Renaissance allegory that the source of true art is in a Platonic vision not perceived by the bodily eye.

Nevertheless, the theorists of the Renaissance were more often Platonic in their phraseology than in their metaphysics of beauty. The perfect Idea was more often understood merely as a mental image of perfection evolved in the artist's mind. No anecdote was more frequently cited than that of Zeuxis, who, in order to paint in Helena the ideal of womanly beauty, gathered the details and proportions for his picture from the five most beautiful virgins he could find. Raphael made the somewhat

ambiguous statement that he fell back upon his inner vision of
beauty because good models were scarce; in a letter to Castiglione he said: "per dipingere una bella mi bisognerebbe vedere
più belle, ma per essere carestia di belle donne, io mi servo
di una certa Idea, che mi viene in mente," — a remark which
became a part of the critical canon for three centuries. Such
artistic procedure, the creation of a perfect whole by aggrega-
ting beautiful parts, touches only the lower levels of Platonism
and may very well be associated with a quite different philosophy.
Thus Federico Zuccari, who published his L'Idea de' pittori,
scultori ed architetti in 1607, had much to say about the rôle of
the Idea in the artist's creative activity, and he devised the
phrase disegno interno to indicate his conception of it; but Panofsky denies that Zuccari was a true Platonist, and shows that
his general ideas were essentially Aristotelian and Scholastic.

In general, much of the Renaissance discussion of the ideal
in art stopped short of the true Platonic conception of beauty as
divine archetype. Nevertheless the Platonic Idea had been added to the resources of criticism and esthetic theory. After a
momentary eclipse during the first half of the seventeenth century, when Michel Angelo displaced Raphael in the first rank
among painters, and Baroque ideals dominated Europe, it again
appeared at the time when, in reaction against the extravagance
of the Baroque, art was seeking a purer and more Classical
style. In 1672 Bellori published in Rome his Vite de' pittori,
scultori ed architetti moderni, restoring the supremacy of Raphael and expounding beauty in terms of the Platonic Idea. But
in the interim the Renaissance had passed and the Neo-Classical age had already reached its meridian.

II

Neo-Classic theory, at least as it concerns the imitative arts,
was not developed under Platonic influences. [8] Its characteristic doctrines were, until near the end of the seventeenth century,
promulgated primarily under the authority of Aristotle. In the
Renaissance, as one scholar has put it,

> Aristotle is the source from which rules for the writing of
> poems can be drawn; in him, the critics found a practical
> art of poetry. On the other hand, Plato is the idealist and
> mystical philosopher; in him the Renaissance could find no
> technical rules of the art: but his speculative philosophy

provided the more subtle of the Italian critics with a theory of poetry, a metaphysical system of esthetics. [9]

In the standardization of Neo-Classical doctrine which went on throughout Europe in the sixteenth and seventeenth centuries, Aristotle's remark that art is an imitation was always regarded as the basic principle. This imitation was, following Aristotle again, conceived of as an idealized rendering. For Aristotle had said that

> poetry is something more philosophic and of graver import than history, since its statements are of the nature of universals, whereas those of history are singulars. By a universal statement I mean one as to what such or such a kind of man will probably or necessarily say or do — which is the aim of poetry, though it affixes proper names to the characters; by a singular statement, one as to what, say, Alcibiades did or had done to him. [10]

It was therefore in entire consistency with Aristotle's meaning that his doctrine of art as an imitation was expanded into the formula, "Art is the imitation of Nature." This formula was not new, but it found ever-increasing acceptance in the seventeenth century. Spingarn has made the misleading suggestion that this conception of Nature is related to the new scientific discoveries and that "the mechanical universe of the philosophy of Hobbes and Locke is thus the basis of seventeenth-century criticism; and the sense of mechanical order in nature was implicit in all thought." [11] But the Nature which was then thought to be imitated by art will be much better understood from Cicero than from Hobbes and the scientists. The conception is at least as old as Stoicism, and had for centuries been a familiar and guiding principle in ethics and law. The secret of living the good life, said the Stoics, is to "follow Nature." To them Nature meant a kind of world-order, an order perceived by the enlightened and disciplined soul, which in turn found within itself a noble capacity for conforming to this ideal world-order, and thus raising itself above sordidness and vice. The Nature which is imitated by art is also of this ideal and normative kind, the

> Unerring Nature, still divinely bright,
> One clear, unchang'd, and universal light,

of Pope's Essay on Criticism. "Omnis ars naturae imitatio est,

all art is but imitation of Nature, " said Seneca (Epistle LXV).
The idealism of the Stoics was impressed upon the doctrine anew
in the seventeenth century, although the precise metaphysical
explanation of this ideal Nature might vary from one writer to
another. The curious by-ways by which this esthetic doctrine
could be transmitted to the seventeenth century may be illustrated by a parallel pointed out by Panofsky. Zuccari, in his Idea
(1607) already referred to, explains thus why art can imitate
Nature:

> La ragione poi, perchè l'arte imiti la Natura è, perchè
> il Disegno interno artificiale e l'arte istessa si muovono
> ad operare nella produzione delle cose artificiali al modo,
> che opera la Natura istessa. E se vogliamo anco sapere
> perchè la Natura sia imitabile, è perchè la Natura è ordina-
> ta da un principio intellettivo al suo proprio fine ed alle
> sue operazioni; onde l'opera sua è opera dell' intelligenza
> non errante, come dicono i filosofi; poichè per mezzi ordi-
> narî e certi conseguisce il suo fine; e perchè questo stesso
> osserva l' arte nell' operare, con l' ajuto principalmente
> di detto Disegno, però e quella può essere da questa imi-
> tata, e questa può imitar quella.

This passage is typically Neo-Classic in spirit; but it is an almost literal translation from Thomas Aquinas (Phys. 2.4.):

> ars imitatur naturam.... Eius autem, quod ars imitatur
> naturam, ratio est, quia principium operationis artifici-
> alis cognitio est.... Ideo autem res naturales imitabiles
> sunt per artem, quia ab aliquo principio intellectivo tota
> natura ordinatur ad finem suum, ut sic opus naturae vi-
> deatur esse opus intelligentiae, dum per determinata me-
> dia ad certos fines procedit: quod etiam in operando ars
> imitatur. [12]

The formulators of the literary doctrine of the seventeenth
century were, then, appropriating a familiar idea which carried
with it an essentially ideal view of the world. When they said
that art is an imitation of Nature, they meant an ideal nature;
later the French coined the phrase la belle nature. This does
not mean that they advocated an avoidance of actuality, but rather a mastery over it, or an interpretation of it. They believed
that art must deal with reality, as opposed to unreality, and also

as opposed to actuality. They well remembered in an age when
Scholasticism was still alive, when its phraseology still entered
into the thought and expression of educated people, that from
the verb esse, which means mere existence, there had been derived such words as essence, essential, which betoken some
sort of degree of reality within the actual. Art must seize this
reality. In one of his letters Poussin thus describes his own
intention as a painter in the Mode, as he puts it, of the Greeks:

> Ici cette parole Mode signifie proprement la raison ou la
> mesure et la forme dont nous nous servons pour faire quel-
> que chose, laquelle raison nous astreint à ne pas passer out-
> re certaines bornes et à observer avec intelligence et mo-
> dération, dans chacun de nos ouvrages, l'ordre déterminé
> par lequel chaque chose se conserve en son essence. 13

Poussin, we observe, regarded the real as in some way residing in the actual; his language reminds us, on the philosophical side, of Medieval Realism, and as studio talk, of modern
artists since Cezanne. But he was only enunciating standard
Neo-Classical doctrine as it was understood by the most representative men of the movement. More than a century after Poussin we find Sir Joshua Reynolds, in his Twelfth Discourse before the students of the National Academy, censuring Boucher,
not only for his innate bad taste, but for his unsound method of
painting from memory alone, without either drawings or models. "A painter with such ideas and such habits," said Sir Joshua, "is indeed in a most hopeless state. The art of seeing Nature, or, in other words, the art of using Models, is in reality
the great object, the point to which all our studies are directed."
This art of seeing Nature, this art of using models, consists,
according to Reynolds, of finding the essential, the ideally real,
which is indeed the painter's vision. In his Ninth Discourse he
told his students that

> the Art which we profess has beauty for its object; this it
> is our business to discover and express; the beauty of
> which we are in quest is general and intellectual; it is an
> idea that subsists only in the mind; the sight never beheld
> it, nor has the hand expressed it; it is an idea residing in
> the breast of the artist, which he is always labouring to
> impart, and which he dies at last without imparting.

Such idealization in the imitation of Nature had, of course, also the authority of Aristotle. In speaking of the characters in tragedy, Aristotle had said:

> As Tragedy is an imitation of personages better than the ordinary man, we in our way should follow the example of good portrait-painters, who reproduce the distinctive features of a man, and at the same time, without losing the likeness, make him handsomer than he is. The poet in like manner, in portraying men quick or slow to anger, or with similar infirmities of character, must know how to represent them as such, and at the same time as good men, as Agathon and Homer have represented Achilles. [14]

But such Aristotelian statement of the esthetic ideal tends to approximate the Platonic vision of a beauty which exists above and beyond the actual world and of which the actual world partakes only imperfectly. Dacier, in spite of his translation of Plato, was not deeply interested in Plato's metaphysics; but when he came in his Poëtique d'Aristote (1692) to Aristotle's remark, just quoted, on the poet's portrayal of the angry man, his explanation took a Platonic turn; this passage means, he said, that the poet "doit plûtôt consulter ce que la colére peut ou doit faire vray-semblablement, que ce qu'elle a fait. Il doit plûtôt travailler d'aprés la Nature, qui est le veritable original, que s'amuser aprés un particulier, qui n'est qu'une copie imparfaite et confuse, ou meme vicieuse, ce que le Poëte doit éviter."[15] Dacier's phrasing may be a mere coincidence, but his conception of Nature as the source of beauty is essentially that of the Platonic Idea.

III

Thus Neo-Classical esthetics, being fundamentally ideal in principle, developed under the authority of Aristotle's doctrine of imitation and the Stoic conception of Nature, to the point where it came very much to resemble Platonism. Toward the end of the seventeenth century, when the various arts were endeavoring to attain a clearer and purer style, when the extravagances of the first half of the century were beginning to be recognized as faults, the revived interest in beauty as perfection inspired also a renewed interest in the Platonic Idea. In the field of painting Raphael was again raised to the highest eminence.

The early seventeenth century had assented to Vasari's praise
of Michel Angelo as "rather divine than earthly." But tastes
and ideals were changing. Fréart de Chambray, an intimate
friend of Poussin, declared in his Idée de la Perfection de la
Perfection de la Peinture (published in 1662 and dedicated to
Poussin), that there "is none but easily perceives, by paralleling the Compositions and Figures of Raphael, with those of Mi-
chael Angelo, that the First was the very sweetness of Grace
it self; whereas, on the contrary, Mic. Angelo was so rude and
unpleasing, that he retain'd not so much as any regard to Good-
manners." 16 Likewise André Félibien, another admirer of
Poussin, historiographer of the French Academy of Painting
and secretary of the Academy of Architecture, in his Entretiens sur les vies des Peintres (1666), thus compared Raphael
and Michel Angelo:

> Pour ce qui est de Michel-Ange, bien que je ne sois
> pas de ceux qui ont une aversion si forte contre lui, qu'ils
> ne le croyent pas mériter le nom de Peintre, mais qu'au
> contraire je l'estime un des grands hommes qui ayent
> été; il faut avoüer néanmoins que quelque grandeur et
> quelque severité qu'il y ait dans son dessein, il n'est
> point si excellent que celui de Raphaël, qui exprimoit
> toutes choses avec une douceur et une grace merveilleuse. 17

For, he says on the same page, "si quelques-uns ont excellé
en une partie de la Peinture, ils n'ont sû les autres que fort
médiocrement, et l'on peut dire que Raphaël a été admirable
en toutes."

The esthetic ideal reflected in this Neo-Classical worship
of Raphael was of course essentially the same as that underlying Boileau's Art Poëtique and Pope's Essay on Criticism. But
Félibien was not content to announce that Art is Truth and Art
is the imitation of Nature. Art, he said, is divine, a sort of
human analogue to the all-mighty power of God, who created
the universe out of nothing:

> Si vous voulez prendre la peine de faire reflexion sur
> les diverses parties de cet Art, vous avoüerez qu'il four-
> nit de grands sujets de méditer sur l'excellence de cette
> premiere Lumiere, d'où l'esprit de l'homme tire toutes
> ces belles idées, et ces nobles inventions qu'il exprime
> ensuite dans ses Ouvrages.

Car si en considerant les beautez et l'art d'un Tableau,
nous admirons l'invention et l'esprit de celui dans la pen-
sée duquel il a sans doute été conceû encore plus parfaite-
ment que son pinceau ne l'a pû executer; combien admire-
rons-nous davantage la beauté de cette source où il a pui-
sé ses nobles idées ? Et ainsi toutes les diverses beautez
de la Peinture, servant comme de divers degrez pour
nous élever jusqu'à cette Beauté souveraine, ce que nous
verrons d'admirable dans la proportion des parties, nous
fera considerer combien plus admirable encore est cette
proportion, et cette harmonie qui se trouve dans toutes
les Créatures. L'ordonnance d'un beau Tableau nous fera
penser à ce bel Ordre de l'Univers. Ces Lumieres et ces
Jours que l'Art sait trouver par le moyen du mélange des
couleurs, nous donneront quelque idée de cette Lumiere
éternelle, par laquelle et dans laquelle nous devons voir
un jour tout ce qu'il y a de beau en Dieu et dans ses Créatures. Et enfin quand nous penserons que toutes ces
merveilles de l'Art qui charment ici-bas nos yeux et sur-
prennent nos esprits, ne sont rien en comparaison des
idées qu'en avoient conceû ces Maîtres qui les ont pro-
duites; combien aurons-nous sujet d'adorer cette Sagesse
éternelle qui répand dans les Esprits la Lumiere de tous
les Arts, et qui en est elle-même la loi éternelle et im-
muable ? Cette Lumiere est la Lumiere d'une Sagesse in-
finiment superieure à la Lumiere de tous les esprits cré-
ez, comme elle le dit elle-même par son Prophete, Mes
pensées ne sont pas comme vos pensées, ni mes voyes
comme vos voyes, etc. [18]

And this celebration of beauty in art as a revelation of Divine
Reality emanated from high authority in the Paris of Racine and
Boileau.

However, this passage from Félibien, remarkable for religious as well as artistic fervor, probably owes nothing to Plato
directly. It was in part inspired by such Platonic phraseology
as had become commonplace in Christian thought; for Félibien,
as we can see from his references, had been turning over the
pages of Augustine. Nor is it entirely fanciful to suppose that
he had heard something of the Platonic enthusiasm of his Italian contemporary, Giovanni Pietro Bellori, who was also a
friend of Poussin. In an important lecture before the Accademia
di San Lucca in Rome in 1664, Bellori had explained beauty in

terms of the Platonic Idea. This lecture he printed as introduction to Le vite de' Pittori, Scultori et Architetti moderni (Rome, 1672), under the title "L'Idea del pittore, dello scultore e dell' architetto, scelta delle bellezze naturali superiore alla natura." He gives an account of painting, said John Dryden, who translated from it in 1695, which "cannot be unpleasing, at least to such who are conversant in the philosophy of Plato." Bellori was a learned antiquarian as well as a Platonist, and he supported his theory of the Idea with a long array of authorities, including Cicero, Proclus, Maximus Tyrius, Xenophon, Quintilian, Aristotle and Pliny among the ancients, and Alberti, Leonardo da Vinci, Raphael, Guido Reni, and Castelvetro among the moderns. Even though most of these were not Platonists, they could be made to bear testimony to the existence in great art of an ideal beauty found only imperfectly in nature. [19]

Dryden's several pages of free translation from Bellori, in his Parallel of Poetry and Painting, are not unsatisfactory; but for the sake of precision it will be necessary to give a specimen from the not very accessible original:

> Quel sommo ed eterno intelletto autore della natura nel fabbricare l'opere sue marauigliose, altamente in se stesso riguardando, costituì le prime forme chiamate Idee, in modo che ciascuna specie espressa fù da quella prima Idea, formandosene il mirabile contesto delle cose create. Ma li celesti corpi sopra la luna, non sottoposti a cangiamento, restarono per sempre belli e ordinati, qualmente dalle misurate sfere e dallo splendore degli aspetti loro veniamo a conoscerli perpetuamente giustissimi e vaghissimi. Al contrario auuiene de' corpi sublunari soggetti elle alterationi e alla bruttezza; e sebene la Natura intende sempre di produrre gli effetti suoi eccellenti, nulladimeno per l' inequalità della materia si alterano le forme, e particolarmente l'humana bellezza si confonde, come vediamo nell' infinite deformità e sproportioni, che sono in noi. Il perche li nobili Pittori e Scultori, quel primo fabbro imitando, si formano anch' essi nella mente vn esempio di bellezza superiore, e in esso riguardando emendano la natura senza colpa di colore e di lineamento. Questa Idea, ouero Dea della Pittura e della Scoltura aperte le sacre cortine de gl' alti ingegni de i Dedali e de gli Apelli, si suela a noi e discende sopra i marmi e sopra le tele; originata dalla

natura supera l'origine e fassi originale dell' arte, misu-
rata dal compasso dell' intelletto diuiene misura della
mano, e animata dall' immaginatiua dà vita all' immagine.
Sono certamente per sentenza de' maggiori filosofi le
cause esemplari ne gli animi de gli Artefici, le quali ri-
siedono senza incertezza perpetuamente bellissime e per-
fettissime. Idea del Pittore e dello Scultore è quel perfetto ed eccellente esempio della mente, alla cui immaginata
forma imitando si rassomigliano le cose, che cadono sot-
to la vista: tale è la finitione de Cicerone nel libro dell'
Oratore a Bruto. [Bellori quotes the sentence beginning,
"Ut igitur in formis et figuris."] Cosi l'Idea costituisce
il perfetto della bellezza naturale e vnisce il vero al ver-
isimile delle cose sottoposte all' occhio, sempre aspirando
all' ottimo ed al marauiglioso, onde non solo emula, ma
superiore fassi alla natura, palesondoci l' opere sue eleganti e compite, quali essa non è solita dimostrarci per-
fette in ogni parte. Questo pregio conferma Proclo nel
Timeo, dicendo: se tu prenderai vn huomo fatto dalla natura e vn altro formato dall' arte statuaria, il naturale
sarà meno prestante, perche l' arte opera più accurata-
mente. Ma Zeusi, che con la scelta di cinque vergini for-
mò l'immagine di Eleno tanto famosa da Cicerone posta
in esempio all' Oratore, insegna insieme al Pittore ed
allo Scultore a contemplare l'Idea delle migliori forme
naturali con farne scelta da vari corpi, elegendo le più
eleganti.

"In these pompous expressions, or such as these," said Dryden at the end of his translation from Bellori, "the Italian has
given you his Idea of a Painter; and though I cannot much comment the style, I must needs say, there is somewhat in the
matter." There is food for thought in the fact that this aged
representative of the Neo-Classical school in poetry and criticism should find the Platonic conception of beauty both pertinent and appealing.

IV

The importance of Bellori in the history of Neo-Classical
art theory in Italy and France has been emphasized recently by
several German scholars.[20] In France his influence was parallel with that of native writers whose ideas and tastes also

reflected those of Poussin, the peintre-philosophe. Among the
more important of these commentators may be mentioned,
along with Fréart de Chambray and Félibien, Hilaire Pader,
the painter Le Brun, and Charles Alphonse Du Fresnoy, whose
poem De Arte Graphica was first translated into English by
Dryden and later by William Mason, with annotations by Reynolds. Bellori, as well as the French writers, had exalted
Poussin as a painter in the Antique Mode, and in the French
Academicism of the latter seventeenth century the Frenchman
was often paired with Raphael. Paris was therefore disposed
to be receptive towards Bellori's ideas.

However, significant as Bellori may be to the modern student of Neo-Classical esthetics, his historical importance must
not be exaggerated; his influence did not extend to the whole
movement of Neo-Classicism, nor can it be said that his Platonism founded a "school." Dryden thought that too much smoke
accompanied his fire; and Dryden there voiced the suspicion of
enthusiasm which marked the whole age. But this being so, we
shall find even greater significance, at least for the special
purpose of this paper, in those scattered instances where the
Neo-Classical esthetic experience was explained in Platonic
terms. For the Platonists were not so much contributing something new to the art experience of the age, as they were explaining and justifying what was already the common intention. The
whole effort of Neo-Classicism was to express ideal truth and
ideal beauty; the Platonists saw in the finished art, so far as
it was great and genuine, a revelation of a transcendent truth
and beauty, a visible embodiment of the unseen Idea.

This affinity between Neo-Classicism and Platonism is all
that we are seeking to establish here. It may be observed even
in certain critical utterances in which men who were not Platonists resorted to a Platonic phraseology. Thus John Dennis
says that Horace, in Ars Poetica,

> makes it as clear as the Sun, what it is to follow Nature
> in giving a draught of human Life, and of the manners of
> Men, and that is not to draw after particular Men, who
> are but Copies and imperfect Copies of the great univer-
> sal Pattern; but to consult that innate Original, and that
> universal Idea, which the Creator has fix'd in the minds
> of ev'ry reasonable Creature, and so to make a true and
> a just Draught. For as ev'ry Copy deviates from the Ori-
> ginal both in Life and Grace, and Resemblance, a Poet

who designs to give a true Draught of human Life and Manners, must consult the universal Idea, and not particular
Persons. [21]

Dennis certainly did not think that Horace was a Platonist; but
the precept of Horace,

Respicere exemplar vitae morumque jubebo
Doctum imitatorem et vivas hinc ducere voces (ll. 317-318),

he explained as "following Nature," and this phrase in turn as
copying from the universal Ideas, possibly recollecting the
passages from Dacier quoted earlier in this paper. For, after
all, in any ideal imitation of Nature, of "la belle Nature," a
governing vision of beauty must first exist in the artist's mind.
Batteux, who said that the artist "est essentiellement observa-
teur," defined the true subject-matter of art, "la belle Nature,"
as "pas le vrai qui est; mais le vrai qui peut être, le beau vrai,
qui est représenté comme s'il existoit réellement, et avec
toutes les perfections qu' il peut recevoir."[22] Or as the English
painter Jonathan Richardson put it: " 'tis a certain Maxim, No
Man sees what things Are, that knows not what they ought
to be."[23]
     But if this tendency towards Platonizing was inhibited by the
general indifference towards transcendental metaphysics, there
is also a further historical reason why such esthetics as Bellori's formed no dominant and continuous tradition. Esthetic
speculation began early in the eighteenth century to shift its
problem from the ideal and over-individual Nature which was
to be imitated, to the subjective conception of art as the product of Genius. Characteristic of this new approach is the famous statement by James Harris that Art is Energy. This new
conception often appeared along with the older one, for it was
not impossible to reconcile the notion of Genius with ideality in
art. Shaftesbury, possibly the most Hellenic mind of the half-
century before Winckelmann and Lessing, and in some ways a
good Platonist, became nevertheless one of the founders of the
new subjectivism. His philosophy parallels Neo-Classical esthetics in important ways. The Beauty which he identified with
the Good is obviously the beauty also of Neo-Classical art and
definable in the customary phraseology of Neo-Classical theory:
it is "a whole, coherent and proportioned in itself, with due
subjection and subordinacy of constituent parts."[24] As a

connoisseur of painting Shaftesbury had studied the ideal beauty of Raphael, although he also believed that the French critics had unduly depreciated Michel Angelo; he had read Bellori and was familiar with his Platonic doctrine of the Ideas. [25] He believed in the validity of standards in art as well as in morals, and in the guidance of artistic cultivation by these standards. And yet Shaftesbury was not greatly attracted by the doctrine of the Ideas; he was not a Platonist of this type; his standards of art and conduct, in spite of his insistence on their objective validity, always resolved themselves at last into the taste of the cultivated gentleman. Fundamentally, Shaftesbury did not escape from the principle that man is the measure of all things; and beauty, he admitted, is after all in the artist, not in the art. "The beautiful, the fair, the comely, were never in the matter, but in the art and design; never in body itself, but in the form or forming power." "So that the beautifying, not the beautified, is the really beautiful." "We have undoubtedly the honor of being originals." [26] Thus Shaftesbury became a founder of the new cult of Genius, and, in spite of his Platonism, his influence rather checked than advanced the esthetic tendencies we are here discussing.

V

Nevertheless these tendencies continued to manifest themselves throughout Europe in the eighteenth century. They sometimes appear in unexpected places, as in a poem On Design and Beauty, an epistle to Highmore from the youthful pen of Isaac Hawkins Browne; "the Platonic idea of Beauty," explained his son, "is pursued through the whole poem." [27] Daniel Webb associated in Rome with Mengs and Winckelmann and incorporated their ideas in An Inquiry into the Beauties of Painting (1760). [28] Of far greater importance is the Platonic theory of beauty in Gravina and Muratori. We shall, however, have to pass even them by, and limit our discussion to three men of great significance for our subject, Père André, Winckelmann, and Sir Joshua Reynolds.

Père André (1675-1764), a French Jesuit, was from his youth a follower of the philosophy of Descartes, and particularly of the development of it by Malebranche, with whom André carried on a correspondence in terms of warm friendship and admiration. In this personal and intellectual adherence to the philosopher who declared that we know, not things, but their

PLATONISM IN NEO-CLASSICAL ESTHETICS

Ideas in God, may be detected at once the idealistic leanings of
André. The Jesuit order in France was hostile to the philosophy
of Malebranche as well as to Cartesianism in general, and André was subjected until late in his life to various petty persecu-
tions, a martyrdom which he courageously suffered. In 1741,
when he was sixty-six years old, he published a small volume
of lectures delivered before the Academy of Caen, under the
title Essai sur le Beau, which he republished twenty-two years
later in an expanded form. This little treatise enjoyed considerable vogue. In the article Le Beau in Diderot's Encyclopédie
the major attention is given to the theories of Crousaz, Hutche-
son, and André. The opening paragraphs of the article, including the discussion of Plato and Augustine, are practically lifted
without acknowledgment from André. And the writer, who is
generally supposed to have been Diderot himself, declares that
André "est celui qui jusqu'à présent a le mieux approfondi cette
matiere, en a le mieux connu l'étendue et la difficulté, en a
posé les principes les plus vrais et les plus solides, et mérite
le plus d'être lu."
    As a disciple of Descartes and Malebranche, André formed
his fundamental philosophy in the rationalistic tradition of his
age and country. And his esthetics, also, are the esthetics of
Neo-Classicism. He refers to Vitruvius and Palladio on architecture, to Félibien on painting, to Rameau and others on music.
He admired as a good Frenchman should the great men of the
seventeenth century, Corneille and Racine, Boileau and Molière, Bossuet and Fénelon. But for the principles of his theory
of beauty he went to Augustine. In Plato, he said, he found
ideas, wit, and eloquence; but in Augustine he found Platonic
thought reduced to system. He lamented that Augustine's youthful treatise De Pulchro et Apto had been lost, but by piecing
together scattered passages from the extant writings he was
able to deduce the fundamentals of Augustine's version of the
Platonic esthetics. The first principle is that there is a certain
original, sovereign, eternal and perfect beauty, which the artist seeks to approach in the practice of his art. Unity is the
form and essence of this beauty. Unity, however, implies also
variety; for it is only in a complex work that unity appears as
a victory of order over chaos. Thus André extracted out of Augustine the principles of Neo-Classicism.
    The idealism of André's theory appears not only in his Au-
gustinian principle, but also in his classification of the kinds of
beauty: essential or divine beauty, natural beauty, and artificial

or arbitrary beauty. Concerning the first two he says:

> On vient de voir, qu'il y en a un que est essentiel, néc-
> essaire, et indépendant de toute institution: un beau géo-
> métrique, si j'ose ainsi m'exprimer. C'est celui dont
> l'idée, comme parle encore saint Augustin, forme l'art
> du Créateur. Cet art suprême, qui lui fournit tous les
> modèles des merveilles de la nature, que nous allons
> considérer. Je dis en second lieu qu'il y a un beau natu-
> rel, dépendant de la volonté du Créateur, mais indépen-
> dant de nos opinions et de nos goûts. Gardons-nous bien,
> de le confondre, comme le vulgaire, avec le beau essen-
> tiel. Il en est plus différent, que le ciel ne l'est de la
> terre. Le Beau essentiel consideré dans la structure des
> corps, n'est, pour ainsi dire, que le fond du beau naturel.
> Un fond, je l'avoue, qui est par lui-même riche et agré-
> able; mais qui avec tous ses agrémens plairoit à la raison
> plus qu'à l'oeil, si l'Auteur de la nature n'avoit pris soin
> de le relever par les couleurs. 29

By drawing this distinction between three orders of beauty, André is able to preserve the authority of his central principle in
the face of such variations in taste as were adduced by the Pyr-
rhonists, just as Dr. Johnson (The Rambler, 156 and 158), with
the same end in view, distinguished between the Law of Nature
and the positive law which should be based on it. It is unnecessary to pursue André's analysis further. We have here an excellent statement of Neo-Classical principles and taste; we can
easily trace in it analogies to the philosophy of Descartes and
Malebranche and to the critical principles of Boileau and Dryden and Reynolds. But this statement is at bottom a form of
Platonic idealism derived from Augustine.

VI

Johann Joachim Winckelmann (1717-1768) has never received
higher praise than in those words of Hegel which Walter Pater
quoted in his essay on him: "Winckelmann, by contemplation
of the ideal works of the ancients, received a sort of inspiration through which he opened a new sense for the study of art.
He is to be regarded as one of those who, in the sphere of art,
have known how to initiate a new organ for the human spirit. "
But although it must be conceded that Winckelmann possessed

an intuitive sense for Greek art which amounted to genius, he
was nevertheless not quite the isolated figure in his age that
Hegel's eulogy would suggest. As some recent German scholars have been pointing out, [30] he was the continuator of the
principles of Neo-Classicism at its best. He knew the work of
Bellori, who may properly be regarded as having prepared the
way for him. In his Gedanken über die Nachahmung der griechischen Werke in der Malerey und Bilhauerkunst (1755) he mentions Poussin along with Raphael and Michel Angelo as men
who had really understood the Ancients. In this essay, published
before his first visit to Rome, he also shows the influence of
Platonism in his conception of beauty: "Die Kenner und Nach-
ahmer der griechischen Werke finden in ihren Meisterstücken
nicht allein die schönste Natur, sondern noch mehr als Natur,
das ist, gewisse idealische Schönheiten derselben, die, wie
uns ein alter Ausleger des Plato lehret, [31] von Bildern bloss
im Verstande entworfen, gemacht sind." After he arrived in
Rome he made a special study of Plato for the purpose of deepening and guiding his appreciation of Greek art.

What Winckelmann sought for in Greek art was intellectual
beauty. "Die Schönheit wird durch den Sinn empfunden, aber
durch den Verstand erkannt und begriffen." [32] It is a vision of
perfection which is divine. Winckelmann's analysis of it forms
a parallel to the Augustinian conception of beauty as expanded
by André:

> Die höchste Schönheit ist in Gott, und der Begriff der
> menschlichen Schönheit wird vollkommen, je gemässer
> und übereinstimmender derselbe mit dem höchsten Wesen
> kann gedacht werden, welches uns der Begriff der Einheit
> und der Untheilbarkeit von der Materie unterscheidet. Die-
> ser Begriff der Schönheit ist wie ein aus der Materie durch
> Feuer gezogener Geist, welcher sich suchet ein Geschöpf
> zu zeugen nach dem Ebenbilde der in dem Verstande der
> Gottheit entworfenen ersten vernünftigen Creatur. Die
> Formen eines solchen Bildes sind einfach und ununter-
> brochen, und in dieser Einheit mannigfaltig, eben dadurch
> aber sind sie harmonisch; eben so wie ein süsser und ange-
> nehmer Ton durch Körper hervorgebracht wird, deren
> Theile gleichförmig sind. Durch die Einheit und Einfalt
> wird alle Schönheit erhaben, so wie es durch dieselbe al-
> les wird, was wir wirken und reden: denn was in sich
> gross ist, wird, mit Einfalt ausgeführet und vorgebracht,

erhaben.... Aus der Einheit folget eine andere Eigen-
schaft der hohen Schönheit, die Unbezeichnung derselben,
das ist, deren Formen weder durch Punkte, noch durch
Linien, beschrieben werden, als die allein die Schönheit
bilden; folglich eine Gestalt, die weder dieser oder jener
bestimmten Person eigen sey, noch irgend einen Zustand
des Gemüths oder eine Empfindung der Leidenschaft aus-
drücke, als welche fremde Züge in die Schönheit mischen,
und die Einheit unterbrechen. Nach diesem Begriff soll
die Schönheit seyn, wie das vollkommenste Wasser aus
dem Schoosse der Quelle geschöpfet, welches, je weniger
Geschmack es hat, desto gesunder geachtet wird, weil es
von allen fremden Theilen geläutert ist. 33

It is true that Winckelmann also recognized the element of Expression (Ausdruck) in the arts which represent human nature;
but he contrasts it with pure Beauty (die reine Schönheit), which
it tends to break down. He thereby raised a problem which was
to perplex later philosophers of art, and which he himself frequently dealt with in his own history and criticism of Greek art.
But the principle of beauty Winckelmann clearly identified with
the ideal form, the Platonic vision of the Idea, not with Expression per se.

It does not matter that Winckelmann in one place asserts,[34]
in contradiction to Raphael, that ideal beauty may indeed be
found, at least fragmentarily, in nature, and that it is no mere
metaphysical abstraction. Such an assertion must be interpreted in the light of his fundamental doctrine that the imitation of
nature can attain true and significant art only if it is guided by
a higher principle. Characteristic of his feeling for supreme
beauty is his rhapsody over the winged Genius in the Villa Borghese:

Hier wünschte ich eine Schönheit beschreiben zu kön-
nen, dergleichen schwerlich aus menschlichem Geblüte
erzeuget werden: es ist ein geflügelter Genius in der Villa Borghese, in der Grösse eines wohlgemachten Jünglings.
Wenn die Einbildung mit dem einzelnen Schönen in der Natur angefüllet, und mit Betrachtung der von Gott ausflies-
senden und zu Gott führenden Schönheit beschäftiget, sich
im Schlafe die Erscheinung eines Engels bildete, dessen
Angesicht von göttlichem Lichte erleuchtet wäre, mit
einer Bildung, die ein Ausfluss der Quelle der höchsten

Uebereinstimmung schien; in solcher Gestalt stelle sich
der Leser dieses schöne Bild vor. Man könnte sagen, die
Natur habe diese Schönheit, mit Genehmhaltung Gottes,
nach der Schönheit der Engel gebildet. [35]

Winckelmann was no metaphysician, and his Platonism was
doubtless as much poetry as philosophy. But it was of profound
service to him in defining the nature of his esthetic experience
and in deepening his insight into the beauty of Greek art.

VII

Sir Joshua Reynolds took from his youth the direction which
his genius was to follow throughout his career. He came upon
one of Jonathan Richardson's treatises on painting, which so
delighted and inflamed his mind, says Malone, "that Raphael
appeared to him superior to the most illustrious names of ancient or modern times, — a notion which he loved to indulge all
the days of his life."[36] Richardson's An Essay on the Theory
of Painting (1715) and Two Discourses (1719) constitute a good
summary of the best current Italian and French theory regarding painting. Richardson knew Bellori and Félibien, [37] and he
was capable of expounding their conception of the role of Ideal
Beauty in the process of artistic creation. He quoted out of Bellori the famous sentence in Raphael's letter to Castiglione. He
understood the paradox of Neo-Classicism that unless Nature
is improved upon it is not truly imitated. "So That is said to
be done by the Life which is done the thing intended to be represented being set before us, tho' we neither follow it Intirely,
nor intend so to do, but Add, or Retrench by the help of pre-
conceiv'd Ideas of a Beauty, and Perfection we imagine Nature
is capable of, tho' 'tis Rarely, or Never found."[38] Of this kind
of art, said Richardson, Raphael "is the great Model of Perfection! All the Painters being rank'd in three several Classes according to the Degrees of their Merit, He must be allow'd to
possess the first alone."[39]

Curiously enough, in addition to having his mind inflamed
by this Neo-Classical idealism, Reynolds came in his youth
under the influence of a Platonist, the Reverend Zachariah
Mudge, Prebendary of Exeter. On this point we have the authoritative testimony of Burke. When Malone in 1797 published
Reynolds' Discourses with a memoir, he gave Dr. Johnson credit for having educated Reynolds in philosophical thinking.

BREDVOLD

Burke, from his last sick-bed, wrote to Malone on May 4, 1797, urging the claims of Mr. Mudge:

> ... I find but one thing material which you have omitted in his Life. You state very properly how much he owed to the writings and conversation of Johnson; and nothing shows more the greatness of Sir Joshua's parts than his taking advantage of both, and making some application of them to his profession, when Johnson neither understood nor desired to understand anything of painting, and had no distinct idea of its nomenclature even in those parts which had got most into use in common life. But though Johnson had done very much to enlarge and strengthen his habits of thinking, Sir J. did not owe his first rudiments of speculation to him. He has always told me that he owed his first disposition to generalise and to view things in the abstract to old Mr. Mudge, Prebendary of Exeter and brother to the celebrated mechanic of that name. I have seen myself Mr. Mudge the clergyman at Sir Joshua's house. He was a learned and venerable old man, and, as I thought, very much conversant in the Platonic philosophy, and very fond of that method of philosophising.... Sir J. Reynolds had always a great love for the whole of that family, and took a great interest in whatever related to them. His acquaintance with the Mudges ought to be reckoned among the earliest of his literary connexions. If the work should come to a second edition, I hope you will not omit this very material circumstance in the institution of a mind like that of our friend. It was from him that I first got a view of the few that have been published of Mr. Mudge's Sermons, and on conversing afterwards with Mr. Mudge I found great traces of Sir Joshua Reynolds in him, and, if I may say so, much the manner of the master. [40]

Burke further penned a memorandum on this subject, which was found in January, 1798, after his death. Malone inserted most of this memorandum in his second edition, which was then going through the press. But in spite of Burke's letter and memorandum, this Mr. Mudge has not received his due from the biographers of Reynolds, and it is a pleasure to call attention to him. No doubt he has been neglected because no one could see any particular significance in such information as that the mind of Reynolds had been formed by a man "much inclined to philosophise in the spirit of the Platonists, " or that Burke could find "great traces of Sir Joshua Reynolds in him, and much the manner of the master. "

At this point the objection may be raised that in the <u>Discourses</u> the analysis of the technique of painting is conducted in a spirit more Aristotelian than Platonic. And it must be conceded that from the sixteenth century on, the analysis and formulation of Neo-Classical principles for each specific art was generally a form of Aristotelianism. But we are not here concerned with the principles or technique of any one art, but with the conception of Beauty — at times presupposed and implied more than expressed — which underlay the theorizing on all the arts. And this ideal beauty, though it is, as we have already seen, thoroughly in harmony with Aristotle's own esthetics, is nevertheless a conception which leads beyond Aristotle, and which Reynolds, like Bellori, Père André, Winckelmann and other men of similar tendencies, definitely thought of as Platonic rather than Aristotelian.

In his Third Discourse Reynolds seized an opportunity to impress his auditors with the antiquity and venerability of this conception of beauty. Whether he had read Bellori or not — and he probably had — he gives here what may be regarded as an excellent summary of Bellori's many citations of authorities:

The principle now laid down, that the perfection of this art does not consist in mere imitation, is far from being new or singular. It is, indeed, supported by the general opinion of the enlightened part of mankind. The poets, orators and rhetoricians of antiquity, are continually enforcing this position, — that all the arts receive their perfection from an ideal beauty, superior to what is to be found in individual nature. They are ever referring to the practice of the painters and sculptors of their times, particularly Phidias (the favourite artist of antiquity), to illustrate their assertions. As if they could not sufficiently express their admiration of his genius by what they knew, they have recourse to poetical enthusiasm: they call it inspiration; a gift from heaven. The artist is supposed to have ascended the celestial regions, to furnish his mind with this perfect idea of beauty. [41]

He then quotes from Proclus, the same passage as Bellori and Winckelmann quoted, and from the page of Cicero's <u>Orator</u>

which had become the locus classicus among the Platonizing
theorists of beauty.

It may, however, be objected further that Reynolds in certain places enunciates what appears to be a denial of the Platonic metaphysics. In his notes on Du Fresnoy's Art of Painting,
for instance, he says that "it is in nature only we can find that
beauty which is the great object of our search: it can be found
no where else: we can no more form any idea of beauty superior to nature than we can form an idea of a sixth sense, or any
other excellence out of the limits of the human mind."[42] There
are passages in his Discourses to the same effect. But Reynolds is speaking on such occasions on a certain level and
against certain errors; we recall that he criticized Boucher for
his vicious habit of painting without models. But if we are to
take these passages literally, and as the expression of the supreme and governing principle in Reynolds' esthetics, we would
be imputing to him the theory that the artist is merely the dex-
terous copier after models. Nothing could be more obviously
false. "My notion of nature," he says in the Seventh Discourse,
"comprehends not only the forms which nature produces, but
also the nature and internal fabric and organization, as I may
call it, of the human mind and imagination. The terms beauty,
or nature, which are general ideas, are but different modes of
expressing the same thing, whether we apply these terms to
statues, poetry, or pictures."[43] Reynolds, in common with the
other Neo-Classical theorists we have been discussing, believed
in a vision of ideal beauty within the mind of man, superior to
actuality, a vision without which the practitioner of any art will
fail to be an artist. It may be said of them all that if they were
not Platonists in a strict philosophical sense, it was merely because in their theorizing they stopped short of metaphysical
problems; had they been metaphysicians, they would have been
Platonists. As it was, the phraseology of Platonism was the
most serviceable they could find for the expression of their esthetic ideal and esthetic experience. Whoever would understand
either the pictures or the Discourses of Reynolds, may well
ponder the eloquent passage in the Ninth Discourse:

> The Art which we profess has beauty for its object;
> this it is our business to discover and to express; the
> beauty of which we are in quest is general and intellectu-
> al; it is an idea that subsists only in the mind; the sight
> never beheld it, nor has the hand expressed it; it is an

idea residing in the breast of the artist, which he is always labouring to impart, and which he dies at last without imparting.[44]

VIII

In conclusion it may be well to guard once more against the all too probable misconstructions which may be put upon any limited and fragmentary treatment of such large and complex subjects as Neo-Classicism and Platonism. This paper makes no attempt at a complete and continuous history of Platonic tendencies within Neo-Classical theory. Nor does it attempt to explain more than one phase of the Neo-Classical movement, important as that phase may be. The one purpose here has been to note certain tendencies among authoritative Neo-Classicists to employ their inheritance of Platonic idealism for the purpose of expressing more cogently and fully what they experienced in the presence of a work of art. We do not always see that behind the rules and formulas of Neo-Classical criticism there glowed a generous enthusiasm and idealism which was as often taken for granted as expressed. Ages differ in what Coleridge called their "anticipated sympathies," which are not always apparent on the surface and may too easily be ignored. And when the historian of esthetic doctrine and of taste interprets a past age in terms of a different set of preconceptions current in his own, nothing but confusion and misunderstanding can possibly result.

The purpose of this paper is therefore to contribute something toward an appreciation of what the esthetic experience of the Neo-Classical age really was, at its best. It was obviously not always at its best, and we are much too prone to be indiscriminating in our selection of representatives of it. Every age has its plethora of artists and critics who are bad or dull or uninteresting. These are not the representative men of a cultural epoch or movement. Bysshe must not be quoted along with Dryden without any difference in weighting. There are many people in this day who, for instance, think that if they condemn Boucher they are condemning the essence of Neo-Classicism; but Reynolds regarded Boucher as representative only of what is bad and false. To understand Neo-Classicism better we need to re-establish some sort of sound hierarchy of artists and critics within the movement. We need, to take one illustration, to raise the reputation of Poussin among us, and study more closely

his art and his ideas; an acquaintance with his work might be
of inestimable assistance to many a modern student struggling
with the eighteenth century. It is remarkable that Hazlitt,whose
literary and artistic perceptions were far more versatile than
his theory, and who could make nothing of the paradoxes of Neo-
Classicism as he found them stated in Reynolds' Discourses,
nevertheless stated them himself with real insight when he
needed them to explain the beauty of Poussin's painting, to
which he was deeply responsive.[45]

The fact that the Neo-Classical age is so often called "artificial" is a testimony to its sense for art. "Artificial" is a complimentary or a derogatory adjective according to the assump-
tions of the person using it. The Neo-Classical age was artificial; the full-bottomed wig is one evidence and symbol of its
taste. But those who condemn the wearing of wigs do not understand an age and generation which preferred not to have either
life or art served up to them au naturel. One important difference between the eighteenth century and our own is that is was
then so easy, indeed almost necessary, to believe in the existence of "le bellezze naturali superiore alla natura"; the principle of ideal beauty was operative in the techniques of all the
arts and handicrafts as well as in life and manners. The gradual refinement and purification of prose style from the early
seventeenth century is one illustration of it; the development of
the delicate inner complexities of the heroic couplet is another.
The rules which we began by quoting from a carpenter's guide
are properly interpreted as arising, not from indifference to
beauty, but from a love of and belief in ideal and perfect beauty.
We have seen how fertile in phrases the theorists were in their
eager desire to define and describe this beauty: Batteux called
it "la belle nature"; Félibien spoke of "ces Lumieres et ces
Jours que l'Art sait trouver par le moyen du mélange des couleurs"; André spoke of "un beau géométrique," Reynolds of
"general and intellectual beauty," Winckelmann of "die reine
Schönheit." They were all trying to convey the Neo-Classical
conception of beauty which, to borrow Sir Joshua's significant
phrase, "comprehends not only the forms which nature produces, but also the nature and internal fabric and organization of
the human mind and imagination."

PLATONISM IN NEO-CLASSICAL ESTHETICS

NOTES

1 Francis Price, The British Carpenter, 4th ed. (London, 1759), pp. 65, 66, and 33.

2 This essay is in effect an expansion and documentation of some paragraphs in my introduction to Selected Poems of Alexander Pope (New York, 1926).

3 Cicero, Orator, 7-10. Atque ego in summo oratore fingendo talem informabo, qualis fortasse nemo fuit. Non enim quaero quis fuerit, sed quid sit illud, quo nihil esse possit praestantius, quod in perpetuitate dicendi non saepe atque haud scio an numquam, in aliqua autem parte eluceat aliquando, idem apud alios densius, apud alios fortasse rarius. Sed ego sic statuo, nihil esse in ullo genere tam pulchrum, quo non pulchrius id sit unde illud ut ex ore aliquo quasi imago exprimatur; quod neque oculis neque auribus neque ullo sensu percipi potest,cogitatione tantum et mente complectimur. Itaque et Phidiae simulacris, quibus nihil in illo genere perfectius videmus, et iis picturis quas nominavi cogitare tamen possumus pulchriora; nec vero ille artifex, cum faceret Iovis formam aut Minervae, contemplabatur aliquem, e quo similitudinem duceret, sed ipsius in mente insidebat species pulchritudinis eximia quaedam, quam intuens in eaque defixus ad illius similitudinem artem et manum dirigebat. Ut igitur in formis et figuris est aliquid perfectum et excellens, cuius ad cogitatam speciem imitando referuntur ea quae sub oculos ipsa non cadunt, sic perfectae eloquentiae speciem animo videmus, effigiem auribus quaerimus. Has rerum formas appellat ἰδέας ille non intellegendi solum sed etiam dicendi gravissimus auctor et magister Plato, easque gigni negat et ait semper esse ac ratione et intelligentia contineri; cetera nasci, occidere, fluere, labi nec diutius esse uno et eodem statu. Quicquid est igitur de quo ratione et via disputetur, id est ad ultimam sui generis formam speciemque redigendum.

4 Epistulae Morales, with an English translation by Richard M. Gummere (London, 1917), 1. 449.

5 Ed. cit. 1. 399.

6 For their history down to the end of the seventeenth century see the valuable monograph by Erwin Panofsky, "Idea," Ein Beitrag zur Begriffsgeschichte der älteren Kunsttheorie (Leipzig, 1924). To this work, which is not so widely known as it should be, I am under deep obligations in this section of my paper.

7   Curiously enough, Bellori's pun, "questa Idea, overo Dea della Pittura," was anticipated by Dante, Convito 2. 5. See Panofsky, p. 88.

8   Any discussion of the theory of music, in which Platonic conceptions played an important part, must be excluded by the limits of this paper.

9   H. B. Charlton, Castelvetro's Theory of Poetry (Manchester, 1913), p. 143.

10 Ingram Bywater, Aristotle on the Art of Poetry (Oxford, 1909), p. 27.

11 Critical Essays of the Seventeenth Century, Vol. 1, Introduction, p. lxviii.

12 Panofsky, p. 109.

13 André Fontaine, Les Doctrines d'Art en France (Paris, 1909), p. 11.

14 Bywater, op. cit., p. 45.

15 La Poëtique d'Aristote (1692), p. 267. Similarly, p. 490, he says: "C'est ainsi qu'on justifie ce qui paroit de prodigieux dans les caractéres qu' Homere a formez; les ignorans les condamnent, parce qu'ils ne voyent rien de semblable dans les ouvrages de la Nature; mais ce n'est pas d'aprés les copies qu' Homere a travaillé, il a travaillé sur le veritable original, qui est la Nature même, et l'esprit rempli des idées fecondes de cet agent universel, il a enfanté ces originaux, qui ont le même avantage sur les hommes ordinaires, que la Nature a sur tous les Etres qu'elle produit; car les originaux doivent toûjours surpasser les copies."

16 Translation by John Evelyn (London, 1668), p. 14.

17 Entretiens (London, 1705) 1. 193.

18 Ibid., 1. 41-43.

19 Bellori plays in his title with the double meaning of the word Nature, as referring now to the ideal, now to the actual.

20 Panofsky, op. cit., pp. 59-63; Julius Schlosser, Die Kunstliteratur (Vienna, 1924), pp. 416 ff., 449 ff., 575 ff.; Werner

Weisbach, "Die klassische Ideologie," in Deutsche Viertel-jahrsschrift 11 (1933).   562 ff.

21   W. H. Durham, Critical Essays of the Eighteenth Century (New Haven, 1915), p. 251.

22   Les beaux Arts reduits à un même Principe (Paris, 1746), pp. 33, 27.

23   An Essay on the Theory of Painting (London, 1715), p. 137.

24   Advice to an Author, Part 1, sec. 3.

25   Second Characters, ed. Benjamin Rand (Cambridge, 1914), pp. 132,145.

26   Moralists, Part 3, sec. 2.

27   Poems upon various Subjects (London, 1768), "To the Reader."

28   Hans Hecht, Daniel Webb (Hamburg, 1920), pp. 7-8, 52.

29   Essai sur le Beau (Paris, 1741), pp. 22-24.

30   See Panofsky, p. 117; Schlosser, pp. 457 ff. and 603; Weisbach, in Deutsche Vierteljahrsschrift 11 (1933). 586-7.

31   Proclus, in his commentary on Timaeus.

32   Geschichte 4. 2. 18.

33   Ibid. 4. 2. 22-3.

34   Ibid. 4. 2. 35.

35   Ibid. 5. 1. 12.

36   Literary Works of Sir Joshua Reynolds, ed. Henry W. Beechy, 1. 38.

37   See Essay, pp. 83, 84, 165; Two Discourses 2. 18, 84.

38   Two Discourses 1. 152.

39   Essay, p. 162.

40   Leslie and Taylor, Life and Times of Sir Joshua Reynolds (London, 1865) 2. 638-9.

BREDVOLD

41 Reynolds, Literary Works, ed. cit. 1. 330-1.

42 Ibid. 2. 351.

43 Ibid. 1. 415.

44 Ibid. 2. 4.

45 See his essay on "A Landscape of Nicolas Poussin," in Table Talk.

SCIENCE AND CRITICISM IN THE NEO-CLASSICAL AGE
OF ENGLISH LITERATURE

Richard Foster Jones

Before proceeding to the substance of my argument, it is
imperative that I define the first term in my title, for upon my
interpretation of it the thesis which I shall present depends. My
conception of the history of science in seventeenth-century England differs in many respects from the usual view. The modern
historian of science develops his subject in a series of descriptions and evaluations of past discoveries in a more or less
chronological order, in which continuity is at best only partially maintained. He may trace the progress of the knowledge of
some aspect of nature from its embryonic beginnings to its finished statement. He may, for instance, explain Copernicus'
theory of the revolution of the planets round the sun, tell how
Kepler determined the elliptical nature of their orbits, show
how Galileo advanced the theory by his observation of the satellites of Jupiter, and discuss the laws governing planetary movements as discovered by Newton. He may show how our present
knowledge of nature is only the sum of all the increments added
at various times in the past to growing conceptions, and describe each increment as it appears. He is primarily interested
in positive contributions to knowledge, and in the appearance
of those elements that have finally been welded into the elaborate scientific method of today.

There is another way of interpreting scientific history, which
considers science primarily as a movement of ideas, which
stresses principles giving rise to discoveries more than the
discoveries themselves, and seeks to trace these principles as
they develop in harmony or conflict with other forces and in relation to contemporary circumstances and needs. In seventeenth-
century England the scientific movement comprised a few definite main principles. First was the demand for a sceptical mind,
freed from all preconceptions and maintaining a critical attitude
toward all ideas presented to it. Second, observation and exper-
imentation were insisted upon as the only trustworthy means of

Reprinted by permission from Journal of the History of Ideas, Vol. 1
(1940), pp. 381-412.

securing sufficient data. And third, the inductive method of reasoning was to be employed on these data. Such were the central or primary ideas in this thought-movement, or, to use an expression borrowed from criticism, the timeless element, for they are as true today — though, perhaps, more generally taken for granted — as they were then. But besides these there was the time element, or those secondary principles which came into being when the primary clashed with their age. To establish experimental science it was necessary to overthrow the principle of authority, especially that of Aristotle and other ancients, who in large part still dominated the human mind. So the anti-authoritarian principle entered the movement. But to undermine the authority of antiquity, it was necessary to attack a prevailing theory of the day, which asserted that modern times represented the old age of the world and the last stages of the decay of nature, in which human powers had degenerated to a level far below those of the ancients, who lived when nature was in its prime. Thus opposition to the theory of nature's decay joins the other principles. Again, the new thinkers, in order to have the opportunity to advance the cause of modern science, found it necessary to insist upon freedom to investigate and to advance their findings against established ideas. So the principle of liberty is insisted upon. And finally, the belief that knowledge could advance if the authority of the ancients were removed, and the realization that some discoveries had already shown the possibility of advancement beyond the ignorance of antiquity, moved the scientists to embrace the idea of progress.

All these values, attitudes, and ideas, together with a few others, combined to form the scientific movement, and they were expressed by an ever increasing chorus of voices throughout the latter half of the seventeenth century, voices not of authentic scientists only, or even chiefly, but of noblemen, state officials, clergymen, and even of the rabble of magicians, astrologers, graceless quacks, and other representatives of the lunatic fringe. Of the four men who probably did more than any others to establish and popularize the idea of the new science, only one, Robert Boyle, was an authentic scientist. John Webster was a Puritan chaplain in the parliamentarian army; Joseph Glanvill was a rector in the Anglican Church; and Thomas Sprat was a noted preacher and later bishop of Rochester. All these men were ardent champions of the great discoveries of the Renaissance, but they were not primarily interested in these discoveries. Their first concern was to promote the idea of

science, to support and give impetus to a thought-movement
which was sweeping away all obstructions. Toward this end they
appreciated scientific discoveries not so much for their intrinsic value as for the support they furnished the movement, either
in proving the ideas of the ancients erroneous or in demonstra-
ting the fruitfulness of the experimental and observational method. One other fact must be briefly stated. The scientific movement was organized around Bacon, and its chief embodiment
was the Royal Society. [1]

Paralleling the rapid development of the scientific movement
was a literary movement, which comprised values and attitudes
quite different from those of science. This was a literary criticism, generally called neo-classical, of which the two cardinal principles were the imitation of nature and the moral purpose of art. Since, however, as Pope was to say, nature and
Homer were the same, the only way to imitate nature was by
following the literary rules and ideas first laid down by Aristotle, Horace, and others, and later elaborated by European critics. Therefore, this criticism maintained that the proper models of writing were to be found only in Greek and Roman literature; that modern writers must follow these models; and that
the rules drawn from them by Aristotle and his followers were
as the law of the Medes and Persians which altereth not. Here,
then, was a critical philosophy which upheld the principle of
authority (though many critics tried to equate it with reason or
common sense), limited the freedom of the poetic imagination,
and rendered impossible any progress beyond the achievements
of the past. It also lent its support to the theory of nature's decay, which indeed became one of its major theses. It would be
difficult to find a more exact antithesis to the views characteristic of the scientific movement than is found in this criticism.
Was it possible for these two thought-movements to proceed
side by side without interaction ?

I

To ascertain the answer to this question it is necessary to
examine the works of some representative critics of the neo-
classical period. The first is Dryden, called by some the father
of English criticism and certainly head and shoulders above any
English critic of the time. But, if we may employ the words with
which he himself described Shakespeare, "he is the very Janus
of critics; he wears almost everywhere two faces; and you have

scarce begun to admire the one, ere you despise the other."
Whenever Dryden passes under the shadow of a French neo-
classical critic, he may become as hidebound and narrow as
any of his contemporaries. At other times, however, he reveals
a critical intelligence of a high order — a sensitivity, insight,
and comprehension unique in his own age and not often surpassed
since. His mind, if at times too subject to influence, was tentative and sceptical, a characteristic of which he was fully
aware, for, in speaking of his translation of Lucretius, he says,
"I laid by my natural diffidence and scepticism for a while, to
take up the dogmatical way of Lucretius."[2] But if this sceptical, undogmatic attitude of mind was his by nature, it was also,
perhaps, fostered and encouraged by his contacts with the scientists of his day. He joined the Royal Society in the year it received its charter from the King, served on two of its commit-
tees, and praised and defended it in his poetry.[3] The critical,
sceptical attitude which Bacon had enjoined upon his followers,
and which the scientists of the Restoration sedulously strove to
attain, could hardly have escaped his notice or been without influence upon him. In describing the spirit which informs his
first important critical treatise, the Essay of Dramatic Poesie,
he denies the charge of dogmatism, which had unjustly been
brought against him: "my whole discourse was sceptical, according to that way of reasoning which was used by Socrates,
Plato, and all the Academics of old, ... and which is imitated
by the modest inquisitions of the Royal Society."[4] Needless to
say, the Society to which Dryden belonged, and to the members
of which he had frequently listened, must have done more to develop the scepticism he speaks of than the far-off models of antiquity.

Not only is the sceptical attitude of science perceptible in
Dryden's criticism; its corollary, the inductive way of reasoning, can frequently be discovered there. The method of reasoning employed by the dogmatic critics of his day was essentially
deductive or syllogistic. They reasoned from general principles
established largely by authority. Dryden, on the other hand,
gathers his data from literature, and from these data draws his
conclusions. A few simple examples will suffice. The dogmatic
critic reasoned thus: poetry is an imitation of nature (a major
premise resting ultimately on the authority of Aristotle); the
supernatural is not an imitation of nature; therefore, poetry
containing it is not correct poetry. But notice how Dryden opposes this narrow idea: "I will ask any man who loves heroic
poetry ... if the ghost of Polydorus in Virgil, the Enchanted

Wood in Tasso, and the Bower of Bliss in Spencer ... could
have been omitted, without taking from their works some of the
greatest beauties in them." From these instances Dryden draws
the general principle that

> an heroic poet is not tied to a bare representation of what
> is true ... but ... he may let himself loose to visionary
> objects, and to the representation of such things as depend-
> ing not on sense, and therefore not to be comprehended by
> knowledge, may give him a freer scope for imagination. [5]

In searching for pertinent data in literature itself, and in drawing from the particular instances found in the three poets mentioned above a principle quite different from that which was
founded on authority, Dryden was following, though in a simple
and elementary fashion, exactly the same procedure adopted
by the experimental scientists who turned their backs on Aristotelian ideas of nature and the syllogistic logic of the Peripa-
tetics, and sought in nature itself the data which by induction
would lead to more accurate ideas or principles.

Another example of this inductive method of arriving at conclusions quite at variance with accepted rules is found in his
preface to the Mock Astrologer, in which he combats the idea
that poetic justice is a law of comedy. To support his own view
he gathers his instances from Terence, Ben Johnson, and Beaumont and Fletcher. [6] Of course, simple induction is a seemingly obvious procedure, but nevertheless strict neo-classical
critics like Thomas Rymer seldom, if ever, employ it to determine their principles, but apply rules secured in other ways
to particular poems, generally with disastrous consequences.
Moreover, there are passages in Dryden which indicate that he
was aware of the nature of the logic he used, for he definitely
calls his reasoning induction. [7] In general, we may say that
when not in his neo-classical moods, Dryden moves about in
literature and collects the data for his opinions; he does not approach it from the outside with a pre-manufactured yardstick
to detect its shortcomings.

Dryden, when in the presence of a French critic, can knuckle
under to authority in the most approved fashion. But when the
influence of the scientific spirit plays upon his mind, he is boldly defiant. When accused of not respecting the authority of Ben
Jonson, he asks: "Or why should there be any Ipse dixit in our
poetry, any more than there is in our philosophy?" (It is

necessary to keep in mind that throughout this period the word
"philosophy" is consistently used where we should use the term
"science.") And in another passage he declares that there are
no Pillars of poetry, a figure taken from the Pillars of Hercu-
les, which was used over and over again by the scientists to
express the limits imposed on knowledge by the authority of the
ancients. [8]

The idea of progress in scientific knowledge, which stimulated the scientists in their experimenting and observing, creates in Dryden a similar attitude toward poetry. One of the
speakers in the Essay of Dramatic Poesie asks:

> Is it not evident, in these last hundred years (when the
> study of philosophy has been the business of all Virtuosi
> in Christendom), that almost a new Nature has been re-
> vealed to us ? — that more errors of the school have been
> detected, more useful experiments in philosophy have been
> made, more noble secrets in optics, medicine, anatomy,
> astronomy, discovered, than in all those doting ages from
> Aristotle to us ? — so true it is, that nothing spreads more
> fast than science, when rightly and generally cultivated.

To this another speaker, who wishes to show that modern poetry may go beyond ancient art, answers: "if natural causes
be more known now than in the time of Aristotle, because more
studied, it follows that poesy and other arts may, with the same
pains, arrive still nearer to perfection."[9] In another passage,
Dryden shows us one way in which he would contribute to the
advancement of poetry, and also the reasons for his hope of
success. What he advocates is the introduction of the supernatural element of guardian spirits into modern epic poetry, concerning which he says:

> I am sufficiently sensible of my weakness; and it is not
> very probable that I should succeed in such a project,
> whereof I have not had the least hint from any of my pre-
> decessors, the poets.... Yet we see the art of war is im-
> proved in sieges, and new instruments of death are inven-
> ted daily; something new in philosophy and the mechanics
> is discovered almost every year; and the science of form-
> er ages is improved by the succeeding. [10]

The progress which the scientists were achieving inspired in

Dryden the desire and hope of a similar advancement in verse. In fact, in one essay he makes this progress the sole aim of his criticism, and to achieve it he is quite willing to remove the bar of ancient authority and supposed perfection:

> I hope I shall not be thought arrogant when I enquire into their errors [i.e., the errors of the ancients]. For we live in an age so sceptical, that as it determines little, so it takes nothing from antiquity on trust; and I profess to have no other ambition in this <u>Essay,</u> than that poetry may not go backward, when all other arts and sciences are advancing. [11]

It was the scientists who were sceptical and took nothing from antiquity on trust, and it was from them and their discoveries that Dryden took his cue.

There are numerous echoes and suggestions of the scientific movement in Dryden's criticism which hardly merit consideration here. His figures of speech are frequently drawn from the activities of science — mathematical, astronomical, chemical, physical, and medical. [12] He was especially fond of illustrations drawn from the Copernican system, though it is true that he occasionally used the Ptolemaic. [13] Yet his last he is careful to introduce with a "they say." Some of his figures reveal familiarity with the keenest battle of the war which the moderns carried on against the ancients, namely, the onslaught of the chemical doctors, who upheld Baconian principles, upon the Galenists, who subscribed to the methods of the great physician of antiquity. [14] Sometimes one versed in seventeenth-century science detects echoes of it in unsuspected passages, as, for example, when Dryden, in expressing his distrust of the rules, says, "many a fair precept in poetry is, like a seeming demonstration in the mathematics, very specious in the diagram, but failing in the mechanic operation." [15] Can there not be heard in this passage the voice of a Baconian scientist, condemning the theoretical and speculative nature of Peripateticism, and its lack of useful or practical application? Dryden is also one with the scientists in respect to the theory of nature's decay, which in every field underlay the feeling of modern inferiority and increased the power of authority. He maintains that "the course of time rather improves nature than impairs her," and in this simple statement a great deal is contained.

In his sceptical attitude, at times in his method of reasoning, and in his revolt against the domination of the ancients in literature and against the principle of authority in general, Dryden owes a considerable debt to his fellow members of the Royal Society, but in nothing more than in that vision of progress in poetry, which he caught from a similar vision in science, and which is a frequent motif in his criticism.

II

Toward the end of the seventeenth century the scientific movement becomes somewhat weaker, [16] in spite of or perhaps because of Newton's great discoveries, which seemed to have left nothing else to be explained. But in the last decade an event came to pass which again brought its values and attitudes clearly before the public. This was the appearance of Sir William Temple's essay Of Ancient and Modern Learning, 1690. Sir William was a retired statesman, who in his cautious political career made no misstep, but who was not so fortunate in his literary activities, for this essay, though it ultimately led to notable literary results in Swift's Battle of the Books, brought only chagrin to the author. The essay is a thinly veiled attack on the new science in general and the Royal Society in particular, in which the author makes a little learning go a long way, in a graceful and charming style. The members of the Society became concerned, and engaged a learned young man, William Wotton, to write a defense of the organization. [17] In it the claims of modern science against ancient are bravely asserted and the controlling ideas of the scientific movement are brought again to the front.

In the very year in which Wotton published his answer to Temple, 1694, Charles Gildon, a young and enthusiastic critic, produced a collection of short critical essays, [18] which, inspired partly by Dryden's criticism, approach critical problems almost entirely from the point of view of the new science. The first essay replies to Thomas Rymer, a critic who represents the extremes to which the dogmatic rules of neo-classicism and the worship of ancient models went in England. [19] Rymer had applied the rules to Shakespeare, and the result of his appraisal was that the bard of Avon knew no more about human nature than a pug in Barbary. Against this judgment Gildon rises up with considerable warmth. He asks if we are to admire Shakespeare, as Dryden does, or place him below the meanest poets, as Rymer has done — Rymer "whom," he says, "nothing it seems can please, but the Antic Forms and Methods of the Athenian Stage,

340

or what comes up, and sticks close to them in our Language."
He does not pause for a reply but proceeds immediately to the
answer: "I can see no Reason why we shou'd be so very fond of
imitating them here, without better proofs than the Critical Historiographer has produc'd." From this negative position he passes to more positive arguments against Rymer.

> 'Tis certain, the Grecians had not the advantage of us in
> Physics, or any other part of Philosophy, which with them
> chiefly consisted in words; they were a Talkative People;
> and being fond of the Opinion of Learning, more than the
> thing it self, as the most speedy way to gain that, stop'd
> their Enquiries on Terms, as is evident from their Sophis-
> try and Dialectic's.

This characterization of ancient philosophy, or science, could
have been taken almost verbatim from Sprat's History of the
Royal Society. "There can be," Gildon continues, "no dispute
among the Learned, but that we excel them in these Points.
Since the time of Des Cartes, when the Dictates of Greece began to be laid aside, what a Progress has been made in the discovery of Nature ? and what Absurdities laid open in the School
Precepts and Terms of Aristotle ?" [20] Gildon sees in the revolt
of modern science against ancient, and in its demonstrated superiority, sufficient reason for questioning the validity of classical rules in literature, and for doubting the superiority of
Greek over English drama. From the same source he also
draws the hope that as knowledge progresses with the new science, so may literature, if the shackles of authority are removed.

There is one argument advanced by this critic which, I am
sure, no student of literature would concede to any scientist;
namely, that the investigation of natural causes and effects is
more difficult than the writing of plays, which in his eyes required only "a nice observation of Mankind." Nevertheless, he
writes that he cannot understand how the Greeks should have so
great an advantage over the moderns in drama, as some would
allow them, when they are so far behind the moderns in matters
of greater difficulty, i.e., science. "But," he says, "it can't be
otherways whilst we make that Age and Nation the Standard of Excellence without regard to the difference of Custom, Age, Climate, etc." [21]

In his next essay [22] Gildon is again answering Rymer, and also the French critic Rapin, who wished to prohibit the introduction

of love scenes into tragedy because Greek drama does not contain them. He insists, and rightly, that the position of the two critics rests only on authority. "The chief Arguments indeed," he says,

> which these Gentlemen bring, are from the Practice of the Ancients, ... whose Authority they are of opinion shou'd outweigh Reason. But since the Ipse dixit has been so long laid aside in Philosophy, as an enemy to our Enquiries into Nature, I can see no reason why it shou'd be of so much greater force in Poetry; since 'tis perhaps almost as prejudicial to our imitation of Nature in This, as to our discovery of it in the Other.

From this analogy Gildon clearly perceived that freedom in art was as essential to the development of poetry as freedom in investigation was essential to the progress of scientific knowledge. He is not arguing only from analogy; he believes that the imposition of authority on literature leads to the same kind of stagnation which it had created in science. He explains rather than modifies his view when he says:

> As far as the Ancients and the Rules Aristotle draws from them, agree with the Character you give these, Of being nothing but good sense and Nature reduc'd to Method, I shall close with them; but when they either deviate from this, or reach not up to what may be done, I must think it but just to withdraw myself from the subjection of the Stagyrite, who has had a Reign long enough o'er the Minds of Mankind, and an Empire that far exceeded the Extent and Continuance of his Royal Pupil Alexander. [23]

Our liberal critic is not contending for what might be called a romantic freedom, but for an enlightened and more liberal neoclassicism, one of the fundamental elements of which, the imitation of nature, he upholds. For this reason he attacks the narrow dogmatic rules, for the support of which ancient authority was invoked, and he insists that there are more ways of imitating nature than those specified by these rules. He also further defines his attitude toward antiquity by acknowledging, as the scientists had done in their field, that the Greeks were the inventors of tragedy and comedy, but, like the scientists, he refuses to let that fact bar the development of the drama, and

stand as a <u>non plus ultra</u> to the progress of poetry. [24]
In his third essay[25] Gildon pursues an argument of a more
novel, if not more significant, nature than any drawn from science. This time he diverts his attack from Rymer to an anonymous author who had maintained that the love poems of the ancients were superior to those of the moderns because, to quote
the author's own words,

> The occasions upon which the poems are written, are such
> as happen to every Man almost that is in Love; and the
> Thoughts such, as are natural for every Man in love to
> think. The Moderns, on the other hand, have sought out
> occasions that none meet with but themselves, and fill
> their Verses with thoughts that are surprising and glitter-
> ing but not ... natural to a Man in Love. [26]

This fundamental classical principle of the universal Gildon counters with the idea of a relative aesthetic, an idea which later was
incorporated in the conception of historical criticism. To understand his reasoning, however, it is necessary to revert to the
clash between the experimental doctors and the Galenists. One
of the arguments produced by the physicians of the new science
against the authority of the ancients in medicine was that diseases
vary according to countries, times, and nations; and, therefore,
the remedies that might have been efficacious in antiquity were
useless when applied to modern ailments. [27] Thus, they contended, it is necessary to discard the supposedly authoritative principles of ancient medicine, and discover new remedies by observation and experiment. This method of reasoning Gildon appro-
priated <u>in toto</u>, and he applied it to love poetry. Repeating the
concession he had made once before, he says:

> I shall never deny the Ancients their just Praise of the In-
> vention of <u>Arts</u> and <u>Sciences</u>; but I cannot without contradict-
> ing my own <u>Reason</u>, allow them the Perfecters of 'em so far
> that they must be our uncontroverted Patterns and Standard:
> For our Physicians have found the Prescripts of <u>Hippocrates</u>
> very Defective: And as in Physic, so in Poetry, there must be
> a regard had to the Clime, Nature, and Customs of the People;
> for the Habits of the Mind as well as those of the Body, are in-
> fluenc'd by them; and Love with the other Passions vary in
> their <u>Effects</u> as well as <u>Causes</u>, according to each Country and
> Age; nay, according to the very Constitution of each Person
> affected.

This fact, he concludes, renders fallacious any idea that the ancients should furnish immutable standards of literary excellence for the moderns. [28] In his insistence upon the principle of relativity, and in his emphasis upon the individual as opposed to the universal, Gildon takes a step toward romanticism. The idea of a relative aesthetic appears again in Gildon's last essay, [29] which upholds the superiority of modern poetry in general over ancient. In answer to the champions of antiquity who would deny the moderns the title of poets because they did not strictly observe Aristotelian rules, he asserts that the dogmatic critics have mistaken the true purpose of poetry, which is pleasure. To achieve this end, he says, "regard must be had to the Humour, Custom, and Inclination of the Auditory; but an English audience will never be pleas'd with a dry, Jejune and formal Method that excludes Variety as the Religious observation of the Rules of Aristotle does."[30] In short, classical principles of art are not good for all time, and if pleasure, the true purpose of poetry, is to be achieved, a different art, determined by the age and nation which produce it, is required.

Gildon does not loom large in the history of criticism, but in his defense of Shakespeare, attack on authority, hostility to imitation, idea of a relative aesthetic, insistence on the aesthetic purpose of poetry, and belief in the possibility of the advancement of literature, what influence he exerted made for the liberalizing of the neo-classical spirit.

Throughout the criticism of this age one finds frequent allusions to the scientific movement and arguments drawn from it. In fact, the frequency with which they occur when any liberal sentiment is expressed, indicates the strength and widespread nature of the influence. One writer, who advocated the spending of more time on the study of English and less on that of the classical languages, remarks that since "our Navigators, Traders, Astronomers and Mathematicians, Physicians and Surgeons, by Benefit of longer Time and Experience, have gone beyond the Ancients in their Arts and Knowledge; is there any good Reason why we should be behind them in Wit and Language ?"[31] The habit of introducing the scientific parallel became so common as to appear in comedy. In the passage referred to, one character remarks that he would as soon receive medical treatment by the rules of Hippocrates and Galen as see a play written by the rules of Aristotle and Horace. [32] To this view Farquhar, a practical and successful dramatist, would certainly have subscribed, for in his essay on comedy he inveighs against Aristotle's authority and tries to undermine

his reputation as a critic. "I will have a tug with ipse dixit, tho'
I dye for 't," he declares. After stoutly denying "that we live in
the decay of Time, and the Dotage of the World is fall'n to our
Share," he exclaims,

> No, no, Sir, ipse dixit is remov'd long ago, and all the
> Rubbish of old Philosophy, that in a manner bury'd the
> Judgment of Mankind for many Centuries, is now carry'd
> off; the vast Tomes of Aristotle and his Commentators are
> all taken to pieces, and their Infallibility is lost with all
> Persons of a free and unprejudic'd Reason.

This being so, he asks, "by what Authority shou'd Aristotle's
Rules of Poetry stand so fixt and immutable ?"[33]

III

In 1716 Sir Richard Blackmore, a physician and a poet of
small ability, published an Essay upon Epic Poetry, [34] the primary purpose of which was to overthrow some of the most cher-
ished neo-classical principles of the epic. A scientist himself
and a fellow of the College of Physicians, he undoubtedly was
familiar with that stream of scientific thought that had come
down from the middle of the seventeenth century. At an earlier
date he had expressed contempt for servile imitators of the ancients, and had voiced the hope that some good genius "would
break the Ice, assert the Liberty of Poetry, and set up for an
Original in Writing in a way accommodated to the Religion, Manners, and other Circumstances we are now under."[35] When after sixteen years no such hero arose, he engaged in this more
elaborate attack on antiquity. He has not proceeded far in his essay before he launches upon a short history of the scientific revolt, which needs to be quoted in full if his position is to be
clearly understood. After speaking of the blind obedience to Aristotle on the part of his earlier followers, he says:

> The voluminous Lucubrations of these idle Students,
> who only copy'd and expounded their Leader's Sentiments,
> which they follow'd with a blind Obedience, were esteem'd
> the only valuable Productions of Philosophy. At length
> arose some famous Worthies, who animated by a generous
> Impulse to deliver Europe from the basest Servitude, that
> of the Understanding, attack'd Aristotle and his Adherents

345

with great Vigour, declar'd against all arbitrary Imposi-
tions on the Mind, and asserted the Liberty of Reflection
and a Power of examining Evidence, and judging for themselves. These excellent Persons, who deserv'd so well
of Mankind, by vindicating the Dignity of Humane Nature,
and standing up for its Rights and Prerogatives, against
the Usurpation of a particular Sect, having by an impartial Search discover'd that the Peripatetick System had
nothing in it for its support, but precarious and unevident
Principles, effectually expos'd its Weakness, and soon
brought the greatest Authority, that was ever establish'd
in the Schools, into general Contempt.

The purpose of this lengthy preamble is clearly visible in the
next passage, in which he expresses surprise that the revolution
in science was not extended to cover literature as well. "But
when," he continues,

these extraordinary Men, by encouraging the free Exercise of Reason, had infus'd an active Ferment into the
Minds of an ignorant and slothful Generation, by the Operation of which they were excited to throw off the yoke
of Aristotle in Matters of Philosophy, it is wonderful
that the Effect was not more extensive. They had as great
Reason to have proceeded to the Examination of his Rules
in the Art of Poetry, and to have made Enquiry if those
were settled on better Foundations.

Blackmore believes that the collapse of Aristotle's authority in
science should have inspired scepticism regarding its validity
in poetry. The realization that such had not been the case moved
him to denounce the dogmatic critics of his day, and to associate them with the incorrigible and subservient Aristotelians of
the preceding age. "But," he says,

I know not how it came to pass, his [i.e., Aristotle's]
Notions and Precepts in this Art have still remain'd un-
question'd and untry'd. The modern Criticks, contemning
the Examples of the Philosophers, have still proceeded in
the old beaten Track, of believing and admiring whatever
Aristotle advances on the Subjects, where the Muses are
concern'd. They are all like their submissive Predecessors, mere Expositors, scarce excepting Bossu himself,

346

of the writings of that great Man, and have made no Improvements, nor asserted the Liberty of Poetry, as the
other freer Spirits have vindicated that of Philosophy.
It's clear, that Aristotle form'd all his Axioms and Doctrines in Poetry, from the Patterns of Homer and other
Greek Writers; and without assigning any Reason of his
Positions, relies for the Truth of them on his own, or the
Authority of those Authors. But it is not the Authority of
the greatest Masters, but solid and convincing Evidence,
that must engage our Belief, and make us subscribe to
any Maxims in any Art or Science whatsoever. [36]

In view of the intensity of the earlier scientific rebellion
against antiquity, and of the number of important men who were
engaged in it, Blackmore's surprise that the revolt was not extended is not strange. But what he does not seem to realize is
that as the seventeenth century advanced, the spirit of literature, and, to a limited extent, the universities, remained humanistic, while science pursued a largely independent course.
It became, in fact, the target for the ridicule of the greatest
writers of the time, such as Swift and, later, Pope. Sir Richard,
however, was only partially correct, as the examples of Dryden
and Gildon show, and his own essay reveals one more critic inspired by the independence of science and rebelling against the
domination of the classics. That his inspiration came from science is further revealed in his attitude toward Aristotle, which
in one passage is expressed in words so reminiscent of the earlier upholders of the experimental philosophy as to seem almost
like direct quotation:

I look upon Aristotle as a great Genius, and a Person of
more than common Erudition; but will no more submit to
him as a Law-giver of the Poets, than of the Philosophers.
I shall always pay Respect and Deference to his Judgment
and Opinions, tho not acquiesce in them as infallible and
decisive Decrees.

It is not that he loves Aristotle less, but liberty more. He
would not in general, he says, condemn Aristotle's rules, but
"I shall use the same Liberty in adding any new Opinions on this
Subject, which in my Judgment will improve the Art of Poetry."[37]
He even looks with some tolerance upon one of the chief ideas of
the supporters of the ancients, namely, that the works of antiquity

have demonstrated their excellence in being approved by so
many nations for so many ages. Yet he strenuously denies that
this fact is proof of their infallibility. "Universality and Antiquity," he says, "are to be look'd on with Respect and Reverence;
but since they have been often produc'd to support manifest Errors in Philosophy as well as in Religion, and have therefore
been often rejected, why should they be regarded as infallible
in Poetry?"[38] Blackmore recognized in this idea of universal
and repeated consent one of the strongest supports of authority.
He introduces it more frequently and answers it more elaborate-
ly than any other opinion. Fortunately, if science had demonstrated anything, it had shown that the life of error may indeed
be long, that many ideas had down through the ages met with
wide approval, only to be overthrown at last by some experimental scientist. Thus the new science offered him the soundest
possible reasons for refuting the idea, and he makes full use of
them. "Aristotle's Notions in Philosophy," he says,

> were, for many Ages, as universally receiv'd by the
> learned World as Homer's Poetry, and esteem'd as the
> Dictates of the most profound Judgment and Oracles of
> Reason; yet, after he had reign'd in the Schools many
> Centuries with uncontested Authority, upon Examination
> he was discover'd to have no just Claim to this great Dig-
> nity; he was found out to be an Usurper, strip'd of his Ti-
> tles and Regalia, and not only degraded, but treated with
> the greatest Contempt.... It is vain to urge the Suffrages
> of Antiquity, against clear and solid Argument. In this
> Case Citations are neither pertinent nor useful, for the
> Authors of former Ages are disqualify'd from giving
> their Votes in a Matter of this Nature; no length of Time,
> no not three Thousand Years, is a sufficient Prescription
> to bar the Claim of Reason, which has an undoubted Pre-
> rogative to seize upon its Rights, when, and wherever
> they are discover'd.[39]

The chief consideration which intensifies Sir Richard's hostility to authority is the loss of liberty which the latter entails,
and with this loss of liberty the impossibility of any development in poetry. Looking upon the great advance which had been
made in science since the overthrow of ancient dictates, he ardently desires the same progress for poetry: "If Men," he says,

from a generous Principle of Liberty, would renounce the unjust, tho prevailing Power of Authority, and claim their natural Right of entring into the Reason of Things, and judging for themselves, it is highly probable that the Art of Poetry might be carry'd on to greater Degrees of Perfection, and be improv'd, as Philosophy has been.

He discovers another happy result of this freedom in the discrediting of the pettifogging critics who would place literature in the strait jacket of neo-classical rules and judge its excellence solely by classical examples. He promises that

> When thus unfetter'd and disingag'd from a slavish Dependence upon celebrated Writers, Men would soon disregard the crude and unreasonable Assertions frequently laid down by injudicious Commentators and superficial Grammarians, whose Attainments consist in a Collection of Examples, and an Ability to explain the Roman and Grecian Authors: Nor will a modern Heroick Work be any longer acquitted or condemn'd merely as it bears a Conformity or Dissimilitude to the Iliad or the Aeneid. "[40]

Instead, Blackmore thinks, critics will find it necessary to advance substantial grounds for their critical appraisals, and a more fruitful investigation of the nature of art will follow.

Sir Richard takes the occasion to answer what is almost the only possible objection to the evidence which he derives from the history of science. "Neither is it sufficient to alledge," he says,

> that Aristotle has express'd greater Judgment and Accuracy in his Discourses on Poetry, than in his Philosophical Productions; and therefore, tho the last, upon a just Tryal, have been exploded, yet the first have been esteem'd in all Ages by the Learned World as masterly Instructions, and continue undisputed to this Day; for this is still to press us only with the Authority of Aristotle and his Commentators. If his Rules and Precepts of Poetry ought to be so highly regarded, it must be upon this Account, That stronger Reasons can be produc'd in Defence of these, than of his System of Natural Science: But how can this appear, if we take his Writings on the Art of Poetry upon Content, and do not by an impartial Examination make it

clear, that the Evidence of Reason is on their Side; which
was wanting to support his Philosophy ? And this, as far
as I know, has not been attempted. [41]

The argument opposed here by Blackmore was potentially the
most powerful one advanced against the deadly scientific parallel, and had been employed in France by such defenders of the
ancients as Dacier. Many years earlier Gildon had acknowledged
that the poets of Greece still maintained their glory though
Greek science had been overthrown, but he had pursued the
theme no further, for he was then writing against the ancients.[42]
In the long interval, however, that elapsed between his early
and later criticism, he underwent a transformation in his critical views, and became one of the narrowest and most dogmatic of neo-classical critics, a complete critical apostate. In a
work published five years after Blackmore's essay, he attacks
the critical doctor severely for maintaining the same opinions
which he himself in the preceding century had espoused with
such enthusiasm. He seizes especially upon the argument which
Blackmore had tried to answer, and which asserts that some
distinction must be drawn between what might be called the na-
turalistic and the humanistic works of Aristotle. But Gildon
muffs his opportunity, for he contents himself with the argument
that Aristotle's philosophy had not received the approbation of
all ages, that it was introduced by the Schoolmen to support
Catholic theology, and that in this limited field only was it given
an authoritative character. Since, he says, its authority did not
arise

> from the universal consent of all men, and in all ages and
> nations where his philosophy had appear'd, ... the instance
> which Sir Richard gives is very defective, not to say un-
> fair, when he puts that, which was forc'd upon mankind,
> on the same bottom with what was voluntarily receiv'd,
> from the evidence of the truth and reason that was found
> in those works of Aristotle, that have met with that uni-
> versal approbation which his poetics, his rhetorics, his
> politics, and his ethics have found.[43]

Because Gildon noticed only the history of Aristotle's scientific
and humanistic works, and did not inquire into the difference
between their natures, he failed to grasp a distinction that might
have furnished him much more cogent proofs than the pitiful evidence he advances.

SCIENCE AND CRITICISM

The development of the thought-movement which we have been following did not proceed independently of France, where the controversy between the ancients and moderns was still active, and was at this time especially concerned with Homer. In fact, Blackmore's essay was partly inspired by this controversy, and reveals distinct indebtedness to a treatise by one of the supporters of the moderns, the Abbé Terrasson, which, in the year Sir Richard's essay appeared, was translated into English by Francis Brerewood under the title A Discourse of Ancient and Modern Learning. It is not my purpose to enter into the complexities of Anglo-French relations in this matter, except to indicate one difference between the movements in the two countries. Terrasson attacks the authority of the ancients as a bar to the progress of poetry and a dishonor to the mind of man, and he introduces the popular parallel from science, but he does all this merely to install Le Bossu in Aristotle's chair of authority — a wretched substitution — and to move French neo-classical poets into the place vacated by Homer and other ancient worthies. The French critic shows how the development of Cartesian science and French classicism went hand in hand, and he argues the superiority of modern writers over ancient, because the former observed more consistently the unities, decorum, and other neo-classical principles, originally based upon the ancients. [44] In short, the freedom from classical authority which the French moderns demanded furnished merely the opportunity to place stronger chains upon themselves. [45] The freedom desired in England was more of a true liberty, and since the moderns whose cause the critics were defending were in large part Elizabethans, especially Shakespeare, the upholders of modernity were essentially contending for a more liberal art. So the controversy in France, deeply influenced by Descartes, made for neo-classicism, while the same controversy in England, reflecting Bacon, moved toward romanticism.

Blackmore, however, did not move far in that direction. But he did insist upon the necessity of a sceptical attitude, upon the liberty of examining and scrutinizing received opinions, and upon the privilege of making additions to critical principles. He does not hesitate to disagree firmly with Le Bossu, to whom Terrasson would hand Aristotle's sceptre. Inspired by the precedent of science, he expresses vigorous dissent from various neo-classical rules, maintaining, for instance, that the epic hero need not be virtuous; that the action need not be prosperous; that the sufferings and calamities of a hero are as fitting material for an epic as his actions and exploits; and that the poem need not embody a moral. [46] Unfortunately, the liberty of departing from received opinions played him false, if his own epics be taken as proof, for they well deserve Pope's satire in the second book of the Dunciad, where they are represented as quite capable of putting the most hardened critic to sleep.

IV

Nowhere is the difference between the French and English revolts from the ancients more clearly revealed and the note of liberty more loudly struck than in the next and last critic to be considered. In 1759, a year so far removed from seventeenth-century science that one might well suppose its influence was already spent, Edward Young published an essay entitled Conjectures on Original Composition, which upholds original as opposed to imitative writing, and which is one of several critical works that definitely mark the turning of the literary tide from neo-classicism to romanticism. Though its own originality can easily be exaggerated, it contains complete, distinct, and confident statements of ideas and attitudes which before had, for the most part, received only brief, sporadic, or subdued expression: hostility to the authority of the ancients; insistence upon freedom from restraining rules; liberty to widen the domain of poetry; depreciation of reason and learning; emphasis upon inspired genius and creative imagination; the organic as opposed to the mechanical theory of art; and belief in the magical and transporting power of verse. All these show how far the treatise is removed from the critical dogmas of the preceding hundred years. Admittedly inspired by Bacon, it is saturated with his spirit and strewn with his ideas, as well as touched by his eloquence. Young speaks of Bacon as one "under the shadow of whose great name I would shelter my present attempt in favour of originals." And, indeed, the general position and attitude of the two men are remarkably similar. Just as Bacon, perceiving the stagnation of learning and the inadequacies of knowledge to be due to servile submission to antiquity, in ringing tones called upon his fellow men to arouse themselves, throw off their fetters, and begin independent investigation of nature; so Young, with the same reforming zeal, urges men to arise, strike off the chains of classical authority, and allow their own genius full play, for "The wide field of Nature ... lies open before it, where it may range unconfined, make what discoveries it can, and sport with its infinite objects uncontrolled, as far as visible nature extends." I cannot refrain from comparing with this passage the promise which the Baconian spirit in Thomas Sprat made to the experimental scientists of his day: "The Beautiful Bosom of Nature will be Expos'd to our view: we shall enter into its Garden, and tast of its Fruits, and satisfy our selves with its plenty."[47]

In analyzing the obstacles standing in the way of the development of poetry, a development which the independent activity of poetic genius could make possible, Young draws heavily upon the reasons Bacon gave for the stagnation of science. In fact, he quotes the Lord Chancellor as follows: "Men seek not to know their own stock and abilities; but fancy their possessions to be greater, and their abilities less, than they really are."[48] "Which," Young adds, "is, in effect, saying, That we ought to exert more than we do; and that, on exertion, our probability of success is greater than we conceive."[49] In another passage Young repeats the idea that men do not know their own abilities. Thus he applies to his own purposes what had been advanced for the reformation of science. Bacon's idea that the advancement of learning is checked by the diffidence and despair which men derive from the belief that it is impossible to go beyond the ancients, finds emphatic expression in the later critic.[50] "Illustrious examples," he says, "engross, prejudice, and intimidate." And he gives this command to modern poets: "Let not great examples, or authorities browbeat thy reason into too great a diffidence of thyself."[51] Like his great predecessor, Young was concerned with inspiring in men confidence in their powers and also a hope of success independent of the ancients. For this purpose Lord Verulam had found it necessary to combat the theory of nature's decay, and later scientists continued to attack it. Young attaches the same importance to a refutation of the idea. Again and again he insists that modern powers lie under no necessary inferiority, that time cannot be held responsible for the lack of modern achievements, and that the mind's teeming time is not past.[52] He utilizes to good effect Bacon's paradox, Antiquitas saeculi juventus mundi; that, as regards the world, the moderns are the ancients.[53] From this he draws the same conclusion as the philosopher, namely, that the moderns must be richer in judgment and knowledge.[54] By nature, our critic says, we are strong as the ancients, by time we stand on higher ground.

Another essential idea of Bacon's and one emphasized by

later scientists, seized upon Young's mind — the idea of the liberty to investigate and to reason upon the results. As we have seen, this attitude inspired all the critics we have discussed with a similar desire for liberty to depart from established rules and models, and to introduce innovations into art. Like them, Young argues for this freedom, which he considers essential to original writing. "Originals," he says, "soar in the regions of liberty; imitations move in fetters." Even more prominent in his essay is the idea of progress, which had inspired and encouraged seventeenth-century scientists, and which had hardened their faces against antiquity because its authority was an obstacle to advancement. Young contrasts the discoveries which originals may make with the sterility of imitations and their inability to go beyond the beaten paths of classical art.[55] Originals, he asserts, extend the republic of letters, and add a new province to its domain. They enable a poet not only to explore more fully the regions of nature, but also to survey the purely imaginary world. "In the fairyland of fancy," he says, "genius may wander wild; there it has creative power, and may reign arbitrarily over its own empire of chimeras."[56] The relatively timid pleas for liberty to go beyond the ancients in imitation of nature has grown into the bold demand for liberty to go even beyond nature. In pleading for literary progress, Young introduces, as earlier critics had done, the encouraging example of progress in scientific knowledge. After painting a bright picture of the future development of art, he concludes: "What a rant, say you, is here? — I partly grant it. Yet, consider, my friend! knowledge physical, mathematical, moral, and divine increases; all arts and sciences are making considerable advance, and why may not poetry go forward with this advancement."[57] As examples of originals he mentions Milton and Shakespeare, but not these only, for he says, "in natural and mathematical knowledge, we have great originals already — Bacon, Boyle, Newton." Thus he draws closer together experimental science and creative poetry, and shows that the essential meaning he gives to the term "original" applies equally well to both.

The reference to Shakespeare merits comment. There is much praise of the poet in the essay, so much that the reader feels that he had a great deal to do with Young's idea of originality, but Shakespeare is not introduced for his dramatic excellence only; he is primarily considered as a means toward an end. Just as in the scientific movement great discoveries were employed, not for their intrinsic value, but because their excellence furnished proof for the validity of the principles of experimental science, which were themselves the matter of most concern, so Shakespeare is introduced to furnish proof of the principles of original composition. This is only an analogy, but it contributes something to an understanding of the similarity between the natures of the scientific and literary programs and between the means used to establish them.

There are other echoes of Bacon and of the scientific movement in Young, such as the belief that imitation of or reliance on antiquity prevents that progress in the liberal arts which the mechanical enjoy, because the latter try to go beyond their predecessors, while the former slavishly follow them.[58] And there are some figures of speech borrowed from Bacon, e.g., "a stream cannot rise higher than its source."[59] That Young was well aware of the scientific movement in the seventeenth century is revealed in a specific reference to "the dispute over ancient and modern learning," a dispute which extended with varying intensity from the founding of the Royal Society in 1662 down to Temple and Wotton. The elaboration of other details is hardly necessary; a thorough treatment of the subject would require an article in itself.[60] Furthermore, what is more important than any details of similarity is the spirit and purpose of Young's proposed reformation. He is really trying to do for poetry what Bacon did for science, free it from the domination of the ancients, and put it on the right road to improvement. He could very well have called his essay The Advancement of Poetry.

V

The ways in which the scientific movement extended its liberalizing aid to literary criticism were various. It did much to develop a sceptical and critical attitude of mind, and, in the case of Dryden, may very well have fostered his inductive method of reasoning. But the most important assistance it offered was directed toward the overthrow of classical authority. Since the end of the Middle Ages the attack on authority had proceeded with little interruption. Authority in religion had been rejected in the Reformation; authority in government had been contested in the Commonwealth; authority in learning or science had been overthrown in the Restoration, and now authority was being expelled from its last stronghold — literature. Since the situation in criticism was exactly analogous to the

earlier situation in science, it is not strange that the revolt of
the latter should have inspired a similar revolt in the literary
world. In this rebellion science assisted in two ways. First, it
set an example of, and furnished a precedent for, the abandonment of submission to the dictates of antiquity. The mere fact
that in one field of intellectual activity an increasing number of
illustrious men had turned their backs upon the ancients could
not but make its influence felt in other fields. Second, it had
demonstrated the fallibility of those who had been considered
infallible authorities. Again and again it had revealed the erroneous nature of traditional theories and ideas in every branch
of science, and had thrown light on places which the ignorance
of past ages left dark. Science had refuted in no uncertain manner that basic argument of conservatism, the consent of many
men and many ages, by proving that many beliefs which had received such consent were totally false. Certainly the literary
critic, looking at the shattered ruins of an erstwhile potent authority, could hardly fail to harbor misgivings regarding its
validity in poetry.

Another way in which scientific attitudes induced like views
in literature is revealed in the idea of progress or advancement.
The title itself of Bacon's Advancement of Learning discloses
the spirit which both inspired and motivated scientific activities
in the seventeenth century. This desire for advancement science
communicated to poetry. But it did more than that. By its discoveries it justified its own attitudes and partly realized its own
hopes, and in doing so presented a stimulating example to literature. Critics came to see in the worship of classical authority the same obstacle to the progress of poetry which had barred
the advancement of learning, and in the progress which science
had achieved by overthrowing this authority, they discovered a
hope that by pursuing the same course poetry could go forward,
its domain could be widened, and its liberty enlarged.

And finally, in combating the enervating idea of nature's decay, science was fighting not only its own battle but that of every aspect of modernity. This obstinate theory was slow to die.
Arising in the sixteenth century and assuming the form of moral
degeneration, it convinced the Elizabethans that theirs was an
iron age, in which vice and wretchedness were the lot of man;
in the seventeenth century it wore the guise of intellectual decay,
and assured the moderns that their inferiority could never hope
to go beyond the ancients in the discovery of scientific truth;
and in the seventeenth and eighteenth centuries it whispered in

356

the ear of the trembling poet that his enfeebled genius left him
no other recourse than to follow meekly in the beaten paths of
classical art, first laid out in the prime and vigor of nature. [61]
Opposition to the theory was by no means confined to science,
but the latter opposed it more vigorously and consistently than
any other antagonist, and when condemnation of the idea is found
in conjunction with other characteristics of the scientific movement, it may very well be ascribed to the influence of the latter.

Indeed, most of the ideas and attitudes which I have attributed to the influence of science may occasionally be found in non-
scientific quarters, but nowhere were they given the publicity
nor so widely and so earnestly advocated as by the scientists.
The experimental philosophy literally had to fight its way through
to final acceptance, and when it emerged victorious, its recognized importance and prestige gave added force to each of its
constituent elements. Furthermore, it may be noted that in regard to the critics discussed in this article no idea has been
ascribed to the influence of the scientific movement except when
attended by a clear and unmistakable reference to it.

In showing the influence of science on the literary criticism
of the neo-classical period, I do not in any way wish to imply
that it was the only liberalizing agent active at this time. Literary history is complex, and its phenomena are not to be explained by a formula nor reduced to the simplicity of a diagram.
The character of neo-classicism in England was by no means
homogeneous. There were inconsistencies and contradictions,
uncertainties and doubts. For the most part, the age found itself in a critical dilemma, inasmuch as it had intellectually em-
braced a critical creed which did not justify its literary tastes.
Dryden says: "Impartially speaking, the French are as much
better critics than the English, as they are worse poets." And
yet the French poets had conformed much more closely to the
rules laid down by their critics than the English, especially the
Elizabethans, whom Dryden has chiefly in mind. The age tried
to escape from its dilemma through its beauties-and-faults criticism, in which beauties were referred to taste, and faults to
the rules, but inevitably the beauties cast suspicion upon the
faults. Throughout the period Shakespeare, Spenser, and other
poets exerted an unremitting pull upon the closed circle of critical dogma, from which they had been excluded, but which under their influence was slowly widening to encompass them.
When to this fact is added the strong nationalistic spirit which
resented the spectacle of English poets being devastated by a

criticism essentially foreign, or, as one critic puts it, English poets being tried by a foreign jury, we can easily see that there were other forces moving in the same direction as the one which we have been discussing. But disregarding the question of the relative strength of the influence which the scientific movement exerted on criticism, we may safely assert that when the experimental scientists of the seventeenth century went forth under the banner of liberty and progress to wage war on authority, they were battling for more causes than their own.

NOTES

1 This analysis of the scientific movement in seventeenth-century England is based upon the present writer's Ancients and Moderns: A Study of the Background of the Battle of the Books (Washington University Studies, New Series; St. Louis, 1936); Bacon's relationship to the movement is discussed in the introduction to an edition of selections from the works of Sir Francis Bacon (New York: Doubleday, Doran & Co., 1937).

2 Essays of John Dryden, ed. W. P. Ker, 1900, I, 260. This work is hereafter referred to under the name of the editor.

3 In "John Dryden and The Royal Society" (P M L A, XLV [1930], 967-76), Mr. Claude Lloyd attempts to show that Dryden possessed no genuine interest in the Royal Society, but he has been convincingly answered by Miss Ella Riske, Professor Louis Bredvold, and Mr. T. B. Stroup. (Ibid., XLVI [1931], 951-61). For a wider discussion of Dryden's scepticism see Bredvold's The Intellectual Milieu of John Dryden, and "Dryden, Hobbes, and the Royal Society," Modern Philology, XXV (1928), 417-38.

4 Ker, I, 124.

5 Ibid., I, 153.

6 Ibid., I, 141-42.

7 Ibid., I, 195; II, 250

8 Ibid., I, 138; II, 149. CF. Richard F. Jones, Ancients and Moderns, p. 302, note 23.

9 Ker, I, 36-37, 43-44. In order to show the possibility of progress in poetry, Dryden denies the theory of the decay of nature. Ibid., II, 25.

10 Ker, II, 33-34.

11   Ibid., I, 162-63.

12   Ker, I, 63, 155, 252; II, 137.

13   Ibid., II, 103, 143, 158; and I, 70.

14   Ibid., II, 158.

15   Ibid., I, 252.

16   William Wotton expressed fear for the future of science be-
     cause "the Humour of the Age, as to those things, is visibly
     altered from what it was Twenty or Thirty Years ago; So that
     though the Royal Society has weathered the rude Attacks of
     such sort of Adversaries as Stubbe, who endeavored to have
     it thought, That Studying of Natural Philosophy and Mathema-
     ticks, was a ready Method to introduce Scepticism at least,
     if not Atheism into the World: Yet the sly Insinuations of the
     Men of Wit, That no great things have ever, or are ever like
     to be performed by the Men of Gresham, and, That every Man
     whom they call a Virtuoso must needs be a Sir Nicholas Gim-
     crack, have so far taken off the Edge of those who have opu-
     lent Fortunes, and a Love to Learning, that Physiological
     Studies begin to be contracted amongst Physicians and Mech-
     anicks." (Reflections upon Ancient and Modern Learning, 1694,
     pp. 356-57.) Much earlier, Sprat had expressed concern over
     the damage which the satirists might inflict upon science.
     History of the Royal Society, 1667, p. 417.

17   See T. R., An Essay Concerning Critical and Curious Learn-
     ing, 1698, p. 47; William Wotton, Reflections upon Ancient
     and Modern Learning, 3d ed., 1705, pp. 393, 475; Richard
     F. Jones, "The Background of The Battle of the Books" (Wash-
     ington University Studies, VII, Humanistic Series II, St. Louis,
     1920, pp. 150-55), and Ancients and Moderns, p. 278. For
     specific references to the Royal Society see Wotton's Reflec-
     tions, 1694, pp. 233, 306-7, 347, 357; and for references to
     the controversy between the ancients and moderns, which
     centered around the Royal Society, see pages 3, 78-80, 156,
     170-71, 293, 257. Wotton gives a brief outline of the develop-
     ment of the scientific movement in the seventeenth century:
     "Now as this [experimental and mechanical] Method of Philo-
     sophizing laid down above, is right, so it is easie to prove
     that it has been carefully followed by Modern Philosophers.
     My Lord Bacon was the first great Man who took much pains
     to convince the World that they had hitherto been in a wrong
     Path, and that Nature her self, rather than her Secretaries,
     was to be addressed to by those who were desirous to know
     very much of her Mind. Monsieur Des Cartes, who came soon

after, did not perfectly tread in his Steps, since he was for
doing most of his Work in his Closet, concluding too soon, before he had made Experiments enough; but then to a vast Genius he joined exquisite Skill in Geometry, and working upon
intelligible Principles in an intelligent Manner; though he very
often failed of one Part of his End, namely, a right Explication
of the Phaenomena of Nature, yet by marrying Geometry and
Physicks together, he put the World in Hopes of a Masculine
Off-spring in process of Time, though the first Productions
should prove abortive. This was the State of Natural Philosophy, when those great Men who after King Charles II's Restoration joined in a Body, called by that Prince himself, the
Royal Society, went on with the Design; they made it their
Business to set their Members awork to collect a perfect History of Nature, in order to establish thereupon a Body of Physicks; what has been done towards it by the Members of that
illustrious Body will be evident by considering that Boyle, Barrow, Newton, Huygens, Malphighius, Leeuwenhoek, Willough-
by, Willis and Abundance more already named amongst the
great Advancers of real Learning, have belonged to it." Reflections, 1694, pp. 306-7.

18   These are contained in Miscellaneous Letters and Essays, on
      several Subjects. Philosophical, Moral, Historical, Critical,
      Amorous, etc. in Prose and Verse. Directed to John Dryden,
      Esq; The Honourable Geo. Granvill, Esq; Walter Moile, Esq;
      Mr. Dennis, Mr. Congreve, and other Eminent Men of the
      Age. By several Gentlemen and Ladies (London, 1694). Gildon
      edited the volume and wrote most of it.

19   "Some Reflections on Mr. Rymer's Short View of Tragedy,
      and an Attempt at a Vindication of Shakespeare, in an Essay
      directed to John Dryden Esq;."

20   Miscellaneous Letters and Essays, pp. 86-87.

21   Loc. cit. Wotton maintains that the superiority of the ancients
      in poetry and oratory does not argue the inferiority of the
      moderns in genius, since the latter have surpassed antiquity
      in science; and he asks, "Does it seem harder to speak and
      write like Cicero or Virgil, than to find out the motions of the
      Heavens, and to calculate the Distances of the Stars?" Reflec-
      tions on Ancient and Modern Learning, 1694, p. 24.

22   "An Essay at a Vindication of Love in Tragedies, against
      Rapin and Mr. Rymer. Directed to Mr. Dennis."

23   Miscellaneous Letters and Essays, p. 146.

24   Ibid., pp. 151-52.

25   "An Essay at a Vindication of the Love-Verses of Cowley and Waller, etc. In Answer to the Preface of a Book Intituled, Letters and Verses Amorous and Gallant. Directed to Mr. Congreve." The author of the "Book" was William Walsh.

26   See the Preface to Letters and Poems, Amorous and Gallant, 1692. In contrast to his staunch championship of the moderns in science, Wotton concedes the superiority of the ancients in poetry and oratory. He takes Perrault to task for holding that ancient love poems, compared with modern, are rude and unpolished, because they lack gallantry: "It may be justly questioned, whether what Monsieur Perrault calls Politeness, be not very often rather an Aberration from, and Straining of Nature, than an Improvement of the Manners of the Age: If so, it may reasonably be supposed, that those that medled not with the Niceties of Ceremony and Breeding, before unpractised, rather contemned them as improper or unnatural, than omitted them because of the Roughness of the Manners of the Ages in which they lived. Ovid and Tibullus knew what Love was, in its tenderest Motions; they describe its Anxieties and Disappointments in a Manner that raises too many Passions, even in unconcerned Hearts." Reflections, pp. 51-52.

27   See Marchamont Nedham's Medela Medicinae, 1665, and Richard F. Jones's Ancients and Moderns, p. 216.

28   Miscellaneous Letters and Essays, p. 210.

29   "To my Honoured and Ingenious Friend Mr. Harrington, for the Modern Poets against the Ancients." Throughout most of the seventeenth century the controversy between the ancients and moderns in England was almost exclusively concerned with science. Even Wotton himself gave the palm to the ancients in the arts. But toward the end of this century and in the next, literature became the center of the quarrel. In a way, my article merely indicates the influence which the first state of the controversy exerted upon the second.

30   Miscellaneous Letters and Essays, p. 223.

31   Many Advantages of a Good Language, 1724, p. 25.

32   The play is Thomas Killigrew's Chit-Chat, 1719, Act IV,

Sc. 2. See Critical Remarks on the Four Taking Plays of this Season ... By Corinna, a Country Parson's Wife, 1719, p. 52.

33 See "A Discourse upon Comedy, in Reference to the English Stage," 1702, in Critical Essays of the Eighteenth Century, 1700-1725, ed. W. H. Durham, pp. 263-64.

34 This essay is found in Essays upon Several Subjects, 1716.

35 See the Preface to A Paraphrase upon the Book of Job, 1700.

36 Essays upon Several Subjects, pp. 10 ff.

37 Ibid., pp. 14-15.

38 Ibid., p. 160.

39 Essays upon Several Subjects, pp. 166-67.

40 Ibid., pp. 12-13.

41 Ibid., pp. 13-14.

42 "I will yield that Greece had Great Poets, notwithstanding all those Monstrous Faults and Absurdities they abound with; tho he [Rymer] will not allow the English any Honour, because they have been guilty of Errors. Nay, I'll say more, that the Poetry of Greece was her most valuable Learning, for that still maintains its Share of Glory and Esteem, whilst her Philosophy is now exploded by the Universal Reason of Mankind. Homer, Pindar, Sophocles, and Euripides will, as long as they are understood, preserve their Characters of Excellent Poets, tho the Stagyrite with all his Volumes, is now shrunk from the Ostentatious Title of the Philosopher to that of a good Critic, or Grammarian." (Miscellaneous Letters and Essays, p. 221.) Other critics than Gildon found it necessary to recognize the overthrow of Aristotle's authority in science. Rymer says, "And however cryed down in the Schools, and vilified by some modern Philosophers; since Men have had a taste for good sense, and could discern the beauties of correct writing, he [Aristotle] is prefer'd in the politest Courts of Europe, and by the Poets held in great veneration." "Preface to Rapin," Critical Essays of the Seventeenth Century, ed. J. E. Spingarn, II, 164.

43 The Laws of Poetry, 1721, pp. 263-64. Wotton points out that though science is unlimited and therefore capable of progressing,

poetry is a limited art and not necessarily capable of advancing. (Reflections, pp. 46-47.) He seems to have recognized the fact that art does not necessarily obey the same law of progress which science follows.

44   See pp. x, xv, lviii-lxi, lxxiii, lxxxvii, lxxxix, xci, xcii-xciv.

45   Cf. Ker, I, xxiii. Wotton says, "In Poetry likewise he [Perrault] sets Monsieur Boileau against Horace, Monsieur Corneille and Monsieur Moliere against the Ancient Dramatick Poets. In short, though he owns that some amongst the Ancients had very exalted Genius's, so that it may, perhaps, be very hard to find any Thing that comes near the Force of some of the Ancient Pieces, in either Kind, amongst our Modern Writers, yet he affirms, that Poetry and Oratory are now at a greater heighth than ever they were, because there have been many Rules found out since Virgil's and Horace's Time; and the old Rules likewise have been more carefully scanned than ever they were before." Reflections, pp. 46-47.

46   Essays upon Several Subjects, pp. 49, 52, 77, 78-79.

47   History of the Royal Society, 1667, p. 327.

48   The quotation is the opening sentence of the Preface to the Great Instauration. Bacon continues: "Hence it follows that either from an extravagant estimate of the value of the arts they possess, they seek no further, or else from too mean an estimate of their own powers, they spend their strength in small matters and never put it fairly to the trial in those which go to the main. These are as the pillars of fate set in the path of knowledge, for men have neither desire nor hope to encourage them to penetrate further." The idea that men do not put their abilities to the test is also clearly expressed by Young: "Its [the mind's] bounds are as unknown as those of creation; since the birth of which, perhaps, not one has so far exerted, as not to leave his possibilities beyond his attainments, his powers beyond his exploits. Forming our judgments altogether by what has been done, without knowing, or at all inquiring what possibly might have been done, we naturally fall into too mean an opinion of the human mind," and think that it is impossible to surpass Homer.

49   Bacon says that more might be expected from the modern age than from antiquity, "if it but knew its own strength and chose to essay and exert it." The Works of Francis Bacon, ed. Spedding, Ellis, and Heath (new ed., 1889), IV, 82.

50 According to Bacon, the principal impediment to knowledge "hath been in despair or diffidence, and the strong apprehension of the difficulty, obscurity, and the infiniteness which belongeth to the invention of knowledge, and that men have not known their own strength." This fact, he says, has caused some to depend on authorities. Elsewhere he asserts that accepted authorities instill in men the belief that they can do nothing either by art or industry, a belief which "tend[s] wholly to the unfair circumscription of human power, and to a deliberate and factitious despair; which not only disturbs the auguries of hope, but also cuts the sinews and spur of industry, and throws away the chances of experience itself." Bacon, op. cit., III, 249: IV, 86.

51 Young makes use of the giant-and-dwarf figure, which appears repeatedly in the seventeenth-century controversy between the ancients and moderns: "Too formidable an idea of their [the ancients'] superiority, like a spectre, would fright us out of a proper use of our wits; and dwarf our understanding, by making a giant of theirs. Too great awe for them lays genius under restraint, and denies it that free scope, that full elbowroom, which is requisite for striking its most masterly strokes."

52 Other references to the theory are found in Young's assertion that an impartial Providence scatters talents indifferently through all periods of time, and that different portions of understanding are not allotted to different periods. For this reason he holds that nature cannot be blamed for modern inferiority.

53 "And to speak truly Antiquitas saeculi juventus mundi. These times are the ancient time, when the world is ancient and not those which we account ancient ordine retrogrado, by a computation backward from ourselves." (Bacon, op. cit., III, 291.) Young says: "though we are the moderns, the world is an ancient; more ancient far, than when they whom we most admire filled it with their fame."

54 "For the old age of the world is to be accounted the true antiquity; and this is the attribute of our own times, not of that earlier age of the world in which the ancients lived; and which, though in respect of us it was the elder, yet in respect of the world it was the younger. And truly as we look for greater knowledge of human things and a riper judgment in the old man than in the young, because of his experience and of the number and variety of the things which he has seen and heard and thought of; so in like manner from our age, if it but knew its own strength and chose to essay and exert it, much more

might fairly be expected than from the ancient times.... "
(Bacon, op. cit., IV, 82.) The last part of this quotation contains the gist of Young's essay, which calls upon men to know
their own powers and exert them fearlessly and independently.

55   "Imitators," Young says, "only give us a sort of duplicates
of what we had, possibly much better, before; increasing the
mere drug of books, while all that makes them valuable, knowledge and genius, are at a stand." And elsewhere he enlarges
upon the fewness of originals: "So few are our Originals, that,
if all other books were to be burnt, the letter'd world would
resemble some metropolis in flames, where a few incombus-
tible buildings ... lift their heads, in melancholy grandeur
amid the mighty ruin." Cf. Bacon, op. cit., IV, 13-14: "For
let a man look carefully into all that variety of books with
which the arts and sciences abound, he will find everywhere
endless repetitions of the same thing, varying in the method
of treatment, but not in substance, insomuch that the whole
stock, numerous as it appears at first view, proves on examination to be but scanty.... Observe also, that if sciences of
this kind had any life in them, that could never have come to
pass which has been the case now for many ages – that they
stand almost at a stay, without receiving any augmentations
worthy of the human race; ..."

56   After quoting Bacon's opinion that the moderns underestimate
their own abilities, Young says, "Nor have I Bacon's opinion
only, but his assistance too, on my side. His mighty mind
travelled round the intellectual world; and with a more than
eagle's eye, saw, and has pointed out, blank spaces, or dark
spots in it, on which the human mind never shone: Some of
these have been enlightened since; some are benighted still."
Bacon's assistance must have taken the form of inspiring
Young to find the blank spots in the poetic world, and to show
how a new province might be added to the literary domain,
"the fairyland of fancy," for he says in the next sentence,
"Moreover, so boundless are the bold excursions of the human
mind, that in the vast void beyond real existence, it can call
forth shadowy beings, and unknown worlds, as numerous, as
bright, and perhaps as lasting, as the stars; such quite original beauties we may call paradisaical."

57   Young finds definite evidence of the superiority of modern
over ancient genius in the fact that the world has progressed
in virtue, and since virtue assists genius, the latter must be
greater than in former times. Thus, for his belief in the possibility of literary progress he draws support from the idea

of progress in the religious and moral world, as well as from
the advancement of science; but since his general indebtedness
to Bacon and the scientific movement is so much more extensive and pronounced than to any other source, we are safe
in inferring that the influence of the latter in this matter was
correspondingly greater. Before Young's treatise appeared
there had been considerable discussion concerning progress
in religion and morality, upon which science exerted no negligible influence. See R. S. Crane, Modern Philology, XXXI
(1933-34), 273-306, 349-82; especially pp. 373-74.

58   In speaking of the evil effects of imitation, Young says,"First,
it deprives the liberal and politer arts of an advantage, which
the mechanic enjoy: In these men are ever endeavoring to go
beyond their predecessors; in the former, to follow them. And
since copies surpass not their Originals, as streams rise not
higher than their spring, rarely so high; hence, while arts
mechanic are in perpetual progress and increase, the liberal
are in retrogradation and decay." Bacon was very fond of the
contrast: "In arts mechanical the first device comes shortest and time addeth and perfecteth. But in sciences of conceit
the first author goeth furthest and time leeseth and corrupteth" (op. cit., III, 226); and in speaking of the way in which
authority prevents progress, he says, "hence it hath comen
in arts mechanical the first deviser comes shortest, and time
addeth and perfecteth: but in sciences the first author goeth
furthest, and time leeseth and corrupteth." (Ibid. III, 289-90.)
Elsewhere he dwells longer upon the comparison: "all the tradition and succession of schools is still a succession of masters and scholars, not of inventors and those who bring to
further perfection the things invented. In the mechanical arts
we do not find it so; they, on the contrary, as having in them
some breath of life, are continually growing and becoming
more perfect.... Philosophy and the intellectual sciences, on
the contrary, stand like statues, worshipped and celebrated,
but not moved or advanced. Nay, they sometimes flourish
most in the hands of the first author, and afterwards degenerate." Ibid., IV, 14; cf. IV, 74-75.

59   Young uses the figure to show that imitations prevent the progress of poetry because they cannot surpass their models, and
Bacon employs it to illustrate his conviction that reliance upon
Aristotle prevents the progress of knowledge, which is "like
a water that will never arise again higher than the level from
which it fell." Op. cit., III, 227; cf. Ibid., III, 290; IV, 16.

60   A few other similarities may be mentioned. Young enlarges

upon the fame accorded originals: "Fame, fond of new glories, sounds her trumpet in triumph at its [an original's]
birth"; Bacon says, "the introduction of famous discoveries
appears to hold by far the first place among human actions;
and this was the judgment of the former ages." (Op. cit., IV,
113.) Young comments upon the assistance which the ancients
can lend the modern in enabling them to surpass the productions of antiquity: "Have we not their [the ancients'] beauties
as stars to guide; their defects as rocks to be shunned?"
Among the reasons given for the hope that his age may surpass the ancients, Bacon lists "the noble monuments of ancient writers, which shine like so many lights before us."
(Op. cit., V, 110.) In explaining the obstacles to progress,
both Young and Bacon use the figure of master and pupil, the
former stating that advancement would be possible "if ancients
and moderns were no longer considered as masters and pupils," and the latter asserting that the traditional philosophy
possessed no life, for "all the tradition and succession of
schools is still a succession of masters and scholars." (Op.
cit., IV, 14.) Bacon says (op. cit., III, 291) that one error
induced by the worship of antiquity "is a distrust that anything
should now be found out, which the world should have missed
and passed over so long"; and Young declares that the reason
why originals are so few is not that "the writer's harvest is
over, the great reapers of antiquity having left nothing to be
gleaned after them." Young merely points Bacon's ideas and
expressions in a new direction. Brandl has noted Young's indebtedness, in thought and style, to the Novum Organum, I,
129. See Jahrbuch der deutschen Shakespeare-Gesellschaft,
XXXIX (1903), 10-11.

61   Cf. Pope's Essay on Criticism, I, 189, 196-98:

Hail, Bards triumphant! born in happier days,
. . . .
The last, the meanest of your sons inspire,
(That on weak wings, from far, pursues your flights,
Glows while he reads, but trembles as he writes)
. . . .
On the history of the theory of decline, see J. B. Bury, The
Idea of Progress, 1928, pp. 44-49, 78-97; Richard F. Jones,
"The Background of The Battle of the Books" (Washington
University Studies, VII, Humanistic Series II [1920], pp. 104-
16), and Ancients and Moderns, pp. 23-42.

RULES AND ENGLISH CRITICS OF THE EPIC, 1650-1800

H. T. Swedenberg, Jr.

For a hundred and fifty years after Davenant and Hobbes published their treatises occasioned by Gondibert, English critics looked upon the epic as one of the most important genres of literature. Many moribund epics were produced and scores of treatises were written about the form. Several forces contributed to this activity. Homer and Virgil were universally accepted as two of the greatest, if not the greatest, writers of antiquity, and Milton, during the eighteenth century, came to be considered worthy of a place beside them. As a matter of course, the epics of these three, admittedly their noblest works, received marked attention. Furthermore Aristotle and Horace had given critical pronouncements on the form, and their works had been embellished and interpreted by critic after critic on the Continent, especially the French of the seventeenth century. Therefore with the Iliad, Odyssey, and Aeneid as classic examples, with Paradise Lost as a native one, with Aristotle, Horace, and the French classical critics as preceptors, English writers almost inevitably turned their attention to the theory of the epic. In fact practically every great critic of the 1650-1800 period, and a vast number of the less great, wrote about the epic poem.

Knowing and using constantly the critical theory of the past, these English writers naturally quite often took notice of such popular subjects as the theory of the rules and the power of critical authority. Since the critics of the epic numbered among their ranks the great and the small, their opinions are fairly representative of their time. In other words, a study of their opinions will indicate not only what they as critics of a certain type of literature thought, but also what they as typical writers of their period believed. A survey of their remarks will, therefore, throw further light on the general theory of the period in regard to rules and critical authority.

The material which is presented below is divided into three sections, each division containing the theory of a fifty-year period. No attempt is made to suggest that any remarkable change

Reprinted by permission from Studies in Philology, Vol. 35 (1938), pp. 566-587.

took place in English criticism in 1700 or in 1750. It is true that a fairly distinct belief is apparent in each of the fifty-year periods, but the exact dates have been chosen primarily for convenience.

I

In writing Gondibert Davenant had consciously departed from certain established methods of epic structure, and therefore he might well be expected to attack certain rules and critics. But he is singularly silent on the subject. His preface to Gondibert (1650), it is true, contains material which indicates clearly that he was quite aware of his departure from Homeric and Virgilian modes. Thus he declares:

> If I be accus'd of Innovation, or to have transgressed against the method of the Ancients, I shall think my self secure in beleeving that a Poet, who hath wrought with his own instruments at a new design, is no more answerable for disobedience to Predecessors, then Law-makers are liable to those old Laws which themselves have repealed. [1]

Again he writes in the same essay that, contrary to his method, most writers "are apter to be beholding to Bookes then to Men."[2] These statements, however, obviously have reference to ancient practice rather than theory. But, at the same time, they indicate that Davenant was skeptical of authority per se.

It is not at all surprising to find Hobbes even more opposed to literary authority than was Davenant. Hobbes exalted the power of reason and concluded that the man of judgment must avoid dependence upon mere authority: "he that takes up conclusions on the trust of authors, and doth not fetch them from the first items in every reckoning, which are the significations of names by definitions, loses his labour; and does not know anything, but only believeth."[3] This general philosophic truth applies, in Hobbes' opinion, to art also. Rather scornfully he writes in his "Answer" (1650) to Davenant's preface about those who "take not the laws of art, from any reason of their own, but from the fashion of precedent times."[4] Therefore he cannot see why a Christian poet should preface his epic with an invocation, except that it is "a reasonless imitation of custom; of a foolish custom."[5]

Hobbes and Davenant, then, are not concerned with customs and authority in practice or theory. Cowley, a friend of both, is likewise doubtful of mere authority. In the Pindaric "To Mr.

Hobs" he shows clearly his opinion by writing:

> The Fields which answer'd well the Ancients Plow,
> Spent and out-worn return no Harvest now,
> In barren Age wild and unglorious lie,
>   And boast of past Fertilitie,
> The poor relief of Present Povertie.[6]

His poem "Reason. The Use of it in Divine Matters" indicates that his praise of Hobbes is not idle courtesy; he was a follower of Hobbes in elevating reason. It is not surprising, therefore, to find him approving Davenant's departure from the epic norm. Some, says Cowley, seem to think everything ill save that which comes from Rome. But Davenant is to be praised for deserting the beaten way. [7] In a note on an ode which he inserted in his Davideis he shows the same tendency toward revolt, saying he had no authority, but declaring that "We must sometimes be bold to innovate."[8] In these remarks Cowley is definitely of a stamp with Hobbes and Davenant in defending reason as opposed to authority. But he does not follow this theory in all his statements about the epic. He declares that he followed the ancients in prefacing his Davideis with an invocation;[9] he explains that he divided the poem into twelve parts after the manner of Virgil;[10] and he notes that he did not carry the poem on to David's anointing because the method of the ancients was to conclude the poem without the final details. [11] Quite obviously, then, Cowley was not a complete convert to the cause of Davenant and Hobbes. His criticism is, in fact, an early example of what was to appear later in epic theory: a blending of authority and reason.

Thomas Rymer took essentially the same stand. As Spingarn has pointed out, [12] Rymer had respect for the theory of Hobbes. Thus in The Tragedies of the Last Age (1678) he writes of the importance of reason in making great poetry. But in his preface to the translation of Rapin's Reflections (1674), just before he begins a survey of English epic poetry, he shows his respect for authority. Furthermore, he blends reason with authority and accepts both:

> The truth is, what Aristotle writes on this Subject are not the dictates of his own magisterial will or dry deductions of his Metaphysicks: But the Poets were his Masters, and what was their practice he reduced to principles. Nor would the modern Poets blindly resign to this practice of the

Ancients, were not the Reasons convincing and clear as any demonstration in Mathematicks.[13]

This is, of course, a statement of the very popular neo-classic doctrine that rules are based on nature and reason and are therefore to be accepted.

Another follower of reason was Edward Phillips, who contended that a poet might know all the laws of epic and tragedy, and still, lacking "Poetic Energie," fail. A critic, in his opinion, must use his reason and common sense as well as his knowledge of the ancients. At the conclusion of his preface to Theatrum Poetarum (1675) he declares that he has judged by what truth has "suggested to my reason, perswading my self, that no right judgement can be given or distinction made in the Writings of This or That Author, in whatever Art or Science, but, without taking ought upon trust, by an unbiass'd and, from the knowledge of ancient Authors, judicious examination of each."[14]

The Earl of Mulgrave had a wholesome respect for reason, "that substantial, useful part"[15] which governs with fancy, and he was even more enthusiastic about the laws of epic structure, in particular those set forth by Le Bossu, who showed the world the "sacred Mysteries" of the epic. In these and other statements Mulgrave blends reason and authority, until authority, leaving reason a little behind, becomes important for itself. Le Bossu, says Mulgrave, has clearly shown the way in epic poetry, but there is no one to follow it.[16]

In the mind of "W. J.," who translated Le Bossu's treatise on the epic, there was no doubt about the efficacy of the rules. In enumerating various reasons for the low state of epic poetry in his time, he gives as one of the most important the disregard for the rules:

> The third and last Reason I shall mention for the declining State of Epick Poetry among the Moderns is, their notorius neglect of following the Rules which Aristotle and Horace have prescrib'd: This, and not want of Genius, has been the true Cause why several of our English Epick Poets have succeeded so ill in their Designs.[17]

But "W. J." does not desert the cause of reason. In defending the method of Le Bossu he points out that Le Bossu has indeed followed the theory of Aristotle and Horace, but he has always employed his judgment in using any of their ideas. Many will

disagree with some of Le Bossu's theories, but, says "W. J. ,"
it is to be hoped that no serious reader will condemn him until

> he has seriously weigh'd his Reasons, and consider'd the
> Arguments he uses to maintain his Cause: and then if our
> Critick can be convinc'd of any Error, he is too modest
> not to submit to the Suffrage of better Judgments. But if,
> on the other hand, he has Reason on his side, it may with
> Justice be expected, that he will be a means of opening the
> Eyes of a great many unprejudic'd Persons. [18]

"W. J. " is obviously much more concerned about the efficacy of
the rules than the sanctity of reason, but he nevertheless remembers that reason and judgment are still important in criticism.

Equally respectful of the rules is Sir Richard Blackmore,
who observes that for seventeen hundred years no one has succeeded in the epic, and then notes: "That the modern Poets
have been so unsuccessful, has not, I imagin, proceeded so
much from want of Genius, as from their Ignorance of the Rules
of writing such a Poem; or at least, from their want of attending to them. "[19] Although, as we shall see, he later made a pre-
tense of revolting against authority, in 1695 Blackmore is awed
by it. He does not seek to justify the rules of epic construction
by reason; he is satisfied that they are correct, because they
have been propounded by great critics. It is useless, he declares,
for him to censure modern epics, for

> whoever will be at the Pains to read the Commentators
> on Aristotle, and Horace's Rules of Poetry; or that will
> but carefully consider Rapin, Dacier, and Bossu, those
> great Masters among the French, and the Judicious Re-
> marks of our own excellent Critick Mr. Rymer, who seems
> to have better consider'd these matters, and to have seen
> farther into them, than any of the English Nation; will be
> soon able to see wherein the Heroick Poems that have been
> publish'd since Virgil by the Italian, French, and English
> Wits have been defective, by comparing them with the
> Rules of Writing set down by those great Masters. [20]

At variance with Blackmore and others on a number of subjects, John Dennis was nevertheless at one with his age on the
subject of rules and reason. He elevated reason, but at the same
time managed to show that nature, the rules, and common sense

are all the same. In The Impartial Critick (1693) he makes one of the characters say: "The Rules of Aristotle are nothing but Nature and Good Sence reduc'd to a Method."[21] And he reiterates even more forcefully in his work on Blackmore's Prince Arthur:

> For the Rules of Aristotle ... are but Directions for the Observation of Nature, as the best of the written Laws, are but the pure Dictates of Reason and Repetitions of the Laws of Nature. For either this must be granted, or Aristotle must be confess'd to have contradicted the Design which he had in prescribing those Rules: Which Design was to teach Men to please, more than they could do without these Rules.... For Poetry is nothing but an Imitation of Nature, which Aristotle, who knew her well, has very well taught us to imitate. And he who keeps up strictly to his Rules, is as certain to succeed, as he who lives up exactly to Reason is certain of being happy. But it is as impossible for any Man who has not a great Genius, strictly to observe the Rules; as it is for any one who has not super-natural Assistance to live up to the Dictates of Reason.[22]

Rules, reason, nature, common sense — all are intertwined, all are closely related in the opinion of Dennis.

Finally there was Dryden, who, as might be expected, took a middle-of-the-road approach. He recognized the value of rules and of reason, but he was skeptical of that reason which would shackle the flights of great poetry. In "A Parallel of Poetry and Painting" (1695) he defends rules as being rational, because they are founded on nature:

> the way to please being to imitate nature, both the poets and the painters in ancient times, and in the best ages, have studied her; and from the practice of both these arts the rules have been drawn, by which we are instructed how to please, and to compass that end which they obtained, by following their example; for nature is still the same in all ages, and can never be contrary to herself.[23]

It is not necessarily true, he goes on, that that which pleases the greatest number is greatest. What "ought to please" is important. Our judgments have become warped, and we sometimes

mistake for an imitation of nature that which has no nature in it. Therefore "rules were invented, that by them we might discern— when nature was imitated, and how nearly. "[24]
Reason, in Dryden's opinion, is all very good, but if it is used to condemn imaginative work it must be the result of a majority opinion, not merely the judgment of one man. Many condemn the flights of heroic poetry as bombast. Such critics had better doubt their own judgment than that of Homer, or Virgil, or Milton. It is true, says Dryden, there are limits to which the poetic spirit may range, "but he must understand those limits who pretends to judge as well as he who undertakes to write."[25]
Mere individual reason is not enough to cast aside the hyperboles of the great masters:

> And if you would appeal from thence to right reason, you
> will gain no more by it in effect, than, first, to set up
> your reason against those authors; and, secondly, against
> all those who have admired them. You must prove, why
> that ought not to have pleased, which has pleased the most
> learned, and the most judicious; and, to be thought knowing,
> you must first put the fool upon all mankind. [26]

Thus also is Dryden a member of the rational-rule group. He will not use reason to carp at the excellencies of imagination, but neither will he allow imagination to run riot. Established judgment, then, is to be the norm for criticism, not the mere whim of each succeeding critic. The judgment established by the great minds is the basis of rules, which are to be considered not because they are rules, but because they are founded on nature, a nature that is always constant.
From the foregoing remarks of various critics of the epic, the fact is obvious that a gradual development toward authority took place in the last half of the seventeenth century. Neo-classic theory of the epic started with Davenant and Hobbes and grew until it reached a fairly mature state in the work of Blackmore, Dennis, and Dryden. During this development opinion on rules and authority changed. Hobbes and Davenant, basing their belief on the importance of reason, scouted the value of authority in epic construction. This respect for reason continued throughout the century, but it soon changed from a thoroughgoing love of reason as opposed to authority to a love of reason and authority as harmonious guides. Even Cowley, an intimate and admirer of Hobbes and Davenant, could not go all the way

with them in rejecting Homer and Virgil as models. As the century progressed and the study of the epic became more popular, established method and rules were looked upon with ever increasing respect. But reason and common sense likewise became more and more a part of every critic's lexicon. It followed, therefore, that rules and reason became companions. By the time of Dryden's death the familiar neo-classic theory that rules are founded on nature and that men of judgment accept them because they are reasonable was established.

II

The first fifty years of the eighteenth century is a period particularly fruitful for an investigation of the theory of rules, for it is universally accepted as the age in which English neo-classicism was at its flood tide. In this period John Dennis continues in the attitude he had expressed prior to 1700. In the "Epistle Dedicatory" to The Advancement and Reformation of Modern Poetry he explains his belief in regularity. There are, says Dennis, some things in great poetry, like some phenomena in nature, which seem at first sight to be "against Reason," but upon close examination those things in nature and poetry prove to be necessary to a "just Design." Thus Homer and Virgil certainly followed the rules of composition, for they had "too much Discernment, not to see the Necessity of knowing and practising the Rules, which Reason and Philosophy have prescrib'd to Poets."[27] Dennis is willing to admit that Milton broke the laws of Aristotle and that he was justified in this course.[28] But apparently this praise of Milton's latitude does not apply to the work of lesser folk who might eschew rules. Dennis goes on to say that poetry has lately fallen to a low level because its devotees are ignorant of the essential laws of the art:

In short, Poetry is either an Art, or Whimsie and Fanaticism. If it is an Art, it follows that it must propose an end to it self, and afterwards lay down proper Means for the attaining that end: For this is undeniable, that there are proper Means for the attaining of every end, and those proper Means in Poetry, we call the Rules. Again, if the end of Poetry be to instruct and reform the World, that is, to bring Mankind from Irregularity, Extravagance and Confusion, to Rule and Order, how this should be done by a thing that is in it self irregular and extravagant, is difficult to be conceived. Besides, the work of every reasonable Creature must derive its Beauty from Regularity, for Reason is Rule and Order, and nothing can be irregular either in our Conceptions or our Actions, any further than it swerves from Rule, that is, from Reason.[29]

Here is, of course, a restatement, in the most explicit terms, of the theory that rules and reason are the same. Addison felt that rules were not always to be honored, and he was particularly irritated with those who judged only by them: "A few general rules extracted out of the French authors, with a certain cant of words, has sometimes set up an illiterate heavy writer for a most judicious and formidable critic."[30] He declares that in writing the critique of Paradise Lost he has not bound himself by the rules of any critic. He has taken something from one and something from another, and at times he has differed from all. That, says Addison, was "when I have thought that the reason of the thing was on my side."[31]

Pope was the first English writer to ridicule the rules of Le Bossu,[32] who was looked upon with great respect by most English critics. In the "Receipt to make an Epic Poem," first published in number 78 of the Guardian, he burlesques Le Bossu's method of criticizing an epic, prefacing his work with a statement about criticism in general. As criticism is known, he says, "it consists only in a knowledge of mechanic rules which contribute to the structure of different sorts of poetry; as the receipts of good housewives do to the making puddings of flour, oranges, plumbs, or any other ingredients."[33] Also, in the "Postscript to the Odyssey" he declares that he is "sawcy enough to think that one may sometimes differ from Aristotle without blundering, and ... I am sure one may sometimes fall into an error by following him servilely."[34] Pope, then, was also skeptical of the rules per se.

Well in the ranks of those who venerated the methods of the classics is Thomas Parnell, who is firm in the belief that the modern can imitate only the ancients. He admits that the modern is not forced to follow the fables of the ancients, but he is certain that he will do well "to observe their Manner."[35] He knows that Milton and Spenser have given evidence that "Invention is not bounded" but he is certain that these two are exceptions and not to be followed by the ordinary man.

On the other side is John Hughes. He finds difficulty in harmonizing strict classic rules with the structure of the Faerie

Queene. Thus, while admitting that one of the major defects of the Faerie Queene is its want of unity, he goes on to say that the poem must not be judged by rules "drawn from the Practice of Homer and Virgil."[36] And having made this statement, he proceeds to draw a parallel in a manner dear to Augustan critics:

> to compare it therefore with the Models of Antiquity, wou'd be like drawing a Parallel between the Roman and the Gothick Architecture. In the first there is doubtless a more natural Grandeur and Simplicity: in the latter, we find great Mixtures of Beauty and Barbarism, yet assisted by the Invention of a Variety of inferior Ornaments; and tho the former is more majestick in the whole, the latter may be very surprizing and agreeable in its Parts.[37]

Henry Felton also had a questioning attitude toward the authority of rules. He is certain that many of the greatest works were written before the rules were evolved: "For those who first prescribed the Rules of Writing, did not take Nature stripped and naked for their Copy; but they looked upon her, as she was dressed and adorned by her Adorers."[38] Rules, then, were simply founded on the models of the greatest writers; and those who have written after these early writers have, in following nature, followed the rules. "And perhaps," concludes Felton rather daringly, "(for I love to doubt in Matters of so hazardous Conjecture) if the Rules had not been given, we had been troubled with many fewer Writers; for then those who had not Nature for their Rule, could have had no Rule at all."[39] As it is, there are many scribblers who think only of the rule and care not at all for the meaning.

We have already noted Sir Richard Blackmore as a staunch defender of authority in 1695. But by 1716 he had reversed his position and was taking a definite stand against the conventional rules. In his "An Essay on the Nature and Constitution of Epick Poetry" he admits Aristotle "as a great Genius, and a Person of more than common Erudition,"[40] but he refuses to accept his dictates as the final decree in poetry. Poets and critics, says Blackmore, should trust their reason and judgment and not rely solely upon authority. If this attitude were taken, men would no longer be slaves to commentators and grammarians. Also modern poetry would not be tried by the laws of the ancients alone. Critics would "produce clear Evidence from the Nature and Constitution of that kind of Poetry, to make good their Opinions; and

not rely on the single Authority of ancient Writers, tho of the
greatest Name, to support them. "[41]

Seven years later Blackmore said essentially the same thing.
In the preface to Alfred he again calls for freedom from ancient
authority. If Homer and Virgil are judged with an exercise of
reason, says Blackmore, it is apparent that they are not free
from faults; and therefore modern writers are under no particular obligation to follow their patterns. A slavish imitation of
them "manifestly sets up Authority and Example, above Judgment and Reason. "[42] It is, after all, only "the half Critick" who
will admit nothing in the epic which is not also in Homer and
Virgil. [43]

Joseph Trapp, first professor of poetry at Oxford and translator of Virgil, also objected to a complete subjection to authority, though he did not believe that poetry can be free of all rules.
In speaking of his own criticism he declares that he has examined various authorities, and goes on to say, "I don't slavishly
adhere to their Decrees. For Books are to be consider'd as
Helps to Learning, not Fetters to it; and it is just, in these sort
of Studies especially, that every Man, after he has weigh'd the
Opinion of others should be at Liberty to follow his own. "[44] But
he goes on to point out that the art of poetry is as susceptible
to laws as other arts, and that these laws are "founded upon
Truth and right Reason. "[45] In another place, however, he shows
that rules may be submitted to reason, for he argues that Aristotle's rules cannot be used to limit all subsequent epic poetry,
since Aristotle based his statements primarily on the work of
Homer. [46]

Of all those who honored the rules, none more completely
revered them than Charles Gildon. He is certain that no man
ever achieved a lasting fame without "coming up" to the rules
of poetry, [47] and he can see no sense in the argument concerning art and nature in a poet, for art is "Nature reduc'd to Form."
It is all very well for the man of genius to exercise his natural
abilities, but he must at the same time use his judgment, which
is based on the rules of art. When the question of Homer's knowledge of rules is proposed, Gildon can only answer that his belief is that the poet proposed rules to himself. [48]

Three years after making these statements Gildon is still
worried about the "low state of Poetry" and the lack of taste of
the people in general. [49] He feels that the rules would alleviate
this condition, if only the public were acquainted with them. And
he is particularly wroth with those "messieurs of Port-Royal"

who question whether Virgil was concerned with the rules. Gildon is convinced that Virgil knew the rules of composition as well as those of grammar. [50]

Though he is concerned only incidentally with epic, Leonard Welsted writes with so much force and directness on the subject of regulation by rule in poetry that he may very profitably be noted here. His essay "A Dissertation concerning the Perfection of the English Language, the State of Poetry, &c." contains some extremely sensible and logical material on the subject. Though Welsted was inclined to the school of taste, he also saw the value of reason and restraint in poetry. But his conception of reason differs somewhat from that held by others of his period, and therefore his pronouncements are particularly interesting.

According to Welsted all that the ancients and moderns together have written on the subject is only what a man of sense would know anyway. The rules have done little except produce a group of very inferior writers. [51] He goes on to say – in striking contrast to Gildon's conception of Virgil's method of composition – that

> Those Observations or Rules were primarily form'd upon
> and design'd to serve only as Comments to the Works of
> certain great Authors, who compos'd those Works without any such help; the mighty Originals, from whence they
> were drawn, were produc'd without them; and unluckily for
> all Rules, it has commonly happen'd since, that those Writers have succeeded the worst, who have pretended to have
> been most assisted by them. [52]

The "arts" of poetry, says Welsted, can touch only the mechanical side of poetry, ignoring the more important internal fire. Rules cannot teach a writer true poetry:

> What Instruction shall convey to him that Flame, which can
> alone animate a Work, and give it to the Glow of Poetry?
> And how, or by what Industry shall be learn'd, among a
> Thousand other Charms, that delicate Contexture in Writing, by which the Colours, as in the Rainbow, grow out
> of one another, and every Beauty owes its Lustre to a
> former, and gives Being to a succeeding one? [53]

Welsted declares that he does not wish to throw poetry into a mysterious vagueness. He understands the necessity for reason. The important point, however, is that reason of poetry should be differentiated from that of mathematics:

> Poetry depends much more on Imagination, than other
> Arts, but is not on that Account less reasonable than they;
> for Imagination is as much a Part of Reason, as is Mem-
> ory or Judgment, or rather a more bright Emanation from
> it, as to paint and throw Light upon Ideas, is a finer Act
> of the Understanding, than simply to separate or compare
> them: The Plays, indeed, and the Flights of Fancy, do
> not submit to that sort of Discussion, which moral or phy-
> sical Propositions are capable of, but must nevertheless,
> to please, have Justness and natural Truth: The Care to
> be had, in judging of Things of this Nature, is to try them
> by those Tests that are proper to themselves, and not by
> such as are proper only to other Knowledges. Thus Poetry
> is not an irrational Art, but as closely link'd with Reason,
> exerted in a right Way, as any other Knowledge; what it
> differs in, as a Science of Reason, from other Sciences,
> is, that it does not, equally with them, lie level to all Ca-
> pacities, that a Man, rightly to perceive the Reason and
> the Truth of it, must be born with Taste or a Faculty of
> Judging, and that it cannot be reduc'd to a formal Science,
> or taught by any set Precepts. [54]

The reason which governs poetry, then, is not to be acquired
by rules; it is rather born in a person. Welsted's opinion seems
to be rather Hobbesian, since his reason is the reason which is
individual, a reason based on the natural endowment of a man,
not that arrived at by the use of set principles. His attitude is
therefore particularly interesting, because of his attempt to harmonize reason and taste, and his rejection of set rules.

Joseph Spence also realized that art may be above rules,
when he wrote "Eloquence has its Je ne scai quoi's, as well as
Beauty."[55] But he was, nevertheless, thoroughly convinced that
certain rules are to be followed in judging a poem. He was particularly irritated with the critics who simply carp at an author's
work. The great critics of antiquity were aware that a poet may
make some minor errors and still be praised, if only he have a
"generous Spirit." "Agreeable to this was the behaviour of these
great Men in laying down rules, or making observations: their
intention was to distinguish the beauties of Language or Sentiments, from the defects and vices of either."[56]

Jonathan Richardson likewise felt that rules may at times be transcended. In regard to Milton's treatment of the rules of epic structure in Paradise Lost he writes:

> if the Sublimity and Peculiarity of the Matter of this Poem, if its Superiority in That Respect has rais'd it above Some of the Rules given by Aristotle, or Whatever Other Criticks, and Gather'd From, or Founded on the Iliad, Odyssey, or Aeneid, it has Distinguish'd it to its greater Glory; 'tis not only an Heroic Poem, but the Most So that Ever was Wrote. Milton did not despise Rules, Such as were Built upon Reason, So far as those Establish'd Reach'd; but as his Free and Exalted Genius Aspir'd Beyond what had Yet been Attempted in the Choice of his Subject, Himself was his Own Rule when in Heights where None had gone before, and Higher than Which None Can Ever go. [57]

Henry Pemberton expressed a similar doubt in the beginning of his Observations on Poetry:

> Were the precepts of critics always consistent with one another, and with truth, nothing more would be necessary towards deciding upon any poetic performance, than to compare it with their dictates. But as the most approved are on some points divided, and, where they are more unanimous, not always in my apprehension free from error; I intend to examine into the genuine principles, whereby our opinion ... ought to be regulated, independent on any authority whatever. [58]

Many, says Pemberton, are still enslaved by "the pedantry of submitting implicitly to ancient authority," but the world is at length largely freed from that bondage. He, therefore, is not afraid to disagree with Aristotle's precepts on the epic.

In this manner the critics of the epic talked about rules in the first half of the eighteenth century. Any attempt to evaluate their position leads inevitably, in the first place, to the conclusion that there was a division of opinion. Some strongly favored the rules, others were equivocal, and others deprecated them. The time-honored explanation that rules were founded on nature appeared often. Those critics who were concerned with defending modern epics naturally could not accept ancient rules as the only correct interpretation of nature. Spenser and Milton, for instance, were so careless of some of the established theories that their works would probably suffer if judged solely by them. And therefore critics like Hughes and Richardson were forced to side-step some of the old laws. Occasionally outright questioning of the value of rules made itself apparent.

It is particularly noticeable that reason was a constant guide, no matter what the critic thought of the rules themselves. He might identify rules with reason or he might put reason against rules, but he was always calling reason to justify his position. Never were rules defended on the basis that they were promulgated by Aristotle or Horace and therefore must be right. As a matter of fact, during this period in which the classics were honored above all, there is a notable tendency among critics of the epic to question the established rules of composition. Not many were ready to declare boldly that these laws should be disregarded, but a goodly number showed plainly that they were restive under the dominion of a system too inflexible. This tendency looks forward to the change in belief that was to come in the last half of the century.

III

In his essay on Pope, Joseph Warton comments on Pope's line "nature methodiz'd," saying that the rules of poetry were all "posterior to practice."[59] Furthermore he adds that "A petulant rejection, and an implicit veneration, of the rules of the ancient critics, are equally destructive of true taste."[60] Warton takes the middle of the way. Critical bigotry is not, he affirms, to be confused with true critical endeavor. Such rules as those that the epic action should begin as late as possible, that the action be great and complete, that the episodes rise from the "main fable," and that the hero be distinguished are "indispensable rules, which nature and necessity dictate, and demand to be observed."[61] He is, however, perfectly willing to damn such absurd theories as those that an epic should have only twelve books, and should end happily.

Thomas Warton was thoroughly convinced that classical rules cannot be applied to the romantic epic:

> But it is absurd to think of judging either Ariosto or Spenser by precepts which they did not attend to. We who live in the days of writing by rule, are apt to try every composition by those laws which we have been taught to

382

think the sole criterion of excellence. Critical taste is universally diffused, and we require the same order and design which every modern performance is expected to have, in poems where they never were regarded or intended. Spenser, and the same may be said of Ariosto, did not live in an age of planning. His poetry is the careless exuberance of a warm imagination and a strong sensibility.... If the Fairy Queen be destitute of that arrangement and oeconomy which epic severity requires, yet we scarcely regret the loss of these, while their place is so amply supplied, by something which more powerfully attracts us: something, which engages the affections the feelings of the heart, rather than the cold approbation of the head. [62]

Arthur Murphy was even more thorough in rejecting the rules of epic structure. In number 92 of the Gray's-Inn Journal for July 20, 1754, he reviews rules for the epic which "Bossu and other Critics" have given the world, such as those of the unity of time, of in medias res, and machinery. These he concludes "do not any Way conduce to the Refinement of Taste, or the Improvement of true Genius. "[63]

Goldsmith sees the ruin of literature in the popularity of rules and critics. He declares that common sense "might suggest, that those rules were collected, not from nature, but a copy of nature, and would consequently give us still fainter resemblances of original beauty. "[64] In a review of Roger Kedington's Critical Dissertations on the Iliad of Homer (1759), Goldsmith[65] expresses a like opinion. Kedington had worshipped Homer abjectly. Goldsmith points out in his review that one of the main reasons for the poor quality of epic writing is that too many people have followed Homer and forgotten nature. As a result all epics

seem to be cast in the same mould: the muse is invoked, she tells the tale, the episodes are introduced, armour rings against armour, games are described, and sometimes a shield; while all the conduct of the passions, and all the mixture of well-conducted intrigue are entirely left out of the question. [66]

Another work with which Goldsmith's name is connected is The Art of Poetry on a New Plan,[67] which shows a similar irreverence for rules. In regard to rules of the epic, the statement is made that

some of the laws of poetry, as well as those of logic, are
better dispensed with than observed; and we see that the
good sense of the present age has so far abrogated the
tyrannic ordinances of logic, that a man who reasons well
may be heard, tho' he does not speak in mood and figure,
or throw every argument into a syllogistic form. [68]

Two reviews of contemporary epics are a little less harsh.
The author of an essay on The Epigoniad rejects the poem because it does not abide by the rules of Le Bossu and Addison. [69]
And William Kenrick, reviewing Fingal, writes that genius may
indeed rise above rules, but at the same time it is necessary to
compare any new work with standards in its field. [70] The rules
of Aristotle, he argues, were formed by a posteriori rather than
a priori methods. Here again, of course, is the apology for the
rules; nature and Homer being the same, Aristotle formed his
rules on the practice of Homer.

With this defense of the rules may be compared several outright repudiations of them. Laurence Sterne had no love at all
for them or critics. He represents the criticism of an epic as
"taking the length, breadth, height, and depth of it ... upon an
exact scale of Bossu's." [71] Of Apollo he asks only "one stroke
of native humour, with a single spark of thy own fire along
with it." [72] Then Mercury can take the rules and go "to – no
matter."

John Gordon feels approximately the same way, though he is
a bit more dignified in his expression. He writes: "But I know
not, how it is; I never in my life, out of complaisance to a set
of rules or terms of art, could affect to be delighted with what
I neither felt, heard, saw, nor understood. This is really the
plain truth, despise me, as much as you please, for it." [73] He
is convinced that those who follow only rules and look not at nature will be misled, and he concludes that many "have bartered
their senses for a few terms of art." [74]

Richard Hurd denounced the rules of epic as they had been
promulgated in England. He was especially irritated with English critics who followed the French vogue of crying down the
Italian epics:

> Sir W. Davenant open'd the way to this new sort of cri-
> ticism in a very elaborate preface to Gondibert; and his
> philosophic friend, Mr. Hobbes, lent his best assistance
> towards establishing the credit of it. These two fine Letters

contain, indeed, the substance of whatever has been since written on the subject. Succeeding wits and critics did no more than echo their language. It grew into a sort of cant, with which Rymer, and the rest of that School, filled their flimsy essays and rambling prefaces. [75]

Hugh Blair and Edward Burnaby Green also showed doubt. Blair labels as pedants those who judge by rule rather than feeling: "For all the rules of genuine Criticism I have shewn to be ultimately founded on feeling; and Taste and Feeling are necessary to guide us in the application of these rules to every particular instance."[76] Greene, in the preface to his essay "Observations on the Sublime of Longinus," wrote that the ancients and moderns have done much to injure criticism: "The former, to speak literally, have, with Aristotle, cramped the imagination within the trammels of rule; and the latter have by indulging a critical affectation, created elegance, but destroyed majesty."[77]

In 1782 William Hayley addressed a poetical epistle to Mason on the subject of epic poetry, in which he showed himself an implacable enemy of the accepted rules and rule-makers, especially Boileau and Le Bossu. Boileau, he says, had elegance and judgment, but his remarks on epic poetry might well have clipped the wings of Milton, if they had affected him. Le Bossu, on the other hand, studied Homer by system,

> And wisely tells us, that his Song arose
> As the good Parson's quiet Sermon grows. [78]

Not even Aristotle is exempt. Hayley believes that a good critic must have understanding, imagination, and sensibility; and he makes bold to say that Aristotle had only the first in abundance.[79] He is certain that no one critic is to be followed, and he writes to Mason

> Thou wilt not hold me arrogant or vain,
> If I advise the young poetic train
> To deem infallible no Critic's word. [80]

He calls upon Mason to help him that they may both free young poets from the bonds of rules, and allow the fancy to range. [81]

In the last decade of the century two other writers on the epic expressed their respect for certain rules. William Belsham was willing to accept Aristotle's rules, but he would have nothing of the regulation of epic theory which had been added to Aristotle's system. The rules of Aristotle, if followed properly, would produce a poem which would "be worthy not only of regard and attention, but of the highest admiration, as manifestly requiring, in order to its accomplishment, the most noble and ardent efforts of the human faculties."[82] Henry James Pye likewise defended Aristotle, but he was not blind in praising him. He declares that Aristotle cannot be expected to account for all the changes in science and art that have taken place since his day. If, however, one makes allowances for the inevitable changes, he will find that, after all, "Aristotle is not so great a blockhead as some take him to be who have never read him."[83]

There is no point in going into further detail, for the writers already noted give sufficient indication of the critical opinion during the second half of the century. As we might expect, there was a marked tendency to doubt the value of the rules. Even those who showed themselves friendly to them were careful to qualify their statements. Thus Joseph Warton could accept some of the rules for the epic, but he could also reject others as completely useless; and Belsham and Pye could praise the law of Aristotle only with qualification. Particularly noticeable is the emphasis on the historical point of view, a theory which stated that Spenser and Ariosto cannot be held accountable to rules which they did not pretend to follow. From 1750 to 1800, then, we see that restiveness which marked the critical attitude toward rules in the preceding fifty years turning into outright revolt.

From the critical opinions expressed during the century and a half just surveyed we may draw several conclusions. First, reason was a dominant force in the criticism of Hobbes and Davenant, and it continued powerful for at least a hundred years. But its application as a critical term varied. The reason which at first was employed to offset the effect of mere authority and rules later became a term to explain and justify rules. Critics of the epic came to feel that they were justified in invoking reason as an ally in defense of or attack on the rules. When used to justify the rules, reason was the logical, sensible opinion of the majority, who looked upon rules and found them good; when employed to attack, reason was the opinion of the individual who examined rules and found them unacceptable.

In the second place, we note that rules became more and more popular with critics of heroic poetry, as the second half of the seventeenth century wore on. But we also see that this popularity definitely began to wane even during the first fifty years of the eighteenth century. During this period – the true classical period of English criticism – there was a constant questioning of the rules, as well as a constant justification of them. It is particularly significant that even those who most heartily approved of rules felt the necessity of defending them. Practically no writer accepted them casually, as beyond doubt. Finally, we notice that the last half of the eighteenth century showed a marked tendency on the part of the critics of the epic to reject rules altogether, a conclusion which, in view of the changes that were taking place in the literature of the time, is hardly startling.

NOTES

1   Critical Essays of the Seventeenth Century, ed. J. E. Spingarn (Oxford, 1908-1909), II, 20. All subsequent references to this work will be designated by the use of the name Spingarn.

2   Ibid., p. 26.

3   "Leviathan" (1651), English Works, ed. Sir William Molesworth (London, 1839-1845), III, 32.

4   English Works, ed. cit., IV, 447.

5   Ibid., p. 448.

6   Works (London, 1668), p. 26, 3d pag.

7   "To Sir William Davenant. Upon his two first Books of Gundibert, finished before his voyage to America," Works, p. 25, 1st pag.

8   Works, p. 37, 4th pag.

9   Ibid., p. 24, 4th pag.

10   Ibid., sig. C3.

11   Ibid.

12   Critical Essays of the Seventeenth Century, I, lxiv.

13   Ibid., II, 165.

14   Ibid., II, 272.

15   "An Essay upon Poetry" (1682), Spingarn, II, 287.

16   Ibid., p. 296.

17   Monsieur Bossu's Treatise of the Epick Poem (London, 1695), sig. b$_2$v.

18   Ibid., sig. b$_5$.

19   "The Preface" to Prince Arthur (London, 1695), sig. a$_2$.

20   Ibid., sigs. c$_1$-c$_1$v.

21   Spingarn, III, 194.

22   Remarks on a Book Entituled, Prince Arthur, an Heroick Poem (London, 1696), pp. 106-107.

23   Works, ed. Sir Walter Scott and George Saintsbury (London, 1882-1893), XVII, 310.

24   Ibid., p. 313.

25   "Apology for Heroic Poetry and Poetic Licence" (1677), Works, V, 116.

26   Ibid., pp. 116-117.

27   The Advancement and Reformation of Modern Poetry (London, 1701), sig. a$_2$.

28   The Grounds of Criticism in Poetry (London, 1704), sigs. a$_6$-a$_6$v.

29   Ibid., pp. 5-6.

30   The Spectator, ed. George A. Aitken (London, 1898), No. 291.

31   Ibid., No. 321.

32   See A. F. B. Clark, Boileau and the French Classical Critics in England (1660-1830) (Paris, 1925), p. 247.

33   The British Essayists, ed. A. Chalmers (London, 1817), XVII, 127.

34   The Odyssey of Homer (London, 1725-1726), V, 314.

35 An Essay on the Different Stiles of Poetry (London, 1713), sig. A4.

36 The Works of Mr. Edmund Spenser (London, 1715), I, lx.

37 Ibid., I, lx-lxi.

38 A Dissertation on Reading the Classics, and Forming a Just Style (2d ed., London, 1715), pp. vii-viii.

39 Ibid., p. ix.

40 Essays upon Several Subjects (London, 1716-1717), I, 12.

41 Ibid., p. 13.

42 Alfred: An Epick Poem in Twelve Books (London, 1723), p. xxxv.

43 It should be noted here that, despite Blackmore's pretended rebellion against rules, he slavishly followed the established scheme of criticizing an epic. His various essays on the epic had practically nothing in them that had not already been said by other critics of the neo-classic school. Blackmore was not alone in this inconsistency. Many of the eighteenth-century critics continued to follow established theory, even though they denounced authority and rules. .The limits of this study preclude a consideration of the theory of the epic in neo-classic England, but the writer plans to publish an extended discussion of the subject at some time in the future.

44 "Author's Preface," Lectures on Poetry Read in the Schools of Natural Philosophy at Oxford. Translated from the Latin, with additional Notes (London, 1742), p. iii.

45 Ibid., p. 3.

46 The Aeneis of Virgil, translated into Blank Verse (London, 1718-1720), I, xx.

47 The Complete Art of Poetry (London, 1718), I, 94.

48 Ibid., I, 97.

49 The Laws of Poetry (London, 1721), p. 39.

50 Ibid., pp. 58-59.

51 Epistles, Odes, &c written on Several Subjects. With a Translation of Longinus's Treatise on the Sublime (London, 1724), pp. xvi-xvii.

52 Ibid., p. xvii.

53 Ibid., p. xix.

54 Ibid., pp. xxii-xxiii.

55 An Essay on Pope's Odyssey: In Which Some particular Beauties and Blemishes of that Work are consider'd (London and Oxford, 1726-1727), Part I, p. 144.

56 Ibid., p. 145.

57 Explanatory Notes and Remarks on Milton's Paradise Lost (London, 1734), p. cxlvii.

58 Observations on Poetry, Especially the Epic: Occasioned by the Late Poem upon Leonidas (London, 1738), pp. 1-2.

59 An Essay on the Genius and Writings of Pope (3d ed., Dublin, 1764), p. 97.

60 Ibid.

61 Ibid., pp. 99-100.

62 Observations on the Fairy Queen of Spenser (2d ed. London, 1762), I, 15-16.

63 Gray's-Inn Journal (London, 1756), II, 251.

64 Works, ed. Peter Cunningham (London, 1854), II, 12.

65 For the identification of Goldsmith as the author, see R.S. Crane, "A Neglected Mid-Eighteenth-Century Plea for Originality and Its Author," Philological Quarterly, XIII (1934), 21-29.

66 Critical Review, 1st ser., IX (1760), 13.

67 See Elizabeth Eaton Kent, Goldsmith and his Booksellers (Ithaca, New York, 1933), p. 64.

68 The Art of Poetry on a New Plan (London, 1762), II, 371.

69   A Critical Essay on the Epigoniad (Edinburgh, 1757), pp. 12-13

70   Monthly Review, 1st ser., XXVI (1762), 41. For the identi-
     fication of the reviewer, see Benjamin Christie Nangle, The
     Monthly Review: First Series, 1749-1789 (Oxford, 1934),
     p. 103.

71   The Life and Opinions of Tristram Shandy, Gentleman, ed.
     Wilbur L. Cross (New York, 1904), II, 42.

72   Ibid., II, 43.

73   Occasional Thoughts on the Study and Character of Classical
     Authors (London, 1762), pp. 89-90.

74   Ibid., p. 134.

75   Letters on Chivalry and Romance, with the Third Elizabethan
     Dialogue, ed. Edith J. Morley (London, 1911), p. 131.

76   Lectures on Rhetoric and Belles Lettres (4th ed., London,
     1790), I, 49.

77   Critical Essays (London, 1770), p. ii.

78   An Essay on Epic Poetry (London, 1782), p. 14.

79   Ibid., p. 132.

80   Ibid., p. 17.

81   Ibid., pp. 4-5.

82   Essays Philosophical and Moral, Historical and Literary
     (London, 1799), II, 523.

83   A Commentary Illustrating the Poetic of Aristotle (London,
     1792), p. xiii.

NATIVE ELEMENTS IN ENGLISH NEO-CLASSICISM

Paul Spencer Wood

In the present article I shall try to show that English neo-Classicism had its roots deep in native soil and that it was in harmony with certain manifestations of the English national genius that were especially prominent in the generation after 1660.

The Restoration brought back more than the House of Stuart. The continuity of English tradition and the rule of reason justified by precedent were also restored in England. The revolution had been completely successful against the king, but it had failed to establish a settled government giving permanent guaranty of the traditional rights of English freemen. British law and constitution alike rested upon the assumption that the government would be carried on by king, lords, and commons. The revolution had swept these aside, but it had not found anything satisfactory to take their place. During the Puritan interregnum England had been governed by men who had departed from immemorial tradition and the common ways of thought — men who desired to pursue ends not customary, and who held power by no prescriptive right. [1]

Charles II was welcomed back to England as the outward and visible sign of the customary ways of government and of the traditional liberty of the British subject:

> Dread Soveraign! I offer no flattering Titles, but speak the Words of Truth: You are the desire of three Kingdoms, the Strength and Stay of the Tribes of the People, for the moderating of Extremities, the reconciling of Differences, the satisfying of all Interests, and for the restoring of the collapsed Honour of these Nations. [2]

Ten years later, at an anniversary sermon, the Reverend John Lake, afterward Bishop of Chichester, praised God "for the happy Restoration of our Dread Soveraign to his Kingdoms, and therein of the Kingdoms themselves, to their Religion, Laws, Liberties, Proprieties again."[3] England, tired of novelty and

Reprinted by permission from Modern Philology, Vol. 24 (1926), pp. 201-208.

excess and caprice, reacted toward constituted authority in church and state and society and literature. Dryden's poem in honor of the Restoration was happily named Astroea Redux.

It was natural that the spirit of the Restoration should be more conservative than that which had preceded the civil wars; there was more to react from. From the riotous individualism of the Puritan interregnum the nation now turned toward the general sense. Disgusted with lawlessness and eccentricity, it reacted toward rules; after enthusiasm and fanaticism, it welcomed sober judgment. The movement was thus conservative and restrictive, tempered by a sense of reason and moderation.

This moderate conservatism is illustrated in the development of English constitutional history after 1660. The lessons of the Civil War period and the protectorate were not forgotten. The reconstituted monarchy was a compromise between autocracy and popular sovereignty, between the tyranny of the monarch and the tyranny of the mob. England had suffered from both, and was learning to hold both in place by means of that intricate series of checks and balances, the developing British constitution. In general, the Whigs most feared the former and the Tories the latter; but both parties and all classes united in expressions of hatred for arbitrary power.

Charles II avowed this principle in his public utterances, and repeatedly declared himself an enemy to all arbitrary proceedings. In his speech at the opening of the Oxford Parliament in March, 1681, he said: "For I, who will never use Arbitrary Government My Self, am resolv'd not to suffer it in Others."[4]

Halifax, in "The Character of a Trimmer," said:

> Our Trimmer owneth a Passion for liberty, yet so restrained, that it doth not in the least impair or taint his Allegiance;[5]

and again:

> The Crown hath power sufficient to protect our Liberties. The People have so much Liberty as is necessary to make them useful to the Crown.
> Our Government is in a just proportion, no Tympany, no unnatural swelling either of Power or Liberty. [6]

Dryden, in The Medal, emphasized British love of a just balance between the extremes "Of popular sway and arbitrary reign."

Samuel Pordage, Dryden's opponent, gave an excellent expression of this moderate conservatism that seeks continuity rather than experiment.

> For Innovation is a dangerous thing,
> Whether it comes from People or from King.
> To change Foundations which long Ages stood,
> Which have prov'd firm, unshaken, sound, and good,
> To pull all down, and cast the Frame anew,
> Is work for Rebels, and for Tyrants too. [7]

Such references could easily be multiplied. However sharply Whig and Tory might differ from each other, both were agreed in resting their cases upon the English law and tradition, the natural constitution of society, and the judgment of reason.

In the English church we can see, no less clearly than in the state, a love of the middle way. On the one side was the Roman Catholic church, which stood for absolute authority and for centralized ecclesiastical government. On the other side were the dissenting sects, which stood for private judgment and for decentralized government. On the one side was respect for tradition, and ordered decorum in services; on the other, disrespect for tradition, and varying degrees of spontaneity and enthusiasm in public worship. In all these respects the Anglican church occupied a middle position. It held both to Catholic tradition and to the open Bible. In ecclesiastical government it rejected alike papal autocracy and independent anarchy. In its order of services it retained a ritual but discarded much ceremonial. The Roman Catholics accused it of rejecting truth; the sectaries accused it of retaining error. Anglican apologists thundered alike against Puritan and Papist, at all times condemning the excess of those who departed from the paths of moderation or who seemed to err by accepting too little or too much. [8]

Against the charges of novelty and singularity the Anglican divines were accustomed to appeal to the decrees of the earliest general councils, the writings of the Christian Fathers, and universal tradition. Over and over again was the appeal made to Scripture, antiquity, and reason. On this combined basis was the church attacked and defended. Chamberlayne, in his description of the Church of England, puts the whole matter clearly, declaring

> That she holds the whole truly Catholick Foundation

according to the Scripture, and the four first general
Councils; That she adheres closely to Tradition truly Uni-
versal; that is, doth willingly receive, quod ab omnibus,
quod ubique, quod semper receptum fuit, which is the old
Rule of Catholicism.... Search all the Religions in the
World, none will be found more consonant to God's Word,
for doctrine, nor to the Primitive example for Govern-
ment...it keepeth the middle way, between the pomp of
Superstitious Tyranny, and the meanness of Fanatick
Anarchy. [9]

The oft-repeated accusation against the dissenters was that
they affected singularity and opposed authority.

Their speech & habits they cannot indure should be like
their Neighbors, and are very curious to be in all things
contrary to the common mode, so that they may be taken
notice of for singular men ... and are so stuft with contradiction that they will do nothing commanded by Authority; so that the only way to have them do anything is to forbid them doing of it on pain of death. [10]

Here, as in other respects, the relations of church and state
were far closer in the seventeenth century than they are today.
Support of the king and the bishops usually went together; the
sanctions of authority and tradition and reason were similar in
church and in state. Of course men were not entirely consistent,
but they could not have separated their politics and their religion even had they so desired. Both were parts of a habit of
thought which affected their whole intellectual and social life.
Long before the outbreak of the Civil War, Roger Ascham had
written:
For he, that can neither like Aristotle in Logicke and
Philosophie, nor Tullie in Rhetoricke and Eloquence, will,
from these steppes, likelie enough presume, by like pride,
to mount hier, to the misliking of greater matters: that is
either in Religion to haue a dissentious head, or in the common wealth to haue a factious hart. [11]

In opposition to the obstinate eccentricity of the dissenters,
we find the churchmen arguing for the general sense and universal consent. "Private opinion or fancy" was sharply disavowed
by the bishops in their debate with the Presbyterian divines on

the commission for the review of the Book of Common Prayer in 1661. [12] When in 1689 Edward Sclater was publicly received back into the English church, after having left it for the Roman, he stated in his public recantation:

> More particularly, I Renounce those disparaging and false Expressions, concerning the Rule of Faith, and the Use of it, in the Church of England. For whereas I then wrote, that the Canon of Scripture in the Church of England was no other, but what her own Members were pleased to allow; that the Private Spirit was the Support of the Protestant Faith; and that I my self, whilst in that Church, might have Choice of an hundred Faiths in Her. I am now fully convinced, That the Church of England does receive the very same Canon of Scripture, and the same Creeds, which have in all Ages of the Church been most Universally received, as containing all things Necessary to Salvation: And that She has due recourse to the Ancient Fathers, and the Authority of the Church; as the most effectual means for repressing the Extravagancies of each Man's private Spirit, and for the maintaining of Truth, and Peace, and good Order in the Church. [13]

Dryden followed a similar line of argument in <u>Religio Laici</u>, where he condemned the fruits of the private spirit in the sects. His conclusion was that "waiving each extreme" we should "learn what unsuspected ancients say," follow the Scripture and the Fathers and the tradition of the whole church, trying all by the light of reason.

> And after hearing what our Church can say,
> If still our reason runs another way,
> That private reason 'tis more just to curb,
> Than by disputes the public peace disturb.
> For points obscure are of small use to learn:
> But common quiet is mankind's concern. [14]

Just as politics and religion tended to fall together, so also religion and manners had close connection in the seventeenth century. The dissenters usually came from the middle and lower classes, which were often deficient in polite manners even if they were not marked by the eccentric habits of the Quaker or the Hebraic diction of the independent. Much of the sharpest

satire in Hudibras deals with manners in social intercourse; it
attacks fanaticism, enthusiasm, social singularity, and obstinate refusal to accord with custom. Such comic writers as Tom
Brown and Ned Ward seem to regard as axiomatic the proposition that there is no gentleman but a churchman. In his character of "The Rude Man" Butler says: "He has neither Doctrine
nor Discipline in him, like a fanatic Church, but is guided by
the very same Spirit, that dipped the Herd of Swine in the Sea."[15]

One important purpose of the seventeenth-century character
writers was to recommend social conformity by ridiculing eccentricity. After the Restoration there was special need to reform the social ideals damaged in the preceding two decades,
when individualism had run riot, untempered by the general
sense. But the restrictive forces after 1660 were not new; they
were merely more pronounced. Earlier in the century, Earle
and Overbury and Hall had thrown their influence on the side of
moderation and decorum. The social ideals recommended by
these men and by Butler were not identical, but they were in a
direct line of development.[16]

Butler's character of "The Over-Doer"[17] is an example of
the man who does not observe moderation, and in consequence
is always wrong. Even more explicit is the statement in his
Notebook: "... for Those that Use Excess in any Thing never
understand the Truth of it, which always lies in the Mean."[17]
In conformity with this belief in measure, Butler satirized "The
Affected or Formal," who carries to excess a belief in rules
and formality.[18] But, on the other hand, he did not recommend
wanton violation of established custom:

> In the Alphabet no letter has any Naturall Right to stand
> before another, but U might as well have taken place of all
> the Rest as A. But Custom has been pleasd to order it oth-
> erwise; and if wee should go about to alter that ranke: the
> Reformation would be as troublesome as ridiculous.[19]

Butler's attitude in this respect was characteristic of the age.
Measure and decorum was set up as social ideals:

> But now our true and noble-spirited Gentleman is one
> that hath taken order with himself and sets a rule to all
> his pleasures and delights; not too precise or too lavish,
> but keeps a just medium and decorum in everything.[20]

The principles thus dominant in state, church, and society were also dominant in the literature of the time. Conditions in all these departments of thought were strikingly similar. [21] As a result of Renaissance extravagance and the undisciplined individualism of the first part of the seventeenth century, English literature needed restriction, reform; it needed purging of excess and return to the normal, the healthy, the sane. It needed order, decorum, measure, respect for the general sense, precisely as England everywhere needed these same qualities. In the effort to attain them, it appealed to authority and tradition on the one hand and to reason and expedience on the other, precisely as the same appeals were made elsewhere. The resultant movement in literature we call "neo-Classicism"; but in constitutional, ecclesiastical, or social history we call it "good sense," "conservatism," "moderation," the "British national temper," or the "spirit of the age."

The relation of these ideals to Jonsonian classicism is evident. They represent the old principles developed logically and affected by the events of the intervening years. The chief addition is in the increased respect paid the general sense and in the corresponding discredit of Renaissance individualism, in so far as the latter tended toward singularity. Jonson's respect for authority, for reason, and for measure had been extending their influence over the land. And when there was added to these the one classical quality in which Jonson had been most deficient, the way was made ready for the literature of the new age.

Now I do not assert that there was nothing of French influence in all this. France and England were both sharers in a movement that affected all Europe; and France had preceded England in its development. My contention is that obviously native institutions such as church and state, which differed fundamentally from the Gallic, manifested ideals strikingly like those shown in the literature of the time. So far as social ideals are concerned, the matter is less obvious; but these agree so well with the political and religious ideals and are so consonant with them that any foreign influence need not be insisted upon even here. If, then, the ideals that we have been noticing are in conformity with the national temper and are normal developments of the times, it is right to call them native elements in English neo-Classicism.

NATIVE ELEMENTS IN ENGLISH NEO-CLASSICISM

NOTES

1   G. M. Trevelyan, England under the Stuarts, p. 272.

2   The Earl of Manchester's Speech to His Maiesty, in the Name
    of the Peers, At his Arrival at White-Hall, The 29th of May,
    1660, London, 1660.

3   A Sermon Preached at Whitehall upon the 29th of May, 1670.
    Being the day of His Majesties Birth and Happy Restoration.
    By John Lake, D.D. Late Rector of S.Botolphs without Bish-
    opsgate, London, London, 1670.

4   His Majesties Most Gracious Speech to Both Houses of Parli-
    ament, At the Opening of the Parliament at Oxford Monday the
    21st day of March 1680/1, Oxford, n.d. The King's sincerity
    is not involved here. Whatever may have been Charles's real
    sentiments, his speech reflected the popular opinion; it was
    nicely adapted to the popular temper.

5   Complete Works (ed. Raleigh), p. 61.

6   Ibid., pp. 62-63.

7   Azariah and Hushai, A Poem (London, 1682), p. 31.

8   "We live secure from mad Enthusiastick Rage
    And fond Tradition now grown blind with Age."—

    Tho. Creech, "To Mr. Dryden on Religio Laici," prefixed to
    the 1682 ed. of Religio Laici.

9   Edward Chamberlayne, Angliae Notitia, or The Present State
    of England (15th ed.; London, 1684), p. 30. See also the letter
    of Jeremy Taylor to John Evelyn, Nov. 21, 1665, in Diary
    and Correspondence of John Evelyn, (ed. Bray), III, 208-9.

10 Richard Head, Proteus Redivivus (London, 1675), p. 236.

11 Scholemaster (ed. Arber), p. 191.

12 The Papers That passed between the Commissioners Appointed
    by his Majesty for the Alteration of the Common Prayer ...,
    in An Accompt of all the Proceedings of the Commissioners ...
    for the Reveiw [sic] of the Book of Common Prayer, etc.,
    London, 1661.

13 Anthony Horneck, An Account of Mr. Edward Sclater's Return To The Communion of the Church of England And Of the Publick Recantation he made at the Church of St. Mary Savoy, the 5th of May, 1689 (London, 1689), pp. 11-12. See also the anonymous pamphlet attributed to Edward Stillingfleet, An Answer to Some Papers Lately Printed, concerning the Authority of the Catholick Church In Matters of Faith, and the Reformation of the Church of England (London, 1686), pp. 8-9. This pamphlet was published in reply to some recently circulated papers attributed to the late king, Charles II, and the first Duchess of York, deceased wife of James II, in support of the Roman Catholic church. Stillingfleet protests against the assumption that those of the Church of England "do leave every man to believe according to his own fancy.... For our Church receives the three Creeds, and embraces the four General Councils, and professes to hold nothing contrary to any Universal Tradition of the Church from the Apostles times."

14 Of course this doctrine of general consent with its opposition to the free exercise of the private judgment in matters religious was not accepted by all. My contention is merely that this doctrine, which strangely parallels the neo-Classical concept of literature, was strongly advanced and was accepted by representative English churchmen.

15 Characters and Passages from Note-Books (ed. A. R. Waller), p. 144.

16 Because of his opposition to Rymer and the extreme principles of Aristotelian formalism, Butler has sometimes been considered romantic — or, at any rate, partly romantic — in criticism. Such a view is based upon the assumption that opposition to the extreme adherents of the school of rules indicates opposition to the fundamentals of neo-Classicism — a view that would rank Boileau himself with the romantic party.

17 Op. cit., p. 179.

18 Ibid., p. 273.

19 Ibid., p. 184.

20 Ibid., p. 407.

21 Sam Vincent, The Young Gallant's Academy, or, Directions how he should behave himself in all Places and Company.... To which is added The Character of a Town-Huff. Together

with The Character of a right Generous and well-bred Gentleman, London, 1674. The quotation is from the last of the
appended characters, which bears in the body of the book the
following title: The Character of a True, Noble, Liberal, and
Stayed Gentleman. See also The Country Gentleman's Vade
Mecum., p. 136.

22   This similarity was more than once observed and commented
upon at this time. Thus Butler characterizes "A Small Poet"
(Characters, etc., p. 49): "He is always repealing the old
Laws of Comedy, and like the long Parliament making Ordinances in their Stead; although they are perpetually thrown
out of Coffee-Houses, and come to Nothing." Just as Butler
here compares the undisciplined poet to the factious parliamentarian, so Dryden in the Prologue to Oedipus draws a
parallel between the contemners of tradition in church and
poetry:

> With some respect to ancient wit proceed;
> You take the first four councils for your creed.
> But, when you lay tradition wholly by,
> And on the private spirit alone rely,
> You turn fanatics in your poetry.

THE OPPOSITION TO NEO-CLASSICISM IN ENGLAND
BETWEEN 1660 and 1700

Paul Spencer Wood

The victory of neo-classicism in England was won only after a struggle against forces which are sometimes called romantic but which are more accurately described as anti-classical. These forces were partly survivals of the past and partly tendencies that pointed forward to nineteenth century romanticism. The latter, so far as they were merely germinal, fall outside the scope of the present discussion, which deals with actual obstacles interfering with the complete dominance of the neo-classical movement after 1660.

There is a striking difference between the opposition encountered by a romantic and by a classical movement. The former, which seeks expansion and individual liberty, is sure to be in conflict with authority – political, social, religious, as well as literary. It is denounced and exposed; its typical figure is a Marlowe or a Shelley. The latter, which seeks repression and social discipline, is likely to receive early and favorable recognition from those in authority. Thus Henry IV favored Malherbe and Louis XIV supported Boileau. The principles these critics advocated were from the beginning respectable.

English neo-classicism, coming in as it did with the restoration of the monarchy, found ready reception in high places. The nation was prepared to welcome an established order in literary as well as in social and political and ecclesiastical affairs. No contrast could be more striking than that between the initial victory of the classical principles immediately after 1660 and the long fight of the romantic principles more than a century later. This fact is clearly evident in the chronology of the two movements: 1660 definitely begins the classical period; but for the romantic there is no agreement upon a beginning date. But after romanticism had won control of the critical citadels the popular battle was over. When neo-classicism had possession of the critical citadels the fight had just begun. The situation was in some respects like that which existed in England after the

Reprinted by permission from Publications of the Modern Language Association, Vol. 43 (1928), pp. 182-197.

conversion of the Saxons to Christianity. Most people were baptized, but the new religion was not yet well established: opposition consisted not so much in advocacy of the old pagan beliefs as in passive retention, in part at least, of the old practices. After 1660, poets, critics, and public alike were ready to accept the principle of order in art as well as in church and state and society, but the classical discipline had to be learned before the new ideal could approach realization. Opposition to this discipline seldom took the form of active revolt; more often it expressed itself as inertia or restlessness under control.

Individualism is characteristic of the English people, the foundation alike of their national liberty and their national eccentricity. With them social discipline does not come easily. The madness of Englishmen was a proverb in the days of Shakespeare. When the First Grave-digger was asked why Hamlet had been sent to England, he replied, "Why, because he was mad; he shall recover his wits there; or, if he do not, it's no great matter there." And he added, " 'Twill not be seen in him there; there the men are as mad as he."

Foreign travellers in England during the last forty years of the seventeenth century generally noticed this tendency. Misson, after describing Bedlam, adds significantly: "Tous les Fous de Londres ne sont pas Là-dedans."[1] Sobière believed that the English were "une Nation, a le dire entre nous, fort bigearre et fort irrégulière."[2] Muralt not only observed the phenomenon but commented shrewdly upon it:

> Les Anglais non seulement ne dépendent, guère de la cour, mais, dans leur manière de vivre ils dépendent fort peu du public et ne se laissent guère tyranniser par la coutume. Ils contentent leurs envies et se plaisent à en formes d'extraordinaires. Ils osent braver l'opinion et la foule, et passer pour fous s'il le faut: grand pas pour deviner raissonable, tandis que chez des peuples moins féroces et plus uniformes, on voit d'enormes sottises devenir générales et héréditaires, par les soins que les gens y prennent de se resembler les uns aux autres, et par la grande frayeur qu'ils ont de tout ce qui s'éloigne tant soit peu de cette uniformité.[3]

Englishmen themselves often recognized this fact. Thus Thomas Gordon, writing early in the eighteenth century on "The Characters of Different Nations," observed:

> If there be any thing that eminently distinguishes the
> English from any other Nation, I think it is the Variety
> there is in their Manners, Humours, Customs, Talents,
> and their Flexibility and Inconstancy in all of these: These
> Diversions in thinking and acting may be observ'd in the
> Religion, the Laws, the Government of our Country. We
> not only in some respects almost generally differ from
> each other, but at times even from our selves.[4]

Statements such as these not only indicate one of the strong
forces which resisted the neo-classical discipline but also show
that this resistance continued throughout the seventeenth century. Though much was done to subject the nation to the discipline of the general sense, England as compared with France
remained a country of eccentricity.

Nowhere is this contrast more clearly shown than in the two
national societies established during the seventeenth century in
Paris and in London respectively. The French Academy was a
powerful force in purifying the language and ordering the literature. The Royal Society, on the other hand, was a body devoted
to experimental science and freedom of discussion. The French
was a limiting, restraining influence; the English, an expansive
one. The respect for authority in the one contrasts with open-
mindedness in the other.

During the latter part of the seventeenth century, there were
numerous attempts to establish an English Academy. In 1664
Dryden in the Epistle Dedicatory of the Rival-Ladies expressed
the wish for such an institution. In December of the same year
the Royal Society appointed a committee of which Evelyn, Waller,
and Dryden were members to take steps "for improving the English tongue."[5] Though elaborate plans were discussed nothing
came of the project. Sprat in The History of the Royal Society
(1667) presented "A proposal for erecting an English Academy."
As time passed and nothing further was done about the matter,
Dryden apparently lost hope of such an establishment, though
he continued to deplore the consequent lack of regularity in the
language.

In 1707 James Beeverell, endeavoring to explain for French
readers in Les Délices de la Grande Bretagne, why there was
no academy in England, declared:

> La Langue Angloise n'a pas la delicatesse de la Fran-
> çoise, mais en récompense elle est plus abondante & plus

riche. Tandis que les François sont atachez servilement
à une Académie, qui leur impose les loix sur les mots,
en sorte qu'ils n'osent presque pas hazarder un mot no-
veau, quand même ils, en ont bien besoin, si l'Académie o
ou l'usage ne l'a aprouvé: les Anglois au contraire, portant leur liberté jusques dans leur Langue, ne font aucun
scrupule d'inventer de nouveaux mots, s'ils en ont besoin,
& par là leur Langue est devenue, non seulement riche,
mais aussi nerveuse, en telle sorte que les Anglois ont
quantité de mots qu'on ne sauroit exprimer en François
que par un longue circonlocution. [6]

Here we have – though in reference to language alone – almost
a perfect expression of the anti-classical reaction. Notce how
exactly these words oppose the spirit of Knightly Chetwood's
lines of 1682. These declare that the need of English poetry is
for

one who license can restrain,
Make civil laws o'er barbarous usage reign,
One worthy in Apollo's chair to sit,
And hold the scales, and give the stamp of wit,
In whom ripe judgment and young fancy meet
And force the poet's rage to be discreet,
Who grows not nauseous while he strives to please,
But marks the shelves in our poetic seas. [7]

The agitation for an English Academy illustrates the whole
matter under discussion: the project failed because it encountered the passive resistance of inertia and the opposition of undisciplined individualism. During the years immediately after
the Restoration, when the establishment of an English Academy
was being urged most actively, it is significant that little or no
protest against it is recorded: the opposition was silent. Similar passive resistance to any social or literary discipline constituted a material obstacle to the triumph of neo-classicism
in the latter part of the seventeenth century.
Another obstacle was the prestige of Elizabethan literature.
Much has been made of this by some critics. Hamelius declared
his belief that apart from the court the older romantic ideals
still lingered.

Schon in der City hielten sich die Kaufleute und Bürger
von fremden Sitten und Anschauungen frei, und in den Graf-

schaften freute sich der Edelmann an seinem Spenser und
Shakespeare, ohne sich darum zu bekümmern, dass die
Hauptstadt neue Muster feierte und nachahmte.... Dieser
Stand empfand wenig Bedürfnisz, seine Ansichten schrift-
lich zu bekunden, und selbst Neudrucke der alten Dichter
waren fast überfflüssig zu einer Zeit, wo Papier und Ein-
bände stark genug waren, um Jahrhunderte zu überdauern.
Der altenglische Geschmack war also night vernichtet,
sondern nur vom geräuschvollen Vordergrunde des Na-
tionallebens verdrangt. [8]

This is indeed moving, from the picture of the nobleman in the
country with his well-loved Spenser and Shakespeare refusing
to bow the knee before the strange, new gods of Whitehall, [9] to
the romantic touch about the durability of the old paper and bind-
ings, and the curiously mixed figure about "der altenglische
Geschmack" crowded out of the noisy foreground of the national
life. It is a striking example of literary criticism based upon
the assumption that whatever bears the label, romantic, contains
all good, and whatever is called classic or "pseudo-classic"
must be bad.

Hamelius' idea about the survival of Elizabethan poetry contains some truth, just enough to make it misleading in its present form. Literary movements are usually slower in making
their presence felt in the country than in the city. To an unusual
degree these classical ideals were social and therefore predominantly urban. A system which involves the arbitrament of the
general sense and which uses as its standards the language and
manners of the court is a system which needs for its development and dissemination the intercourse of cultivated people. Thus
it is reasonable to assume that country readers − so far as they
existed at all − were not entirely in accord with the new movement in literature. But on that account one should not assume
that they were devoted adherents of romanticism. That country
gentlemen neglected their hunting to pore in rapture over the
Renaissance allegory of Spenser or that they spent their leisure
in rapt contemplation of the pages of Shakespeare − anachronism
is a mild word to apply to such a conception. Country readers
whose literary accomplishments extended beyond the pages of
the prayer-book and the almanac were reading The Merry Conceited Jests of George Peele and Tarlton's Newes Out of Purga-
torie and The English Gusman: or the History of that Unparalleled
Thief, James Hind and The Monk's Hood Pulled Off and debased

chapbook versions of The Seven Champions of Christendom and
of Guy of Warwick. People in the country were seldom engaged
in lamenting the degeneration of the stage but, whenever a strol-
ling company gave them the opportunity, were indulging the old
English taste for Jack Swabber, Simkin in the Chest and Simple-
ton the Smith.

As for "Die Kaufleute und Bürger," they were quite free as
yet from the contamination of La Bruyère and Corneille: they
were reading The Belman of London in revamped editions and
Deloney's best sellers, such as The Pleasant and Princely History of the Gentle Craft and The Pleasant History of John Winch-
comb in His Younger Years Called Jack of Newberry. At Bar-
tholomew Fair the spectators were not troubled about the dramatic unities but were attending native English farces where the
wit consisted in "the putting out of Candles, kicking down of tables, falling over Joynt-stools."[10] Ned Ward said of the "Musick
Booth" there:

> I thought it an Abuse to Humane Shape, for anything that
> bore the Proportion of either Sex, to behave themselves
> so Ostentatiously Foolish, so Odiously Impudent, so Intol-
> erably Dull, and void of all Humour, Order, or Design.[11]

There were merchants and country-gentlemen with a taste for
literature, fewer than at present certainly but still to be found.
For appreciation of the Elizabethans, however, one must look
chiefly to the men of letters such as Mulgrave, Dennis, Collier,
and Dryden. These critics, who were in touch with the literary
movements of the day, were the men who best knew and respected the older poetic tradition, who, though they did not entirely
accept it, yet took it into account in their judgments and gave it
praise. They admired even while they protested against its
breaches of literary decorum.

On the subject of decorum, historians of English literature
seem to have what the semi-technical jargon of the present day
describes as a psychological complex. The term suggests to
them Rymer's famous dictum about who may kill whom decently
in tragedy, and the "improvements" of Shakespeare through the
elimination of his low expressions. Now the facts of the matter
seem to be that the campaign against lowness and lack of decorum was directed primarily against farce and burlesque and the
unpruned excesses of the popular taste. The old English taste
for Merry Andrew and Jack Pudding[12] will be no mystery to one

who reflects upon the moving pictures of the twentieth century.
It has a dramatic history at least as old as the Chester play of
Noah's Flood. If, in the campaign against such perennial manifestations of bad taste, some critics pushed their praise of decorum to extravagant lengths, the phenomenon is not unparalleled among the annals of reform. It is one of the best evidences
of a real classical spirit in late seventeenth century England
that immoderate demands of decorum were treated in the same
way as other violations of the law of measure.

It was but natural that the discussion of literary decorum
should center about the practice of the Elizabethan dramatists,
not because this was primarily under attack but because it was
a test case. What sanction did the example of Shakespeare and
his congeners give to the prevalent disregard for propriety and
regularity? Such a question inevitably presented itself in the
latter part of the seventeenth century. There could be no doubt
that the Elizabethan dramas fell short of classical standards in
these respects. In our own day we have chosen, more or less
deliberately, to ignore these things because we believe them to
be mere mint and cumin as compared with the weightier matters
of the Law. Another generation may view them more seriously.
But for the Restoration they constituted a real crux in criticism.
Dryden raised his voice against too much deference to the Elizabethan tradition.

> But it was only custom which cozened us so long; we
> thought, because Shakespeare and Fletcher went no farth-
> er, that there the pillars of poetry were to be erected.[13]

It was not that Dryden loved Shakespeare less but poetry more.
Even Thomas Rymer was not moved primarily by a desire to
attack the Elizabethans. Dr. G. B. Dutton, after an elaborate
study of Rymer's criticism, has reached the conclusion that it
was not intended as a full and rounded estimate of the various
authors treated, but was meant rather to reform future practice by pointing out the faults in the works of more or less de-
servedly popular writers. [14] Though John Dennis wrote The Impartial Critick to defend Shakespeare against Rymer, he put into
the mouth of Jack Freeman, who seems to represent his own
views, an explicit avowal of the correctness of such an attitude.
In response to Beaumont's objection, "But methinks the very
faults of a Great Man ought to be respected upon the account of
his Excellencies," Freeman says:

The very contrary of which is true: Upon that account they ought to be the rather expos'd. His Faults are the more dangerous on the account of his Excellencies. For young Writers, before they have Judgment to distinguish, are sometimes so far mistaken as to copy the very Faults of famous poets for Beauties. One thing I will easily grant you, that to expose a Great Man's Faults, without owning his Excellencies, is altogether unjust and unworthy of an honest Man. [15]

Dennis' real accusation against Rymer is that the latter exposed faults without voicing compensating praise.

To appreciate Elizabethan literature and at the same time to hold a theory of poetry directly opposed to its spirit: this was the great critical problem of the Age of Dryden. The prestige of Shakespeare had to be accounted for without invalidating neo-classical principles or weakening their application to contemporary production. In the reconciliation of these opposites, modern English literary criticism had its beginnings. The influence of the Elizabethans in the end made for a tempered and thoughtful discrimination, not for a rebellion against neo-classical standards.

Another anti-classical tendency of the last part of the seventeenth century was the protest against the strict rules of Aristotelian formalism. Some literary historians, who fail to distinguish between different schools of neo-classical criticism, have assumed that any critic of this period who spoke harsh words against the rules was a romanticist born out of due time. As a matter of fact, the last years of the seventeenth century saw much debate about the value of the rules and a decided reaction against the extreme formalistic position which implied, if it did not state, that one might become a poet by diligent study and application of the rules. The reaction was in part caused by the influence of the French school of taste, particularly by the Longinian influence exerted through Boileau. But even before this influence was much felt in England, there was protest against the rules. English critics and men of letters generally did not place so much dependence upon the positive value of the rules as did many of the French. There was a tendency to regard the rules in their extreme form as un-English. They were associated with the names of Italian and French and Dutch critics, and thus were felt to be foreign.

> But for my part, I desire to be tried by the laws of my
> own country; for it seems unjust to me that the French
> should prescribe here, till they have conquered.

So wrote Dryden in the Preface to All for Love.

But some have called Dryden a romanticist or partly a romanticist. No one, so far as I am aware, has voiced any such
suspicions about Oldham. Yet Oldham in an Ode Upon the Works
of Ben Johnson makes a similar protest:

> Sober and grave was still the Garb thy Muse put on,
> . . . .
> No refuse, ill-patch'd Shreds o' thè Schools,
> The motley wear of read and learned Fools;
> No French Commodity, which now so much does take,
> And our own better Manufacture Spoil;
> Nor was it ought of forein Spoil
> But Staple all, and all of English Growth and Make.

Such a protest in a poem written in full sympathy with the classical features of Jonson's work, a poem that pays tribute to the
"known and uncontested Rules of Poetry," shows clearly the
danger of mistaking the import of protests against the rules.

Sir Robert Howard has been claimed by Hamelius as a romanticist because of his Preface to The Great Favorite. [16]
Howard blames "the unnecessary understanding of some that
have labor'd to give strict rules to things that are not Mathematical," and concludes that

> who ever wou'd endeavour to like or dislike by the Rules
> of others, he will be as unsuccessful as if he should try
> to be perswaded into a power of believing, not what he
> must, but what others direct him to believe. [17]

This protest is so close a parallel to that of Molière in the sixth
scene of La Critique de l'Ecole des Femmes, published about
five years earlier, that there can be little doubt of its origin.[18]
Howard's objections are rationalistic — not to rules themselves
but to rules that in his opinion are "so little demonstrative."
After all, Howard was not an important poet and scarcely a critic at all. His chief aim in his two best-known prefaces was to
attack rime. His remarks about the rules were slight in substance, probably little digested, and certainly not intended to be

revolutionary. Personal pique at his brother-in-law, Dryden, may have motivated them to some extent. That Howard was not consistently opposed to all neo-classical rules is shown by his protest in the Preface to Four New Plays against the English fault "in usually mingling and interweaving Mirth and Sadness through the whole course of their Plays." In any event, Dryden's answer, A Defence of an Essay of Dramatic Poesy, was entirely adequate and seems to have disposed at once of Howard's objections.

Butler has also been called a romantic critic[19] because he said hard things about the rules and the critics in Hudibras and more especially in the lines — originally without title — which Spingarn reprints under the heading, Upon Critics Who Judge of Modern Plays Precisely by the Rules of the Antients.[20] The last named poem is a brief reply to Rymer, attacking the formalistic school in the name of "wit and sense." It is perfectly clear to any one acquainted with the spirit of Butler's work that he is here opposing what he considered excess. For him the pedantic critic is no better than the despised virtuoso or any one else who violates the law of measure.[21]

Two other lines of attack upon the rules should be considered here, for though neither was fully developed until later, both received contemporary notice, and both have been treated by recent writers as signs of romanticism in the period now under consideration.

First there was the influence of Boccalini, whose Ragguagli di Parnasso (1612) was widely read throughout Europe at the close of the seventeenth century. This influence of Boccalini was of two distinct sorts: upon form and upon content. Ragguagli di Parnasso is made up of semi-independent essays purporting to give news from Parnassus where Apollo holds his court in a strangely unreal world in which Greek divinities and the spirits of famous men — chiefly poets and critics — are in intimate relations with the world of art, letters, and politics. This conception, which probably derives to some extent from Lucian, may be made the vehicle of any sort of critical views, and was used for widely different purposes in England by such unlike authors as Suckling, Sheppard, Buckingham, Rochester, Swift, and Addison.

Boccalini's free treatment of critical dogma was followed to some extent, however, by some of his imitators. The form readily adapted itself to a slashing criticism. For if a case may at any moment be referred to the personal judgment of Apollo,

the rules are constantly subject to amendment or at least to re-
interpretation; and on a Parnassus where Homer and Aristotle
and Tasso and Shakespeare and Dryden are contemporaries, the
respect due to antiquity is minimized. At the same time, the
ground-work of the Ragguagli involves the idea of a literary
autocracy. Apollo is a benevolent despot, to be sure, but he
rules Parnassus none the less absolutely. From one point of
view, the arrangement is the apotheosis of order. The gospel of
Aristotle and even the living church of criticism yield to the personal command of the god of poetry laying down infallible law.

In 1656 Henry Carey, Earl of Monmouth, published an English translation of Boccalini under the title, Advertisements
from Parnassus. This work was reprinted in 1669, 1674, and
1706. In 1704 "N. N. Esquire" published Advertisements from
Parnassus. Written Originally in Italian by the Famous Trajano
Boccalini. Newly Done into English, and Adapted to the Present
Times. As the title indicates, this latter is a free adaptation
which substitutes English names for the Italian of the original.
In the three volumes of this work protest against neo-classical
dicta takes an advanced form.

In Advertisement XXVIII there is a criticism of the Aristotelian rules in the form of the following story. Otway[22] having been
debarred from the honor of having his plays deposited in the
Delphic Library because the critics appointed to consider the
case decided that he had violated the rules of Aristotle, appealed
to Apollo on the ground that there is no law on Parnassus to limit the poet's fancy. Apollo, incensed, summoned Aristotle and
demanded how he durst "pretend to write Rules for Poetry and
to go about to debarr the Virtuosi[23] of the Christian Liberty of
Fancy, which had been free and uncontroul'd as Air in all Ages,
and ought to continue so?" Since Otway's works, he argued,
"had met with general Applause from all Mankind, it was apparent he had observ'd all the Rules Poets are oblig'd to take Notice of." Aristotle pleaded that his rules had been misinterpre-
ted through the ignorance of later ages. He had merely pointed
out methods which "the most accurate Writers before his time
had follow'd; and withal confessed that he believed 'twas possible a Poet, might at this Day, write so excellent a Poem, without following his Rules, as might serve to give Laws to future
Ages." Finally he confessed that he had been led into error
through pride, "for finding how many Peoples Ignorance, in the
Misconstruction of his Design, had heightened his Reputation in
the World, he had suffer'd 'em to go on in their Mistake; which

was the more pardonable in him, since his Credit, as to matter of Politicks had so long been lost."

This judgment is radical because it avers not only that modern critics misunderstand Aristotle but also that Aristotle's rules, even when rightly understood, are no longer necessary. When this Advertisement is compared with Monmouth's translation of the same passage (which is a pretty faithful rendering of the original) the fact is evident that the edition of 1704 has not only used English names but has heightened the contrasts and altered the language to make the attack upon the rules the more vigorous. Thus the original protest has been developed into something that looks like a revolutionary document.

Striking as some of these critical opinions are, they have less significance for our present purpose than might appear. In the first place, they are in a foreign work which, though well known, seems to have been little regarded critically in England at this time. [24] Boccalini was remembered primarily as a political and personal satirist who had popularized an interesting form of expression.

In the second place, the translation which most emphasized opposition to the rules did not appear until the opening years of the eighteenth century. Of course, one must not draw chronological lines too narrowly; a book published in one century may be none the less inspired by the thought of that preceding. But there is significance in the fact that the version of Boccalini read in the seventeenth century and demonstrably popular then did not exaggerate the anti-classical tendencies of the original as did the edition read in the eighteenth century. Thus the influence of Boccalini between 1660 and 1700 does not invalidate the general statement that adverse criticism of the rules – especially in their extreme formulation – does not necessarily indicate a romantic tendency.

Another strong attack upon the rules was made by the French exile, Saint-Evremond, who, during the forty-two years of his residence in England, exerted a strong influence upon English criticism. In many respects Saint-Evremond was "un honnête homme," a lover of moderation delicately ridiculing excess of every sort. But he never completely subjected himself to the social and critical discipline of the Age of Louis XIV; his long residence in England broke his relations with French literature and society to such an extent that he was at once reminiscent of the past age and, as a result of his free speculation, typical of the future.

Though he was a classicist in most essentials, Saint-Evremond had little respect for Aristotelian formalism. In De la
Tragédie Ancienne et Moderne, he attacked the rules of the Abbé
d'Aubignac:

> On n'a jamais vu tant de règles pour faire de belles
> tragédies; et on en fait si peu, qu'on est obligé de repré-
> senter toutes les vielles.

He then proceeded to speak of Aristotle's theory of katharsis,

> que personne jusqu'ici n'a entendue, et qu'il n'a pas bien
> comprise lui-même, à mon jugement.... Entre mille per-
> sonnes qui assisteront au théâtre, il y aura peut-être six
> philosophes, qui seront capables d'un retour a la tranquil-
> lité, par ces sages et utiles meditations; mais la multi-
> tude ne fera point ces réflexions. [25]

In his attack on the rules, Saint-Evremond was an early exponent of historical criticism. Neo-classical absolutes gave
place in his mind to relative considerations. He believed that
times change and men change with them; what pleases the genius of one nation may be displeasing to that of another, since
each is affected by national habits of life and thought. His famous statement that the best ancient tragedy, even the Oedipus
itself, if it were performed in French in his day would appear
utterly barbarous and opposed to modern taste is but one of several utterances on the subject. [26] In Sur les Poëmes des Anciens,
he argued that if Homer were alive to-day he would write dif-
ferently, and consequently our poets do badly to rule themselves
"par des règles, qui sont tombées avec des choses que le temps
a fait tomber." To be sure, he admitted that there are certain
unchanging rules founded upon good sense and reason, but these
he thought were few in comparison with those which grow out of
changing conditions. Poets are too much bound by the rules of
the past; they imitate servilely and combine incongruous elements. Two sentences from De la Tragédie Ancienne et Moderne sum up his rebellious attitude as a result of the theory of
relativity:

> If faut convenir que la Poétique d'Aristote est un excel-
> lent ouvrage: cependant il n'y a rien d'assez parfait pour
> régler toutes les nations et tous les siècles. Descartes

et Gassendi ont découvert des vérités qu'Aristote ne con-
noissoit pas; Corneille a trouvé des beautés pour le théâ-
tre qui ne lui etoient pas connues; nos philosophes ont re-
marqué des erreurs dans sa Physique; nos poëtes ont vue
des défaute dans sa Poëtique; pour le moins à notre égard,
toutes choses étant aussi changes qu'elles le sont.

This principle of relativity was frequently discussed during
the last forty years of the seventeenth century. Bacon had long
before declared his belief in a causal relation between all learning and the forces, racial, physical, religious, political, and
social that determine its development; but he had not applied
this theory to literature in any thoroughgoing fashion.[27] Cowley
in the Preface to Poems (1656) and Sir Robert Howard in the
Preface to Four New Plays (1665) showed that they were interested in it. Sprat in the History of the Royal Society (1667) spoke
of the influence of climate, air, heaven, blood, and geographical situation, – all uniting to make England a "Land of Experimental knowledge." Toward the close of the century, we find the
idea of relativity most clearly expressed by Sir William Temple,
especially in his essay, Of Poetry. Here he endeavours to account for a national literature by reference to a national character and this, in turn, by reference to national environment. Wot-
ten, though arguing against Temple in Reflections upon Ancient
and Modern Learning, follows him to some extent in accounting
for Greek poetry and oratory. Dennis in The Impartial Critick
lays some stress on the influence of climate and custom in accounting for the differences between Athens and London.
    Such ideas were, however, still undeveloped in the seventeenth
century. True, they had been recognized both in France and in
England as opposed to classicism and had been attacked, especially by the Aristotelian formalists. But the full implications
had not yet been realized. It remained for the eighteenth and especially the nineteenth century to develop these ideas to the full,
thereby striking at the very roots of classicism. But though in
the period now under discussion this doctrine of relativity was
well known and widely accepted, it seems to have been taken up
rather as a useful means of combating extreme formalism than as a
theory considered hostile to the prevailing neo-classicism. Such
men as Howard and Butler and Dennis and Temple, who protested
against this excessive formalism, were the Whigs of criticism, ob-
jecting to the divine right of Aristotle and the high Tory doctrine of
non-resistance to his rules. But they were neither commonwealth

men nor theoretical republicans. They wished to restrict the royal prerogative of Aristotle but not to overturn his throne.

There is no more dangerous pitfall in criticism than that which lies before the searchers after late seventeenth century romanticism. Those who have believed that romanticism is perennial and therefore has never been quite crushed out in any classical period have gone forth with eyes sharpened to discern those ten thousand of the faithful in Israel who never bowed the knee to Baal. Those who have believed that romanticism is the one literary faith by which men may be saved have expected to find little candles of this true faith hidden away behind obstructing bushels.

Although between 1660 and 1700 there were many forces in England opposed to neo-classicism, there were few or none that may be correctly described as romantic. There was no romantic body of doctrine that dissenters from the orthodox critical creed could set up as a justification for their heterodoxy. Since Renaissance individualism had broken down, there was no choice except between some sort of classical restriction and literary anarchy. Just as in 1660 Englishmen of all political faiths had united in support of the restored monarchy as the alternative to political chaos, so at about the same time they made the same decision in favor of literary order. The choice was not between romanticism and classicism but between confusion and the only order possible at the time.

It was not until well into the eighteenth century that those ideas were formulated which made possible the critical defence of any kind of romanticism. During the interval there were many instances of dissatisfaction with individual articles of the classical creed which some have confused with revolt against the system. But whether they proceeded from inertia or were inheritances from the Elizabethan period or were the products of British opposition to excessive formalism or were as yet undeveloped seeds of systems that would be germinant in the future, they were disturbances within the system rather than attempts to destroy it.

NOTES

1   Mémoires et Observations Faites par un Voyageur en Angle-
    terre, article "Bedlam," p. 29.

2   Voyage en Angleterre, p. 79.

3   Lettres sur les Anglais, pp. 58-59.

4   The Humourist, vol. 2, pp. 235-36.

5   Cf. Edmund Freeman, "A Proposal for an English Academy
    in 1660," Mod. Lang. Rev., xix, 291-300.

6   Vol. 5, p. 904.

7   Quoted by Gosse, From Shakespeare to Pope, p. 32.

8   Hamelius, Die Kritik in der Eng. Lit., pp. 50-51.

9   One wonders if there is here a reminiscence of the great folio
    Shakespeare, editio princeps, which Scott in Woodstock rep-
    resents as lying on the reading desk in the sitting apartment
    of Sir Henry Lee. That Scott should have endowed his charac-
    ters with his own literary and bibliophilic interests is not sur-
    prising; but Scott distinguished sharply between romance and
    serious criticism.

10 Shadwell, Dedication of A True Widow.

11 London Spy, Part XI, p. 260.

12 Cf. Soame and Dryden's adaptation of Boileau's Art of Poetry,
    closing lines of canto III.

13 Of Heroic Plays, Ker, I, 148-49. Dryden is here speaking of
    rime, but the principle that he invokes is of wide application.

14 See his unpublished Harvard dissertation, Rymer and Aristo-
    telian Formalism, passim and especially pp. 205-206.

15 Spingarn, Crit. Essays of the Seventeenth Century, III, 176.
    Cf. Dennis' remarks, in his own person, in the Third Letter
    "On the Genius and Writings of Shakespeare," Smith, Eigh-
    teenth-Century Essays on Shakespeare, p. 45.

16 Die Kritik in der Eng. Lit., p. 48; cf. Routh, The Rise of
    Classical Eng. Criticism, p. 22.

17   Spingarn, Crit. Essays, II, 106-07.

18   Pointed out by Spingarn, Ibid., II, 336.

19   Routh, op.cit., p. 22.

20   Op. cit., II, 278 ff.

21   No other writer of the period has been so frequently hailed as
     a brother romanticist – in part or at times – as Dryden. (See
     Hamelius; Routh; Bohn, P M L A, XXII, 56 ff.; Elton, The
     Augustan Ages, p. 195; etc.) Since I am discussing Dryden's
     criticism at some length in another article, it will be suffi-
     cient to suggest here that Dryden's case does not materially
     alter the present conclusions.

22   Op. cit., pp. 74-77. In the original, Tasso is the hero of the
     story.

23   This word is taken directly from the Italian with a favorable
     connotation rare in the English use of the period.

24   J. E. Spingarn, Critical Essays of the Seventeenth Century,
     III, 313, in a note on Gerald Langbaine's Essay on Dryden,
     speaks of Ragg. 28 as being "often cited by seventeenth cen-
     tury opponents of the Rules." The evidence of Spingarn's own
     collection is the other way. But two passages in the three vol-
     umes make serious reference to Boccalini's criticism, and
     only the essay by Langbaine, previously referred to, quotes
     Ragg. 28, or indeed connects him in any way with an attack on
     the rules. Dryden mentions Boccalini but once in the essays
     included in Ker's collection (II, 193) and then the reference
     is to an unnamed imitator merely. During the seventeenth cen-
     tury, there were many imitations of Boccalini's form. (For
     an incomplete list of these imitations see the article by R.
     Brotanek, Archiv für das Studium der neueren Sprachen, CXI
     (1903), 409-414.) But these imitations did not necessarily or
     usually involve an attack upon the rules.

25   Oeuvres Mêlées, II, 329.

26   De la Tragédie Ancienne et Moderne and Sur nos Comédies.

27   See Miller, The Historical Point of View in Eng. Crit., p.72.
     Cf. also Odell Shepard's review of C.Rinaker's Thos. Warton
     in J E G P, XVI, 153, for many other references.